RESTORING THE GLOBAL JUDICIARY

Restoring the Global Judiciary

WHY THE SUPREME COURT SHOULD RULE IN U.S. FOREIGN AFFAIRS

Martin S. Flaherty

PRINCETON UNIVERSITY PRESS

PRINCETON & OXFORD

Copyright © 2019 by Princeton University Press

Published by Princeton University Press
41 William Street, Princeton, New Jersey 08540
6 Oxford Street, Woodstock, Oxfordshire OX20 1TR

press.princeton.edu

ISBN 978-0-691-17912-4
ISBN (e-book) 978-0-691-18612-2

British Library Cataloging-in-Publication Data is available

Editorial: Bridget Flannery-McCoy and Alena Chekanov
Production Editorial: Kathleen Cioffi
Jacket Design: Layla Mac Rory
Production: Erin Suydam
Publicity: Tayler Lord and Kate Farquhar-Thomson
Copyeditor: Evan White

Jacket art: (Background image) Standard map of the world. Geographia Map Company, 1942 /
Library of Congress Geography and Map Division, Washington, D.C.

This book has been composed in Miller

Printed on acid-free paper. ∞

Printed in the United States of America

10 9 8 7 6 5 4 3 2 1

To Emily

CONTENTS

THIS BOOK BRINGS together several longstanding interests, each of which happens to address an ever more obvious and grave threat to constitutional government, fundamental rights, and international stability.

The threat goes by many names: illiberal democracy, elective authoritarianism, populist despotism. The varied labels reflect its pervasiveness. So too do its manifestations. In my capacity as sometime legal advisor at the UN, I am occasionally forced to hear their exposition by various mouthpieces of sadly familiar autocracies. (Of course, these demonstrations are hardly the most onerous incarnations of such threats.) The growing chorus includes lackeys of Vladimir Putin's Russia, Xi Jinping's China, Rodrigo Duterte's Philippines, Victor Orban's Hungary, Jair Bolsonaro's Brazil, Nicolas Maduro's Venezuela, Omar al-Bashir's Sudan, and Recep Tayyip Erdoğan's Turkey. These and other regimes, more or less harsh, manifest certain tendencies that historically ebb, flow, and have lately combined. One is the age-old problem of concentrating power in one leader, whether king, dictator, party chair, or chief executive. Another such tendency, a somewhat more recent discovery, is the tyranny of an electoral majority. Concern over abuse of power, among other things, motivated the Founders of the American republic. They would hardly have been surprised at the periodic rise of these dangers elsewhere in the world. They would be dismayed that their framework had let through a figure such as Donald J. Trump. Yet Trump is merely the *reductio ad absurdum* of a concentration of elective authority that should have concerned more Americans more consistently for more time than it has to date.

A situation this dire demands resistance on many fronts. In my case, happenstance has given me the good fortune to experience disparate fields, each of which (as I hope this work will suggest) is useful for the task.

The mention of the Founders brings up what is, appropriately, my most longstanding interest, history. Growing up in New Jersey, I was fortunate to live relatively far from "the cages on Highway 9," and dwelt instead amid numerous Revolutionary War sites. That happy accident instilled a lifelong fascination with colonial America, the fight for independence, and the founding of the American republic. Sometimes I pursued these topics in a fairly hands-on fashion. The only gun I know how to or care to use is an eighteenth-century flintlock; this ability dates to my "service" as a ranger in the Continental Army at a national historical park in Morristown. But mostly I've explored the period academically. Studying with Father Giles Hayes while in high school at Delbarton, John Murrin as an undergraduate at Princeton, Louis Cullen while on a fellowship to Trinity College Dublin, and Edmund M. Morgan while in graduate school at Yale provided an invaluable and enduring foundation. Countless colleagues, too numerous to mention, continue to add to that base.

All this has enabled me to both extol and critique the "dead white male slaveowners" I tell my students helped found the nation. Given their flaws, not to mention the intervening centuries, the drawing of any lessons from their legacy should proceed with caution. But neither should our precaution lead us to ignore them, or worse, allow them to be twisted beyond recognition to shape a modern agenda. Whatever their faults, those who resisted imperial rule gained recognition as an independent nation; hammered out constitutional frameworks, state and federal; and combined book learning and practical experience in a way seldom equaled in world (let alone American) history. Handled with care, their insights endure. Well handled or not, their legacy looms large, especially, for better or worse, in U.S. constitutional law. An understanding of early American history, in short, is a prerequisite for confronting the pathologies of modern American government.

The mention of law reflects a subsequent interest of mine that informs this volume. As I also tell my students, at some point in graduate school I had the epiphany that law professors make twice the money—for doing half the work—as do historians. So off to law school I went. At Columbia I was also fortunate to study with a varied array of constitutional law experts in particular, including Bruce Ackerman, Vince Blasi, Henry Monaghan, Barbara Black, and Kendall Thomas, as well as a host of others in related fields. As in history, subsequent dialogue with numerous colleagues once I began teaching has built on this foundation immeasurably. Eye-opening in a different manner was that American law school version of a postdoc, serving as a clerk to a judge. Here my constitutional education continued with the opportunity to learn from two very different, very formidable jurists: Judge John J. Gibbons of the Third Circuit and Justice Byron R. White of the Supreme Court.

Summarizing constitutional law's clashing viewpoints, arguments, and approaches leads directly to a place where angels rightly fear to tread. Some apparent lessons, however, do stand out. One deals with the process of interpreting our very terse Constitution and so deriving specific rules that can alter the destinies of millions of people. As my students also hear more than once, perhaps the least useful tool in modern constitutional controversies is the actual text of the Constitution, especially in foreign affairs. Much of this volume addresses this predicament by drawing upon the interests and experiences just outlined. One other insight deals with the substantive role of the judiciary. My legal education came at a time when the last echoes of the Warren Court were dissipating. With them faded the idea that the judiciary, within the bounds of the law, could be an agent of positive social change, or even a significant check on the Congress and the executive, the so-called political branches. That idea first came under withering criticism from the Right, but it was later challenged from the Left as well. I remain enough of a child of my time to stick with the old-time religion. As this book will argue, these two lessons can be brought together to defend the idea that the judiciary should reclaim and embrace its role as a defender of fundamental rights against government overreach under a properly interpreted constitutional order. Cutting further against various trends, it also argues that that role is more, not less, urgent in cases touching upon matters beyond the nation's borders.

Another interest animating this study, one that has long been dominant in my work, is international human rights. It took going beyond classrooms and judicial chambers to appreciate how readily governments overreact to perceived threats, and to grasp the value of checks on such efforts, including and especially an independent judiciary. My start here came about in law school, thanks to opportunities and encouragement from Louis and Alice Henkin and Jack and Deborah Greenberg, towering figures all in civil and human rights. Through their good offices I got the chance to work with leading local and U.S. NGOs in Northern Ireland when there seemed to be no end in sight to the "Troubles." This lifelong engagement allowed me to learn on the ground from such advocates as Mike Posner, former assistant secretary of state for democracy, human rights, and labor, Fionnuala Ní Aoláin, UN special rapporteur on counterterrorism, Diego García-Sayán, UN special rapporteur on the independence of judges and lawyers, and Kemal Bokhary, former permanent judge of the Court of Final Appeal in Hong Kong. These days I concentrate on human rights in China through, among other platforms, the Woodrow Wilson School at Princeton, the New York City Bar Association, and a small NGO named the Committee to Support Chinese Lawyers. In between I've had the chance to participate in human rights missions to Turkey, Hong Kong, China, Mexico, Malaysia, Kenya, Romania, and, not least, the United States. These latter opportunities mainly came about through the Leitner Center for International Law and Justice at Fordham Law School in New York, where, with Tracy Higgins, I am a founding codirector.

What is surely most valuable about these first-hand experiences is that they offer a radically different perspective than that of many foreign relations scholars, many of whom have encountered the "real world" working safely ensconced in executive branch offices of the U.S. government. In Belfast I first interviewed victims of torture and mistreatment, surviving family members of slain human rights advocates, and government officials who blithely denied or justified (not infrequently at the same time) the events and experiences I'd heard described. I recall a bright young translator in Diyarbakir rushing out of the room in tears after hearing the stories of Kurdish human rights lawyers who had been detained in cold, concrete cells with no clothes and who were subjected to shocking physical abuse. For the past decade even more harrowing accounts have come from human rights lawyers in China; some of them, such as Teng Biao and Chen Guangcheng, have been exiled, while lawyers such as Wang Yu and Wang Quanzhang were arrested in country. In these and many other instances, a consistent phenomenon was official abuse of power that was knee-jerk and counterproductive. And a near-universal plea from victims and their advocates was for access to independent courts, where they might finally have a chance to end, or at least mitigate, their mistreatment. Confirming this plea were the actions of international tribunals, or certain local judges, whose stance did just this. This is why, when I do return to the classroom, arguments that courts have little or no role to play in matters involving national security or the violation of international human rights tend to ring hollow. So too do recent glib and trendy critiques of the human rights movement that issue from scholars more concerned with scaling the heights of the academy than plumbing the depths of abuses encountered on the ground. These experiences also inform this work.

My involvement in international human rights necessarily led me to international relations, an additional, corollary interest featured in the following pages. Since the legal realist movement emerged last century, it has been a truism that neither the law nor its impact can be understood outside their social context. That observation applies with the greatest force in international law, which lacks the enforcement mechanisms of its domestic counterparts. It follows that the implementation of global human rights law cannot be understood without knowing something about how nations behave. Fortunately, I received a crash course in international relations by virtue of my time researching and teaching over the past dozen years at the Woodrow Wilson School of Public and International Affairs at Princeton, first as a fellow in its Law and Public Affairs program, then as something of a permanent visiting professor teaching human rights. Encountering such scholars as Anne-Marie Slaughter and Bob Koehane firsthand has been invaluable. Their work—spoiler alert—inspired what are probably the most original chapters that follow.

Any one of these interests—early American history, constitutional law, international human rights, or international relations—could easily have sustained a book-length version of the argument made here. Perhaps doing so would have been more effective. My hope, however, is that synergy makes for a more compelling case than specialization. In this I follow my late father, one of the most widely read individuals I've ever known, who used to decry the compartmentalization of knowledge in academic departments. Interdisciplinary work has come a long way since that time. Combining these multiple interests continues the efforts made along that path. As noted, the resistance to popular and populist threats, themselves the extension of longstanding trends, needs all the help it can get.

Any effort this deliberately varied requires an equally varied set of acknowledgments, over and above the many influences already cited. At my principal institution, I am indebted to numerous colleagues for offering insights, not withholding criticism, running institutional interference, and providing general encouragement. In particular I'd like to thank Thomas Lee, Andrew Kent, Tracy Higgins, Catherine Powell, Clare Hunnington, Jed Shugarman, and Saul Cornell. It also borders on embarrassing to admit that this work could not have been done without a splendid set of tireless law student–research assistants, including Chris Pioch, Michael Fronte, Morganne Barrett, and Sijin Choi. I would also be remiss if I failed to thank my superb assistants, Larry Bridgett and Emma Mercer.

One of the many glories that makes putting up with New York's less glorious aspects worthwhile is the number of legal scholars and colloquia situated within a short subway ride. Of these, I have accrued a special debt over the years to the NYU Law School Legal History Colloquium, and especially to Bill Nelson, John Phillip Reid, and R. B. Bernstein, as well as the group's more recent hosts, Daniel Hulsebosch and David Golove. Uptown, I have had the chance to give a number of presentations at Columbia, where I am grateful for the input of Sarah Cleveland, Philip Bobbitt, and Henry Monaghan. A slightly longer subway ride was well worth the opportunity to present aspects of this work at St. John's Law School, where I've enjoyed teaching periodically and have benefitted from the insights of Peggy McGuinness and Chris Borgen.

Crossing the river to the Jersey side, I'm immensely indebted to Princeton and the Woodrow Wilson School for ongoing support; unfettered access to facilities, resources, and faculty; and an immersion course in international relations, as noted. There one of my co-teachers, Deborah Pearlstein, provided guidance and inspiration. Special thanks to Anne-Marie Slaughter, who kindly reviewed the chapters building upon her work. I also owe an immeasurable debt to Chris Eisgruber for his friendship, insights, and encouragement of this project over the years.

Further afield, Harvard and Yale also helped shape my thinking at various points in time. Thanks to Bill Alford and Gabby Blum for allowing me to float early versions of certain chapters at their workshop in Cambridge. In New Haven, Harold Koh and Bruce Ackerman have ever been lively inspirations. Peter Spiro and Duncan Hollis at Temple also deserve mention for the opportunity to present there. The Federalist Society, for which I have served as something of a house progressive over the years, has provided a well-heeled forum to test my arguments. My erstwhile sparring partner John Yoo has been an especially valuable foil. More generally, I also benefited greatly from the humor, encouragement, and scholarly critique of Liam O'Melinn.

U.S. foreign relations law is, for various reasons, a particularly vibrant field, as witnessed by the always useful gatherings of the American Society of International Law's International Law in Domestic Courts group. There I've benefited from exchanges with such scholars as Mike Ramsey, Bill Dodge, Paul Stephen, Jack Goldsmith, and many others. I owe a special debt of gratitude to David Sloss. Most of all, I am indebted to my former co-clerk and erstwhile coauthor, Curtis Bradley.

Chris Eisgruber, not surprisingly, extolled Princeton University Press, and I could not be happier with the choice. This book would not have appeared without the advice and counsel of Eric Crahan, Bridget Flannery-McCoy, Kathleen Cioffi, and Evan White. I'd be remiss if I didn't also thank Jim Fleming, who helped guide me though the process of submitting this manuscript, which led me back to Princeton. Boundless gratitude to the protean Mark Graber, who revealed himself the author of two rounds of rigorous and immensely useful comments on the draft manuscript.

With all this assistance, no errors of any sort should appear in what follows. To the extent they do, alas, the fault is mine alone. Of these the most grievous would be omitting those who deserve mention here, to whom I offer my sincere apologies.

On the personal side, I cherish the smiles and laughter of Aisling and Ciara Flaherty over the years. Finally, words cannot express my debt to Emily Lee, without whom this book would never have been completed.

New York City
January 2019

RESTORING THE GLOBAL JUDICIARY

CHAPTER ONE

Introduction

TO APPRECIATE THE role of American courts in foreign affairs, it pays
to go abroad. For me, the place to start was Beijing. Just before the turn
of the millennium, I had the opportunity to spend a semester teaching
law at China University of Political Science and Law, one of the country's
leading law schools. China then was sufficiently open to now-discouraged
"foreign influence" that *Fada*, as it is known in Chinese, welcomed a course
in English on U.S. constitutional law. For its part, the Chinese Constitution,
or *xianfa*, could not be raised in court. Nor were courts independent, in
any case. Undaunted, however, several brave reformers would soon try,
with indirect success, to defend the rights of Chinese citizens by raising
the xianfa before judges in specific cases.[1] Fada, whose previous dean had
defended student involvement in the 1989 Tiananmen Square demonstrations, presumably knew just what it was doing by inviting an American to
share a very different constitutional tradition, one that commanded respect
around the world.

After some thought, I decided *not* to start with *Marbury v. Madison*,[2]
the great Supreme Court decision with which almost every American
constitutional law course begins. Instead I selected *Youngstown Sheet &
Tube Co. v. Sawyer*, the "Steel Seizure case."[3] The controversy arose when
President Truman, facing a national steelworkers strike during the Korean
War, ordered an emergency federal takeover of steel mills to keep them
running. The choice to lead off with *Youngstown* had in part to do with several iconic opinions. Justice Hugo Black wrote a majority opinion that is
a model of what is sometimes known as "strict construction." Justice Felix
Frankfurter's concurrence remains frequently cited for the idea that how the
various parts of the federal government have operated over time serves as
a "gloss" on the Constitution's text. Most importantly of all, Justice Robert

Jackson wrote a typically eloquent opinion that has ever since served as a classic framework for thinking about how the judiciary should resolve rival claims of authority between the president and Congress. But starting with *Youngstown* also had to do with the judgment itself. In essence, six unelected lawyers in black robes told a president of the United States that he was powerless to take an action he thought to be essential for conducting a war. What better case than *Youngstown* to show the awesome power of the American judiciary to maintain the rule of law, the Constitution, and, with them, basic rights?

Just a few years later, the lessons of *Youngstown* had apparently disappeared back home. After the attacks of 9/11, the administration of George W. Bush notoriously ordered the use of "enhanced interrogation techniques" on suspected terrorists, including hooding, sleep deprivation, subjection to extreme heat and noise, sexual humiliation, and waterboarding. Nearly all of these methods violated international law, whether human rights prohibitions or the humanitarian laws of war. On any credible reading, they also violated the federal antitorture statute. Many government lawyers, especially in the State and Defense Departments, agreed. Higher-placed executive branch lawyers, however, argued otherwise, including Attorney General Alberto Gonzales, John Yoo, head of the Office of Legal Counsel, and Assistant Attorney General Jay Bybee (now a federal judge). In what came to be known as the "torture memos," these officials asserted that the techniques in question did not amount to torture under the statute. They did not bother with the international law. More importantly, they argued that even if Congress did prohibit the methods in question, the president had the authority to disregard the command of Congress based upon his authority as chief executive and commander in chief. Nowhere did the memoranda mention *Youngstown*, nor how the Supreme Court would apply that precedent to a violation of federal law.

Youngstown may have been eclipsed so far as the White House was concerned, but it was not forgotten elsewhere. When the torture memos were leaked to the *New York Times*, the reaction was swift and stinging. The clear majority of politicians, pundits, and scholars argued that the "enhanced" interrogation techniques amounted to torture in fact and in law, and that a president could not disregard a federal statute making it a criminal offense to engage in the practice. A few disagreed. But at least among legal scholars, *nearly* everyone criticized the memos for not citing *Youngstown*, the leading Supreme Court case providing a framework for analyzing executive action to meet foreign affairs threats in light of any relevant steps taken by Congress.[4] Soon enough, the Supreme Court would rely on the case in a series of landmark decisions that checked other measures ordered by the president in response to 9/11. That *Youngstown* went missing in action within the executive branch was nonetheless remarkable. Even more striking, the case was nowhere to be found in key lower court decisions after 9/11; this omission helped to uphold the executive's actions.

This conflicting picture reflected a trend that long predated *Youngstown*, a trend which that decision sought to stem. Arguments highlighting the president's advantages in conducting the nation's foreign affairs are as old as the presidency. Alexander Hamilton, perhaps the most proexecutive of the Founders, enumerated several of these in articulating what a body such as the Senate lacked: "accurate and comprehensive knowledge of foreign politics; a steady and systematic adherence to the same views; a nice and uniform sensibility to national character; decision, *secrecy*, and despatch."[5] Yet such arguments were not originally deployed to subordinate either Congress or the courts, much less to marginalize them. Those attempts were made consistently only as the United States took its place as a global power, then as a superpower, and finally (for now) as a hegemon. By the early twenty-first century, *Youngstown* notwithstanding, this push for an ever more powerful presidency, both within and outside the executive, had brought matters to a crossroads. With Congress acting as an occasional check at best, the task of reigning in what had long since become the most powerful branch of government would fall to the branch that Hamilton characterized as "the least dangerous"[6]—the judiciary. Yet decades of presidential advocacy and pressure, along with supporting scholarship, had brought the courts to a crossroads as well. The Supreme Court in particular appears especially conflicted. At times, as in the post-9/11 cases, it maintains its traditional role as a restraint on excessive government power. Conversely, and with apparent growing frequency, it bows to the other branches, above all in foreign affairs and, most notably, when the actions issue from the executive.

Scholarship often provides those with a measure of power a theory or theories that can be transformed into practice. So, at least, do many scholars hope. As with modern case law, the current scholarly literature on the courts, separation of powers, and foreign affairs also presents a conflicted picture. Here, however, the balance tilts more decidedly against a robust judicial role. Whatever their differences, this dominant view includes such leading scholars as Anthony Bellia, Brad Clark, Jack Goldsmith, Andrew Kent, Julian Ku, Saikrishna Prakash, Eric Posner, Michael Ramsey, Adrian Vermeule, and John Yoo.[7] Their works advocate, reflect, or complement the idea of a so-called unitary executive. On this view, the president should wield unfettered power over the executive branch proper, such as the Departments of State, Justice, or Commerce, as well as administrative agencies such as the Food and Drug Administration and the Environmental Protection Agency—all with minimal control by Congress and the courts. More relevant for this study is the corollary that almost inevitably results. The president should rightly and all but unilaterally dominate decision-making in foreign affairs. These views are perhaps not surprising given that a number of these scholars served in the executive branch.

A deceptively numerous yet dissenting set of scholars plays the part of loyal opposition, distinguished yet out of power, or at least less influential, in the face of ever-increasing executive power. Countering the dominant school include such commentators as Bruce Ackerman, Curtis Bradley, David Golove, Daniel Hulsebosch, Heidi Kitrosser, Martin Lederman, Thomas Lee, Julian Mortenson, Deborah Pearlstein, David Rudenstine, Gordon Silverstein, David Sloss, and Beth Stephens.[8] Yet even their work tends to emphasize Congress rather than the Supreme Court, and still less the lower courts, as the key check.

Still other writers evade easy categorization. No less prominent a figure than Justice Stephen Breyer, in his recent book, *The Supreme Court and the World*, argues forcefully but incorrectly that the judiciary over time has become a more active constraint in foreign affairs, while at the same time conceding various institutional limitations.[9] Harold Hongju Koh, drawing on his varied career in and out of government and the academy, argues for the political branches' capacity for more principled foreign policy–making, while preserving the judiciary's capacity to serve as a check when they fall short. On one hand, the executive in particular can and has taken constitutional and international legal constraints more seriously than has been typical of late. In such cases, the need for judicial intervention correspondingly diminishes. Yet, on the other hand, courts can and should step in when the executive flouts those limitations that, among other things, are meant to preserve constitutional balance.[10]

It remains at least an impressionistic truth that, based upon the sheer volume of books and articles on the question, skeptics of judicial authority in foreign affairs increasingly prevail. Should the theories they offer truly presage action, the prospect of further judicial retreat in this area appears even more likely. This book seeks to tip the balance in the other direction and reorient informed discussion to take the judiciary's foreign affairs role more seriously.

That task has become painfully and obviously urgent given the presidency of Donald J. Trump. With a chief executive lacking the knowledge, experience, and temperament of even his most "imperial" predecessors, the pressures on the federal judiciary to abandon the role symbolized by *Youngstown* have grown exponentially. Just the initial litany of controversial presidential actions, taken or proposed, that implicate foreign affairs is staggering: the "Muslim" travel ban(s), reinstatement of torture, withdrawal from the Paris Climate Accord, nuclear retaliation, the proclamation of an emergency on the nation's southern border. Not coincidentally, these actions have come hand in hand with unprecedented attacks on federal courts and individual judges, as well as nominations to the federal bench of candidates likely to defer to the executive, especially in foreign affairs. Where 9/11 may have illustrated the judiciary in foreign affairs at a crossroads, the Trump presidency has taken the path of unchecked executive power toward a precipice.

This state of affairs would have shocked, but not surprised, the nation's Founders. They did anticipate at least some of the forces that brought things to this point. That those forces resulted in the executive dominance we see today they would nonetheless find shocking. This is because the Constitution they framed and ratified embraced the idea of separation of powers precisely out of the fear that concentrated power could become tyrannical. As they refined it, that doctrine in particular contemplated a judiciary with sufficient independence and power to check the states as well as the other federal branches of government. By definition, the exercise of that power would require considering the assertion of some right necessary to create a legal case or controversy.[11] In the end, neither separation of powers nor judicial authority came to be applied as fully to foreign as to domestic affairs.[12]

The precedents that the Founding generation established under the Constitution were faithful to this vision. When President Washington sought the interpretation of a critical treaty during a global crisis, he had two brilliant legal advisors, Secretary of State Jefferson and Secretary of the Treasury Hamilton, reach out to the Supreme Court rather than try to avoid it. (Chief Justice John Jay famously declined, but only because the queries did not arise in the context of a litigated case.) When the captain of the USS *Constellation*, during an armed conflict with France, attempted the common practice of claiming a captured vessel as a prize for himself and his crew, the Supreme Court rejected the claim, and indirectly checked Congress, by holding that interpretation of the federal statute authorizing the capture should not lead to the violation of international law if at all possible. When, during the same hostilities, another navy ship seized a Danish vessel, the Court again held against the nation's armed services personnel, this time holding the captain liable for any damages caused on the grounds that he exceeded an act of Congress limiting when such captures could take place. When a British subject in the United States during the War of 1812 objected to the executive seizing his property, the Supreme Court similarly voided that action, on the grounds that the president did not have the authority to violate international law.[13] These episodes stand in stark contrast to modern calls for the judiciary to defer to the "political branches," and especially the president, in foreign affairs, or better, to stay out of such matters altogether.

This book argues that the Founding generation and, for almost a century and a half, its successors had it right. As *Youngstown* recognized, however, pressure on the original framework had long been building, and it has only grown more severe since that decision. Among the reasons for this, not least is the nation's increased engagement in world affairs. After a period of isolation, the United States ascended to the status of global power in the late nineteenth century with its military victory over Spain. World War I confirmed the nation's place as a power equal to any other, however much it attempted to withdraw from that role. With World War II, the United States rose to the status of superpower, and with the fall of the Soviet Union, it became the sole superpower. As such, it has been engaged in nearly constant armed conflict. These developments have shifted power from the states to the federal government. As *Youngstown* warned, actors within the federal government tend to shift power to the executive, given all-too-frequent congressional inaction or acquiescence. Fresh insights into modern international relations reveal that the way nation-states currently interact only tends to exacerbate the problem of executive overreach. The result has been precisely the concentration of power in one branch, and the consequent threat to liberty, that the Founders feared.

We have all the more reason, then, to turn the clock backward in order to move forward. Modern concerns about the "imperial presidency" date at least, and not insignificantly, to World War II.[14] Yet in foreign affairs, cold wars spiked by hot wars and succeeded by a "war on terror" have rendered the term "imperial" woefully inadequate to capture the presidency today, especially when the executive is aided and abetted by a subservient Congress. Ironically, the chaos, bluster, and exaggerated assertions of the Trump administration may give pause to those who previously advocated the effective supremacy of the executive as a necessary means to deal with the nation's challenges in a dangerous world. If so, no shortage of potential reforms exist, including electoral reform to lessen party polarization and stalemate in Congress, reform of the Electoral College, and checks within the executive branch itself.

Yet one more measure is as straightforward as it is essential. The judiciary must commit itself to reclaiming its historic role precisely because—rather than despite the fact that—a case or controversy involves foreign affairs. That is the goal of this volume.

Toward that end, some initial clarifications are in order. First, this study views broadly matters that encompass foreign affairs. *Youngstown* demonstrates the difficulty in drawing a bright line between the foreign and domestic. On one hand, the case involved the seizure of a factory in Ohio. Yet on the other, the seizure was ordered so that the same concern would continue to produce steel to fight a war half a world away. In this light the best that can be said is that any dispute that raises significant foreign affairs consequences fairly merits consideration. Second, this work concentrates on the federal judiciary, with a particular focus on the Supreme Court. State court decisions can sometimes have important foreign affairs implications. Nonetheless, the conduct of foreign affairs is overwhelmingly concentrated in the federal government and, as will be argued, is apportioned among its three branches. It follows that concentration on the federal judiciary entails, for better or worse, highlighting the Supreme Court, if only because its decisions establish the framework in which the lower courts must operate. The Court has left open a surprising number of issues that bear upon foreign affairs, which means, at the very least, that the decisions rendered below demand attention.[15] Finally, a restoration of the judiciary to its proper role in foreign affairs in theory demands that it checks both of the so-called political branches, Congress and the executive, alike. The growing power of the presidency that the following pages describes nonetheless ordains that the principal struggle in reestablishing the judicial role will pit the judiciary against the executive, the Supreme Court against the president.

This book proceeds in four parts. Part I considers the Founding. What constitutes "the Founding," a period that to many offers the promise of settling constitutional controversies, is itself an open question. A narrow definition focuses on the Federal Convention of 1787 and the subsequent ratification debates.[16] Broader treatments not infrequently look further back to explore the legal and political thought of the so-called Glorious Revolution of 1688 or even to the English Civil War of the 1640s.[17] Looking in the other direction, many scholars, advocates, and judges view the Founding as not fully concluded until the First Congress, while others point even later to the Jefferson administration, which sought to undo many of the constitutional practices established by his two Federalist predecessors, George Washington and John Adams.[18] This study will navigate a middle course. Appreciating the Constitution's origins requires, at the very least, some consideration of the constitutional experiments Americans attempted upon declaring independence in 1776. Conversely, the Founding generation often did not work out an initial understanding of a constitutional issue—or at times even leave behind a particular range of understandings—through the new government's first decade and (in some instances) well beyond.

Dealing with the Founding at all raises the perennial question of its relevance to modern constitutional controversies. What purchase do the views of an exclusive, nondiverse elite living in a mainly agricultural society under a weak government buffeted by global superpowers have on a modern, multiracial and multicultural population in the postindustrial economy of a nation that is itself a superpower, one that regularly buffets other countries yet is also strangely vulnerable? Or, as I put it more simply to my students: Why care about a bunch of dead, white, male slave owners?

There are at least three sets of reasons to do so. First, no less true for being hackneyed, are the same reasons we look to history at all. These have been captured in various phrases which are themselves clichéd: from Santayana's "Those who cannot remember the past are condemned to repeat it," to the folk proverb "You don't know where you're going unless you know where you've been," to the more general motto of Faber College, "Knowledge Is Good."[19] All capture the basic idea that consulting history can confirm solutions to modern problems that have demonstrably worked and help avoid missteps that have not.

A more specific set of reasons has to do with the Founders themselves. To the modern eye, to be sure, they are a disturbingly exclusive, racist, sexist, and elitist lot. Still, they enjoyed two advantages denied most modern activists and thinkers thanks to the accidents of time and place. For one thing, they lived during a time when a cultivated person could master several fields and so enjoy a more multifaceted view of human experience. Jefferson, whatever his moral failings—and they were ghastly—could be both a leading political theorist and first-class architect.[20] His great rival Hamilton could himself pioneer political theory, master economics, and in the meantime excel as perhaps New York City's leading attorney. Franklin, of course, was Franklin. These men, and lesser contemporaries, arguably enjoyed a breadth of perspective unavailable to today's law professor, federal judge, cabinet official, or member of Congress.[21]

In addition, the Founding generation further benefited from an unparalleled period of experimentation in the art of government. Consider the career of John Adams. As a lawyer in the Massachusetts Bay Colony, Adams established his credentials as a political thinker through extensive popular essays making the case for the colonies' autonomy under the British constitution, writings that were themselves part of a ten-year colonial struggle to define the American colonies' proper constitutional place in the empire. After independence, in which he played a central role, Adams served as a diplomat, took a leading role in reforming his state's government with the landmark Massachusetts Constitution of 1780, and collected his ideas on proper governmental structure in his influential *Thoughts on Government.* While he was abroad during the Federal Convention and ratification, he returned to serve as vice president and president in the newly reformed republic. Adams's own contributions are distinctive, but his general experience is not.[22] Many of those involved in the making of the Constitution had some background in either the constitutional resistance to Parliament before the Revolution, the creation of the new state constitutions, the dangerous challenges of foreign affairs, or the ultimate framing, ratification, and initial implementation of the new constitutional order. Few generations in history have been presented with so many opportunities to consider how best to constitute government.

Finally, for better or worse, the Founding demands attention in light of constitutional theory. Among constitutional "professionals"—judges, lawyers, professors, even politicians—nearly everyone holds that the views of the Founders merit some weight in resolving current controversies. Not a few who are especially influential believe that the "original understanding" should be dispositive. Much ink has been spilled over this latter end of the spectrum, otherwise known as "originalism." Suffice it to say for many, if not most, of its practitioners, its justification lies in a certain kind of democratic foundation in many ways forged by the Founders themselves. This theory posits that "We the People of the United States . . . ordained and established this Constitution" through processes that required "super"-democratic approval and greater deliberation than ordinary laws. On this basis, since known as "popular sovereignty," it follows that the best place to resolve any of the numerous ambiguities and gaps in the Constitution's text is the views of the Founding generation—"the People" who framed, and especially those who ratified, the framework. [23]

Instances of originalism date back to the Founding era, though so too do other methods of constitutional interpretation. Over the centuries, originalists have adopted both liberal and conservative positions. More recently, various, often competing forms of originalism have been on offer. It used to be fashionable to refer to the "original intent" of the "framers," that is, the specific expectations of the men in Philadelphia who proposed the Constitution. That view has largely given way to the notion that what matters is the general, public understanding of the Constitution once it was submitted for ratification.[24] Often these distinctions become scholastic. It is hard to see how a common understanding of a term at the Federal Convention would diverge radically from its understandings in the ratification debates, and still less from any projected public understanding. Far more important is an underappreciated historical reality all too familiar to historians acquainted with history's messiness. More often than not, the Founders at best achieved agreement on contentious matters only in the most general terms, only to disagree vigorously on details. Justice Jackson had this in mind when he famously stated that "just what our forefathers thought, or would have thought, had they known of modern conditions must be divined from sources almost as enigmatic as the dreams Joseph was called upon to interpret for Pharaoh. . . . They largely cancel each other."[25] Jackson overstates; sometimes a dominant view even on more specific matters can be discerned. Closer to the mark is Jack Balkin's latest, if not last, word on originalism. On his view, "Constitutional interpretations are not limited to applications specifically intended or expected by the framers and adopters of the constitutional text. . . . Adopters use . . . standards or principles because they want to channel politics through certain key concepts but delegate the details to future generations."[26]

Whatever its internal debates, originalism exerts an exceptional pull on how Americans approach the Constitution. Yet the truth is that even at the other end of the spectrum, where history is minimized, most theories of constitutional interpretation hold that the views of the Founders merit respect, even if they don't compel blind obedience. Conventionally, approaches that emphasize the Constitution's (super)democratic foundation are juxtaposed with schools of thought that instead find its ultimate legitimacy in the extent to which constitutional law reflects fundamental justice.[27] On this view, working out what principles are moral, fair, and just outranks discerning the understandings of the Founding generation. Perhaps the leading proponent of this "justice-seeking" school remains the late Ronald Dworkin. Dworkin, to be sure, rarely made extended historical arguments in his magisterial works. For him, the philosopher John Rawls loomed far more prominently than James Madison or Alexander Hamilton. Yet even Dworkin accepted that some knowledge of the Founding period could only enhance what he called the project of discovering what best justified and fit our constitutional order.[28]

All of which goes to part I's concentration on the Founding, starting with chapter 2's focus on separation of powers. Americans are, theoretically, familiar with the idea that the Constitution assumes that there are three types of government power—legislative, executive, and judicial—and assigns these powers to three separate sets of hands or branches—Congress, the president, and the federal judiciary. Yet even standard historical accounts do not fully appreciate how central these ideas were in the ferment that led to the Constitution. Separation of powers first of all served as a newly central tool in diagnosing perceived failures in the first state constitutions, drafted following the issuing of the Declaration of Independence. Previously, Americans had thought primarily in terms of the British constitution,[29] which keyed to social classes rather than government functions. Independence effectively meant that the new American governments would have to forego institutionalizing monarchy, as in the British Crown, and aristocracy, as in the House of Lords, and make the best of democracy through legislative assemblies. State legislative majorities, however, soon proved capable of violating fundamental rights in a way previously thought the exclusive province of kings and nobles. Separation of powers, hitherto a secondary idea, came to the fore to demonstrate that too much power had been concentrated in the legislatures. The same idea that exposed the problem also pointed to the solution. Separation of powers suggested that both the executive and judicial branches needed to be made sufficiently independent and equipped to check the dominant legislatures. For the judiciary in particular, that meant, among other things, salary protection, life tenure, and the emerging idea of constitutional judicial review.

Chapter 3 argues that separation of powers was understood to apply to foreign no less than domestic affairs. In so doing, it provides a long overdue corrective for both the history of the Founding and certain Founding myths that later constitutional approaches have projected upon that history. The chapter first of all brings together two dominant accounts of the Constitution's origins that almost always pass one another like eighteenth-century frigates in the night. One, as will have been seen in the previous chapter, emphasizes the failure of Americans' initial experiments in independent government in the states. The other, more familiar generally, stresses that the Constitution came about in response to the national government's weakness under the Articles of Confederation, especially in foreign affairs.[30] This chapter weaves together these two still surprisingly separate strands. The Constitution clearly established a framework for a national government strong enough to hold its own in a world of vastly more powerful states. The prospects of an effective army and navy, enforcement of national treaty obligations, and the power to retaliate against foreign commercial sanctions through commercial regulation motivated just some of the reforms that created a vastly more powerful national government. Yet concentration of power also meant a corresponding threat to liberty. Precisely for this reason, separation of powers mattered *more*, not less, with regard to the national government's enhanced powers in foreign affairs. The constitutional text and debates together confirm that the Founders sought to divide foreign affairs powers among the three branches in the same original ways they had for authority seen as ordinarily domestic. As in domestic affairs, moreover, the expectation was for the judiciary to play a critical role, especially in checking the other branches, the better to reign in excess power and safeguard fundamental rights.

Part II turns to how well, or poorly, subsequent generations realized the Founding's commitments. The manner in which the original framework has actually been implemented has often been termed "constitutional tradition" or "custom." With regard to separation of powers and foreign affairs, such custom takes shape as the branches work out to what extent their specific powers overlap or are exclusive. For courts, the common-law idea that a decision should ordinarily stand as binding precedent can render judicial custom especially powerful. Conversely, judicial determinations not to hear certain kinds of cases turn this power on its head and work to entrench previous determinations that courts do not have the authority to settle certain kinds of controversies, an argument made with increasing frequency about cases implicating foreign affairs. Justice Frankfurter captured the idea of constitutional custom when he stated that "the way the [constitutional] framework has consistently operated fairly establishes that it has operated according to its true nature. Deeply embedded traditional ways of conducting government cannot supplant the Constitution or legislation, but they give meaning to the words of a text or supply them."[31]

As such tradition evolves, however, numerous problems can arise. Most importantly, when does custom merely realize the Constitution's "true nature," and at what point might it diverge so as to "supplant"—and indeed violate—the Constitution? The power to make war provides a vexing illustration. Assume, as does this study, that the Founding's commitments merit some consideration in determining the Constitution's legitimate meaning. Assume further, as most scholars do, that one such commitment was that the determination to use military force abroad fell primarily to Congress under the power to "Declare War."[32] What then to make of a tradition in which Congress has authorized major wars but allowed the president to unilaterally initiate small ones? This problem, in turn, emerges only after solving the threshold problems of what government actions count to determine a tradition, how consistent or unbroken that tradition has to be, and how to determine the acquiescence of the other branches.[33]

This study again takes a middle position among differing poles. At one end of the spectrum is the view that tradition must remain subordinate to other sources of constitutional meaning. For an originalist, any tradition that broke away from "the" initial constitutional understanding would be a violation, not an elaboration. Likewise, anyone committed to a "justice-seeking" vision would reject any custom that parted from notions of fairness or right reason.[34] Conversely, other interpreters believe that evolving custom *is* constitutional law. Something like this idea is often associated with Edmund Burke's argument that the virtue of the British constitution was that it developed by way of measured evolution through evolving tradition, rather than as some reflection of justice or periodic adoption of constitutional text.[35]

This study assumes that neither extreme reflects our constitutional culture. As noted, Founding commitments simply weigh heavily under almost any theory. Yet, as Frankfurter noted, it seems "an inadmissibly narrow conception of American constitutional law to confine it to the words of the Constitution"—or even to a narrow application of the original understanding even where one exists. To confine it in such a way would be "to disregard the gloss which life has written upon [the text]."[36] This book therefore assumes that the Founders' commitments, especially their broadly envisioned separation of powers framework, commands fidelity absent a formal constitutional amendment or an equivalent "constitutional moment" in which something approaching a national consensus deliberately endorses major constitutional change. At the same time, it is open to the possibility that a "systematic, unbroken . . . practice, long pursued with the knowledge [of the other branches] and never before questioned"[37] within that framework might work legitimate constitutional change.

On these bases, chapter 4 contends that for much of our history, constitutional tradition confirmed the Founders' basic commitments about separation of powers, foreign affairs, and the courts. In particular, the Supreme Court and the federal judiciary more generally played their part as originally envisioned. That meant, among other things, fulfilling their assigned roles of checking both Congress and the president, not to mention the states, in the service of protecting individual rights under both domestic and international law. These general patterns, moreover, persisted though the mid-twentieth century. Given the time frame, this account necessarily must be general, especially in light of the other matters this book covers. It therefore makes its case mainly though a consideration of certain landmark controversies and decisions that are nonetheless representative. These cases suffice to confirm the overall fidelity of subsequent constitutional tradition to the Constitution's initial vision.

Chapter 5 serves as an interlude that seeks to establish the symbolic terms of a transition that remains incomplete. By the outset of the twentieth century, America's ascendance as a major power exerted corresponding pressure on the Constitution's original conception of meaningful separation of powers applied to foreign and domestic affairs alike. Increased engagement in world affairs, diplomacy, colonization, imperialism, and wars major and minor inevitably shifted power to the executive at the expense of Congress and the courts. At the same time, courts had become less equipped to play their still-traditional role. In a change of course from its early days, the Supreme Court, in particular, now featured fewer justices with diplomatic experience. For various reasons, international law had become less central, thanks in part to the nation's previous relative isolation from world affairs. By the mid-twentieth century, these and other factors pressured the judiciary to retreat from its envisioned role. At least a partial retreat did begin, and this would become more marked as the century progressed. It would not, however, become sufficiently systematic, unbroken, or unopposed to count as a legitimate customary amendment to the Constitution's original scheme. Then and now, two iconic cases embody the challenge in best determining the Court's role in foreign affairs and its ongoing repudiation. The Supreme Court's most dramatic retreat came in *United States v. Curtiss-Wright Export Corp.*,[38] which has served as a manifesto for executive supremacy in foreign affairs.[39] With *Youngstown Sheet & Tube Co. v. Sawyer*,[40] the Court powerfully recommitted to maintaining the historic role of Congress and the judiciary. So frequently do opponents cite each case that what the decisions say, and why they say it, has become obscured. This chapter attempts to recover their deeper significance, the better to understand the as-yet failed constitutional transformation.

Chapter 6 brings the survey of custom to the beginning of this century. That survey shows how U.S. foreign policy has continued to pressure the judiciary to go in the direction of *Curtiss-Wright*, an invitation it has still generally refused in light of the recommitment to the original constitutional framework set out in *Youngstown*. That the courts, and the Supreme Court in particular, maintained their position as well as they did stands as a testament to the original constitutional design and nearly a century and a half of constitutional custom. Starting roughly midcentury, World War II, the Cold War, and the creation of a national security state placed the nation on a type of near-permanent war footing. These developments accelerated the trend toward greater claims of executive power in particular. In this setting, arguments that the judiciary was ill suited to second-guess executive foreign policy, and to intervene in foreign affairs more generally, were sounded with greater frequency. At times the Court bowed (not least in the face of executive assertions), much to its later regret. Yet, for the most part, it has shown itself capable, sometimes dramatically so, of protecting individual rights, applying international law in claims made against the several states, resisting congressional overreach, and, above all, checking executive aggrandizement. In the end, the survey of constitutional custom falls short of showing constitutional demotion of the judiciary's role in foreign affairs as originally envisioned and long practiced.

Part III shifts perspective to explore the nature of modern international relations. In contrast to the Founding or later constitutional tradition, modern international relations theory does not offer any direct source for the Constitution's meaning. Rather, the sometimes strikingly new ways in which nation-states interact with one another speaks to the setting in which constitutional principles are applied. As the previous parts will have shown, the United States remains committed to a model of separation of powers in foreign affairs that includes a key role for the courts, especially in the protection of fundamental rights under the law. Nor is the United States singular in this regard. Many constitutional democracies have adopted the tripartite system pioneered in Philadelphia. Yet even parliamentary systems, which fuse legislative and executive power, still typically establish independent judiciaries, usually with some form of judicial review.[41] How does the way that these and other states conduct foreign affairs affect these domestic frameworks? International relations experts do not say. But much of their work suggests that the processes they describe spell trouble for any regime committed to some form of separation of powers. Put starkly, modern international relations tends to further empower already dominant executives, leaving judiciaries behind (while legislatures are even more dramatically marginalized). Understanding this development turns recent challenges to judicial participation in foreign affairs upside down. Opponents of an active judicial role typically argue that since courts have little expertise in foreign affairs, they should stay away.[42] International relations, to the contrary, suggests that courts should guard their assigned role of maintaining balance among the branches of government precisely because the cases that may properly come before them involve foreign affairs.

Accordingly, chapter 7 looks to what Anne-Marie Slaughter has termed the real "New World Order."[43] Conventionally, international relations as well as international law concentrated on the interactions of nation-states. On this model, the United States, China, Russia, the United Kingdom, Kenya, Mexico, and the Bahamas, for example, are principally the irreducible units. Recent thinking emphasizes that instead, international relations more and more consists of executive, legislative, and judicial officials directly reaching out to their foreign counterparts to share information, forge ongoing networks, coordinate cooperation, and construct new frameworks. The traditional nation-state has today become "disaggregated," dealing with its peers less as monolithic sovereign states than through these more specialized "global networks." Notably, the counterparts that officials of one state seek out in others tracks the divisions of separation of powers: executives to executives, judges to judges, legislators to legislators.[44] How such transnational, interdepartmental networking affects each branch of government within a given state is another matter.

International relations theory does not take up that question, but chapter 8 does. It argues that relations between modern "disaggregated" states empower the different branches within any nation to different degrees. The executive far and away benefits the most. This enhanced primacy in large part results from structural advantages, including the "secrecy and despatch" identified by Hamilton, meeting modern demands, such as the need for global regulation and the challenge of global terrorism. Perhaps surprisingly, the judiciary follows next, as judges share views in face-to-face meetings and in mutual citations from abroad. Collective-action problems, among other factors, ensure that the legislature benefits least. The consequence is a comparatively more powerful executive, further outstripping its rivals as a direct consequence of new ways to conduct foreign affairs. The resulting imbalance contributes to the precise evils separation of powers is designed to combat. It follows that the need for a judicial check, and, for that matter, a legislative counter as well, becomes more, not less, pressing in light of foreign affairs in a world of disaggregated states and global networks.

Part IV shows what a judiciary restored to its proper role in foreign affairs would mean. To do this, it reviews contemporary controversies implicating foreign affairs in which judicial intervention has been sought, especially those invoking fundamental rights or international law. This increasingly large group usefully breaks down into several broad categories: cases that require determining whether some aspect of foreign affairs precludes the courts from hearing them in the first place; cases for which (if they are in fact admitted) it must be determined how and to what extent the courts should assert their authority on the merits; and finally, claims based upon international human rights law. Across these categories, part IV offers additional support for decisions in which the judiciary has remained faithful to its role, pointed critique for judgments that signal its retreat, and direction in areas where it appears wavering at the crossroads.

Chapter 9 therefore begins with areas presenting threshold questions of effectively getting cases into court in the first instance. It notes the emergence of an array of doctrines to shut the courthouse doors that has formed a part of the custom that remains insufficient to undo entrenched constitutional understandings. Among these are standing requirements, the "state secrets privilege," and the so-called political question doctrine, among others.[45] Not surprisingly, they have been asserted by the executive; unfortunately, they have been accorded increasingly serious consideration by the courts. This chapter aims to counter this trend by showing how such backsliding is inconsistent with the Founders' vision, the bulk of our constitutional tradition, and the effects of modern international relations.

Chapter 10 undertakes much the same task regarding foreign affairs matters that arise once a case has been accepted for review. Here, easily the most threatening potential wrong turn has concerned potential judicial deference to the executive's interpretations of agency regulations, international law, statutes, and the Constitution itself. In each of these areas, the pressures have grown only stronger for courts to cede their responsibility to say "what the law is" to executive officials, on the grounds of their supposed superior grasp of foreign affairs over judges. At times the Supreme Court, and courts below it, have bowed to such arguments. Yet in a series of landmark cases in the wake of 9/11, the Court has remained true to its constitutional role. This chapter relies throughout on the trilogy of Founding pledge, overall tradition, and international relations context to commend the justices' fidelity and contend that, if anything, they have not been steadfast enough.

Chapter 11 concludes the survey of contemporary issues by considering a phenomenon that has consistently been among the most contentious of modern legal controversies—the application by American courts of international human rights. Recent years have witnessed high-profile conflicts over international human rights law. One major battle involves whether, when, and how U.S. courts should recognize rights set out in the nation's treaty obligations. Another heated area of contention has arisen under an act of Congress, the Alien Tort Statute, which has for decades served as a means for foreign victims of human rights abuses to seek redress for violations of their rights under customary international law in federal court. Perhaps most heated of all have been debates over the use of foreign legal materials, including customary international law, to interpret the Constitution of the United States. In these areas as well, the Supreme Court, and the judiciary generally, has wavered. Yet once more, a fresh appreciation of the principles the Founders entrenched, the subsequent custom that on balance confirms that original vision, and the consequences of the way nations interact in a globalized age—all these imperatives point away from the path that the judiciary appears more and more to be considering, and back to the course first established.

The book concludes, as it began, with *Youngstown*. It concedes that in many of the areas considered—including getting into court, interpreting the law once there, and implementing international human rights—on certain issues the federal judiciary has already proceeded perilously far in the wrong direction. Justice Jackson's opinion helps explain why, citing the distinct advantages of the executive in particular in asserting foreign affairs powers in a dangerous world, especially given a subservient legislative branch. The executive's advantages, moreover, may be even more ominously robust than Jackson supposed, and not just because of the nature of modern international relations. The combination of aggressive executive and supine Congress has for some time reached into the composition of the Supreme Court itself. Typical among recent appointments are candidates with executive branch experience and an ensuing commitment to judicial deference to the president, especially in foreign affairs. Thanks to the Trump administration pressing the Senate's own deference to the full, Justices Neil Gorsuch and Brett Kavanaugh have become only the most recent and obvious examples. In this light, reliance on a revived judiciary to restore any balance seems no less forlorn as relying on Congress.

Yet Jackson also sounded a note of guarded hope. Central to that hope was the judiciary holding fast to its duty to apply the law, regardless of its source, against encroachments by the other branches. So pressing could the foreign affairs assertions of the president become, especially when backed by Congress, that even Jackson could elsewhere argue that sometimes it might be better for the Court to stand aside rather than ratify an unconstitutional action. Exactly that fear was realized when a majority of the justices effectively approved Japanese-American internment. This volume ends with the argument that several powerful factors mitigate this concern. The life tenure that justices enjoy can lead to a measure of independence. Serving in the judiciary can likewise inspire institutional loyalty. Turning to the courts domestically can lead to complementary proceedings in international institutions, what Harold Hongju Koh calls "transnational legal process."[46] Finally, the prospect of some constraint is, at the end of the day, better than the certainty of no constraint at all. In part for these reasons, the modern Court has shown itself capable of keeping alive the hope that it can reclaim its historic role as a check even and especially in foreign affairs. So too did *Youngstown* itself advance this aspiration by providing later justices a framework and example.

This volume aims to keep that hope not merely alive and well but compelling. To the extent that the hope is realized, the judiciary will do more than regain its role within the United States. It will also again serve as an inspiration beyond the nation's borders, wherever lawyers, judges, and citizens struggle to defend fundamental rights through the rule of law, whether in Venezuela, Turkey, Russia, Hungary, Egypt, Cuba, or, indeed, in China.

PART I

The Supreme Court, Foreign Affairs, and the Founding

CHAPTER TWO

Inventing Separation of Powers

EIGHTEENTH-CENTURY AMERICANS BELIEVED that they knew as much—or more—about the art of government as any people on earth. Not only did they inherit rich and varied learning from the Old World, from Britain above all. They also benefited from unparalleled practical experience in establishing, adapting, and implementing governmental frameworks, first for colonies and then for states. Still unappreciated, however, especially by legal scholars dabbling in history, is that Americans were late in appreciating one doctrine that would become central to all these efforts and culminate in the Constitution of the United States. That doctrine was separation of powers. Americans would not fully embrace separation of powers until the end of the century precisely because they were so well versed in constitutional law and thought. The only problem was that the constitution they had mastered was not American, but British.

Mixed Government

The American commitment to constitutional government did not begin with the Constitution. Nor did it begin with the constitutions of the several states. From the time their first settlements were founded, colonists in what would become the United States thought, debated, and wrote about how government ought to be framed.[1] Americans could, and did, also draw upon an array of sources to guide their thinking: Enlightenment thinkers such as Locke, Montesquieu, and Hutcheson; English common law; and the "Radical Whig" or "Commonwealth" tradition forged by Harrington, Sidney, Trenchard, Gordon, and Bolingbroke.[2] What these sources all tended to confirm was that, of all the governments on the globe, easily the best was formed by the constitution of Great Britain. Originally this framework went under the label "English"; later, after the Act of Union bringing together England and Scotland in 1707, it was sometimes called "British," and it was also referred to as "Whig," after the political faction most often associated with its development. Whatever the name, a young John Adams called it "the most perfect combination of human powers in society which finite wisdom has yet contrived and reduced to practice for the preservation of liberty and the production of happiness."[3] One of the many things that made it so was its devotion not to separation of powers but to the more old-fashioned ideal called "mixed government."

Mixed government reflected the idea that the balance between necessary governmental power and essential human liberty could be struck through constitutional structure. This idea, an ancient one, gained renewed vigor during the Renaissance. Yet the mixed government approach did not attempt to structure government based on governmental functions. It instead sought to frame government in order to balance the basic social forces within any society. Those forces consisted of three orders, "each embodying within it the principles of a certain form of government: royalty, whose natural form was monarchy; the nobility, whose natural form was aristocracy; and the commons, whose form was democracy."[4] Experience unhappily showed that each of these "pure" forms would almost always degenerate into either an excess of power—monarchy into tyranny; aristocracy into oligarchy—or into an excess of liberty, or at least of licentiousness: democracy into anarchy.

The English constitution escaped these fates in two ways. First, it developed institutions—the Crown, the House of Lords, and the House of Commons—that embodied each social estate. Next, it structured these institutions in such a way as to ensure that they would direct power not only to preserve order, nor just to provide essential services, but also to check each other. American Whigs saw their own colonial frameworks as replicating mixed government in miniature. Each of the North American colonies would come to have a royal governor as well as an upper and lower house of the legislature, striking a similar balance to that of the king, Lords, and Commons. Through this balance, both the English state and its colonial offspring could rule efficiently enough to satisfy the dictates of power while protecting traditional rights sufficiently to satisfy the demands of liberty.[5]

Whig constitutionalists on both sides of the Atlantic were all but unanimous in celebrating England's brand of mixed government as "a system of consummate wisdom and policy."[6] So powerful was support for this system that when American Whigs became American patriots—when, that is,

Americans in the 1760s begin to resist perceived parliamentary encroach-ment on their rights as Englishmen—the furthest thing from their minds was repudiating the English constitution as they understood it. To the con-trary, the patriots opposed Parliament not because the English constitution oppressed them but because Parliament violated the English constitution. Adams, for example, argued exactly this on the very eve of Lexington and Concord.[7] Nor even did the shooting change matters, at least not at first. Even after independence appeared on the horizon as a genuine possibility, few Americans realized the profound implications that the break with Great Britain would have on their understandings of government.

They could not evade these implications for long. Thomas Paine, with typical fire, was among the first to explore what independence would mean for mixed government. In *Common Sense*, the best-selling tract of the era, Paine lampooned what had been seen as the consummately wise and poli-tic system, proclaiming as "farcical" the notion of the English government as a "union of three powers, reciprocally checking each other."[8] Thanks in part to this onslaught, Americans began to question their allegiance to mixed government.[9] But Paine's onslaught was not the only reason for this shift. More fundamentally, it was independence itself that led to the ulti-mate abandonment of mixed government. Breaking the link with Britain in the first instance presented Americans with the problem of framing their own governments on the state level. Yet independence also deprived them of exactly those societal foundations on which the most successful framework that had ever been seen was built. Gone was royalty. There were no plausible candidates—or desire—for a king of Massachusetts, queen of Virginia, or royal family of New Jersey. Gone was the nobility. While different colonies boasted leading families, colonists retained a deep-seated aversion to the kind of titled, landed class required to sustain mixed government outside the empire. Gone, therefore, was the chance of repli-cating the mixed government that American patriots so prized.[10]

Republican Experiments

With mixed government no longer a plausible option, Americans turned to the one possibility their classical education still afforded them—democracy. For any but the smallest polity, this choice meant experiment-ing not with democracy in its pure form, on the model of Athens, but with democracy in the form of representative republics.[11] Ominously, the same Whig political theory that taught Americans that republics were all they could realistically hope to establish also taught that republics had little

realistic chance for success. Without the checks of monarch and aristocracy, republics almost always fell prey to the excess of liberty known as anarchy. But just as American society presented the problem, it also afforded a
solution. America's lack of royal families or titled nobility—in fact, its relative lack of very rich and very poor compared to Europe (not, as few did,
taking into account the enslaved)—helped ensure an abundance of civic
"virtue," the critical quality that made republican experiments feasible at
all. Seen as a selfless, participatory commitment to the public good, civic
virtue issued from within the hearts of citizens themselves to keep liberty
in check. A virtuous sense of public spirit worked to prevent individuals
from seeking self-interested goals—based on religious, class, or local
commitments—at the expense of the whole.[12] Europe suffered from too
many of these types of factional divisions for its republics to succeed for
very long. But Americans, at least white male Americans, prided themselves on their relative homogeneity, what Franklin called "a general happy
Mediocrity."[13] Especially in the even more homogeneous context of each
state, American republicans believed that they could cheat the received
political wisdom and establish thirteen versions of what Samuel Adams
described as a virtuous and republican "Christian Sparta."[14]

It followed that republics in America would have to emphasize certain
political principles and downplay others. With respect to liberty, American republicans to a significant extent felt free to sacrifice the balance
so critical to the English mixed constitution in favor of accountability to
the democratic commons.[15] In light of American virtue, this emphasis on
democratic accountability no longer seemed fated to descend into chaos.[16]
One reason the English constitution required balance as a means of turning power against itself was that it needed power to prevent anarchy. Sufficient virtue, however, could do much of the work traditionally set aside for
power by checking factionalism and disorder.

Better still, reliance on virtue could avert anarchy without posing a threat
to liberty in the way that trusting in power did. Americans could therefore
promote liberty in the form of a government as responsive to the general
public as possible. As they knew better than anyone, self-government was
at once a right in itself and the best means for safeguarding other rights.
Power had subdued liberty in their own lifetimes when a distant, unrepresentative, oligarchic Parliament, at the same time and often through the
same measures, both denied Americans the right to control their own destinies and infringed on their individual rights.[17] A virtuous, self-governing
people, in short, could foster only liberty, not tyranny.[18] A New Jersey com-
mentator voiced the common wisdom in saying, "A virtuous legislature

will not, cannot, listen to any proposition, however popular, that [comes] within the description of being unjust, impolitic, or unnecessary."[19] When it came to liberty, the title of a New England pamphlet put it best: *"The People the Best Governors."*[20]

American republicans also had to reconsider the role of power. They acknowledged that ensuring liberty though representative government came at the expense of government power. Unable and unwilling to replicate either the monarchical or aristocratic features of the English constitution in any straightforward way, republicans realized that their own state governments would be more modest, limited, and small. Accordingly, those governments might well be less effective in delivering many services and preserving order. But this was a price that republicans were willing to pay. Their own experience of energetic government as England had practiced it made Americans even more leery of government than they otherwise might have been. Better to have a less powerful government than one capable of suspending the New York legislature,[21] closing the port of Boston,[22] and employing standing armies, as had the king and Parliament.[23]

These principles became concrete in the early state constitutions, most of which in some way featured legislative supremacy, magisterial impotence, and judicial enfeeblement.[24]

Consider first those devices, both abandoned and embraced, that English Whig constitutionalism viewed as fostering liberty. American republicans manifested their retreat from the idea of balance by concentrating power in the legislatures. As Gordon Wood writes, "The American legislatures, in particular the lower houses of the assemblies, were no longer to be merely adjunct or checks to magisterial power, but were in fact to be the government—a revolutionary transformation of political authority. . . ."[25] Virginia's Constitution of 1776, in many ways typical of the first-generation state frameworks, provided that all legislation must arise in the lower house, empowered both houses to appoint most judges, and tacitly permitted the legislature to change the constitution by statute. Pennsylvania's first constitution, generally seen as the most radically republican ever produced,[26] went further and concentrated these and other powers in the lower house of the assembly, abolishing the upper house altogether. Not only did these initial constitutions concentrate power in the assemblies, they prevented the other branches of government, both governors and courts, from checking the legislatures.

The first constitutions consequently sought to prohibit the executive from corrupting the legislature through informal influence, commonly prohibiting any person holding government office or receiving government patronage from sitting in the assembly. More dramatically, they also removed formal checks on the legislature that the magistracy had traditionally wielded both in Parliament and in the colonial legislatures. In most states the republican governor, unlike his royal predecessor,[27] could neither adjourn nor prorogue the assembly.[28] Nor, more dramatically still, could he veto legislation.[29]

These early constitutions also shackled the courts. They did so in large part because most American republicans at this time still viewed the judiciary with either suspicion or skepticism. Many constitutional thinkers still associated courts with the executive; this view had predominated for centuries before Montesquieu first proposed that judicial power be seen as distinct. Others did see an independent judiciary as a check on government abuse but believed that abuse would come not from legislatures but from kings or governors, which had been the dominant experience on both sides of the Atlantic during the colonial era.[30] Accordingly, early state constitutions typically vested the appointment of judges, as well as the power to impeach them, in the assembly, on such elastic grounds as "mal-administration."[31] No less significant were provisions bearing upon the judiciary which were not there. Most of the first generation of state constitutions failed to accord state judges either salary protection or "tenure on good behavior," the eighteenth-century term of art for life tenure.[32] Like the early state executives, the early judiciaries effectively were subservient to the more accountable and republican legislatures.

The early state frameworks, in short, rejected the idea that the various government institutions that they created should check and balance one another. Instead, American republicans embraced civic accountability, which in practice meant that the democratic part of government, the lower house of the legislature in particular, should represent the people as closely as possible.[33] American republicans therefore employed an array of constitutional mechanisms long championed by their Whig predecessors. Among these were annual elections,[34] term limits to guarantee rotation in office,[35] a relatively broad franchise,[36] and even a right of localities to issue nonbinding instructions to their representatives.[37] Not surprisingly, nowhere did the rage for representation go further than in Pennsylvania. In addition to all the other devices, that state's first constitution did its best to make the people part of the legislative process, providing that "the doors of the house in which the representatives of . . . this state shall sit in general assembly, shall be and remain open for the admission of all persons," that "the votes and proceedings of the general assembly shall be printed weekly during their sitting," and that "all bills of public nature shall be printed for the consideration of the people, before they are read in general assembly the last time for debate and amendment."[38]

Where the early constitutions traded one libertarian strategy for another, they sacrificed the traditional devices meant to assure state power. Especially notable was the treatment accorded the magistracy, the body that, for better and often for worse, wielded power most efficiently. Not only did the early constitutions prevent the governors from checking the legislature, but time and again they empowered the legislatures to check the governors.[39] The Virginia Constitution, once more reflecting the national trend, permitted the legislature to choose the secretary of state, the attorney general, the governor's cabinet (styled the "Privy Council"), and, finally, the governor himself.[40] Virginia republicans further sought to limit magisterial power by prohibiting the governor, "under any presence, [from exercising] any power or prerogative, by virtue of any law, statute, or custom of England"; by specifying a three-year gubernatorial term limit; and by subjecting the governor to impeachment for "mal-administration."[41] Pennsylvania, again pushing the limits, simply got rid of a unitary governor altogether. In its place, Pennsylvania's republicans created an unwieldy "supreme executive council," consisting of twelve persons directly elected by the people but headed by a president and vice president chosen by the unicameral assembly.[42]

Finally, many of the same devices that undermined judicial independence from the legislature necessarily undermined the judiciary's effectiveness as well. Legislative appointment of judges had the natural effect of making them think twice about robustly enforcing unpopular measures. Impeachment on such vague grounds as "mal-administration" would inevitably have a similar effect. Add to this another grant of legislative power typical for its time—the ability to restrict or eliminate the jurisdiction of different courts—and the groundwork for cautious judicial branches was laid.

Enter Separation of Powers

Americans quickly discovered that their republican solutions did not work as well as they hoped. To many observers, the governments that operated under the first state constitutions had ushered in what John Quincy Adams called a "critical period"[43] and what others simply referred to as a "crisis."[44] Of the many evils that had arisen, perhaps the most dismaying was the behavior of the legislatures. In state after state, self-interested and rapacious factions, it seemed, had managed to seize the assemblies and enact ill-advised laws that confiscated property, transferred wealth through schemes of calculated inflation, eliminated existing contractual obligations, and even limited the sacred right of trial by jury.[45]

Most observers agreed that these and other ills arose because the American people were not so virtuous after all. In addition, many commentators predictably viewed these developments in classical republican terms and decried what appeared to be an inevitable popular degeneration into "anarchy and confusion."[46] Others, however, diagnosed a novel and far more troubling malady. To these individuals, the problem was not an excess of liberty but rather that the people, through the legislatures, were doing what English constitutional theory posited as a solecism—*the people were tyrannizing themselves*. As Forrest McDonald observes, the reason for the crisis facing the nation, "in the eyes of many Americans, was that governments were now committing unprecedented excesses, even though—or precisely because—governments now derived their powers from compacts amongst the people."[47] Americans, in short, began to consider that representative self-government and rights did not always go hand in hand.

With the republican model exposed as inadequate, a number of prominent thinkers groped toward new solutions, a search that included rethinking the hitherto "relatively minor eighteenth-century maxim" of "separation of powers."[48] Americans had long been familiar with the doctrine through the writings of ancient Greek and Roman philosophers, English Commonwealth radicals, Locke, and, above all, Montesquieu.[49] Still, the development of the doctrine in seventeenth- and eighteenth-century Europe, to say nothing of its reception in America, is an enormous, complex, and often counterintuitive topic. Several basic features, however, remained constant. First was the assumption that government entailed discrete functions. Exactly what these were, however, was not always self-evident. The idea of separate legislative and executive powers went back to antiquity. The precedents for any further power were not so clear. The often-invoked Locke, for example, wrote of legislative, executive, and "federative" power.[50] The idea of a discrete "judicial power" came relatively late in the doctrine's development.[51] Second was the idea that these powers were best assigned to different persons or government institutions. Finally, it was perceived that separation of powers brought several advantages. Most obviously, it created a balance among institutions that prevented a concentration of power that would threaten liberty. At the same time, it would generate greater specialization and efficiency for putting into effect legitimate government actions. By making different government departments responsible for different functions, it could also make it easier to hold officials accountable.

Despite superficial similarities, separation of powers was distinct from mixed government and had long been overshadowed by it. In mixed government, institutions reflected different orders of society. In separation of powers, government departments were differentiated by function. With independence, Americans would struggle making the shift from the familiar model to the new alternative. For one thing, much about separation of powers would remain ill-defined and contested. More immediately, the shift presented several false analogies and fresh conceptual challenges.

Take legislative power. American constitutional thinkers had to grapple with the realization that the House of Lords was not fully analogous to the upper house of a republican legislature. Under a mixed government conception, the House of Lords embodied the aristocracy in the form of a landed, titled, and still mostly hereditary nobility. But what would the upper house of, say, the New Jersey legislature represent? Some initial answers came in the form of representatives elected from larger districts that would presumably produce candidates of greater accomplishment and broader vision.[52]

Judicial power did not present so much the problem of false analogy as the need for new understanding. For millennia, the power to adjudicate disputes had been viewed as an aspect of executive power. Not until the middle of the eighteenth century did the French philosopher Montesquieu assert that judicial power was a discrete government function, distinct from executive or legislative authority. Montesquieu himself, creatively construing the British constitution though a separation of powers lens, was himself responding to Parliament's efforts to insulate judges from royal control by according them tenure *quamdiu se bene gessirent*—on good behavior—rather than *durante bene placito regis*—at the pleasure of the king.[53]

In terms of partial analogies, executive authority afforded perhaps an even thornier pitfall. Of all the possible constitutional adaptations, monarchy seemed most readily translated—as executive power. Yet, at least in theory, the extensive powers of the British monarch, on many (if not most) definitions, went farther. More or less everyone agreed that the king possessed executive power, defined as the power to implement laws. But the British monarch possessed numerous additional powers classed under the rubric of the royal prerogative. These included the nominal powers to make war and peace, to make treaties, to appoint and dismiss royal officials, to veto legislation, to prorogue and dissolve parliaments, and to grant pardons, to name just a few. Over the course of the eighteenth century, on both sides of the Atlantic, some constitutional thinkers would view executive power as, strictly speaking, no more than the power to ensure that laws were followed. Some would go to the other end of the spectrum to argue that executive power encompassed most, if not all, prerogative powers. Many more would struggle toward intermediate conceptions based on trial and error in the various state constitutions.[54]

Perhaps ironically, more than a few scholars both fail to fully appreciate the conceptual shift from mixed government to separation of powers and to concentrate too heavily on one or another point along the spectrum of possible definitions of executive authority. Especially simplistic are modern apologists for presidential power who argue that the Founding generation all but universally equated "executive power" with the nominal powers of the British king.[55] In a more sophisticated (yet still problematic) approach, Eric Nelson has usefully questioned whether American and British conceptions of royal and executive power were the same. His work nonetheless overly simplifies American attitudes as equating prerogative and executive power, in part out of eagerness to assert the engagingly ironic yet too-neat theory that Americans would develop a kinglier conception of their chief executive than the British themselves had of their king.[56]

Perhaps the best that can be said is that by the 1770s, Americans who invoked separation of powers generally agreed that the doctrine turned on three now-familiar types of governmental power: legislative, executive, and judicial. According to Montesquieu, to whom Americans usually turned, legislative power comprised the enactment, amendment, or abrogation of permanent or temporary laws; executive authority included the power to implement laws, to make peace or war, and to ensure public security; and judicial power entailed punishing criminals and resolving disputes between individuals.[57] But even here, at the core of the doctrine, these definitions did not command universal assent. Most often, discussion of governmental structure assumed rather than explicated such definitions.[58] And beyond this imprecise core, the rest remained up for grabs—including most issues that generate modern controversy.

American constitutionalists nonetheless bravely attempted to apply separation of powers early on as best they could. Their efforts, however, often reflected the challenges, difficulties, and downright confusion of shifting rapidly from one dominant constitutional model to another and then implementing it in practical detail. For this reason, initial attempts strike modern eyes as more rhetoric than reality. Four of the early state constitutions, for example, included express separation of powers clauses.

Virginia's was typical, providing that "the legislative, executive, and judiciary department, shall be separate and distinct, so that neither exercise the powers properly belonging to the other."[59] Perhaps the most concrete manifestation of the doctrine is one taken for granted today. In general, early republican constitutions expressly prohibited members of the legislature from holding any remunerative position elsewhere in government. They did this, as the New Jersey Constitution declared, so that "the legislative department of this government may, as much as possible, be preserved from all suspicion of corruption."[60]

Given their commitment to legislative supremacy, however, the states effectively honored their commitment to these declarations in the breach. "What more than anything else makes use of Montesquieu's maxim in 1776 perplexing," writes Gordon Wood, "is the great discrepancy between the affirmations of the need to separate the several governmental departments and the actual political practice the state governments followed. It seems, as historians have noted, that Americans in 1776 gave only verbal recognition to the concept of separation of powers in their Revolutionary constitutions, since they were apparently not concerned with a real division of departmental functions."[61]

Taking separation of powers more seriously pointed to ways of explaining where the states had gone wrong. This critique in turn sharpened many Americans' apparently hazy conception of the doctrine. From this process a number of leading critics realized that they had placed too little faith in balance, had devoted too much attention to democratic accountability, and had given insufficient concern to the need for government power.

The most insistent critique of the early state constitutions targeted the lack of balance among the branches. Time and again, critics of state constitutions decried their asymmetry and proposed separation of powers as a means to restore balance and preserve liberty. One early critic, Benjamin Rush, complained that the Pennsylvania Constitution ensured that "the supreme, absolute, and uncontrolled power of the whole State is lodged in the hands of *one body* of men."[62] Jefferson famously sounded the same theme when criticizing his state's constitution in *Notes on the State of Virginia*:

> All the powers of government, legislative, executive, and judiciary, result to the legislative body. The concentrating [of] these in the same hands is precisely the definition of despotic government. It will be no alleviation that these powers will be exercised by a plurality of hands, and not by a single one. 173 despots would surely be as oppressive as one. . . .

[Government] should not only be founded on free principles . . . the powers of government should be so divided and balanced among several bodies of magistracy, as that no one could transcend their legal limits, without being effectually checked and restrained by the others.[63]

Despite occasional rhetorical excess, advocates of separation of powers rarely argued for keeping the three government departments absolutely distinct. Even when they did, it is doubtful whether they meant it with much more clarity than did the men who drafted Virginia's original—and effectively ignored—separation of powers clause. As Willi Paul Adams notes, "Montesquieu, the authority used by critics, had not advocated a separation of powers pure and simple."[64] Likewise, Montesquieu's "much praised model, the British constitution, permitted several functions to be exercised jointly or in a partially overlapping manner by the several branches."[65] The more sophisticated commentators understood that governmental power needed to be separated sufficiently to ensure that no one branch would ever again become as powerful as the state legislatures had.[66]

As it promised balance, separation of powers also reflected a reconceptualization of accountability. Simple accountability had proven to be too dangerous. As the Critical Period progressed, many thinkers could agree with Aedanus Burke when he observed that "a popular assembly," framed to respond to unmediated popular will and "not governed by fundamental laws, but under the biass [sic] of anger, malice, or a thirst for revenge, will commit more excess [sic] than an arbitrary monarch."[67] This followed, others concluded, because simple accountability had also resulted in government that was paradoxically unaccountable. Recent experience demonstrated that radically representative legislatures fell easy prey to demagogues, to localism, and—perhaps most importantly—to factions. It was for these reasons that state legislatures could pass too many laws too quickly in ways that threatened liberty. As Madison noted, "The short period of independency has filled as many pages as the century which proceeded it" with ill-considered, unjust, and unrepresentative laws.[68]

Separation of powers was the key to addressing these unhappy discoveries. It could do so not by abandoning the idea of democratic accountability but by recasting it in such a way as to render it less dangerous and more truly representative, or at least representative of the people's more virtuous selves. Proponents of the doctrine therefore tended to worry less about attempting to replicate the populace as nearly as possible in the halls of the legislature. Attempting this, it was declared, would ensure that "all power residing originally in the people, and being derived from them, the several

magistrates and officers of government vested with authority, whether legislative, executive, or judicial, are the substitutes and agents, and are at all
times accountable to them."[69] This more complex view of accountability
meant shifting attention from such republican strategies as annual elections, local instructions, and requirements that "all bills of a public nature,
shall . . . be printed for the consideration of the people."[70] In their stead, it
yielded such devices as direct election of the governor and upper houses of
the assemblies, as well as selection of judges by some combination of elected
executives and legislators.

For all that separation of powers promised as a safeguard of liberty, it
also held out ways for making government power more effective, republican government's more traditional problem. Mostly those ways pointed
toward rehabilitating those offices that executed and adjudicated the
laws. Here, however, the concern was not so much for achieving balance
or spreading representation but for ensuring that the government could
promote order. Many Americans viewed the vices of the Critical Period
as the inevitable degeneration of republics into anarchy. Some events, in
fact, were best seen as just that. Most spectacular in this regard was Shays's
Rebellion, during which farmers in western Massachusetts rioted against
state authority in 1786. The famous revolt, as Wood notes, was received with
excited consternation mingled with relief by many Americans precisely
because it was an anticipated and understandable abuse of republican liberty. "Liberty had been carried into anarchy and the throwing off of all
government—a more comprehensible phenomenon to most American
political thinkers than legislative tyranny."[71]

Seen this way, as anarchy, Shays's Rebellion suggested the solution.
Happily, state government had been able to restore order to western
Massachusetts thanks in part to that state's reformed and more vigorous executive. As Charles Thach puts it, concern about authority in part
meant "a corresponding change of emphasis" and confirmed the wisdom
that—contrary to the Pennsylvania approach—"the one-[person] executive is best." It also suggested "the necessity of executive appointments,
civil and military; the futility of legislative military control . . . [and the]
value of a fixed executive salary which the legislatures could not reduce."[72]
That a rebellion occurred at all sent shockwaves straight to Boston. One
consequence of the Shaysites' actions was a renewed appreciation of a vigorous judiciary, since one object of their wrath was the local courts, which
upheld the claims of creditors over rural debtors. It was in part to reopen
these courts that the recently empowered governor of Massachusetts effectively marshaled the local military.

A new spate of state constitutions, most notably the Massachusetts Constitution of 1780, put developing separation of powers principles into practice. So too, however, did the earlier New York Constitution of 1777, a document that was ahead of its time, anticipated or even exceeded the approach later taken in other states, and is often cited, alongside the Massachusetts framework, as a precursor of the Federal Constitution.[73] Both state documents, among others,[74] displayed a profound commitment to a functional balance that was nonetheless short of a rigid, formal division.

The Massachusetts instrument, the work of such notable reformers as John Adams, stated—or, to be more accurate, overstated—the new commitment in the most ostensibly formalist separation of powers clause written to that point:

> In the government of this commonwealth, the legislative department shall never exercise the executive and judicial powers, or either of them; the executive shall never exercise the legislative and judicial powers, or either of them; the judicial shall never exercise the legislative and executive powers, or either of them; to the end it may be a government of laws, and not of men.[75]

This prescription meant strengthening the governor and the courts at the expense of the assembly, the lower house in particular. Unlike fellow chief magistrates, the governor of Massachusetts—to be styled "His Excellency"[76]—was therefore accorded an array of protections against despotic legislative power, including express salary protection, the ability to prorogue and adjourn the legislature, and a provisional veto that could be overridden by two-thirds of each house.[77] Along similar lines, the New York governor had the authority to convene (on extraordinary occasions) and prorogue the assembly, along with a complex power to "revise" bills in conjunction with the state chancellor and judges of the supreme court to prevent laws that were "hastily and unadvisedly passed."[78]

In both states the judiciary also benefited. Massachusetts vested the power to appoint judges in the governor (with the advice and consent of the upper house of an executive council) and granted judges life tenure.[79] New York, though more modest in its protections, also accorded the governor a qualified power to appoint judges and guaranteed that judges would serve during good behavior until the age of sixty.[80]

Critically, in states both with and without newer reform frameworks, courts continued to develop the doctrine of constitutional judicial review as a check on legislative excess. Previously, and then only recently, this idea had been understood to develop as a reaction to majoritarian tyranny in the states. More recently still, however, scholarship indicates that courts in America had begun asserting the doctrine even before independence. In particular, William Nelson has demonstrated that courts in several colonies refused to enforce the notorious 1765 Stamp Act on the ground that it violated the British constitution.[81]

With independence, written constitutions, and home-grown democratic despotism, such newly independent states as Virginia, Rhode Island, Connecticut, North Carolina, and New Jersey[82] all played host to cases that in some way anticipated or established the idea that a court could declare void a legislative act that conflicted with a given constitutional framework. And though Massachusetts did not take part in this trend, New York did. In *Rutgers v. Waddington*,[83] a New York City court engaged in what today would be termed constitutional avoidance by construing a state statute in a manner that conflicted with the law of nations, as incorporated into New York law by the 1777 constitution. Successfully putting forward this position was a young New York commercial lawyer named Alexander Hamilton.[84] *Rutgers* not only confirmed a judicial power which had been developing on the local level for a generation. The decision also demonstrated a readiness to employ that power to vindicate claims under international law.

Beyond balance, separation of powers meant adopting devices that reflected a more complex conception of accountability. New York and Massachusetts did this most dramatically by rejecting legislative selection of the governor in favor of direct election by the people. The constitutions also diffused accountability within the assemblies themselves. Where a number of earlier constitutions had gone so far as to either empower the lower house to elect the upper houses,[85] or to get rid of the upper houses completely,[86] New York and Massachusetts confirmed the majority view by specifying that this body too would be directly elected by the people.[87] Conversely, neither instrument extended the principle to the election of judges, a strategy with which state constitutions generally would not experiment for at least a generation and the Federal Constitution would reject outright.

Finally, both the Massachusetts and New York frameworks also reflected a comparative concern for efficient administration of state affairs. Given the Pennsylvania option, it is significant that these and other systems chose to retain a single person as "supreme executive magistrate" or "governor."[88] As noted, Massachusetts in particular greatly circumscribed the governor's executive supremacy, especially with regard to appointments. Nonetheless, the state's retention of a "unitary" governor reflected a fresh appreciation throughout the republic that a single chief executive promoted energetic enforcement of the laws in a way that a plural executive could not.[89] Likewise, Massachusetts, as well as New York,[90] also provided that the governor would be "the commander in chief of the army and navy . . . and shall have full power . . . to train, instruct, exercise, and govern the militia and navy" to defend the commonwealth.[91] If anything, New York enunciated its commitment to executive energy even more plainly in stating that it was the duty of the governor "to transact all necessary business with the officers of government, civil and military; to care that the laws are faithfully executed, to the best of his ability; and to expedite all such measures as may be resolved upon by the legislature."[92]

Separation of Powers, Federalized

The developments of the previous two decades of trial and error culminated in the Federal Constitution. The document that emerged from the Philadelphia Convention lacked a separation of powers clause of the sort that many of the state constitutions had. The omission, however, could not possibly be more misleading. The gap probably resulted in part from the Constitution's overall economy of text. Another possible factor is that the Constitution expressly "mixed" powers, which would have made the type of absolute language seen in state constitutions' separation of powers clauses inaccurate. Whatever the reason, the background, text, structure, and discussions of the new framework make clear that separation of powers would be a—if not *the*—cornerstone of the new system. This reality should stand as a cautionary tale against the temptation, to which lawyers and judges are especially prone, of drawing lessons from what is *not* in the Constitution's text.

As it was, the lessons painfully learned on the state level would now be elaborated on a national scale. Here, too, the Constitution reflected a basic concern to further create balance within the government, secure accountability throughout its various bodies, and ensure its effectiveness. The means toward these ends would again be a more constrained legislature, an enhanced executive, and, not least, an independent and robust "supreme Court, and . . . such inferior Courts as the Congress may from time to time ordain and establish."[93] The document accomplishes this strategy, metaphorically, by using ink at the top, pencil in the middle, and blank paper at the bottom. The ink appears assigning the three core powers of legislation, execution, and adjudication to the three separate branches. In addition, the Constitution expressly assigns to each branch additional powers that either were difficult to categorize, were contested, or which facilitated the main goals that separation of powers was to further, such as balance. More of a pencil-sketch approach may be found in the many areas in which the document assigns powers to different branches that have no precise or obvious borders. Unclear, at least on the surface, is where Congress's power to declare war ends and the president's authority as commander in chief begins when it comes to deploying the armed forces. Blank are vast areas that suggest no consensus whatsoever. The Constitution addresses appointing federal officers, but not their firing. Likewise, it prescribes the making of treaties, but not their termination. All told, the framework's overall sketchiness confirms that much about the basics, not to mention the details, of separation of powers remained contested, under-developed, or both.

Even so, the legislative branch would remain formidable. The Federal Congress, in fact, managed to eclipse the Confederation Congress in two fundamental ways. It would, first of all, have a direct electoral mandate in the House of Representatives, and retain an indirect democratic basis through the election of senators by state legislatures. On this foundation, the new Congress would at least have the authority to tax and legislate directly, rather than through humble requests to the state. To achieve a ver-tical balance of authority with the states, the powers of Congress would not be plenary, but instead would encompass broad but not unlimited leg-islative powers "herein granted."[94] Yet despite, or because of, Congress's increased authority, the Constitution's most striking feature was the cre-ation of an executive and judiciary that would be worthy and powerful counterparts to the legislature and each other.

The most striking result was a "supreme magistrate [that] was truly awesome."[95] The president's specific powers started with "the executive Power." Whatever else it may have meant to some, the only definition of the term that commanded a clear consensus was its core—implementation of the laws. Conversely, at least no significant American thinker believed that the term included all prerogative powers associated with the British monarch. But just what "executive Power" meant in between was hotly debated, contested, attempted, amended, and variously interpreted throughout the period. For this reason the Constitution accords the presi-dent various specific powers beyond implementing the law that, taken together, make for a unique package. These include the power to grant pardons and reprieves, to make treaties and appoint ambassadors and judges of the Supreme Court (with the advice and consent of the Senate), to fill vacancies during the recess of the Senate, to recommend measures for congressional consideration, to convene Congress upon extraordinary occasions, to receive ambassadors, to take care that the laws be faithfully executed, and to appoint and commission federal officers.[96]

The Constitution pursued balance even more directly when it provided the top of each branch with specific means of self-defense. Often, this came at the expense of accomplishing a clean division of powers. Most dramatically, the president could exercise a qualified veto over legislation.[97] While delegates supported the veto on a number of grounds, James Wilson articulated the dominant rationale when he stated, "Without such a Self-defense the Legislature can at any moment sink [the executive] into non-existence."[98] Another defense mechanism that is now taken for granted is the Constitution's express protection of the president's salary from congressional diminution or increase. In the same manner, the Federal Convention included express salary protection for federal judges, providing as well that they "shall hold their Offices during good Behaviour."[99] Further provisions specified additional protection for the president in providing for impeachment as the only method of removal.

No less important, the idea of extending accountability promoted separation of powers still further. Like the state frameworks, the Constitution reflected a suspicion of simple electoral mandates as demagogic.[100] Under the new understanding, the executive was able to stake its own claim as representative, the better to check even the national legislature's attempts to rush through ill-considered laws on the strength of a self-serving and distorted reliance on the popular will.

The Constitution's strategy with the president is as well known as it is confused. As in Massachusetts, the chief executive would not be selected by the legislature. Yet by contrast, the Constitution rejected the option of direct popular election in favor of the elaborate and convoluted Electoral College.[101] The convention opted for this indirect method partly to placate the advocates of state sovereignty and partly to ensure that only the most virtuous, disinterested individuals—in James Wilson's phrase, "Continental Characters"[102]—would gain the office. As a direct function of the president's newly enhanced accountability, the delegates also decided to give the president a hand in several powers, a number of them dealing with foreign relations, that had originally been slated for the Senate alone. Among these were the power to make treaties and appoint ambassadors and "judges" of the Supreme Court.[103]

The Constitution's version of separation of powers again ensured that the government would respect liberty and nonetheless discharge its duties with energy. Most important here was the creation of a unitary presidency— "unitary" in the sense of being headed by one person rather than, as in

Pennsylvania, a committee. Advocates for this position prevailed over noisy opposition, primarily with arguments that a single chief magistrate would provide the executive branch with the most "vigor" and "dispatch."[104] For just these reasons, the Constitution went even beyond the Massachusetts model in granting the president further—but by no means complete— control of the military. Toward this end, the document made the president commander in chief and provided that he "shall Commission all the Officers of the United States"[105] yet kept an array of powers concerning military finance and regulation vested in Congress.[106]

Along with the new executive, similarly impressive was the national judiciary, especially given that, like the executive, none had existed before. The Constitution provided for the Supreme Court and assumed a lower federal judiciary. It also specified a limited yet broad federal court jurisdiction, including the following: cases arising under the Constitution, laws, and treaties; cases affecting diplomats; admiralty and maritime cases; and controversies in which the United States is a party; as well as controversies between two states, between a state and citizens of another state, between citizens of different states, between citizens of the same state claiming lands under grants from different states, and between a state and foreign citizens.[107] Finally, the framework assumed the power of constitutional judicial review.[108] As with the executive, the Constitution accorded the judiciary both protection and the means for self-protection. In the same manner, the Federal Convention included express salary protection for federal judges, providing as well that they "shall hold their Offices during good Behaviour."[109] And, like the president, they could not be removed other than through impeachment.[110]

Less appreciated, those Supreme Court "judges" and their lower federal counterparts would also reflect the goal of accountability. For all the later slogans concerning "unelected judges," the federal judiciary actually reflects an enhanced democratic pedigree, though one that would help ensure that selection would not be the result of mere popular whim. The judges, first of all, would be nominated by the president, the one figure who could claim at least indirect election by the entire nation. Yet the Senate, the house expected to have a higher proportion of "Continental Characters," would also have to sign off. In this way, the federal judiciary could now claim democratic accountability through two elected branches. But precisely for that reason, it would not be beholden to either branch, given that the branches would not necessarily have identical views on what types of jurists should sit on the federal bench. Beyond independence, the complex nature of the federal courts' democratic pedigree would greatly reduce the chances that the popular will reflected in judicial selection would manifest as demagoguery as opposed to deliberation.[111]

In similar fashion, the Constitution set the stage for a judiciary that would be effective. In the main, the decisions that facilitated balance likewise furthered judicial energy. A mandated Supreme Court, an expected lower federal judiciary, life tenure, and salary protection[112] all militated for a court system that would efficiently—and independently—meet whatever challenges it would have to face. Perhaps ironically, the Constitution would commandeer the state judiciaries in adjudicating federal law through the supremacy clause, which mandates that the Constitution, federal statutes, and treaties shall be the "supreme Law of the Land; and the Judges in every State shall be bound thereby."[113] More directly, Congress would realize the Constitution's expectation of a full-blown court system in the First Judiciary Act, which created a three-tier system of district and circuit courts, since reformed and made even stronger, with the Supreme Court at the summit.[114]

Much like separation of powers itself, what would prove to be the most formidable judicial power did not appear expressly in the text at all. It does not require extensive reflection to see how the authority to declare legislative and executive acts unconstitutional facilitates all three functions that separation of powers was meant to advance. The power to check the other branches, especially in the name of rights, obviously promotes balance to prevent abuse of power. It also gives the courts a powerful tool of self-protection. In addition, judicial review serves accountability in at least two ways. As noted, the federal courts actually have a democratic pedigree through appointment of judges by the president with Senate approval. In addition, reliance on the Constitution means applying law not just enacted by Congress or implemented by the president but entrenched by "We the People of the United States," through difficult procedures that require something approaching a national consensus. Finally, judicial review further makes for a vigorous judiciary, as critics of "judicial activism" never cease to point out.

Given its importance, constitutional judicial review has generated perhaps more written analysis than any other topic in American law. The doctrine's origins account for a hefty share of the overall total. Academic debates on the emergence of judicial review may outlast the Constitution itself. Yet certain broad points are by now reasonably settled. First, at root, constitutional judicial review is distinctly an American invention, flowing from the ideas that a constitution is superior to ordinary law (hence "constitutional") and that the judiciary has the duty to apply the higher law over inconsistent ordinary law, at least in cases before it (hence "judicial review").[115] Add the common-law notion of *stare decisis*, or precedent, and any judgment that an ordinary law is unconstitutional will have a ripple effect far beyond the immediate case that triggered it. As noted, numerous state courts had been groping their way toward constitutional judicial review well before the drafting of the Constitution, not least in cases involving international law.[116]

That said, few who have studied the matter would contend that the Founding generation would have foreseen that judicial review would have achieved anything like the scope, frequency, and importance it has gained since. Rather, the anticipated role for judicial review under the Federal Constitution was primarily as a check on the states, not to mention state violations of treaty obligations.[117] It would, however, be a mistake to conclude that judicial review was not also meant to apply horizontally, to possible unconstitutional acts by the other branches of the federal government. For one thing, the previous state cases pointing toward judicial review themselves applied the idea horizontally to limit the political branches of their states. As an analytic matter, moreover, that the Founders focused on the problem of unconstitutional state acts does not mean that they would have exempted from judicial scrutiny unconstitutional federal acts, any more than the drafters of the Fourteenth Amendment would have countenanced violations of an equal protection principle by the federal government just because state violations of that principle demanded their immediate attention. Finally, scholars of early judicial review are agreed that the Founders generally thought that the need for the judiciary to protect itself from legislative or executive encroachments on its jurisdiction represented another reason to constitute the doctrine.

Whatever else it did, therefore, *Marbury v. Madison* neither invented judicial review nor established judicial review in anything like its modern form, in which it is extensive and routine. Rather, it was one not-insignificant step for the Court that pointed to subsequent giant leaps for the judiciary.

There has been no shortage of keystrokes expended debating *Marbury*. Reacting to its mythic status, many scholars emphasize the narrowness of the Court's holding. The decision applied only to the parties before the Court, rejected an invitation to expand its jurisdiction, and for that reason required no affirmative action from the political branches to enforce it. Nor, infamously, would the Court again decline to apply another act of Congress it deemed unconstitutional until a generation later, in *Dred Scot v. Sanford*, which held that the federal provision abolishing slavery in the Minnesota territory violated the due process clause of the Fifth Amendment.[118]

However narrow its originally anticipated scope, *Marbury* merely confirmed an increasingly established principle that "it is emphatically the duty of the judicial department to say what the law is" in cases properly before it.[119] What the judiciary said "the law is," moreover, in such cases could check actions of the states themselves as well as those of the other political branches, as had been pioneered at the state level.

Though the fact is often overlooked, *Marbury* held this line in the face of a combined assault by both Congress and the president. In its waning days in power, the Federalist "party" managed to enact the Judiciary Act of 1801. The measure in part was a true reform initiative which, among other things, established standing federal circuit courts of appeals that relieved Supreme Court justices of the onerous task of riding circuit. Yet by creating numerous new judgeships under Article III, the act would also have cemented a Federalist hold on the judiciary for years, if not decades, to come. That prospect did not sit well with the newly elected Jeffersonian Congress, much less the newly elected President Jefferson. They responded by repealing the Federalist and passing new legislation that together reconstituted the circuit courts without the new circuit judges. These actions presented momentous constitutional issues. Not least of these was the question of how Congress could eliminate judgeships whose occupants were guaranteed life tenure and salary protection under the Constitution. The Supreme Court, in *Stuart v. Laird*,[120] nonetheless allowed this frontal assault on the judiciary to succeed. To have done otherwise might well have invited a constitutional crisis had the Jeffersonians been bent on ignoring a decision that held otherwise, given their electoral triumph. In this light the same Supreme Court, led by the Federalist Chief Justice John Marshall, leaped on the opportunity to preserve the idea of judicial review put forth in *Marbury*, a case in which the act of Congress that was struck down had, paradoxically, sought to increase the jurisdiction of the Court.[121]

Marbury, in short, in asserting judicial review, confirmed a power that was neither novel by that time nor modest in light of the circumstances. It may be true that the initially anticipated role for the doctrine at the federal level centered on the judiciary's power to check the states and on preserving the judiciary's own independence. It may also be true that, after *Marbury*, the Court would not exercise the power against Congress for over a generation. Yet nothing in the constitutional text, these initial expectations, or the underlying logic of the doctrine limits its application to constitutional violations in other areas. Still less do they limit the broader idea for which *Marbury* stands—that the judiciary has the duty to say what the law is in cases that properly come before it, even or especially if doing so checks the actions of the other branches. Such instances are not confined to holding that the Constitution prevails over an act of Congress. They may also involve construing statutes, where possible, to be consistent not just with the Constitution but also with existing statutes or international law, whether treaties or custom. And the exercise of judicial review in this broader sense would surely apply to violations of any of these sources of law, where applicable, by the executive.

As it happens, nowhere would the early Supreme Court exercise this authority more dramatically than in cases involving international law and foreign affairs.

CHAPTER THREE

Separation of Powers in Foreign Affairs

DOMESTIC CONCERNS MAY have fostered constitutional innovation—most dramatically, perhaps, in the Founding generation's commitment to separation of powers. But it was the vices of the *national* system in *foreign affairs* that spurred the true sense of crisis. Most modern writing about the Constitution overlooks the role that the nation's failures abroad played in the lead-up to the Philadelphia Convention. Still less does scholarship attempt to relate the Founders' foreign affairs worries to their fears of majoritarian tyranny in the states. This disconnect would have stunned Madison and many of his future Federalist reformers. To them, the incapacity of the United States to conduct foreign affairs in a dangerous world made imperative the creation of a vastly stronger national government.

Yet with the prospect of enhanced national power came the threat of a truly epic tyranny on a continental scale. Fortunately, the Founders' encounter with democratic despotism in the states gave them the tools to check excessive power even as they created a more effective and accountable national government. Chief among these was separation of powers. Faith in precisely this doctrine enabled those advocating a new constitution to believe that a more powerful national government could establish not just an empire but also an "Empire of liberty."[1] Contrary to current misunderstandings, separation of powers would apply as fully, if not more fully, to foreign affairs as to domestic matters. And as in domestic matters, a key to the system would be a robust role for an independent and vigorous national judiciary in foreign affairs.

The Disunited States

Americans learn the truths that the Declaration of Independence held to be self-evident. They do not have as firm as grasp on what it actually declared:

> That these United Colonies are, and of Right ought to be, FREE AND INDEPENDENT STATES . . . and that as FREE AND INDEPENDENT STATES, they have full Power to levy War, conclude Peace, contract Alliances, establish Commerce, and to do all the other Acts and things which INDEPENDENT STATES may of right do.[2]

The Declaration, in other words, announced the establishment of one (or at least one) new nation-state as defined under the law of nations.[3] Of the many attributes of international statehood, the Continental Congress significantly specified three. Armed with the powers to make war, peace, and alliance, the United States would be able to safeguard its national security. The nation would also be able to engage in international commerce, critical for an economy that rose or fell with transatlantic trade. Finally, though this was a less tangible attribute, statehood would bring the pride, honor, and respect of assuming an independent and equal place among the world's nations.[4]

From the first, however, the new nation's government fell short of its ends. The Declaration points the way here as well. As scholars have long pointed out, the document maintains almost a studied ambiguity as to whether it is declaring the independence of one state or thirteen. The Declaration claims to issue from "the thirteen united States of America." Yet elsewhere it refers "one People." Nor does the operative clause help. It proclaims that the "United Colonies" are free and independent states.[5] But what does it mean to say that as free and independent states they may engage in foreign affairs? The phrase might mean that the new nation can do whatever other independent states can do. Or it may mean that the thirteen distinct states will deal with the rest of the world as a unit. It might even be taken to claim that the thirteen states are just that under the law of nations—thirteen entities that each may conduct foreign affairs separately.[6] The challenge of how best the colonies could be engaged in united action predated the Revolution, and it would endure now that they were "united" states.[7]

Unfortunately, this ambiguity would prove to be more than just rhetorical. So long as the United States faced its common British enemy, the United States mustered enough cohesion to keep up the fight. With peace, the Declaration's ambiguity manifested itself in often crippling disunity, through the structure of a national government in which the domestic states that composed it gave up limited authority. This weakness notoriously crippled the nation's foreign commerce. It so compromised national security that a genuine threat of dismemberment emerged. Not least, the disunity threatened the sense of pride and honor that Americans forged during the Revolution. These foreign affairs crises, far more than majoritarian tyranny at home, led nationally minded Americans to seek a genuine national constitution. As a leading foreign affairs scholar put it, "More than anything else, [Americans'] inability to effectively address crucial foreign policy problems persuaded many leaders that a stronger national government was essential to the nation's survival."[8]

The United States acted more effectively without a formal framework during war than it would with a formal framework during peacetime. Few things bind a nation together more strongly than an external threat, and the new, compound republic was no exception. Confronting Great Britain enabled the Continental Congress to manage, often just barely, to keep the Continental Army in the field.[9] That achievement in turn helped the Congress to obtain loans and conclude commercial treaties with European states, and above all to conclude a treaty of alliance with France. Not least, the war helped further forge a national identity.[10] Yet even the war was not enough to prompt the states to agree on an actual national framework until the fighting had nearly concluded. Mindful of the urgent need for such a blueprint, Congress adopted the Articles of Confederation on November 15, 1777. They would not formally go into effect until March 1, 1781, with the ratification of Maryland, the last state to approve.[11]

Often overlooked are the Articles' genuine steps toward creating a working national government, especially in foreign affairs. Among other things, the document prohibited any state from entering into any treaty without Congress's approval, prevented the states from levying imposts or duties in violation of treaties, and prohibited making war without congressional approval.[12] Affirmatively, the Articles gave Congress the power to make war and peace, receive ambassadors, make treaties, prescribe the rules relating to the taking of prizes, grant letters of marque and reprisals, and regulate the army and navy.[13] Likewise overlooked, the Articles went beyond the state constitutions in concentrating power in a legislature, lacking either an executive or standing judiciary to provide even a weak check.

The one nod the Articles did make to separation of powers was with respect to both judicial power and international law. Article IX, by far the most relevant provision, set out, among other things, detailed procedures for the creation of an ad hoc court to adjudicate individual boundary disputes between the states. After petitioning Congress, state parties would first "be directed to appoint by joint consent, commissioners or judges to constitute a court for hearing and determining the matter in question."[14] If they could not agree, judges would be drawn by lot from a list provided by Congress, which would then "hear and finally determine the controversy; ... and the judgment and sentence of the court to be appointed, in the manner before prescribed, shall be final and conclusive."[15] With less detail, Article IX also gave Congress the power to establish ad hoc national courts to determine "controversies concerning the private right of soil claimed under different grants of two or more States."[16] The Articles made no mention of the law that would resolve these controversies. Yet the principal (and in border disputes the *only*) rules of decision would come from the law of nations.[17]

But overall, the substance of the Articles reflected the states' long hesitation in delegating too much power to any national government. The first substantive provision made clear that any such delegations would be narrow, stating, "Each state retains its sovereignty, freedom, and independence, and every power, and jurisdiction, and right, which is not by this Confederation expressly delegated to the United States, in Congress assembled."[18] More crucial were the delegations that the states did not make. The Articles failed to grant Congress the power to pass legislation that directly bound anyone in the nation it purported to represent. Nor did Congress have the authority to levy direct taxes. Perhaps most striking, the Articles did not grant Congress the power to regulate commerce with foreign nations or among the states. David Golove and Daniel Hulsebosch aptly summarize the resulting constitutional halfway house: "Under the Articles, Congress had no taxing power. This reveals two key assumptions behind Revolutionary-era notions of sovereignty: Taxation and commercial regulation were essential markers of sovereignty, but foreign policy could be coordinated without violating state independence."[19]

Absent the authority to legislate, tax, and regulate commerce, the best Congress could do was request that the states employ these powers themselves to promote specified national ends. As Madison would later point out, the "failure of the States to comply with the Constitutional requisitions ... [has been an] evil ... so fully experienced both during the war and since the peace, results so naturally from the number and independent authority of the States and has been so uniformly exemplified in every similar Confederacy, that it may be considered as not less radically and permanently inherent in, than it is fatal to the object of, the present System."[20] As a result, the new United States proved to be incapable of safeguarding its security, its economy, and its national honor.

National security involved the highest stakes and the greatest failure. As Frederick Marks writes, "The most elemental duty of the Confederation government, its very *raison d'être*, was the protection of the country against foreign attack."[21] It was a duty, however, that the new government could not fulfill for two fundamental reasons. First, Congress had the authority to make treaties, but could not ensure that the nation would hold up its end of any international bargain. Second, should resulting U.S. treaty violations invite foreign intervention, the national government had no means to raise a credible military force for the nation's defense. What the system invited, events confirmed.

Despite its potential, the United States began life as an exceptionally weak nation, operating under what at the time was by definition unstable republican government, vulnerable by land and sea to such European superpowers as Britain, France, and Spain. New states susceptible to foreign encroachment, then and now, seek refuge in international law,[22] and the United States was no exception. During the Revolution, Congress made treaties, most notably with France, to ensure military victory. It also agreed to the 1783 Treaty of Paris with Britain to secure the fruits of that victory, above all British recognition of American independence. The nation's leaders further looked to treaties and the law of nations—today, the latter mainly refers to customary international law—to safeguard free trade across the Atlantic that was vital to the U.S. economy.

Peace, ironically, would demonstrate how the flaws of the national framework would transform essential international commitments from safeguards to threats. Nowhere was the problem more evident, or dire, than in the implementation of the Treaty of Paris ending the Revolution. The treaty, which arrived while Congress temporarily met at Princeton, contained several favorable terms. Beyond independence itself, Great Britain agreed to, among other things, fairly expansive American land claims in the West, fishing rights off Newfoundland, and navigation rights on the Mississippi River (which nonetheless was controlled by Spain), and it pledged to "withdraw all [the King's] armies, Garrisons, and Fleets from the said United States, and from every Post, Place, and Harbour within the same."[23] But the British also negotiated important concessions. Though phrased in reciprocal terms, article 4 aimed primarily to protect British interests, stating that it "is agreed that Creditors on either Side shall meet with no lawful impediment to the Recovery of the full Value in Sterling

Money of all bona fide Debts heretofore contracted."[24] Even more point-edly, article 6 sought to protect Americans who had remained loyal to the Crown, calling for "Restitution of all Estates, Rights, and Properties, which have been confiscated belonging to real British Subjects; and also of the Estates, Rights, and Properties of Persons resident in Districts in the possession on [sic] his Majesty's Arms and who have not borne Arms against the said United States."[25]

Yet ensuring payment of British creditors and, even more notably, pro-viding compensation for confiscated loyalist property remained beyond the powers of the Congress that had made these commitments. As Jack Rakove notes, "Freed from the patriotic constraints that had always oper-ated, although unevenly, during the war, the states were no longer obliged to defer to the wisdom of Congress and the overriding demands of the com-mon cause."[26] Few groups, moreover, could be less popular among the constituents of state legislators than those the treaty sought to protect. Not surprisingly, the states refused to enact laws making good on the nation's obligations. No less surprisingly, the British cited these failures as a justi-fication for keeping their garrisons along the nation's northwest border, including forts at Michilimackinac, Detroit, Niagara, Point du Fer, Dutch-man's Point, Oswego, Oswegatchie, Sandusky, and Presque Isle.[27] Not only did the British military presence remain, it increased, and included attempts to foment hostility toward the United States among Native Americans. In the meantime, American settlers continued to push north and west. The combination was toxic, resulted in several border confrontations, and, to some observers, threatened outright war.

A "Canadian Friend of the United States" captured the situation, alert-ing his American audience that:

> Your pusillanimity in suffering Britain to retain the frontier posts—the want of energy in your federal head—the contracted state of your commerce—the British reinforcing the garrisons of Canada—the many thousands of troops which were disbanded and became settlers in this province at the end of the war, and who are ready to fly to arms at a moment's warning being tired of cutting down trees and endeavoring to cultivate unfruitful land—are circumstances which unless guarded against will rend America in pieces.[28]

Such warnings were not lost on the government. No American official railed against the situation more sharply or consistently than the ambassador to the Court of St. James. John Adams made it known that state laws pre-venting payment to British creditors or compensation to loyalists ensured the Great Britain's intransigence on a host of issues, including withdrawal from the northwestern forts. "It is my Duty," he railed to Foreign Minister John Jay, "to be explicit with my Country, and, therefore I hope it will not be taken amiss by any of my fellow Citizens, when they are told that it is in vain to expect the Evacuation of Posts, or Payment for the Negroes [i.e., slaves freed by the British without compensation to American slaveowners], a Treaty of Commerce, or Restoration of Prizes, Payment of the Maryland or Rhode Island Demand, Compensation to the Boston Merchants, or any other relief of any kind, until these Laws are all repealed."[29]

Congress, moreover, did try to respond. Significantly, one solution was a federal court that would resolve disputes under treaties and the law of nations. In one of the last congressional attempts to propose amendments to the Articles, a "Grand Committee" proposed that Congress have "the power to institute a federal judicial court . . . to which court an appeal shall be allowed from the judicial courts of the several states, in all causes wherein questions shall arise on the meaning and construction of treaties entered into by the United States with any foreign power, or on the law of nations."[30] As with previous efforts, the idea went nowhere.

Greater progress along these lines took place, paradoxically, at the state level. Just as certain states pioneered separation of powers reforms generally, including judicial review, New York—and Alexander Hamilton— demonstrated how courts could play a critical role in holding the new nation to controversial commitments under the law of nations.[31] *Rutgers v. Waddington* involved a claim by a patriot whose New York City brewery had been occupied, with military authorization, by a British merchant after she fled as the city fell to British forces in 1776. The displaced owner brought suit under New York's recent Trespass Act. The act not only allowed such a claim but denied any defense based upon British military orders.[32]

Hamilton, who represented the British merchant, argued that the law of nations permitted such a defense. He further contended that the local court had to apply the law of nations over the state statute on two grounds. First, the Articles of Confederation transferred all foreign affairs matters to the national government; today this might be called a dormant foreign-affairs-power argument. As Hamilton put it, "Congress have the exclusive direction of our foreign affairs, & of all matters relating to the Laws of Nations."[33] Second, the Treaty of Paris implicitly adopted the relevant law of nations defense, and that treaty was supreme over state law. Finally, Hamilton asserted that the New York Constitution's adoption of the common law included the law of nations, and that at least the latter could not be altered by statute.[34]

The Mayor's Court sided with Hamilton. Mayor James Duane's opinion "most clearly embraced Hamilton's argument that the law of nations operated directly on the legislature by way of Confederation law, referring repeatedly to the 'foederal compact.'"[35] For this reason, he refused to read the Trespass Act as violating the law of nations absent an express abrogation, since it would be unthinkable for the legislators to knowingly violate the law of nations without some clearer indication. Again in modern terms, Duane engaged in a form of constitutional avoidance in light of a dormant foreign relations power. More importantly, Hamilton, Duane, and the *Rutgers* case, which would become widely known, illustrated how courts could usefully apply international law to vindicate individual rights even in the most sensitive foreign affairs cases, notwithstanding popular opinion as expressed in political branches.

American treaty and more general international law violations might not have mattered were it not for the national government's other fundamental flaw—its inability to muster a credible army or navy. As Marks plausibly speculates, the British "might well have withdrawn *in spite of* American violations had they been confronted with substantial military power."[36] The prospect of such power, however, fell prey to other gaps in the national framework. Congress could not itself raise an army or establish a navy. Nor could it directly raise money to pay troops or sailors even if it had such a capacity. Once more, the states neither deferred to Congress nor the demands of the common national cause. By 1787, the United States lacked the means to mount any credible defense. The number of troops under national control had withered to a token establishment of seven hundred. The lack of funds and troops forced Secretary of War Knox to eliminate the departments of the quartermaster, commissary, hospital, marine, and clothier.

As a result, the nation faced containment, defeat, even dismemberment. As with Britain in the Northwest, Spain determined to check American expansion to the Southwest. In particular, the Spanish ambassador Don Diego de Gardoqui strung along U.S. Foreign Minister John Jay concerning possible U.S. navigation rights on the Mississippi, determined all the while never to yield, given American weakness. Spain and Britain augmented their efforts by encouraging Native American forces to check U.S. expansion, not that much encouragement was needed. Native efforts led to numerous deadly setbacks. Leaders such as the Six Nations' Joseph Brant and the Creeks' Alexander McGillivray directed numerous successful raids against settler populations, with U.S. forces too thin and poorly equipped to either counter or prevent casualties that numbered in the thousands. No less dire, military weakness combined with the nation's inability to credibly negotiate treaties threatened the Union itself. Here Jay's repeated failed attempts to secure American navigation rights to the Mississippi River from Spain fueled dark sectional suspicions, as Southerners accused Northerners of bargaining away the interests of settlers pushing westward from Kentucky and Tennessee in favor of the commercial needs of New England fisherman and New York merchants. These divisions, in turn, further encouraged both Spain and Britain in pursuing policies of "dividing and conquering" the increasingly disunited states in the hope that the fragile new nation would break apart.[37]

Grave as was the state of national security, most Americans more directly felt the Articles' failure to deal with foreign commerce. As Chief Justice Marshall would later note, "It may be doubted whether any of the evils proceeding from the feebleness of the federal government contributed more to that great revolution which introduced the present system, than the deep and general conviction, that commerce ought to be regulated by Congress."[38] Echoing the challenges to national security, parallel institutional deficiencies regarding commerce guaranteed corresponding economic crises.

The structural flaws soon became glaring. Congress could regulate neither foreign trade nor commercial relations among the states. This weakness first and foremost meant that the national government could not retaliate against, and still less deter, foreign trade restrictions. Lack of national trade regulation further meant that the enforcement of any commercial treaties was left to the state legislatures and state courts, features that could only make foreign governments think twice about the value of trade agreements with the United States at all. Finally, the Confederation's inability to raise an effective military affected both potential retaliation and prospective treaties. As the British occupation of the Northwest forts suggested, military action could counter hostile economic measures, such as American failure to pay debts to British creditors. Likewise, a navy could be an effective tool in preventing smugglers from evading duties or tariffs set out in commercial agreements. As Marks writes, "The great question, though, was how could Congress prevail upon unwilling states since it lacked both judicial and military power under the Articles of Confederation?"[39] Put another way, the absence of just one of the foregoing powers would be enough to prevent a nation from countering hostile trade practices. Without any of these powers, an already weak, disunited nation, heavily dependent on blue-water shipping, positively invited them.

The foreign power that took up this invitation to the most devastating effect was Great Britain. For all the grievances leading to the Revolution,

the British Empire nurtured American prosperity. American ships dominated trade routes in which American agricultural goods would go first
to other British colonies, above all the West Indies, then to Britain, then
back to North America. Notorious, and profitable, was the "triangle trade,"
in which New England would ship rum to West Africa in exchange for
slaves, who would then be taken to the West Indies and traded for molasses. Ships would then return with the molasses to New England, where
it would be made into more rum. For a time, newly independent Americans thought they would remain in the imperial system. That dream came
crashing down on July 2, 1783, when the Privy Council ordered the closing
of American ships, sailors, and most profitable goods to the British West
Indies. Other orders in council added injuries to injury. One restriction
banned American ships from Newfoundland and Nova Scotia. Another
imposed high duties on certain U.S. products and banned others entirely.
Still another laid open the possibility that ships from one state could not
carry goods from another state to Great Britain itself.[40]

The results bordered on economic depression. American merchants,
shipowners, shipbuilders, riggers, chandlers, rope makers, sailmakers,
blacksmiths, and even many farmers all endured significant decline. More
generally, the U.S. balance of trade with Britain remained woefully one-
sided, holding to a ratio of four to one British imports to U.S. exports. Keeping matters bad, if not making them worse, American trade to nations such
as France and the Netherlands never grew enough to offset expulsion from
the empire. American trade with Spain actually fell, thanks in large part to
the North African Barbary States, which controlled the Mediterranean.[41]

U.S. diplomats decried the situation, and for good reason. As Golove
and Hulsebosch point out, the new nation was often the object of diplomatic contempt from friend and foe, none more so that the British.[42] At
the Court of St. James, Ambassador John Adams notably failed to secure a
commercial treaty, which might have restored to the United States some
aspects of imperial trade. Lord Grenville, speaking in Parliament, noted one
of the reasons for Britain's stance, observing, "We do not know whether they
are under one head, directed by many, or whether they have any head at
all."[43] Lord Sheffield elaborated the point, declaring:

> No treaty can be made with the American States that can be binding
> on the whole of them. The act of Confederation does not enable Con-
> gress to form more than general treaties: at the moment of the highest
> authority of Congress, the power in question was with-held by the sev-
> eral States. . . . When treaties are necessary, they must be made with

the States separately. Each State has reserved every power relative to imports, exports, prohibitions, duties, &c. to itself.[44]

Adams did attempt to rally the individual states to enact retaliatory trade restrictions against Britain. The collective action problem, however, always undermined any possible united front.

For just this reason, American officials and national figures also saw opportunity. Once more Adams led the way, suggesting that Congress be given the power to regulate foreign and national commerce. He soon would be joined by the likes of John Jay, Rufus King, Gouverneur Morris, and George Washington.[45] In Congress, James Monroe pushed for reform through the Articles' near-impossible amendment process.[46] This resulted in a report of the "Grand Committee," the same one that proposed a national court, devoting eight out of its ten amendments to national commercial regulation.[47] These reforms, likewise, went nowhere. Richard Henry Lee, among others, opposed them on the ground that they simply and dangerously shifted too much power to the national government, however dire the country's foreign-trade problems. Better Congress remain, he declared, "a rope of sand than a rod of iron."[48] Bowed but not defeated, others decided to push outside Congress. Foreign commerce issues led directly to the Annapolis Convention, which was to propose more trade amendments yet failed to reach a quorum. From that failure came the Federal Convention in Philadelphia, which would produce a framework that went far beyond what Lee feared but which addressed those concerns with the same doctrine—separation of powers—that emerged to counter the rise of majoritarian tyranny domestically.

Separation of Powers Abroad

The new Constitution may have heralded a government that could at least conduct foreign affairs effectively, one that would, moreover, be more directly accountable. Yet with the prospect of greater central power came the possibility of continental tyranny. And it is just here—in a vastly underappreciated phenomenon—that the value of separation of powers learned on the domestic front became a key to taming the stronger national government required to ensure the new republic's survival both as a viable nation and a free republic.

This connection belies a persistent historical misunderstanding that treats the Founders' commitment to separation of powers as purely a domestic story. The doctrine, to be sure, came into its own first to diagnose, and then cure, the vices of democratic despotism in the states. The idea nonetheless transcended its origins to serve as a device both to check tyrannical power and promote efficiency. As such, it was ideally suited to ensuring that the concentration of foreign affairs authority in a stronger national government would not threaten liberty, while still leveraging the expertise of each branch for effective foreign policy.

Those engaged in constitutional reform simply drew no distinction between domestic and foreign affairs authority. Typical in this regard is Madison's classic analysis of separation of powers in *The Federalist* No. 48. There he famously sets out to demonstrate that "unless the [legislative, executive, and judicial departments], though separate, be so far connected and blended as to give each a constitutional control over the others, the degree of separation which the maxim [of separation of powers] requires, as essential to a free government, can never in practice be duly maintained."[49] At no point, however, does he exempt powers related to foreign affairs from his consideration. To the contrary, one of the other faces of Publius, John Jay, affirmatively discussed the propriety of combining the president and two-thirds of the Senate in creating treaties, stressing that the virtues of the combination outweighed any concerns about concentrating the treaty power in a combination of two departments.[50]

This is not to say that separation of powers concerns applied exactly the same way in foreign as in domestic matters. As noted, the "most dangerous branch" on the state level was clearly the legislatures, which were, in Madison's phrase, "everywhere extending the sphere of [their] activity and drawing all power into [their] impetuous vortex."[51] Accordingly, the Constitution enhanced the executive and judicial branches to curb this evil. In foreign affairs the Founders clearly thought that the chief threat to liberty would come from the executive. That said, certain Federalists, such as the Hamiltonian incarnation of Publius, did famously stress the "secrecy, energy, and despatch" that the president would bring to foreign affairs in particular. Yet just for this reason, the dominant theme discussing the proposed president stressed the need to hold the new office in check. Toward that end, the new Constitution took an innovative tack in here strengthening, rather than weakening, the legislature. No less important, it further enhanced the judiciary against foreign affairs encroachments by either entity or both.

The Constitution's text confirms that separation of powers flourished as fully in foreign affairs as in domestic. As is almost a ritual to note, the document does not deal with the new government's powers abroad as fully as it does at home. But contrary to advocates of foreign affairs exceptionalism, the difference is of degree and not kind. Instead, all three branches receive foreign affairs grants in rough proportion to their internal counterparts.

Article I grants Congress the following powers: to tax for, among other things, the "common Defense"; "to regulate Commerce with foreign Nations, and among the several States, and with the Indian tribes"; "to constitute Tribunals inferior to the supreme Court"; "to define and punish Piracies and Felonies committed on the high Seas, and Offenses against the Law of Nations"; "to declare War, grant Letters of Marque and Reprisal, and make Rules concerning Captures on Land and Water"; to raise "Armies"; "to provide and maintain a Navy"; to call forth "the Militia"; and to regulate the militia.[52]

These grants did not just fortify Congress in external relations. They also took authority that some commentators had previously categorized as "executive" and with these strengthened Congress still further. Then as now, the power to regulate national and international commerce made for a vastly more powerful central government. But perhaps even more striking, where the Constitution generally moved domestic power to the executive, the better to check the legislature, in foreign relations important powers went in the other direction. Of these, none was more important than the declare war clause. Countless specific matters involving separation of powers reveal no Founding consensus but instead furnish apt quotations supporting different sides. The declare war clause is not one of these. With the exception of a few idiosyncratic voices, a near scholarly consensus agrees on the basics of this assignment.[53] Under the British prerogative and many of the state constitutions, the authority to commit soldiers or sailors to hostilities fell to the Crown or governor. The Federal Convention rejected this assignment and, in a Constitution that generally shifted power away from the legislature, shifted this authority to Congress. This shift was first and foremost understood to lodge the power to authorize the president to conduct hostilities consistent with the law of nations. It was further taken to entail the power to formally declare the nation's status as belligerent under the law of nations, and it altered, among other things, who might conduct trade and whose ships would be subject to seizure. The debates at the Federal Convention later revealed that the document had originally proposed to grant Congress the power to "make War." On the motion of Madison and Elbridge Gerry, the delegates voted to change "make" to "declare," not to exclude Congress's power to authorize war but instead to leave "to the Executive the power to repel sudden attacks," given that Congress would usually not be in session and would take weeks to convene.[54]

A key reason for the declare war clause was the desire to slow the path to conflict by granting the decision to authorize entry to a collective body. Such deliberation would be prudent in any case, but it was especially so for a fledgling republic in a world of warring superpowers. Yet the grant was also understood to be a specific separation of powers check on a chief executive who would also hold the title "commander in chief."[55] The Founding generation especially feared individuals who would rush armies into the field in pursuit of personal glory, in the manner of a Caesar or Cromwell. The handling of this power demonstrated the Constitution's application of separation of powers to allay this concern.[56]

A terser portion of the framework, Article II confers upon the president the following: "executive Power"; status as "Commander in Chief" of the army, navy, and militia when those bodies are called into national service; "Power, by and with the Advice and Consent of the Senate, to make Treaties, provided two thirds of the Senators present concur"; the power to appoint, with the advice and consent of the Senate, "Ambassadors, other public Ministers, and Consuls"; the authority to "receive Ambassadors and other public Minsters"; and the responsibility to "take Care that the Laws be faithfully executed."[57] The mere creation of a federal executive where none had existed before necessarily addressed many of the weaknesses that had plagued the Articles. That said, the executive that the Constitution created was itself limited and subject to separation of powers constraints, even in foreign relations. Of the many factors that compel this conclusion, three in particular are worthy of note. First, several of the president's foreign affairs powers were last-minute additions. Through August, for example, the Federal Convention had lodged treaty-making authority exclusively in the Senate. Only after the means of selecting the president became better defined was the president given the principal role of negotiating treaties, subject to Senate advice and consent. This eleventh-hour shift suggests that the Founders did not view executive power as either plenary or unconstrained unless otherwise indicated when it came to foreign affairs.

Second, the actual list of granted powers fell short of the most obvious model for a robust foreign affairs "executive," the British Crown. The text divided the power to make treaties and appoint diplomats between the president and Senate. Articles I and II taken together likewise divided the responsibility of federal deployment of the militia, in this instance between Congress and the president. The first instance in which this took place, an armed insurrection under the Washington administration, would reveal a further expectation for a central judicial role as well.[58] Most dramatically, the American chief executive, as noted, was stripped of the power to make war other than to respond to attacks when Congress was not in session. Nor, as some would have it, are any of these provisions plausibly understood as express exceptions to some universally understood baseline of otherwise executive powers.

This is because, whatever else Article II's grant of executive power meant, it did not imply plenary foreign affairs authority unless otherwise indicated. Sometimes called the "vesting clause thesis," this idea simply has no basis in the Constitution's text, structure, or original understanding. In the eighteenth century as today, the core meaning of "executive" was implementing laws; beyond that, agreement broke down utterly. The Constitution's structural grants of foreign affairs powers to each of the branches belies the notion that any one enjoys an unlimited well of authority when it comes to the nation's external relations. Most importantly, in the thousands of statements about the role of the executive in foreign affairs from independence through the Washington administration, exactly two speakers expressly stated that a grant of executive power conveys foreign affairs power—Alexander Hamilton and New York Congressman Egbert Benson. For his part, the notably proexecutive Hamilton made the argument only in passing after defending the president's assertions of authority in foreign affairs with respect to specific textual grants.[59]

Properly read, in short, Article II—including the vesting of "executive Power" in a "President of the united States"—confirms the application of separation of powers to all of the Constitution's grants of authority, domestic and foreign.

A Foreign Affairs Judiciary

The Constitution's last assignment of a general authority, Article III vests "the judicial Power" in the "supreme Court." It goes on to extend the judicial power to federal laws and treaties; to "all Cases affecting Ambassadors, other public Ministers, and Consuls"; "to all Cases of admiralty and maritime Jurisdiction"; and to suits between a state "or Citizens thereof, and foreign States, Citizens or Subjects." Notably, the Supreme Court receives original jurisdiction in "all Cases affecting Ambassadors, other public Ministers and Consuls."[60]

And again, as with domestic matters, the new Constitution assigned the anticipated new federal judiciary a vital foreign affairs role, suggesting if anything more obviously that the judiciary was best suited to protect individual rights under international law. As noted, that last role could and should have been fulfilled by state courts and state legislatures. The president of the Confederation Congress, Charles Thomson, earlier argued in vain that even under the Articles, "every state in the confederacy & every individual in every state is bound to observe [the law of nations]. It is a law paramount in the state so long as the state continues a member of the confederacy. The legislature have no right to interfere with it. . . . On the contrary it is their duty to remove every obstacle (if any there be) within their state to the faithful performance and observance of the treaty."[61] But interfere the state legislatures did, resulting in U.S. treaty violations that compromised national security.

The Constitution solved this problem simply and directly. Critically, it also declared treaties "the supreme Law of the Land." This designation applied not just to "Treaties . . which shall be made" but also to treaties already made "under the Authority of the United States." In a stroke, compacts such as the Treaty of Paris, which the states had violated with impunity, and which in turn led to the Federal Convention to begin with, were now federal law, making "the Judges in every State bound thereby, anything in the Laws of Constitution or Law of any State to the Contrary notwithstanding."[62] Given previous experience with enforcement at the state level, the Constitution, as noted, also mandated a "supreme Court" and anticipated a federal judiciary. It also extended the "judicial Power" to cases involving laws and treaties as supreme federal law. Taken together, these assignments addressed the foreign affairs concerns that Madison had raised years earlier. Now a federal judiciary could ensure that the United States would at last live up its international commitments, including and especially when these established individual rights. Ironically, this solution did not go as far as Madison had originally hoped. At Philadelphia, he had sought to give the new national legislature a "veto" power over all state laws, which would have included those that violated the nation's treaties. This the convention voted down, leaving the supremacy clause, backstopped by a national court system, as the next best option. As it was, what disappointment Madison had was the result of according the federal judiciary an especially important and sensitive role.[63]

Less obviously, the Constitution also extended the courts' authority to what now would be termed customary international law. Article III's vesting of the judicial power was understood, among other things, to include the authority of judges to apply the common law. In the late eighteenth century, as in the United Kingdom today, this authority included the ability of courts to recognize not only domestic doctrines but also rules from the law of nations and even natural law. On this view, the extension of federal jurisdiction to "Laws" of the United States would mean not just statutes but federal common law that judges discovered, adapted, and applied, including the law of nations.[64] One area in which this expectation would be important was disputes between the states, whether over borders, rival land claims, or authority beyond their territory. The several states merited the honor in part because it would "ill suit [their] dignity to be turned over to an inferior tribunal,"[65] but also because controversies between states involving rival land or border claims would require the highest command of the international law principles used to resolve disputes between sovereigns. So significant were other categories that they were reserved for the Supreme Court's original jurisdiction.

Likewise worthy of the Court's original jurisdiction were cases involving "Ambassadors, Consuls, and other public Ministers." Such cases, too, typically implicated the law of nations. As Hamilton explained, "All questions in which they are concerned are so directly connected with the public peace, that as well for the preservation of this, and out of respect to the sovereignties they represent, it is both expedient and proper that such questions should be submitted in the first instance to the highest judicatory of the nation."[66] Matters involving diplomats, once taken away from the states, might have been thought better handled by the executive on the ground of its ostensibly greater sensitivity to possible foreign affairs consequences. As in other areas, the shift to the national government reflected not just federalism concerns but the application of separation of powers as well. Once more that meant that, where the federal courts were properly seized of an actual case or controversy that implicated foreign affairs or international law, resolving the matter would fall to them alone rather than Congress or the president.

The Constitution did not leave what was arguably the most important component the law of nations in any doubt. This was Article III's extension of federal judicial power to "all Cases of admiralty and maritime Jurisdiction."[67] First and foremost, admiralty involved prize cases—the liquidation and sale of captured vessels during hostilities under the law of nations. Few areas touched upon more delicate matters of foreign affairs and national security, as numerous early landmark decisions of the Supreme Court would illustrate. Hamilton rightly observed that such cases "so generally depend on the laws of nations, and so commonly affect the rights of foreigners, that they fall within the considerations which are relative to the public peace."[68] Next, the Constitution's structure confirms the early understanding that the federal courts were to apply the law of nations even without direct incorporation by federal statute. This understanding follows from Article III's grant of admiralty jurisdiction without a parallel grant to Congress to legislate in the field in Article I. In addition, the Constitution, in a further attempt to depoliticize prize cases, declined to extend the right of jury trials to admiralty disputes. As Golove and Hulsebosch note, "The grant of admiralty jurisdiction to the federal courts—with their constitutionally guaranteed independence from the legislative and executive branches—was an important signal to European powers of the willingness and capacity of the new nation to uphold its legal obligations."[69] Judicializing the enforcement of such obligations—particularly in the high-stakes area of prize and admiralty—not only ensured that the states would no longer undermine those obligations. It further added an initial check against the Congress and the executive violating those obligations. All that said, the Constitution nonetheless did not assign these cases to the Supreme Court alone. This was not because they were unimportant. To the contrary, their importance lay in the knowledge that admiralty and maritime cases were so numerous that they would require the full federal courts system once it was established.

It fell to John Jay, the nation's premier diplomat and soon to be its first chief justice, to capture the expected role that the federal courts would play in the nation's external relations. Sounding the importance of a strong central government, Jay wrote that it is "of high importance to the peace of America that she observe the laws of nations towards all [powers with whom she has treaties and other relations], and to me it appears evident that this will be more perfectly and punctually done by one national government than it could be either by thirteen separate States or by three or four distinct confederacies."[70] Yet he also suggested the importance of the judiciary in separation of powers terms. "Under the national government," he wrote, "treaties and articles of treaties, as well as the laws of nations, will always be *expounded* in one sense and *executed* in the *same manner*."[71] Given the Constitution's structural assignments, the task of expounding would fall to the courts; that of executing would fall to the president. On this basis, Jay concluded, "The wisdom of the convention, in committing such questions to the jurisdiction and judgment of courts appointed by and responsible only to one national government, cannot be too much commended."[72]

PART II

From Developing Country to Global Power

CHAPTER FOUR

Holding Steady

THE FOUNDING VISION held for much of the nation's history. For the most part the Supreme Court led the federal judiciary in playing its assigned separation of powers role of robust enforcement of individual rights under laws, treaties, and the law of nations in cases with clear foreign affairs implications. A study covering what amounts to over a century of constitutional evolution would require a volume in itself. A survey of representative landmark cases and controversies must suffice to outline the general story of constitutional continuity that, in the main, lasted well into the first half of the twentieth century.

This story begins with the dispute known as the Neutrality Controversy, perhaps the earliest major foreign affairs challenge that the nation faced under the new Constitution. Whatever else it entailed, this initial crisis reflected an underappreciated expectation of judicial involvement, an expectation so thoroughgoing that the Supreme Court itself had to decline the invitation. Yet the general idea that the judiciary would enforce constitutional, statutory, and international law, especially with regard to rights, regardless of the foreign affairs implications, endured. For present purposes, the judiciary's commitments are perhaps best conveyed categorically, by showing highlights in the ways the federal courts would enforce federal law and rights in the context of foreign affairs. The courts would first of all do so for the purpose of checking the states. Second, they would also consistently do so for the purpose of limiting congressional excesses through artful interpretation of quasi-wartime federal statutes. Third, and particularly striking today, the judiciary would also check the executive by refusing to defer to that branch's interpretations of treaties, rejecting the executive's claims that it could violate the law of nations absent congressional authorization, and generally upholding Congress's own checks on presidential foreign affairs assertions. What's more, in several instances, the Court performed these functions at the literal expense of heroic U.S. Navy officers and crew on whose behalf the executive pressed its assertions of presidential foreign affairs authority.

Appealing to the Court: The Neutrality Controversy

The United States instituted its new government just in the nick of time. No sooner had the Constitution been ratified than the foreign affairs threats to the nation became infinitely worse. Inspired in part by its American forerunner, the French Revolution by 1793 had led to what in many respects was the first true world war. At its center, the conflict pitted against each other Europe's two leading imperial superpowers, France and Great Britain. As it would again over a century later, the United States first attempted to remain neutral. This time, however, the still fledgling republic would mainly succeed. As with most fledgling nations, the United States found refuge in international law as a check, however imperfect, against powers greater than itself. Better adherence to the law of nations, of course, was a critical impetus for the new Constitution. That goal was more important than ever as the institutions that the document outlined began to operate. Consistent with this framework, neither Congress nor the Washington administration sought to monopolize foreign affairs or, still less, keep cases implicating such matters out of the hands of the judiciary. Instead they accepted, and even solicited, action by the courts as a safeguard in favor of rights both for U.S. citizens and foreigners. They did so, moreover, even though many cases the new Supreme Court handled had enormous implications for the new republic's delicate place in world affairs.[1]

None of this is to say that governing under the new Constitution generated no disputes. To the contrary, the stakes of establishing precedents were substantial and produced battles whose intensity matched the importance of the matters under consideration. Nowhere was this phenomenon clearer than in matters in which the Constitution met foreign relations. It is all the more striking, therefore, that one question that did not produce significant debate was the Supreme Court's extensive involvement enforcing rights in exactly this area.

Probably nothing established these patterns more clearly than the disputes that came to be known at the Neutrality Controversy. As soon as war erupted between the French and British superpowers, President Washington determined that the only course the United States could steer was to remain at peace with both. With neither a credible army nor navy, the nation could scarcely risk choosing the wrong side. No less importantly, the United States survived on transatlantic trade. Under the law of nations, nonbelligerents could continue to engage in commerce so long as the goods involved were not military contraband. The determination to seek peace abroad would be easier said than done, but it was the country's only realistic option. It would nonetheless trigger at least four heated constitutional controversies at home. Two of these would not directly involve the courts, but two others would.[2]

The first and most enduring conflict involved Washington's decision to declare the nation's nonbelligerent status without seeking the approval of, or even convening, Congress. Toward this end he issued the so-called Neutrality Proclamation early in 1793. The document actually avoided the term "neutrality," since the country was already starting to choose sides between Britain and France. The statement did, however, make clear that "the duty and interest of the United States require, that they should with sincerity and good faith adopt and pursue a conduct friendly and impartial to the belligerent powers."[3] The cabinet, including the Anglophile secretary of the treasury, Alexander Hamilton, and the pro-French secretary of state, Thomas Jefferson, had supported this declaration unanimously.

By the summer, however, tensions between British and French supporters divided the cabinet and country. On one side, Hamilton, writing as "Pacificus," defended the president's power to in effect declare peace. From Congress, James Madison, writing as "Helvidius" and urged on by Jefferson, replied that the power rightly rested with the legislature.[4] Hamilton's view prevailed, not least thanks to Washington's support.[5] Also victorious, unfortunately, has been the myth that the future Broadway phenomenon primarily based his position on the theory that the president had all but plenary power in foreign affairs, through the clause that granted the office "executive Power."[6] For their part, Madison and Jefferson could point to Congress later passing a "Neutrality Act," which for them undermined Washington's unilateral proclamation as a precedent.

Meanwhile, a second nonjudicial controversy had arisen in the cabinet itself. However much Washington wanted to maintain neutrality, France was the nation's first ally, and the treaties with Louis XVI that established the alliance back in 1778 were still in place. Did those treaties require that the United States support France? Washington submitted the matter to Hamilton and Jefferson, who in effect wound up acting as opposing counsel. Hamilton argued that the revolutionary change in regime meant that the treaties could be deemed "suspended." Jefferson, for once the more careful lawyer, contended that the treaties applied in full force, but did not require U.S. intervention unless the British attacked France's possessions in the Caribbean. International law enabled the United States to be neutral, which in turn helped safeguard the nation's trade and even survival.[7]

Other, and controversial, aspects of the policy did demand judicial action. Yet they were not controversial for involving the judiciary in foreign affairs. Aside from declaring "impartiality," Washington's proclamation also made known that "whosoever of the citizens of the United States shall render himself liable to punishment or forfeiture under the law of nations"[8] for assisting any of the belligerent powers. He added, "I have given instructions . . . to cause prosecutions to be instituted against all persons who shall, within the cognizance of the Courts of the United States, violate the law of nations, with respect to the powers at war, or any of them."[9] This part of the proclamation meant that any American who assisted France, Britain, or their allies, would be subject to criminal prosecution. The problem was that Congress had not enacted a statute making such assistance a crime. Rather, "the Courts of the United States" would be left to apply the law of nations, the international cousin of the common law.

That problem burst into a nationwide dispute when Gideon Henfield was prosecuted in federal court in Philadelphia for serving as an officer on a French privateer that had captured a British ship. Justice James Wilson, who, along with other Supreme Court justices, oversaw neutrality prosecutions while riding circuit, instructed the jury that the defendant "was bound to keep the peace in regard to all nations with whom we are at peace. This is the law of nations."[10] Such prosecutions had been a standard feature in English law. In the polarized political atmosphere of the day, they nonetheless met with substantial popular opposition, and Henfield was acquitted. Congress addressed the problem by enacting the 1794 Neutrality Act, which criminalized assisting nations with whom the United States was at peace in statutory text, after which prosecutions went forward with less incident. Whatever else had made Henfield's and other such cases controversial, the idea of courts applying international law in sensitive foreign affairs matters was not one of them. Opponents instead criticized the executive for attempting to make criminal law without the legislature. More generally, Americans inside and outside the legal community were coming to oppose any criminal sanctions not set down precisely in statutes. For just this reason the Supreme Court would eventually disallow prosecutions based on the common law rather than legislative acts. To the extent the Court rejected judge-made criminal law, the repudiation had little to do with foreign affairs.[11]

Neutrality led to still another problem, one that would demonstrate how significant rather than marginal a role the Supreme Court was expected to play in foreign affairs. The event that would highlight this expectation came about with the arrival of the French Republic's new ambassador to the United States, Edmond Genet. Among many other initiatives, Genet upon his arrival commissioned American vessels with American crews as French privateers, established prize courts on U.S. territory to oversee the condemnation of enemy British vessels, and, while in Philadelphia, even converted a captured British merchant vessel into a French privateer.[12] All these actions appeared to violate the law of nations, invite a British attack, and drag the United States into war.

Still, the president needed to be sure. Three of Washington's four cabinet members were lawyers. Aside from Hamilton and Jefferson, the president could also turn to Attorney General Edmund Randolph. In Hamilton, moreover, Washington has access to one of the best legal minds in the country, not to mention the one he trusted most. Yet unlike many successors, this president was not content to rely on legal advice from within the executive branch, even on a foreign affairs matter that could mean the difference between war and peace. Instead he turned to the Supreme Court. He had Hamilton draft twenty-nine queries, most of them asking to what extent, under the treaties between the United States and France, and international law in general, French citizens could or could not use the United States as a base for privateering operations against a nation with which the United States was at peace. Jefferson wrote the cover letter, which stated:

> These questions depend for their solution on the construction of our treaties, on the laws of nature and nations, and on the laws of the land; and are often presented under circumstances which do not give a cognisance of them to the tribunals of the country. Yet their decision is so little analogous to the ordinary functions of the executive, as to occasion much embarrassment and difficulty to them. The President therefore would be relieved . . . to know, in the first place, their [the justices'] opinion.[13]

Chief Justice Jay famously responded that the justices could not answer this request on the ground that they could not "extrajudicially" decide legal questions. Instead, the Constitution expressly gave the president the power to call for opinions off all sorts from "Heads of Departments." In this way, the precedent against the Court issuing "advisory opinions" was established.[14]

But that may not be the story's most important lesson. Today executive officials, from the president down, seek to avoid the courts' judicial intervention in foreign affairs, even in litigated cases or controversies in which individuals claim the violation of important rights under domestic and international law. Gateway doctrines are simply the most efficient way to do this. Contrast this approach with the assumptions of the Founding generation. Jefferson, Hamilton, and Washington all sought out the legal opinions of the justices even though there was no pending claim. They did so, moreover, on at least two grounds. As Jefferson suggests, the judiciary has superior institutional competence in interpreting the law. The "Judges of the supreme court of the US," Jefferson wrote, enjoy "knowledge of the subject [that would] secure us against errors dangerous to the peace of the US." Relatedly, the judiciary's expertise and neutrality would "ensure the respect of all parties," including, potentially, "the public."[15] Ironically, it was the Court that felt compelled to limit its pronouncements to actual cases. Yet this Founding bottom line, that at the very least courts must adjudicate cases despite and even because of their foreign affairs implications, is exactly the commitment that modern executive officials and their apologists seek to dodge—even at the cost of keeping otherwise justiciable cases out of court in the first place.

The Neutrality Controversy (or controversies) reflected, among other things, a far different constitutional culture, one in which the executive sought to engage rather than avoid the courts. This culture would be confirmed in a sequel during which all three branches embraced a judicial role in a crisis that involved, if not foreign affairs, an armed challenge to national security. That challenge arose out of the new federal government's first tax on a domestic product, an excise on whiskey and other distilled spirits. The tax met with violent resistance by farmers in western Pennsylvania, who had relied on distilling their excess grain for additional revenue, not to mention consumption. By 1794 resistance had escalated from rioting to a full-scale armed insurrection known ever since as the Whiskey Rebellion. For the first time, state militias were federalized, and for the only time, a sitting president, George Washington, at one point led troops in the field. The show of federal force succeeded.[16] What is less well known is that the president scrupulously followed the provisions of the Militia Act, which Congress had enacted in 1792. Under the statute, a federal judge had to certify that "the laws of the United States [had been] opposed, or the execution thereof obstructed, . . . by combinations too powerful to be suppressed by the ordinary course of judicial proceedings, or by the powers vested in the marshals by this act."[17] Not only did Washington duly submit such a statement to Justice James Wilson. The president also dutifully deferred mustering troops until he received the justice's certification.[18]

The Neutrality Controversy (or controversies) reflected larger patterns that would recur for much of the next century. A trio of experts on foreign relations law ably note several of these in analyzing just the Supreme Court's international law docket. The case law, they argue, demonstrates that the Court never suggested that the judiciary's role in applying international law differed significantly from its role in applying domestic law, that the Court frequently used international law to constrain governmental power, that it used international law to vindicate private rights, and that it strove to facilitate the nation's compliance with its international legal obligations.[19] Applying international law almost by definition implicates foreign affairs. It would follow that what applied to international law cases was likewise reflected in decisions that turned on domestic law; yet these principles nonetheless had significant foreign policy consequences.

Saying What the Law Is in Foreign Affairs

REVIEWING STATE ACTION

The Supreme Court, in other words, remained faithful to the Founders' commitments. One of its earliest landmark cases illustrates this fidelity. In *Ware v. Hylton*, the Court reviewed a Virginia statute that effectively blocked payment of debts owed to British creditors by Virginia citizens.[20] The Court held that the statute was invalid under the 1783 Treaty of Paris, which ended the Revolution and guaranteed that creditors on either side would meet with "no lawful impediment" to the full recovery debts owed. As Justice James Iredell's opinion explained, "The extreme inconveniencies felt from such a system [under the Articles of Confederation] dictated the remedy which the constitution has now provided, 'that all treaties made or which shall be made under the authority of the United States, shall be the supreme law of the land. . . .' Under this Constitution therefore, so far as a treaty constitutionally is binding, upon principles of moral obligation, it is also by the vigour of its own authority to be executed in fact."[21] Often overlooked is the fact that *Ware*, not *Marbury*, is the first judicial review case insofar as in *Ware* the Court invalidated the act of a legislature in the name of higher law. No less importantly, the judgment reflected a key reason the Constitution had been framed in the first place. A national judiciary, not the legislature or the executive, invalidated a state law to place the United States in violation of its international law commitments. This was so, moreover, regardless of whether or not it made better foreign policy sense at that moment to err on the side of Britain or France.

That national judiciary showed itself capable of intervening even when it did not have the formal power to do so, and on the most explosive issue possible. One of many outrageous chapters in America's shameful legal enshrinement of slavery came when the slave states in the nineteenth century sought to bar free African Americans from the North and from abroad. As in many such cases, South Carolina took the lead with the so-called Negro Seaman's Act, which, among other things, mandated the detention of any free African American sailor while his ship were in port, with release conditioned on his captain paying the state for the expenses of his incarceration.[22] By 1823 a challenge to this law had made its way to federal court, a case with the added feature of diplomatic protest by the world's greatest naval power. The controversy arose when state authorities imprisoned Henry Elkison, a free British sailor born in Jamaica, from his trading ship, the *Homer*, sailing out of Liverpool. Elkison sought a writ of habeas corpus in the U.S. Circuit Court for the District of South Carolina. During the proceedings, the British consul not only intervened on Elkison's behalf. He also introduced a letter from British Foreign Minister George Canning protesting the law to Secretary of State John Quincy Adams.[23]

Justice William Johnson, riding circuit, loudly declared the "Negro Seaman's Act" to be in violation of the Constitution and international law. The law first violated the principle that "the right of the general government to regulate commerce with the sister states and foreign nations is a paramount and exclusive right."[24] "The case does not rest here," however. The justice continued, "In order to sustain this law, the state must also possess a power paramount to the treaty-making power of the United States, expressly declared to be a part of the supreme Legislative power of the land; for the seizure of this man, on board a British ship, is an express violation of the commercial convention with Great Britain of 1815, which effectively prohibited South Carolina's practice."[25] Though hailing from South Carolina himself, Johnson concluded that his state in effect had converted a federal right into a state crime.

To their undoubted dismay, however, Elkison and the British officials intervening on his behalf did not succeed in obtaining the writ. An evidently frustrated Johnson rightly concluded that Congress had authorized his ability to grant habeas only when an individual was in federal custody. But Johnson had made his point nonetheless. Much like Marshall in *Marbury* itself, the justice logically could and should have begun and ended his opinion by noting his lack of authority to grant relief, which made further opining on the merits unnecessary. Both justices, however, went out of their way to assert their views on the substance of the controversy. In Johnson's case, that assertion could not have easily reached more sensitive areas in foreign and domestic affairs combined.

Limiting the states in foreign affairs—though not necessarily with regard to slavery—may have been the Founders' most immediate concern, but they were also mindful of limiting the federal government itself through separation of powers. So too was the Supreme Court. Amid global war, the justices did not hesitate to enforce limits on both Congress and the president in cases implicating international affairs, whether those limits were based on the Constitution, statutes, international law, or various combinations thereof.

REVIEWING CONGRESSIONAL ACTION

Several early landmark cases enforced limits on Congress—not that Congress provided the Court with many opportunities. When it came to foreign affairs, in the republic's first decades Congress stayed within its ample grants of constitutional authority and, more strikingly, sought to comply with the nation's international law obligations. The Senate did this through approving treaties that were, as *Ware v. Hylton* held, the "Law of the Land," or by incorporating the customary law of nations. Today the most famous instance of this latter approach is the 1789 Alien Tort Statute.[26] In similar fashion, Congress later enacted the Prize Act, which was understood to incorporate customary international law with regard to naval captures by privateers operating for the United States.[27] The Supreme Court made this understanding explicit by applying law of nations rules under the statute in several prominent decisions.[28] Congress was later more explicit in the 1819 Piracy Act, which criminalized piracy "as defined by the law of nations."[29] Here, too, the Court dutifully filled in the international law provisions that Congress referenced.

Yet when the Court believed an Act of Congress might violate international law, and so undermine assumed foreign policy commitments, the Court pushed back. The most enduring instance arose during one of the periods in which the nation ran afoul of a warring superpower, despite its best efforts at neutrality. As the eighteenth century closed, France and the United States engaged in an undeclared "quasi war" on the high seas. During these hostilities, the USS *Constellation*, one of the six "super" frigates that formed the core of the reinvigorated navy, captured a schooner named the *Charming Betsy*.[30] The *Constellation*'s captain, Alexander Murray, believed he had acted lawfully. Congress had enacted the Federal Non-Intercourse Act, which, among other things, prohibited trade "between any person or persons resident within the United States or under their protection, and any person or persons resident within the territories of the French Republic, or any of the dependencies thereof."[31] Instructions from the president "comprehended the case of a vessel found in the possession of the French captors," though "they seemed to intend a vessel belonging to citizens of the United States."[32] The *Charming Betsy*, once a neutral Danish vessel, had been captured by a French privateer when the *Constellation* recaptured it. The *Constellation* then sought to have the *Charming Betsy* sold, with the proceeds to be dispersed between the captain and crew, as was standard practice. The owner of the *Charming Betsy* challenged the sale. He argued that the statute did not cover vessels that were originally American but were later sold to owners from neutral countries. The navy men argued that it did.

Chief Justice Marshall famously decided against the intrepid captain and his men. In *Murray v. Schooner Charming Betsy* he famously declared that "an act of congress ought never to be construed to violate the law of nations, if any other possible construction remains."[33] If interpreted in favor of Captain Murray, the statute would place the United States in violation of the law of nations by permitting the capture of neutral vessels. The Supreme Court, in other words, went out of its way to constrain Congress's ability to violate international law, in a decision that deprived American sailors of compensation during an armed conflict. Marshall did not say that Congress lacked the authority to pass an act that violated international law. If it desired to do so, however, Congress would have to jump the hurdle of making its intention clear. The *Charming Betsy* canon has been a feature of Supreme Court jurisprudence ever since. The Court has not uniformly followed it, especially in light of more recent attempts to curtail its foreign affairs authority. It nonetheless remains the starting point for interpreting any Act of Congress that implicates international law and, by extension, foreign affairs.

The Supreme Court drew upon international law to establish other limits on Congress as well. In *The Appollon*, Justice Joseph Story set out a presumption against federal statutes applying extraterritorially. Yet he did not do so out of conviction that the Court should not intrude in matters beyond American shores.[34] To the contrary, he drew upon settled international law. In his words, "The laws of no nation can justly extend beyond its own territories, except insofar as it regards its own citizens."[35] As leading scholars have pointed out, at the time the principal international law authorities on this topic "agreed that within a nation's territory its jurisdiction was absolute . . . but that outside a nation's territory it generally did not have binding force."[36] That said, the basis for *The Appollon* does not mean that courts should slavishly apply this presumption today. Since the early nineteenth century, international law's commitment to exclusive territorial sovereignty has eroded significantly, nowhere more so than in the rise of modern international human rights law. It follows that as international law more and more permits the extension of a state's laws beyond its borders, a presumption constraining Congress that rests upon international law should likewise diminish.[37]

Much the same story arose from another limitation the Court imposed upon Congress, the doctrine of foreign sovereign immunity. In *The Schooner Exchange v. McFaddon*, the Court yet again dealt with a prize capture.[38] This time the French Navy captured the American merchant vessel *Exchange* and armed it as a warship. When the ship had to put into Philadelphia during a storm, its original American owner brought suit for its return. Chief Justice Marshall held that the suit could not go forward because the practice under the law of nations for domestic courts was not to grant suit against, among other things, foreign sovereigns, foreign ministers, or warships of friendly nations entering domestic ports. Against this backdrop, Marshall construed the relevant statutes as not granting jurisdiction. Once more, Congress could authorize suit against a foreign sovereign if it made its intention clear. It would have to do so, however, not because of the Court's timidity about engaging in foreign affairs cases but, paradoxically, because it looked to contemporary international law. Once more, it would be a mistake to apply this landmark as frozen in time. Since *The Schooner Exchange*, international law has opened several exceptions to foreign sovereign immunity, first for a state's commercial activities, more recently, and incompletely, for human rights violations. Today's Court should approach the doctrine mindful of the relevant international law context, just as Story's did.

REVIEWING EXECUTIVE ACTION

The Court showed an even greater readiness to enforce restrictions on the executive. It did so regardless of whether the constraints derived from the Constitution, statutes, treaties, or the customary law of nations. It further did so regardless of the executive's assessment of the foreign affairs consequences, even when the stakes involved war and peace.

An early judicial shot across the bow resulted from the capture of the French schooner *Peggy* by the USS *Trumbull* during the quasi war. This initial decision, handed down in 1801, actually dealt with the end of the hostilities. The captain and crew as a matter of course brought a libel action against the *Peggy*, so a federal district court could determine that the seizure comported with the law of nations, order the sale of the vessel as a prize, and have the proceeds distributed among the officers and crew. This the district court did. Such, after all, was the standard method for rewarding naval personnel for successful actions. The men of the *Trumbull*, however, had to contend not just with the *Peggy* but also with the treaty the brought the quasi war to an end. The key provision stated that "property captured and not yet definitely condemned or which may be captured before the exchange of ratifications . . . shall be mutually restored." On this basis the Supreme Court held against the intrepid crew. Chief Justice Marshall's opinion first unproblematically applied the treaty as the supreme law of the land. It further reasoned that the district court's condemnation of the *Peggy* was not yet "definite," as the matter had been pending on appeal at the time the treaty was concluded.[39]

A slightly later case went significantly further. *Little v. Barreme* was yet another result of the nation's fraught position between the warring British Empire and French Republic.[40] As with *Charming Betsy*, this landmark case also involved the heroic actions of a U.S. Navy frigate during the French quasi war. In this case, the USS *Boston*, commanded by Captain George Little, captured a Danish vessel, the *Flying-Fish*, as it sailed from a French port in Haiti. Congress's Non-Intercourse Act had authorized the president to order naval commanders "to stop and examine any ship or vessel of the *United States* on the high sea . . . if upon examination it should appear that such ship or vessel is bound or sailing *to* any port or place within the territory of the *French* republic or her dependencies," in which case "it is rendered lawful to seize such vessel, and send her into the *United States* for adjudication."[41] Congress, however, had left an obvious loophole by failing to authorize seizure of vessels sailing *from* French ports. Acting on President John Adams's authority, the secretary of the navy gave a "construction [of the act] much better calculated" to give it full effect, by authorizing capture of American vessels sailing both to and from French ports.[42]

The Supreme Court held that the capture had been illegal and that Captain Little was liable for any damages the owner suffered. Chief Justice Marshall reasoned that "however strong the circumstances might be, which induced Captain Little to suspect the *Flying-Fish* to be an *American* vessel, they could not excuse the detention of her, since he would not have been authorized to detain her."[43] Once more, the Supreme Court did not hesitate to rule against a valiant American captain during armed hostilities. This time, however, the ruling did more than narrow an act of Congress. Instead, it rejected the executive's interpretation of a federal statute to disallow an executive action at the ostensible military core of its expertise.[44]

Not long after the hostilities with France ended, the United States engaged in a markedly more heated conflict with the pirates of the Barbary States on the North African coast of the Mediterranean. Those states, in particular Algiers, Tunis, and Tripoli, had long been notorious for exacting tribute from nations for unimpeded passage of their merchant ships. Those countries, lacking an adequate navy, or obtaining protection from countries that had one, left their ships and sailors open to capture or destruction unless they paid the extortion demanded. Victims and opponents railed against the Barbary "pirates" given that their actions violated the law of nations.

One prominent victim was the United States, especially since it lost the protection of the Royal Navy with the Treaty of Paris and lacked anything like an adequate navy of its own until after Congress authorized the construction of six "super" frigates in 1794. Years of payments and captures notwithstanding, President Jefferson sent a squadron on a peace mission, but with instruction to "protect our commerce & chastise their insolence—by sinking, burning or destroying their ships & Vessels wherever you shall find them" in the event of attack.[45] Jefferson, however, did not know that Tripoli had already declared war as penalty for the United States' refusal to pay further tribute. In consequence, the president sought and obtained authorization from Congress to seize all ships under Tripoli's rule and "also to cause to be done all such other acts of precaution or hostility as the state of war will justify." In the ensuing conflict, the United States suffered a major loss when the frigate *Philadelphia* was captured and had to be burned. Yet the new navy won a series of other battles. Final victory did not occur, though, until the marines mounted a successful attack "on the shores of Tripoli."[46]

None of these proceedings resulted in a landmark case or precedent. But that is the point. With Jefferson careful to seek Congress's approval for aggressive military action, the judiciary did not have to consider whether fearless naval officers in this instance had exceeded their legislative mandate, as in *Little v. Barreme*. Nor did the courts have to avoid construing an authorization to act against the pirates in a way that violated the law of nations, as in *Charming Betsy*. The other branches played their assigned parts, within their proper boundaries, so the judiciary did not have to play its own role.

The Marshall Court was, however, perfectly willing to limit a wartime executive, and in a full-fledged, declared war. More importantly, it indicated that not just statutes but also the law of nations constrained the president's actions. In *Brown v. United States*, the justices considered an incident in which pine timber located within Massachusetts and belonging to a British subject was seized by a U.S. attorney after Congress had declared war on the United Kingdom in 1812.[47] The Court disallowed the seizure. Chief Justice Marshall, writing for the majority, reasoned that neither the declaration of war nor any other act of Congress authorized the condemnation.

In addition, *Brown* followed the Founding views of Hamilton, Madison, and Jay that the law of nations also could operate as an affirmative constraint. Marshall himself observed that, while the lack of congressional authorization was dispositive, the law of nations had been evolving to a principle prohibiting the seizure of property owned by citizens of belligerent powers. He added, however, that "this usage is a guide which the sovereign follows or abandons at his will."[48] By sovereign, Marshall explicitly meant Congress: whether or not to adhere to the law of nations rule was "proper for the consideration of the legislature, not of the executive or the judiciary."[49] In a rare departure from his senior colleague, Justice Joseph Story dissented on the ground that the condemnation of the property could go forward. In his view the declaration of war in essence authorized the president to undertake any actions consistent with the law of nations. Unlike Marshall, Story read international law as permitting immediate seizure. The two justices, therefore, disagreed on the legality of this particular executive act. This disagreement should not mask their more fundamental accord. Unless Congress authorized a departure, the president had to act in accord with the law of nations, and the judiciary was perfectly equipped to make this determination.

Brown merits fresh consideration for another reason. It may be argued that the decisions arising out of the quasi war with France occurred only after hostilities concluded. At best, therefore, the Court stood up to a postwar executive, and then only after a change in administrations had already confirmed a less belligerent policy. Such a view would reflect a longstanding view that the judiciary fulfills its checking function precisely when there is no longer much to check.[50] Yet at least in this instance, this type of assessment runs into several problems. In contrast to many instances today, the lower courts took these wartime cases while the war still raged. That the Supreme Court considered them afterward stands more as a comment on the length of the appellate process than on the Court's substantive views. As for those views, discounting such decisions as *Little* and *Charming*

Betsy privileges the counterfactual of how a true wartime court might have deferred over its express reasoning. Even conceding all this, the critique does not apply to *Brown*. That decision, applying the law of nations to limit the authority of the president, occurred well before the War of 1812 ended, and indeed even before the British burned down what was then known at the Executive Mansion.[51]

Nor would the judiciary stop here. Federal courts showed themselves capable of limiting executive authority not only under the international laws of war but also under what today would be considered a forerunner of international human rights law. Just under a decade after the War of 1812, the USS *Alligator*, a schooner under the command of Robert Stockton, seized the *La Jeune Eugenie*, a schooner sailing under the French flag, off the west coast of Africa. Stockton suspected the ship was engaged in the slave trade, seized it, and brought it to Boston, where he filed a libel action in federal court to have it condemned and sold, the proceeds to go to himself and his crew in due course. But the French government intervened on behalf of the vessel's owners and filed a protest against the proceedings. The French consul argued, among other things, that any offense by a French ship with French owners could be properly considered only in French courts.[52]

Justice Story, sitting as a circuit justice, rejected this contention. He held instead that Stockton had the right to seize *Le Jeune Eugenie*, even though the United States and France were at peace, for the simple reason that by 1821 the slave trade violated the law of nations. As he put it: "It appears to me, therefore, that in an American court of judicature, I am bound to consider the [African slave] trade an offence against the universal law of society and in all cases, where it is not protected by a foreign government, to deal with it as an offence carrying with it the penalty of confiscation."[53] Notably, the court took it for granted that it could apply this norm in and of itself, without any need for either a federal statute or treaty incorporating it into domestic law.

Yet neither did the court hand Stockton, or the executive, a victory. Continuing, Story held that no applicable law, international or domestic, accorded Stockton the right to have the ship that he lawfully seized, condemned and sold. As a result, the vessel would have to be forfeited either to the United States or, if it asserted a right to proceed against the property in its own courts, to France. Story chose the latter course on the understanding that the French authorities would pursue this avenue. Once again, a federal court in a prominent case did not hesitate in reviewing an executive action, even though such review prompted an express objection from a major power. On one hand, the court authorized the navy's action, though importantly, on the ground that the commander was authorized to enforce a prohibition that served to protect individual rights under customary international law. On the other, the court also relied on the absence of either a domestic or international law authorization to prevent the executive officers from reaping the usual reward that a seizure would bring during war.[54]

The judiciary's readiness to hold the executive to account was not confined to statutes, the law of nations, or even cases that have since become landmarks. In an important study, David Sloss examined every case in the first four decades of the republic that turned on applying a treaty of the United States and in which the federal government was a party. Of the nineteen cases that the Court decided on the merits, the U.S. government prevailed in only three. No less significantly, the justices accorded the executive no deference in the treaty interpretations that it put forward.[55]

Yet perhaps the strongest confirmation of the judiciary's independent role in foreign affairs came from the executive itself. While neutrality still held, the French ambassador to the United States asked Secretary of State Edmund Randolph to intervene in cases pending in American courts on the ground that they violated the nation's treaties with France. Randolph's statement could not have made the case for the judiciary's role in foreign affairs more clearly:

> The courts of justice exercise the sovereignty of this country in judiciary matters, are supreme in these, and liable neither to control nor opposition from any other branch of the Government. . . . For, if the President were even to decide that a prize ought not to be prosecuted in our courts, the decision would be treated as an intrusion by those courts, and the judicial proceedings would go on notwithstanding. So speak the constitution and the law.[56]

Semper Fidelis: Keeping the Faith in the Late Nineteenth Century

As the nation's first century progressed, the Court's docket changed, but its commitment to foreign affairs did not. Napoleon's defeat at Waterloo in 1815 ended a generation of global war, which the United States had mostly sought to avoid. The subsequent era of relative peace, at least in Europe, enabled the still new republic to face west and turn to domestic matters and continental conquest. Fewer cases, therefore, reached either the Supreme Court or the rest of the federal judiciary that implicated national security or U.S. relations with other states. Even the international law aspects of the Civil War failed to prompt judicial retreat. To be sure, as the century went on, cases would initiate or reflect certain changes in relevant doctrines or understandings of the law. Yet the basic commitments established in early foreign relations jurisprudence endured. The courts would embrace the opportunity to take cases, consider individual-rights claims, and enforce limitations on the other branches without hesitating due to concern for the consequences in foreign affairs.[57]

REVIEWING STATE ACTION, CONTINUED

The Court continued to address the Founders' fundamental concern that the states not impede the nation's international obligations. *Geofroy v. Riggs* illustrated this continuity in striking fashion even as the nineteenth century was drawing to a close.[58] Congress in 1801 had established that Maryland law "as it then existed" would govern the District of Columbia. At that time the state, like most others, had maintained the common law rule that aliens could not inherit real property. Almost a century later, French citizens living in France challenged this prohibition. The Court held for the French claimants, relying on an 1800 treaty with France that guaranteed French citizens the right to inherit property regardless of state laws. Justice Stephen Field declared for the majority that "the treaty, being part of the supreme law of land, controlled the statute and common law of Maryland whenever it differed from them."[59] In this, *Geofroy* followed the reasoning of *Hauenstein v. Lynham*, a decision ten years earlier that involved a conflict between state law and a treaty with Switzerland.[60]

More importantly, both cases followed *Ware v. Hylton*, the "first" judicial review case, which initially applied the principle of treaty supremacy in delicate foreign affairs circumstances. In one sense, however, the cases showed an even greater commitment to international law in the abstract. As Duncan Hollis has observed, "The treaty supremacy at stake in *Hauenstein* and *Geofroy* differed from earlier concerns that state noncompliance would lead the United States into disputes, war, or worse. Conflict with France—let alone Switzerland—[at the end of the nineteenth century] seemed unlikely. . . ."[61]

REVIEWING CONGRESSIONAL ACTION, CONTINUED

More important today, the Court also continued to uphold individual rights by limiting Congress in matters touching upon foreign affairs. Often the justices did so by applying treaties or customary international law. This is not to say that the Court denied the power of Congress to violate international law. *Brown* had established that the national legislature could place the United States in violation of the law of nations. As for treaties, the Court prior to the Civil War had never settled the debate between advocates who asserted that treaties must always be superior to federal statutes and those who argued that they were equivalent. Then, just a year after the Civil War ended, a majority for the first time adopted the "last-in-time" rule, holding that when a treaty and a federal statute came into conflict, the more recent should be applied.[62]

Yet if Congress could violate international law, the Court continued to make it hard for it to do so, especially when individual rights were concerned. Ironically, its most ringing declaration of its role came in a case in which it actually ruled against the parties asserting certain rights. In *Head Money Cases*, the Court applied the last-in-time rule to uphold an act of Congress even if it conflicted with prior treaties. Even so, Justice Samuel Miller made clear that the Court was fully prepared to vindicate treaty rights even though such cases by definition involved foreign affairs:

> A treaty is primarily a compact between independent nations. It depends for the enforcement of its provisions on the interest and the honor of the governments which are parties to it. If these fail, its infraction becomes the subject of international negotiations and reclamations, so far as the injured party chooses to seek redress. . . . *But a treaty may also contain provisions which confer certain rights upon the citizens or subjects of one of the nations residing in the territorial limits of the other, which partake of the nature of municipal law, and which are capable of enforcement as between private parties in the courts of the country. . . . A treaty, then, is a law of the land, as an act of Congress is, whenever its provisions prescribe a rule by which the rights of the private citizen or subject may be determined. And when such rights are of a nature to be enforced in a court of justice, that court resorts to the treaty for a rule of decision for the case before it as it would to a statute.*[63]

The Court would go some distance to enforce treaty rights of such "a nature to be enforced in a court of justice." In a certain category of cases it would even ignore the last-in-time rule. These instances mainly involved treaties that directly granted "vested" property rights to individuals. In one example, the Court upheld property rights granted to certain Chippewa Indians (including to "Chief Moose Dung") by a treaty even though a later act of Congress attempted to convey the land in question to others. The repeated doctrinal trope in this area articulated that "Congress is bound to regard the public treaties, and it had no power . . . to nullify titles confirmed many years before. . . ."[64]

Otherwise, the Court's strategy remained the limiting of Congress through the softer means of statutory construction. Having established the last-in time-rule for most treaty and statute conflicts, the late-nineteenth-century Court would apply a type of *Charming Betsy* canon to later statutes that appeared to conflict with earlier treaties. In *Whitney v. Robertson*, the case most often cited for the last-in-time rule, the Court added that "when the two relate to the same subject, the courts will always endeavor to construe them so as to give effect to both, if that can be done without violating the language of either."[65] In one striking example, the Court construed the notorious 1882 Chinese Exclusion Act, which appeared to require Chinese returning to the United States to have a certificate, not to apply to a laborer named Chew Heong, on the ground that the statute did not apply to those who left the country before Congress enacted its certification requirement.[66] The majority adopted this reading, which was by no means obvious, in large part to keep the statute on the right side of an 1880 immigration treaty between the United States and China.

The Court also continued to place limits on Congress in more subtle ways. As two leading scholars have observed, "Between 1861 and 1900 . . . the Supreme Court frequently invoked the unwritten law of nations to aid interpretation of statutes and regulations."[67] In this regard, "the Court generally applied international law in a way that constrained the exercise of governmental powers."[68] The Court imposed these constraints, moreover, precisely because the statutes at issue involved "international subject matter" rather than "broad domestic applicability."[69]

In other words, the *Charming Betsy* canon remained alive and well, even if not always cited. To take one example, John Henry Hollander sued Jacob Baiz, who briefly acted as U.S. consul-general of Guatemala and Honduras. Baiz sought to dismiss the suit as filed in the U.S. district court, citing a federal statute that gave the Supreme Court exclusive jurisdiction over ambassadors and public ministers. Consulting several law of nations treatises, the Supreme Court concluded that the suit in the district court could go forward because Baiz did not qualify as a public minister for the purposes of the act.[70] More dramatically, the Court decided numerous post–Civil War cases under the Captured and Abandoned Property Act, which dealt with confiscations by the Union Army in the South.[71] Frequently the court looked to international law to determine whether the original property owner should receive compensation. Some claimants lost, but significantly, others prevailed.

As before, the Court also continued to use customary international law to limit congressional power through doctrines that tended at that time to undercut rights but which, in light of modern international law, would tend to expand them. As a general matter, the justices continued to grapple with applying *The Schooner Exchange*'s presumption against the extraterritorial application of statutes. Similarly, the Court did at least cite the doctrine of foreign sovereign immunity, though it would not actually apply it in a case until the next century.

REVIEWING EXECUTIVE ACTION, CONTINUED

More notable, however, was the Court's review of presidential assertions. That latter half of the nineteenth century saw comparatively fewer challenges to executive foreign affairs authority. Two landmark cases nonetheless bookend the period. As seen earlier in the century, each involved claims that the executive had exercised war powers in violation of individual rights guaranteed by customary international law, none of which the Court hesitated to decide on the merits.

The Prize Cases arose from President Lincoln's April 1861 proclamation deeming it "advisable to set on foot a blockade of all the ports within the [Southern] States aforesaid, in pursuance of the laws of the United States and of the law of nations in such case provided."[72] Congress had not been in session, but when it met several months later it passed two relevant statutes, one prospective and one retrospective. On July 13 it authorized the president to maintain the blockade; on August 6 it passed another statute declaring that Lincoln's prior military decisions "are hereby approved and in all respects legalized." *The Prize Cases* dealt with claims made by the owners of four vessels that had been captured prior to the July 13 authorization.

The Court rendered its decision in 1863, as the Civil War still raged. The holding most remembered dealt with the separation of powers issue of whether Lincoln had the power to unilaterally suppress a rebellion. On this, Justice Robert Grier's opinion answered yes, reasoning that such a power arose when Lincoln was confronted with a "state of war" through foreign invasion or rebellion, which was, in essence, a factual determination left to the president.[73]

Less well known today is the related issue of whether the laws of war authorized the executive to seize not just foreign ships but domestic vessels and cargoes as well. Here the Court also said yes, even though the property at issue had been owned by a Virginian who had pledged loyalty to the Union, and the capture had taken place before Virginia had actually voted to secede.[74] The president therefore won this particular battle. The Court, however, maintained its place in the overall struggle. It did not hesitate to take up a case with not just national security but, by its own analysis, foreign relations implications in the midst of an armed struggle. No less importantly, it showed that it was prepared to consider whether a president still conducting that struggle had violated an individual's rights as potentially limited by, among other sources, customary international law. As one scholar has noted, "The Court validated Lincoln's blockade of Confederate ports," but only because "it regarded the blockade as *consistent* with the law of nations."[75]

There would be further judicial landmarks over the next century. Then again, even at this point there were a number of foreign affairs controversies that raised significant legal questions that did not occasion judicial intervention. Earlier in the century, Jefferson himself harbored constitutional concerns over his authority to effect the Louisiana Purchase from France by means of a treaty, concerns that led his Federalist opponents in Congress to nearly defeat the acquisition.[76] Congressman Abraham Lincoln first made a name for himself nationally by successfully arguing that President Polk had misled the Congress and the country to obtain a declaration of war against Mexico.[77] The subsequent annexation of Texas prompted a further constitutional controversy when President Tyler, having failed to secure approval of two-thirds of the Senate for annexing the Lone Star Republic by treaty, gained the prize through the dubious means of winning Congress's approval to admit Texas as a new state.[78] The later annexation of Hawaii would raise similar concerns.[79] In none of these cases, however, would those concerns result in formal cases in the federal courts, still less the Supreme Court.

In these and comparable instances, litigants evidently did not turn to the courts. The explanation for why they failed to do so is elusive. An infinite number of reasons can be put forward in the attempt to explain a negative and still fall short. The failure to resort to the courts may have resulted from a perceived lack of resources, opportunity, or vision. More likely it reflected the sense that, at least in the controversies mentioned, thorough debate and struggle between the two political branches, including decisive votes and elections, obviated the judicial option. Put another way, proponent or opponents of given executive or legislative initiatives may have viewed their most promising path to be through the political branch whose action they supported. A pitched, decisive battle would leave all sides spent, at worst, and with a sense of legitimate cloture, at best.

Or it may be that in these instances the judiciary was not considered the appropriate forum. Without more evidence, however, this negative says nothing at all to support the idea that foreign affairs controversies were exceptional. To the contrary, several early domestic controversies that today would inevitably wind up in court did not do so at the time. Probably the most obvious instance was the Sedition Act, passed during the quasi war with France during the Adams administration. This statute notoriously introduced seditious libel into federal law. Today the idea of criminalizing criticism of the government would be seen as an axiomatic violation of the First Amendment, ripe for judicial intervention. Several of those prosecuted did make this argument as one—though not a primary—defense. No court, however, formally considered the issue nor permitted a jury to do so. Several points follow. First, no serious constitutional scholar would suggest that the failure of the federal judiciary to resolve a critical assault on free speech in the early days of the republic would preclude the courts from entertaining First Amendment challenges today. Second, and more importantly, the episode suggests that the key factor in the judiciary's failure was not whether a controversy was foreign or domestic, but rather that this failure was a function of the narrower scope of questions that judicial review was expected to address, in particular state intrusion on federal authority and assaults on federal court jurisdiction. Certainly the foreign affairs controversies left unresolved by the courts yielded up no consequent principle in modern judicial expressions to the effect that the judiciary should defer to the political branches in foreign affairs. To the contrary, the Sedition Act controversy suggests that, if anything, courts were more likely to resolve foreign affairs controversies as a result of the landmark cases that grew out of the same quasi conflict with France.

As it was, the century ended with another landmark case that showed that the Court could still go further in applying this reasoning and issue the executive an actual defeat. *The Paquete Habana* is famous for the statement that "international law is part of our law, and must be ascertained and administered by the courts of justice of appropriate jurisdiction as often as questions of right depending upon it are duly presented for their determination."[80] As has been seen, that declaration merely confirmed what had been a standard view since the Founding. Beyond this, the case ended one century and began another by effectively reaffirming the Court's earliest foreign affairs cases.

The Paquete Habana, like *Little*, *Brown*, and *Charming Betsy*, dealt with the capture of a purportedly hostile vessel during armed conflict. During the Spanish-American War, U.S. merchant ships participating in the navy's blockade of Cuba seized two small fishing vessels, the *Paquete Habana* and the *Lola*. They were taken to Key West as prizes, where they were to be sold, with the proceeds to go to the capturing captain and crew. The owners challenged the seizure on the ground that the seizure violated customary international law. The Court agreed, holding that international law indeed prohibited the capture of coastal fishing vessels not engaged in carrying prohibited contraband.[81] As before, the Court vindicated the rights of foreigners against the actions of a wartime executive, once more using international law.

The Paquete Habana nonetheless contained the seeds for subsequent misunderstanding. Just as the Court reconfirmed that "international law is part of our law," it added that "where there is no treaty and no controlling executive or legislative act or judicial decision, resort must be had to the customs and usages of civilized nations . . . as evidence of"[82] customary international law. Today this statement has generally been taken to mean that the executive, or at least a high executive official, can unilaterally authorize the violation of an applicable customary international law standard. One of the most careful international law scholars, however, has convincingly argued otherwise. The late David Bederman instead read the passage merely to mean that where a customary international law standard is unclear, the president may ignore it though a "controlling executive . . . act."[83] But where such a standard was clear, the president should follow it. This concern might be one reason that the majority opinion in *The Paquete Habana* is also famous for its excruciatingly exhaustive, four-hundred-year survey of how "civilized nations" treated coastal fishing vessels during wartime. Precisely because the rule was clear, it was to be followed. In short, "Justice Gray was by no means holding that the President had unfettered authority to violate customary international law."[84]

Other cases also pointed to changes that were born, if not of misunderstanding, then at least of ambiguity. In particular, the Court later in the century began to at least acknowledge treaty interpretations put forward by the executive. As early as 1867, in *United States v. Hathaway*, the majority held against the claims an individual had made under a treaty in part because it "concur[red] in the interpretation given . . . by the Secretary of the Treasury."[85] More significantly, toward the century's end *In re Ross* devoted considerable space to the views of the executive concerning a treaty provision that empowered a U.S. consul in Japan to conduct a criminal trial without presentment by a grand jury. Justice Stephen Field's opinion makes clear that the Court came to the same conclusion, based on its own analysis, as the majority in *United States v. Hathaway*.[86] *In re Ross* would nonetheless become the basis for the modern argument that, contrary to early practice, the judiciary should give "great weight" to the executive's treaty interpretations.

How and why the Court's approach, here and elsewhere, began to drift away from its role in foreign affairs as envisioned at the Founding will be the subject of the next chapter.

CHAPTER FIVE

Curtiss-Wright versus *Youngstown*

A TURNING POINT THAT DIDN'T TURN

THE FOUNDING VISION would not last unchallenged. With the advent of the twentieth century, the factors that had once helped ensure a robust judicial role in foreign affairs reversed and accelerated. Externally, the United States rose from power to superpower to hegemon. Engagement in world affairs, including foreign wars, shifted initiative to the executive, which in turn sought to maximize its authority in relation to Congress and the courts. Meanwhile, factors internal to the law left the judiciary less and less equipped to maintain its traditional role. In particular, the influence of legal positivism and the effects of nineteenth-century isolation led to the relative diminution of the law of nations in the American legal community. One consequence was a partial retreat by the judiciary from its previous foreign affairs role. The Court demonstrated its growing ambivalence in two landmark cases. *United States v. Curtiss-Wright Export Corp.*[1] came to stand for the proposition that the executive was the "sole organ" in foreign relations, standing outside ordinary constitutional analysis and judicial scrutiny. By contrast, in *Youngstown Sheet & Tube Co. v. Sawyer*,[2] the Court notably reasserted its role as a check on presidential power, even during wartime.[3] *Youngstown* remains a potent doctrinal force. Yet the considerations raised by Justice Jackson, in particular, factors that led to the erosion of the Founding vision, have only grown stronger since.

Curtiss-Wright

In 1936, a federal prosecution of a U.S. corporation for an illegal international arms shipment led to an oft-cited Supreme Court decision that was jarringly at odds with almost all that had come before, and much that would come after.

Two years before, President Franklin Roosevelt issued a proclamation stating that, "acting under and by virtue of the authority conferred in me by . . . [a] joint resolution of Congress, [I] do hereby declare and proclaim that I have found that the prohibition of the sale of arms and munitions of war . . . to those countries now engaged in armed conflict in the Chaco may contribute to the reestablishment of peace . . . and I do hereby warn [all persons] that all violations . . . will be vigorously prosecuted."[4] As FDR noted, he acted based upon—and based solely upon—a joint resolution of Congress that authorized him to prohibit arms sales subject to a fine of up to $10,000, two years imprisonment, or both.[5] It was for violation of the president's proclamation that the Curtiss-Wright Export Corporation faced federal prosecution for conspiring to sell fifteen machine guns to Bolivia—a sign of less destructive times, if nothing else.

The district court dismissed the case, largely on the ground that Congress's delegation of authority to President Roosevelt was unconstitutional. At the time, the question of how much power Congress could delegate to the president, and to the executive branch generally, featured prominently in national politics and jurisprudence. Ever since the Progressive era, if not earlier, concern had arisen over how much ostensibly legislative or even judicial power Congress could give to administrative agencies that appeared to legislate through regulations or adjudicate through the resolution of disputes, yet which remained under control of the executive. The Supreme Court had never struck down such a delegation by Congress until the New Deal. Then it did so twice, and dramatically, invalidating portions of FDR's centerpiece National Industrial Recovery Act because Congress's delegations had no intelligible limiting standards. When *Curtiss-Wright* went directly to the Supreme Court, it was precisely over the delegation doctrine that the parties thought the case would turn, as it had at the trial level.

The case did not, in fact, turn on this question, or at least not in a straightforward way. Rather, Justice George Sutherland's majority opinion assumed that the delegation would be invalid if it were confined to "internal" affairs. But it went on to ask, "May it nevertheless be sustained on the ground that its exclusive aim is to afford a remedy for a hurtful condition within foreign territory?"[6] Sutherland famously, or infamously, answered yes, based on two claims that are in turn grounded on a version of original understanding that is, let us say, distinctive.

Sutherland first argues that "the powers of the federal government in respect of foreign or external affairs and in respect of domestic or internal affairs" are fundamentally "different, both in respect of their origin and their nature."[7] With respect to domestic powers, "the primary purpose of the Constitution was to carve from the general mass of legislative powers then possessed by the states such portions as it was thought desirable to vest in the federal government, leaving those not included in the enumeration still in the states."[8] In short, the Constitution outlined a national government with limited and enumerated domestic powers. So far, so adequate.

However, Sutherland continues, since neither the colonies nor the states possessed foreign affairs powers, there was nothing to carve out there. Rather, foreign affairs powers originally rested with the Crown. With independence, those general powers passed to the United States and were originally exercised by the Continental Congress. Foreign affairs powers, therefore, "did not depend upon the affirmative grants of the Constitution."[9] Instead, the powers to declare war, conclude peace, and conduct diplomatic relations would rest with the federal government even "if they had never been mentioned in the Constitution"![10] Otherwise, Sutherland went on, the United States would not be "completely sovereign" as a nation. Previously, the Court had upheld federal powers nowhere specified in the Constitution as deriving from a constitutional or even extraconstitutional notion of national sovereignty. A particularly unfortunate example was the *Chinese Exclusion Cases*, confirming Congress's "plenary" power to control immigration, a holding that plagues those who would subject this unenumerated power to constitutional rights constraints to this day.[11] But never had the Court said that foreign affairs powers were categorically different altogether and beyond the limits of conventional constitutional interpretation.

But Sutherland was only half done. It remained to determine which branch or branches of the federal government properly exercised sovereign foreign affairs authority. Sutherland might have answered this question by assuming that the Constitution's commitment to separation of powers divided that authority among Congress, the executive, and the judiciary. In *Curtiss-Wright* itself, this assumption would suggest that Congress had delegated the power to prohibit international arms sales to the president to implement should he deem that measure would contribute to peace in the region specified. Certainly that is what Congress and FDR thought they were doing. Yet this conclusion would have run up against, among other things, the Court's recent attempts to enforce the nondelegation doctrine. Sutherland got around this problem with a move as bold as it was simple. Delegations to the president in foreign affairs were subject to few if any limits. That followed because of the even more provocative suggestion for which the case has been cited by executive branch lawyers ever since. The sovereign foreign affairs powers that the United States inherited from the British Crown nearly all fall within the exclusive domain of the president.

Here too Sutherland based his conclusion on original understanding. On this basis he attributed to the Founders at least three arguments that presidents have typically advanced to burnish their foreign affairs authority. First, "the President alone has the power to speak or listen as a representative of the nation."[12] True, "he makes treaties with the advice and consent of the Senate; but he alone negotiates."[13] To drive home the point, Sutherland famously relies on none other than John Marshall when he was still a congressman: "As Marshall said in his great argument . . . in the House of Representatives, 'The President is the sole organ of the nation in its external relations, and its sole representative with foreign nations.'"[14]

Second, the president rightly succeeded the Crown in foreign relations based upon superior institutional competence. According to Sutherland, "He, not Congress"—and, a fortiori, not the courts—"has the better opportunity of knowing the conditions which prevail in foreign countries, and especially is this true in time of war. He has his confidential sources of information. He has his agents in the form of diplomatic, consular and other officials."[15]

Finally, the sensitivity of foreign affairs often required confidentiality, particularly in negotiations. As Sutherland put it, "Secrecy in respect of information gathered by [U.S. diplomats] may be highly necessary, and the premature disclosure of it productive of harmful results."[16] For this proposition, he quoted no less a figure than President Washington, who explained his refusal to turn over documents relating to his negotiations of the 1796 Jay Treaty by declaring that "the nature of foreign negotiations requires caution, and their success must often depend on secrecy, and even when brought to a conclusion."[17]

All these considerations supported the conclusion that "we are here dealing not alone with an authority vested in the President by an exertion of legislative power, but with such an authority plus the very delicate, plenary and exclusive power of the President as the sole organ of the federal government in the field of international relations—a power which does not require as a basis for its exercise an act of Congress. . . ."[18] Among other things, Sutherland had transformed the president from the "sole organ" in communicating with other nations into the sole organ of the United States in foreign affairs. Every subsequent president has cited this language for that proposition in the course of a foreign affairs dispute. As Harold Hongju Koh wryly puts it, for presidents Republican and Democrat, the case has come to mean "*Curtiss-Wright*, therefore I'm right."[19]

As an account of the Founding alone, *Curtiss-Wright* could scarcely get things more wrong.[20] For starters, nothing in the relevant sources, let alone the document itself, supports the contention that the Constitution's constraints apply any less in foreign affairs than domestic matters. Rather, Federalist theory posited that "We the People" granted broad yet discrete powers to the national government without distinguishing between the two realms and would have done so even if a bright line could, in fact, have been drawn between them. Of more immediate relevance, nothing in constitutional text or contemporary sources supports the implication that the prerogative foreign affairs powers of the British Crown somehow passed through the Confederation Congress directly to the president of the United States. As set forth at length, "We the People" divided governmental authority in both internal and external arenas among the three branches, reflecting the core constitutional commitment to separation of powers.

Nothing better illustrates *Curtiss-Wright*'s tendentious history better than the "sole organ" language that keeps it famous. Sutherland's ultimate use of the term all but invites executive branch lawyers to cite his opinion as a source for presidential foreign affairs authority where no specific grant of power suffices. That this invitation appears to have originated with John Marshall makes it all the more enticing. But undifferentiated foreign affairs power is not what the future chief justice meant. Congressman Marshall was making the far narrower assertion that the president properly served as a point of communication between the United States and foreign governments. This he did to oppose Jeffersonian congressmen communicating directly with representatives of the French Republic.[21] And he was correct. The Constitution's provision that the president "receive Ambassadors," along with understandings going back to Blackstone, amply supported the point. Ironically, Sutherland's first reference to the "sole organ" appears to acknowledge this more precise interpretation. Yet neither he nor later presidents were able to restrain themselves from making the term synonymous with near-plenary executive authority in foreign affairs.

For all its originalist trappings, *Curtiss-Wright* reflected its time. The opinion in particular arose from the recent ideological commitments of

Justice Sutherland himself.[22] More importantly, the decision illustrates the rise of the comparative power of the executive that attended the rising global power of the United States as the twentieth century progressed.

On several levels *Curtiss-Wright* presents a puzzle. Most of the justices in the majority adhered to a narrow view of the Constitution's grants of authority. Sutherland in particular was a leader of the "Four Horseman," who combined to strike down many key measures of FDR's New Deal as exceeding the Constitution's grants of power to the government.[23] Why would he and most of the others assert that the government, and in particular the same president whose measures they had struck down, had nearly unconstrained, plenary power in foreign affairs? Recently, the noted historian Edward Purcell convincingly argued that Sutherland for most of his career had viewed the executive as similarly constrained in internal matters as external.[24] The justice's very different views in *Curtiss-Wright*, Purcell argues, can be traced to two sources. First, Sutherland drew upon the ideas of Chief Justice Charles Evans Hughes, who had long advocated a vision of extensive presidential foreign affairs authority, in no small part based upon his years as secretary of state after World War I. Second, the majority "adopted sweeping but vague executive power language . . . to provide practical support for President Franklin Roosevelt in his contemporaneous struggle with Congress over the nation's foreign policy, especially his efforts to implement an anti-Nazi foreign policy. . . ."[25]

These specific concerns in turn reflect a more fundamental challenge that has been more enduring and significant. If the majority hoped that the United States would check fascism abroad, it was because the nation had demonstrated that it could exercise global power decisively. With the turn of the century, the republic had already assumed the role of an imperial power with its victory in the Spanish-American War. World War I confirmed the nation's position as a global power now the equal of any in the Old World. At least to the Court, postwar isolationism proved that the United States should turn inward only so far. Significantly, Chief Justice Hughes, as secretary of state, played a leading role in seeking to keep the nation at the forefront of international affairs, for example, by convening the Washington Naval Conference to control the worldwide naval arms race and prevent another world war.[26]

Unfortunately, *Curtiss-Wright* illustrates a corollary. As far as the majority was concerned, U.S. leadership abroad required strong leadership at home, which only the executive appeared capable of delivering. Sutherland's opinion makes clear that the president's ostensible superiority derives from what is typically termed "institutional competence," including the ability to act with greater secrecy, better information, and superior decisiveness. The various justices for various reasons viewed these qualities as having never been more important in light of the rising threat of fascist and authoritarian regimes. The opinion of the Court, however, did not assert that new times called for a reimagined scheme in which the president would exercise a near monopoly on foreign affairs. Rather, it mainly projected that view onto the Founders, who would have been astonished at the characterization.

For all that, *Curtiss-Wright's* significance is more symbolic than legal. It endures as an early and noted—perhaps the most noted—landmark demonstrating a willingness of the Court to defer to the president in light of the nation's rise as a global power. Yet it has played a far more limited role as precedent than as rhetoric. Among its other limitations, it does not actually involve unilateral executive action, still less any asserted violation of a constitutional right. Beyond that, Purcell rightly notes that the justices left their language on independent executive foreign affairs power almost deliberately amorphous. "They may have done so," he adds, "because their goal was not to provide clear and detailed doctrinal guidance, but to provide moral support for the national executive in an ominous and deeply troubled time."[27]

Youngstown

Against *Curtiss-Wright* is a slightly later landmark that stands as its opposite in almost every significant way. *Youngstown Sheet & Tube Co. v. Sawyer* also dealt with a unilateral executive action that implicated both constitutional rights and the conduct of foreign affairs. It famously struck down President Truman's attempt to seize the nation's steel mills to keep them operating under federal control in the face of a threatened national strike during the Korean War. In so doing, *Youngstown* reflects a basic fidelity to the Founding just as *Curtiss-Wright*, ostensibly steeped in original understanding, departed from it. Writ large, the two cases frame the story of the Supreme Court in foreign affairs as the United States ascended to the status of superpower.

During the spring of 1952, the United Steelworkers union called for a nationwide strike. Such an action would have caused significant disruption at any time, but here it came in the midst of the Korean War. In that light, the "indispensability of steel as a component of substantially all weapons and other war materials led the President to believe that a work stoppage would immediately jeopardize our national defense and that governmental seizure of the steel mills was necessary in order to assure the continued availability of steel."[28] Just few hours before the strike, President Truman issued an executive order that directed the secretary of commerce to take possession of most of the nation's steel mills. The steel companies obeyed the seizure under protest but challenged the measure in federal court.[29] Neither the lower courts nor the Supreme Court sidestepped the case based on a so-called political question or any related gatekeeping doctrine.[30] To the contrary, the Supreme Court bypassed the court of appeals and granted direct review of the district court's ruling.

The justices ruled that a wartime executive did not have the authority to take steps that he deemed essential to prosecuting a war.[31] Such an assertion was hardly novel. The Court had done much the same in a number of contexts, as early as the quasi war with France and at least as recently as the Spanish-American War. *Youngstown* remained true to these precedents. More importantly, the case dramatically reaffirmed the Founders' commitment to separation of powers in foreign affairs, including and especially the Court's role both as a check against excess government power in general and as a safeguard of rights in particular. Ironically, none of the lead opinions did so with significant reference to the Founders themselves. Instead, they reflected fidelity to the original expectations by emphasizing other classic methods of constitutional interpretation: one focusing on text; another on subsequent custom; and the most famous one on structure.

Justice Hugo Black wrote the sometimes-underappreciated opinion of the Court. Reputedly, though not always consistently, a strict textualist, Black stated simply, "The President's power, if any, to issue the order must stem either from an act of Congress or from the Constitution itself."[32] The majority answered neither. No act of Congress plausibly conferred the power to seize the steel mills, nor did any Constitutional grant. The commander in chief clause did not work in the government's favor because the "theater of war" did not extend to Ohio. The provision that "the President shall take Care that the Laws be faithfully executed" did not hold sway because it fell to Congress to authorize the taking of property in an emergency since "the Constitution does not subject this lawmaking power of Congress to presidential or military supervision or control." Finally, the clause vesting "Executive Power . . . in a President of the United States" likewise failed to support the government's case because there was no pertinent law that Congress had enacted for the president to execute.[33]

Easily overlooked is what the opinion does not say. First, Black at no point questions whether separation of powers applies as fully to cases that involve foreign affairs as domestic matters, even when the decision might materially affect the outcome of a war. If anything, *Youngstown's* facts suggest that drawing a line between domestic and foreign affairs may frequently be impossible. Second, the majority sees no reason to avoid hearing the case. Black's opinion pauses to consider whether the Court should consider an immediate injunction against the seizure or defer the matter and let the companies proceed later to recover damages, but it does so only briefly.[34] Third, the majority views the president's authority as deriving from the Constitution's specific textual grants. Glaringly absent is any hint that the executive's powers rest on some notion of national sovereignty, as Sutherland asserted in *Curtiss-Wright*. Finally, and characteristic of Black when in his strict textualist mode, the Court reads the Constitution's express grants narrowly. Conspicuously missing in this regard is any notion that the president exercises some vaguely defined reservoir of foreign affairs powers through the clause vesting the office with "the executive Power." When it comes to securing steel to fight a war, the president was anything but the "sole organ" of U.S. foreign affairs.

Justice Frankfurter agreed, but through a different route that reflected his belief that "the legal enforcement of the principle of separation of powers seem[s] to me more complicated and flexible than what appears"[35] in the majority opinion. Both the greater complexity and flexibility resulted from the justice's belief in the necessity of considering not just the text but also constitutional custom. What Frankfurter wrote about the Founders fully applied to himself: "The doctrine of separation of powers was not a mere theory; it was a felt necessity."[36] One problem, however, was that the text hardly enumerated every power that the government could legitimately exercise, particularly for the president. "But," his concurrence argues, "unenumerated powers do not mean undefined powers. The separation of powers built into our system gives essential content to undefined provisions in the frame of our government." Where, then, to find the defined limits to the three branches' respective powers? The answer that makes the concurrence endure points to "the way the framework has consistently operated. . . ." It follows that:

> it is an inadmissibly narrow conception of American constitutional law to confine it to the words of the Constitution and to disregard the gloss which life has written upon them. In short, a systematic, unbroken, executive practice, long pursued to the knowledge of the Congress and never before questioned, engaged in by Presidents . . . making as it were such exercise of power part of the structure of our government, may be treated as a gloss on "executive Power" vested in the President by § 1 of Art. II.[37]

Frankfurter differs from Black in believing that a longstanding governmental practice could establish a presidential power even where the text could not—but not in this instance. After extensive research presented in a proto-spreadsheet, Frankfurter's opinion concludes that no such constitutional custom established any presidential power to seize property, even in times of national emergency.

Often overlooked, however, is the common ground the two justices share. Frankfurter, like Black, draws no distinction between "foreign" or "domestic" separation of powers. Moreover, Frankfurter expressly defends the judiciary's duty to consider the constitutionality of the president's wartime measure when presented in a genuine case or controversy, even if the remedy might be an injunction. Otherwise, the opinion warns, "To deny inquiry into the President's power in a case like this, because of the damage to be feared from upsetting its exercise . . . would in effect always preclude inquiry into challenged power, which presumably only avowed great pubic interest brings into the action." Lastly, Frankfurter is no more willing than Black to hint that the president (or Congress) may draw upon some undefined reservoir of foreign affairs powers, either though national "sovereignty" or some expansive reading of "executive Power."

For all that, *Youngstown* lives on mainly thanks to the concurrence of Justice Jackson, among the most notable opinions in the Court's history.[38] The concurrence became influential largely because of the useful framework it provided for analyzing separation of powers cases, though Jackson's elegant writing style played a part. Eventually, it rose to the level of doctrine after the Court, less rather than more, adopted its approach thirty years later.

As Black focused on text, and Frankfurter on custom, Jackson ostensibly united the two under a structural approach. The concurrence rightly, though perhaps excessively, dismisses Founding sources as usually too unclear to resolve conflicts between the president and Congress "as they actually present themselves."[39] "Just what our forefathers envisioned, or would have envisioned had they foreseen modern conditions," Jackson lyrically opines, "must be divined from materials almost as enigmatic as the dreams Joseph was called upon to interpret for Pharaoh."[40] Instead, the concurrence remains true to the Founding commitment to separation of powers on a more general level. In essence it unites textual grants and, at least ostensibly, custom under a broad framework that "diffuses power the better to secure liberty" but also "contemplates that practice will integrate the dispersed powers into a workable government."[41]

On this basis, Jackson set out what would become a famous three- level matrix for the Court to use in analyzing conflicts between the president and Congress. The president's power would be at its "zenith" when "the President acts pursuant to an express or implied authorization from Congress . . . for it includes all that he possesses in his own right plus all that Congress can delegate." At the other end of the spectrum, the executive's power would be at its "low ebb" when "the President takes measures incompatible with the expressed or implied will of Congress." In between, the president "can rely only upon his own independent powers" when he (or one day, presumably, she) "acts in the absence of either a congressional grant or denial of authority." Critically, he added that "there is a zone of twilight in which he and Congress may have concurrent authority, or in which its distribution is uncertain." As a result, "congressional inertia, indifference, or quiescence may sometimes, at least as a practical matter, enable, if not invite, measures on independent presidential responsibility."[42] Applied to *Youngstown* itself, Jackson concluded that President Truman's actions fell into the "low ebb," largely because Congress had implicitly denied the president's power to seize industrial property, even in an emergency, since it had considered a bill delegating that authority but rejected it.[43]

Ironically, the fame of Jackson's three categories tends to obscure the aggressive foreign affairs role for the judiciary that his concurrence shares with the other main opinions. As with Black and Frankfurter, he draws no distinction between separation of powers in external versus internal measures.[44] With them, he sees no difficulty in enforcing the doctrine even when the stakes involve prosecuting a war. And, like them, he declines to allude to any notion that undefined foreign affairs authority is a subset of "executive Power," and still less that it derives from the nation's sovereignty.

It is therefore ironic that Jackson's opinion has been consistently "under-read" in ways that mute its vision of both the Court and Congress checking an increasingly powerful president. Commentators typically interpret the "zone of twilight" analysis as adopting the notion, made clear by Frankfurter, that a longstanding custom of congressional silence in the face of executive assertions of power may serve as a legitimate source of executive authority. Indeed, this was the reading favored by the Supreme Court decades later when it adopted a version of Jackson's framework.[45]

Yet this reading is nearly the opposite of the concurrence's central point. Jackson instead sought to warn Congress that, "as a *practical* matter," the executive would fill any vacuum that Congress's inaction would create. The concurrence, in fact, rejects reliance on custom, instead asserting the Constitution's general grants of power to the president, broadly interpreted, suffice.[46] Instead, the opinion attempts to awaken Congress to the pressing reality that its checking function is all the more critical in light of the enormous power that the American executive has amassed. Jackson presciently cites several reasons for this expansion: the concentration of power in one person, the shift in power from the states to the federal government, the president's access to the media, a party system that divides a legislator's allegiance between Congress and a chief executive of his or her own political affiliation, and perceived public emergencies—foreign and domestic—that invite decisive action. All this, however, is exactly why the need for the other two branches is even *more* imperative. Drawing upon foreign legal materials, the opinion draws a sobering contrast between the recent history of the United Kingdom and France, where legislative checks remained, and Hitler's Germany, no less, where they did not.[47]

All this Jackson states expressly, but the import of the opinion does not stop there. The president's power may be at its "zenith" when the president is acting pursuant to an act of Congress, but nothing in the opinion indicates that the Court should abdicate its duty to police executive and legislative assertions, even when combined. Rather, Jackson expressly acknowledges the possibility that even when supported by Congress, a president's act "may be held unconstitutional" and, if this is the case, "it usually means that the Federal Government as an undivided whole lacks power." He does concede that in such a scenario "the burden of persuasion would rest heavily" on anyone attempting to establish such a position. [48] In a footnote he even cites to *Curtiss-Wright* to concede the idea that congressional delegations in foreign affairs should be broadly construed. He does, however, note that such statements by the Court to this effect are "recent." More importantly, he assumes again that the Court may invalidate actions at the "zenith," even as he cautions that it should "hesitate long before limiting or embarrassing such powers."[49]

Youngstown itself belies even this attempt to find some common ground with *Curtiss-Wright*. The facts of the case show the futility of drawing sharp lines between the government's exercise of "domestic" and "foreign affairs" powers, which is almost certainly why Jackson makes no attempt to rely on the distinction in the opinion's text. Jackson, moreover, makes no effort to find congressional authorization for the seizure. To the contrary, he instead (somewhat creatively) discovers a congressional prohibition against the measure. He does not do so by foraging in legislative history, as does Black. Jackson instead relies on a sort of "field preemption" theory, arguing that Congress has legislated in the relevant area without delegating the relevant power (i.e., the seizure of private property) to the president.[50]

Elsewhere, Jackson also makes clear that the judiciary has the capacity to hold the president to account in "the zone of twilight" when Congress is silent. Just where Jackson does this, however, can be misleading. After concluding that Congress has neither authorized the seizure nor remained silent on the matter, he turns to analyze whether the president had authority to take the action where his power was at "its lowest ebb," that is, in the face of Congress's effective prohibition. Here the only way the president could prevail would be if the seizure were exclusively "within his domain and beyond the control of Congress." Jackson answers in the negative. Yet the way he does so demonstrates that he would also have denied Truman the authority even had Congress remained silent.

Jackson dismisses all other possible sources of relevant executive authority on offer. First, he rejects the notion embraced in *Curtiss-Wright* that the president enjoys only powers that the Constitution expressly delegates and "does not enjoy unmentioned powers." Like Black, he then dispatches the clauses that the executive put forward. But he does so more thoroughly than Black. The executive vesting clause, he concludes, cannot "be a grant in bulk of all conceivable executive power but [is an] . . . allocation to the presidential office of the generic powers thereafter stated." As for the commander in chief clause, he declares that

> no doctrine that the Court could promulgate would seem to me more sinister and alarming than that a President whose conduct of foreign affairs is so largely uncontrolled, and often even is unknown, can vastly enlarge his mastery over the internal affairs of the country by his own commitment of the Nation's armed forces to some foreign venture.[51]

For good measure, he adds that his view comports with "the early view of presidential power" as espoused by President Jefferson in seeking congressional approval to use naval force against the Barbary States in the Mediterranean.[52] Jackson further denied that the Constitution's stricture that the president "shall take Care that the Laws be faithfully executed" can supply the requisite authority. The laws, he points out, also include provisions of the Bill of Rights that limit any authority granted. Finally, the opinion ventures beyond specific clauses to dismiss the idea of "nebulous, inherent powers never expressly granted but said to have accrued to the office from the customs and claims of preceding administrations."

In all these ways Jackson decimates the arguments that the president had any exclusive constitutional authority in the "lowest ebb" to order the seizure in the face of a congressional prohibition. Yet each of the arguments he makes applies as fully to any claim that the president would have had that authority—and indeed general foreign affairs powers—in a "zone of twilight" in which Congress had said nothing. Congress serves as an important check. But it is not the only one. In the end, there is the judiciary as well.

The coda of Jackson's performance accordingly beseeches the legislature to again play its part, yet it ends by insisting that the judiciary must do its duty regardless. The final passage of the concurrence is dedicated primarily to challenging Congress to live up to the role envisioned by the Founders. "We may say," it concludes, "that power to legislate for emergencies belongs in the hands of Congress, but only Congress itself can prevent power from slipping through its fingers."[53] And lest there be any doubt, Jackson finishes with a sobering reminder of the role the judiciary should play, as it had in this very case. He notes that people "have discovered no technique for long preserving free government except that the Executive be under the law, and that the law be made by parliamentary deliberations."[54] None of this may be enough if Congress remains missing in action. The legislative institutions for such deliberations, he darkly laments, "may be destined to pass away." There is, however, at least one other safeguard: "*It is the duty of the Court to be last, not first, to give them up.*"[55]

CHAPTER SIX

Article III versus the National Security State

THE FOUNDING VISION would not last forever unchallenged. With the advent of twentieth century, the factors that had helped ensure a robust judicial role in foreign affairs effectively reversed. Externally, the United States rose from regional to global power. Engagement in world affairs, including foreign wars, shifted initiative to the executive, which in turn sought to maximize its authority in relation to both Congress and the courts. Meanwhile, factors internal to the law left the judiciary less equipped to maintain its traditional role. In particular, the influence of legal positivism and the effects of nineteenth-century isolation diminished the place previously held by the law of nations in the American legal community. Out of this dynamic sprang the Supreme Court's partial retreat from its traditional role, the turning point that did not fully turn, as symbolized by the pairing of *Curtiss-Wright* and *Youngtown* detailed in the previous chapter.

By midcentury the pressures for further retreat accelerated. At the most general level, the United States continued its ascent from global power, to superpower, to virtual hegemon by the century's close. That ascent, moreover, came in tandem with armed conflict. The coming of World War II, followed by a near-perpetual state of cold and hot conflicts following the war, led, critically, to a "national security state," in which Congress authorized and acquiesced to executive authority to a degree that would have shocked even Alexander Hamilton. *Youngstown* itself, coming just as the national security state was being established, confirmed that the Court could still defend its Article III authority in foreign affairs. Yet the considerations raised by Justice Jackson in his concurrence, factors that led to the erosion of the Founding vision, have only grown stronger since. With the new millennium, it should have come as no surprise that *Youngstown* might still characterize a dominant theme in the Court's jurisprudence, but in key areas and in key cases, the spirit of *Curtiss-Wright* and judicial retreat became increasingly insistent.

Gavel versus Sword

The judicial ambivalence that *Youngstown* and *Curtiss-Wright* together represent reflects the culmination of several factors that had been at work for some time. Outside the Court itself, by far the most important development was the rise of the United States as a world power. This ascent both echoed and fostered a shift in power to the federal government in general and to the executive in particular. These shifts, combined with domestic parallels, put increasing pressure on the traditional separation of powers analysis. Not surprisingly, the Court's more consistently mixed response coincided with the nation's more consistent engagement as a leading power with the coming of World War II, followed in quick succession by the Cold War and global terrorism. Within the Court, moreover, still another factor undermining the judiciary's traditional foreign affairs role was the decline of international law among the American legal elite. This erosion of a principal basis for the judiciary's intervention in foreign affairs further contributed to the Court's increasing hesitation to play its traditional role.

Whatever their differences, almost every history of U.S. foreign affairs agrees that the nation consistently claimed a leading role in world affairs as a major power only with the onset of World War II. Perhaps the leading work on the subject refers to the break as "the great transformation."[1] The nation had always been committed to international trade. And it had fought its share of formal and informal wars. The conventional wisdom nonetheless holds that, thanks to the Atlantic Ocean and the British Royal Navy, Americans for most of the nineteenth century could ignore conflicts among the world's major powers and concentrate on fighting weaker neighbors, wiping out indigenous peoples, and decimating one another. Nor did the nation's traditional "isolationist" posture fundamentally change with the Spanish-American War or even World War I. As Mary L. Dudziak has argued, these conflicts ushered in and perpetuated the nation's participation in some form of overseas armed conflict for the next century and right up to today.[2] Those conflicts further demonstrated the nation's power and greater potential. Each time, however, U.S. policy returned to the "normalcy" of few alliances and an almost embarrassingly small military establishment.[3]

This changed, of course, in the lead-up to World War II. As one scholar has written, the Nazi conquest of France and assault on the United Kingdom meant that "for the first time since the early republic, many Americans feared that in a world shrunken by air power their safety was threatened by events abroad and concluded that defense of other nations was vital to their own."[4] Pearl Harbor served to confirm this belief, "marking the end of one era and the beginning of another." Thereafter, as another prominent historian observes, the United States has in essence been involved in perpetual foreign conflict.[5] The Cold War yielded, among other overt and covert adventures: Berlin, Korea, Iran, Cuba, Congo, Vietnam, the Dominican Republic, Laos, Cambodia, Chile, Lebanon, Grenada, Guatemala, El Salvador, and Nicaragua. Shortly thereafter, the struggle formerly known as the "global war on terror" has produced Afghanistan, the Iraq War, Yemen, and Syria. Nor should Panama, the Persian Gulf War, and Libya, which do not fall neatly under either heading, go unnoted.[6]

The consequence has been enormous pressure on separation of powers as originally conceived and traditionally applied. Ongoing strategic engagement abroad necessarily enhances federal authority. As early as the U.S. triumph over Spain, Congress began exercising a novel power of enacting imperial legislation over the lives of millions of former Spanish subjects, authority that the Court only partially checked in the *Insular Cases*.[7] Since "the great transformation," Congress has formally exercised its power to approve armed conflicts as least four times, made major appropriations for most others, and created numerous bodies devoted to national security, including the Joint Chiefs of Staff, the CIA, the National Security Council, and the National Security Agency.[8] These assertions of power are formidable in their own right, but related exercises also have relative implications. Most dramatic in this regard was Congress's attempt to significantly reduce the habeas corpus jurisdiction of the judiciary, which otherwise could be used to hold the government accountable for excesses that might result from too zealous a focus on national security.

Yet by far the greatest beneficiary of the nation's rise to global primacy has been the executive. The *Curtiss-Wright* Court actually sought to foster this shift given President Roosevelt's desire to aid the United Kingdom against the fascist states in the face of Congress's opposition through the 1930s. Once the United States embarked on a consistent policy of global engagement, no branch was better equipped than the executive to take advantage, thanks to the president's ability to act with "despatch" and "secrecy" based on information gained as "the sole organ" of communications—as opposed to all foreign policy—with foreign states. FDR pressed that advantage even before U.S. entry into the war by concluding an increasing number of international agreements outside the Constitution's difficult procedures requiring two-thirds approval by the Senate. Notable here was the 1940 "destroyers for bases" deal, in which the executive unilaterally exchanged dozens of U.S. Navy ships for bases on territory within the British Empire.[9] FDR's successors went even further, initiating interventions ranging from a major war in Korea to "minor" incursions into, among others places, the Dominican Republic, Laos, and Nicaragua, without or even contrary to congressional authorization.

Even more enduring was the creation of ongoing policies and institutions with the onset of the Cold War. The result has been variously termed the "national security state" or, even more provocatively, the "warfare state."[10] Previously, the end of formal conflicts such as the Spanish-American War and World War I meant a return to isolationism and a vast reduction of U.S. armed forces.[11] The long struggle with communism after World War II broke this pattern and has kept military spending and deployment at unprecedented levels ever since.[12] No less significant was the creation of the national security administrative state. The landmark National Security Act, enacted in 1947, alone consolidated executive foreign affairs power with the creation of the Department of Defense, the Joint Chiefs of Staff, and the National Security Council.[13] These initiatives, moreover, cannot be fully separated from the earlier expansion of domestic federal agencies any more than internal affairs can be walled off from external matters. Worthy of mention as well is the creation in 1934 of the Office of Legal Counsel, designed to, among other things, advance the constitutional perspective of the executive.[14] To bring the story full circle, the OLC has played a consistent role in pressing an expansive vision of presidential authority in foreign affairs, not least by transforming *Curtiss-Wright*'s "sole organ" into its virtual motto.

Consistent global engagement did not only work to comparatively empower the political branches, the executive in particular. It also served to weaken the force of international law, one of the principal bases for the judiciary's involvement in foreign affairs. International relations theory conventionally holds that weak states seek refuge in international law as a potential constraint on stronger states. Stronger states, by contrast, may generally adhere to international law but are also in a better position to bear the diplomatic and reputational costs should they decide to violate it. As noted, one principal reason for the Constitution's embrace both of international law and the role of the judiciary to enforce it stemmed from the new nation's need to adhere to treaties and custom, the better to argue that the more powerful states it confronted did the same. Since World War II, the United States has assumed the role that Britain and France played after the American Revolution.

The legalist tradition in American foreign policy making did remain significant. It clearly prevailed in trade agreements, where the nation could often press its postwar economic dominance. It also remained alive more generally in the work of FDR's secretary of state Edward Stettinius in the forging of the UN Charter, Eleanor Roosevelt's foundational efforts in human rights, the leading role of U.S. military lawyers in the creation of the 1949 Geneva Conventions, and the persistence of an array of arms control negotiators, especially with regard to nuclear weapons.[15] It is, nonetheless, safe to say that the dominant policy-making perspective once the nation assumed its superpower role looked upon international law as useful but hardly central. George Kennan, the noted architect of containment, best summed up this view, stating, "The idea of the subordination of a large number of states to an international juridical regime, limiting their possibilities for aggression and injury to other states, implies that these are all states like our own, reasonably content with their international borders and status. . . . Actually, this has generally been true only of a portion of international society. We tend to underestimate the violence of national maladjustments and discontents elsewhere in the world if we think that they would always appear to other people as less important than the preservation of the juridical tidiness of international life."[16]

At the same time, international law itself changed, especially from an American perspective. On one hand, its scope was newly broad. The emergence of international human rights law in particular invaded numerous areas in which states had previously been sovereign, including the extent to which governments could detain, arrest, mistreat, control speech, and regulate religious practice. Above all was the prohibition of discrimination based on race, sex, language, or religion—a result of the Holocaust and kept central by decolonization.[17] The revolutionary nature of human rights law was real. Yet its novelty within the U.S. constitutional order can be and has been exaggerated. The property and contract rights protected by eighteenth-century treaties were comparable invasions into a nation's sovereignty at the time. The key difference was that violations of those rights, which protected unpopular British aliens, meant that a still-weak nation could have been dragged into war, whereas violating an international commitment to racial equality, which protected marginalized African Americans and Asians, was a price a superpower could pay.[18]

That difference, however, raises a paradoxical aspect of postwar international law. Though ostensibly more intrusive, within the United States its foundations would prove to be weaker than before. Much of the reason for this had to do precisely with racial equality. The prospect of a treaty such as the UN Charter prohibiting Jim Crow in the South or anti-Asian laws on the West Coast would produce an immediate and powerful racist backlash against international law itself.[19] More longstanding and rarefied factors also contributed. By the time of America's great transformation as an engaged global power, natural law had long ceased to be a foundation for international law, depriving it of at least a theoretical source of authority. Ironically, the horrors of World War II would highlight the inadequacies of positivism alone and lead to a minor resurgence of natural law, at least for human rights. The decline of natural law would affect customary international law especially, at least in the United States.[20] Courts, moreover, increasingly treated international custom as subsumed under general common law, which the Supreme Court would reject in the landmark 1938 decision *Erie Railroad Co. v. Tompkins*.[21] Finally, a century and a half of isolationism, development, and internal conquest and ethnic cleansing, among other factors, meant that international law had not maintained its previously central place in the American legal community.

America's newfound commitment to the international stage, in short, inevitably put unprecedented pressure on separation of powers in foreign affairs, including and especially the historic role of the judiciary. Engagement in overlapping, ongoing conflicts as a world power yielded a national security state in which the executive above all would seek to leverage newfound power that Congress had granted and that successive presidents sought. Meanwhile, international law, one of the common bases for the Court's intervention in foreign affairs, staked out newly bold postwar claims on foundations that would prove surprisingly shaky within the United States. Still to be determined was how much the great transformation in the nation's foreign policy would transform separation of powers in foreign affairs.

"Continuity and Change"

The answer to this question recalls the diptych framed by *Youngstown* and *Curtiss-Wright*. On one hand, several prominent scholars have argued that the Court has largely retreated from its historic mission. Harold

Hongju Koh, for example, decries the case law that, in the decades after *Youngstown*, demonstrated that "the federal courts, through action and inaction, . . . adopted an increasingly deferential attitude to the president in foreign affairs."[22] This deference, he elsewhere noted, came to extend to the institutional conclusion that courts are "somehow incompetent . . . to make the very determinations regarding international and foreign affairs law that they had been making since the Republic began." Bruce Ackerman agrees, diverging from his colleague mainly in seeing the judicial retreat as even more thoroughgoing and dire.[23] G. Edward White, for his part, suggests that the judicial acceptance of executive primacy came even earlier, with roots dating back through World War I and established by 1936.[24] Other prominent specialists assert that the Court's capitulation, like Mark Twain's death, is greatly exaggerated. Paul Stephen emphasizes the postwar Court's readiness to maintain a pronounced degree of independence in such traditional areas as property, contracts, and injuries to persons and property.[25] He nonetheless views much of the Court's postwar foreign affairs jurisprudence as "a complex mixture of deference and judicial self-confidence."[26] William Dodge best captures the ambiguity of the Court's more general record as a story "of continuity and change."[27]

That assessment raises the question of whether the change has outweighed the continuity. The Court's encounters with the new national security state suggest not. To the contrary, the challenge to the long-established constitutional framework in foreign affairs, as reflected in *Curtiss-Wright*, cannot yet be taken to effectively amend that framework, as defended in *Youngstown*—at least not on any theory that demands a sustained change in constitutional custom to displace formal text, original understanding, and over a century of custom faithful to the initial vision. A change in constitutional tradition on this scale has yet to take place. The Court's postwar record instead reveals a dominant theme consistent with the foreign affairs role assigned the judiciary, notwithstanding decisions and opinions establishing a clear challenge to that understanding. This pattern, moreover, can be seen in the various foreign affairs responsibilities the Court had played previously: as a check on the states, as a break on Congress, and, most of all, as a safeguard against executive overreach.

REVIEWING THE SEVERAL STATES

The Court's response to the nation's ascendency in foreign affairs properly begins with its historic role of constraining the several states. Recall that judicial enforcement of exactly such constraints lay at the heart of the call for the Federal Convention, the eventual supremacy clause, and the first case in which the Court struck down the act of a legislature, *Ware v. Hylton*.[28] To an extent, the Court continued to remain true to this historic mission. It did this in part by enforcing certain kinds of treaties. It even augmented its power by introducing a doctrine that enabled it to invalidate state laws even in the absence of a treaty or federal law. Most strikingly, the Court lent its approval to international agreements overriding state law made by the president alone. Conversely, the Court did surrender a core aspect of its foreign affairs power by accepting an assault on the Founding doctrine that treaties were automatically supreme over state law. This distinctive retreat did not come in consequence of growing congressional or even presidential power. Instead, it resulted from the collision of international law's growing commitment to equality and too many states' entrenched systems of racial segregation.

The most important restraint the Court would apply to the states during this period came at the earliest stage. The Founding, and the supremacy clause it produced, had anticipated that judicial enforcement of full treaties would be the primary way in which states would be brought into line with national foreign policy. In the years leading to World War II, the Court vastly expanded the types of international agreements that could bind the states. The Constitution's text notwithstanding, the federal government had from its earliest days entered into compacts with other countries outside of treaties concluded by the president and two-thirds of the Senate. The alternatives were congressional-executive agreements, agreed to by the president and a majority of each house, as the name implies, and sole executive agreements, made by the president alone, as the name makes obvious.[29]

Not long after *Curtiss-Wright*, and for similar reasons, the Court approved of the sole-executive alternative in two cases that reigned in the states.[30] *United States v. Belmont* presented the question whether an agreement made by FDR and the just-recognized Soviet Union overrode the laws of New York State. With Justice Sutherland (of *Curtiss-Wright* fame) in the lead, the Court answered yes. The sole-executive agreement was a valid exercise of federal foreign affairs power, in the face of which "state lines disappeared."[31] The Court reaffirmed this conclusion a few years later during World War II in *United States v. Pink*. That decision likewise held that FDR's sole-executive agreement was both valid and supreme over New York law that ordinarily would have protected property held by American interests in the face of Soviet claims.[32] Consistent with *Curtiss-Wright*'s concerns, both decisions gave formal approval to a tool that FDR could use in resisting the fascist powers. Not coincidentally, that new tool gave the Court an additional category of international agreements to vindicate federal foreign affairs powers over state policies that might undermine the nation's interest.

Significantly, the judicial enforcement of foreign affairs restrictions on the states did not fare as well without a sole-executive basis. Instead, there emerged a postwar pattern in which the Court initially relied on different aspects of federal foreign affairs authority but, over time, turned to domestic constitutional or regulatory power. Such was the case with traditional treaties made by the president with the advice and consent of two-thirds of the Senate. In several postwar cases, the justices cited treaties when invalidating state laws that discriminated against aliens inheriting property.[33] Then, in the idiosyncratic 1968 case *Zschernig v. Miller*, the Court appeared to do itself one better. There it announced the novel doctrine that it did not even need a treaty to override a state law. The immediate problem was an Oregon statute that discriminated against aliens inheriting property, on the ground that foreigners from communist states that prevented Americans from inheriting property in those countries should not be able to succeed to property in the United States. No treaty or (for that matter) federal statute, let alone a constitutional provision, preempted Oregon's foray into the fight against global communism. That did not stop the justices from striking it down anyway. Their novel move was to rely on a "dormant" federal foreign affairs authority that alone sufficed to override any state law.[34] However novel the doctrine, the Court has not relied on it since. Instead the justices have found that either the Constitution, acts of Congress, or federal regulations have sufficed to strike down state measures that arguably encroach on federal foreign affairs policies.[35]

In one area, however, the Court dramatically retreated from its historic foreign affairs role, though not because of either the national security state or the relative ascent of the executive. As we have seen, under the supremacy clause as originally understood, all treaties were automatically the supreme law of the land when in conflict with state law. Otherwise known as "treaty supremacy," this idea became a solution to states violating national treaty commitments, one of the principal problems leading to the Constitution in the first place. Later the Court introduced the idea that some treaties were "non-self-executing" and needed implementation by Congress to become domestic law. Yet this idea extended only to the matters binding on the federal government, not the states.[36]

All this changed just after World War II. In essence, international law's postwar commitment to human rights ran headlong into America's countercommitment to racial segregation. At the state level, at least one court relied on the UN Charter to invalidate a discriminatory California law.[37] At the Supreme Court, briefs and the writings of certain justices likewise referred to the Charter with reference to Jim Crow laws in the South. As David Sloss has shown, this judicial dalliance with postwar international human rights law produced a complex yet strong reaction in Congress and among certain elite lawyers that nearly resulted in the so-called Bricker Amendment, versions of which would have required all treaties to be implemented domestically through federal statutes.[38] The amendment went down to a narrow defeat in Congress, but the cost was a new understanding that automatic treaty supremacy over state law would no longer be the rule. Instead, the question whether a treaty automatically applied domestically, an inquiry previously relevant only to federal law, would now apply to state laws as well.

The result was that the few human rights treaties the United States would sign and ratify would be deemed non-self-executing thanks to Senate declarations to that effect, and so not directly binding on the states. Ironically, this insulation of Jim Crow from international law did not exactly help the nation win over the developing world during the Cold War. To this extent, this foreign affairs cost vindicated the Founders' original insight about the importance of preventing the states from undermining the nation's treaty commitments. As Mary Dudziak has shown, the Court partially, though consciously, mitigated this problem by striking down Jim Crow laws, most notably with *Brown v. Board of Education*. Yet however much foreign policy concerns may have provided additional motivation to promote civil rights, the Court relied exclusively on the Constitution, not human rights treaties, to get that job done.[39]

Not surprisingly, the rise of a perpetual national security state did nothing to undermine the Court's historic remit to ensure that the states did not undermine the nation's foreign policy. To the contrary, the Court augmented the constraints it could use in upholding international agreements made by the president alone, a move that itself enhanced executive foreign affairs authority. Only when postwar international law embraced racial equality did the Court balk, declining to apply relevant treaties or the centuries old doctrine of treaty supremacy. The American original sin of slavery and segregation, in other words, was sufficient to deflect the Court from otherwise ensuring that the states would not violate the nation's international obligations.

The real test that the advent of the national security state would pose to the courts would, theoretically, come from the national political branches.

As before, less significant were assertions by Congress. Previously, and especially in the early days of the republic, the Court did not hesitate to impose soft constraints on Congress, mainly through the *Charming Betsy* canon's imperative to interpret federal statutes consistent with international law. The post–World War II case law suggests that the Court imposed limits on Congress even less frequently, not so much because the justices backed away from their duty but because Congress itself stood on the sidelines. Justice Jackson's *Youngstown* concurrence foretold just such a situation in calling upon the legislature to fulfill its constitutional role and not cede authority to the executive. The result was that in few instances did the Court and Congress clash over legislation implicating foreign affairs. One searches this period in vain for an analog to the Court's early, restrictive readings of federal statutes authorizing various military measures during hostilities.

REVIEWING CONGRESS

That said, one clear area in which the two branches did come into conflict involved the extraterritorial application of federal statutes. Previously, the Court had developed a presumption against applying acts of Congress abroad, but mainly because international law and comity mandated as much. Under the *Charming Betsy* canon, therefore, federal legislation should be interpreted accordingly. In the postwar era, the justices continued to limit the application of U.S. laws overseas. From a foreign affairs perspective, however, the continued imposition of such limits grew increasingly perverse. First, many of the statutes at issue involved the creation of rights rather than the extension of regulations. Second, postwar international law itself evolved to permit any particular state to extend the reach of its laws abroad. The case law in this area is rich and complex, and further comprises the distinct areas of maritime and nonmaritime law. For a fairly representative example of the overall phenomenon, however, consider *EEOC v. Arabian American Oil Company*, in which the Court considered the application of the 1964 Civil Rights Act to an American employee of an American company working abroad who claimed he had been fired on the basis of race. The Court rejected the claim, citing the presumption against extraterritoriality, but with no reference to international standards—which themselves were consistent with a prohibition on racial discrimination—or *Charming Betsy*.[40]

Why the Court in this and other areas more and more relied on a domestic presumption against extraterritoriality divorced from *Charming Betsy* and international law is not clear. Yet one possibility should not be discounted. As noted, postwar international law not only expanded to cover whether states violated the fundamental rights of persons within their jurisdiction, but also made equality the centerpiece of the process. At least in the United States, this expansion directly countered the nation's enduring tradition of segregation. That conflict in turn produced a dramatic backlash, sufficient even to effectively repeal the Founding commitment to the supremacy of treaties over state law. For various reasons, the Court evidently found it safer to promote racial equality with purely domestic, constitutional materials. In this context, a more general retreat from international to domestic norms is not surprising, especially when the international norms worked to promote human rights from abroad.

Another area that brought the Court and Congress into conflict involved statutes granting the federal government the authority to strip persons of their U.S. citizenship involuntarily. There the pattern was not erosion of judicial oversight over time, but instead initial retreat and then reassertion. At first the Court upheld legislation authorizing the forfeiture of citizenship. In that instance a U.S. citizen had moved to Mexico to avoid the draft during World War II. While there he also voted in a Mexican election, which triggered the statutory provision that triggered his loss of U.S. citizenship. By the 1960s, however, the Court began to consistently invalidate such legislation, and then did so purely on constitutional grounds. They first struck down a law that mandated loss of citizenship for draft dodgers. They next overturned a provision that designated the same penalty as applied to a naturalized citizen who moved back to her prior country and resided there for three years. Finally, the Court effectively held that U.S. citizens could not be deprived of their citizenship involuntarily in general. Some of the justices in these cases referred to treaties that supported the government; others appealed to international standards supporting the claim to citizenship. But in no instance was international law determinative, especially when it cut against the government.[41]

Several factors may account for this pattern. It accords with the phenomenon, seen most clearly during the Civil War, in which the judiciary at times steps aside during active hostilities, to then reassert its authority later. The failure to rely on international law as a check in these instances may have reflected the more general reluctance to cite international human rights law given the reaction it produced for having championed racial equality. Most importantly, the citizenship cases are best seen as dealing with domestic authority in any event. Though they implicate internationally protected rights, in the end they deal with a state's authority to define who is a full member of its political community. As such, the Court's eventual reliance on the domestic constitutional sources made sense here as well.[42]

REVIEWING THE EXECUTIVE

More than Congress or the states, conflict, whether hot or cold, tends to empower the executive above all. Previously, the nation's discrete foreign conflicts meant this tendency was episodic, as was the resulting pressure on separation of powers in foreign affairs. With World War II, the Cold War, and the "global war on terror," both foreign conflict and consequent assertions of executive power grew constant, as reflected in the creation of the national security state.[43] The Supreme Court's response was not surprising. *Youngstown* reflects the dominant theme of the Court remaining faithful to its assigned role. Yet various justices, and at times the Court as a whole, also responded with doctrines and decisions that signaled retreat in the face of executive assertions. In some areas, the resulting encroachments were halting; in others they were more constant. Either way, the challenge to separation of powers as originally designed and long practiced merits attention and response, especially given the absence of formal amendment, informal yet legitimate constitutional moment, or sufficient alternative custom.

World War II invited what was perhaps the executive's most egregious abuses, and with them some of the Court's most shameful retreats.[44] Months after Pearl Harbor, Franklin Roosevelt invoked his authority as president and commander in chief to issue the now infamous Executive Order 9066, which authorized the secretary of war, and any military commanders he may designate, "to prescribe military areas . . . from which any or all persons may be excluded" and further provide them with "accommodations" during the period of exclusion.[45] On this basis General John DeWitt first ordered a curfew for Japanese Americans and lawful Japanese aliens on the West Coast, followed by an order excluding them from the West Coast states and sending them to internment camps for the balance of war.[46] Prior to the general's orders, Congress had weighed in with an act making it a federal crime to disobey any restrictions promulgated under the president's order.[47] Ultimately, at least 120,000 men, women, and children were sent to various internment camps solely on the basis of their Japanese ancestry.[48]

The Supreme Court infamously upheld the curfew, the exclusion, and effectively the internment. In *Hirabayashi v. United States*, the justices unanimously though inaccurately reasoned that the president and Congress had authorized the curfew. Weighing that authorization against the due process clause, the Court concluded that the measure was "reasonable" in light of the attack on Pearl Harbor, the number of military installations on the West Coast, and the particular "solidarity" Japanese Americans felt for Japan.[49] *Korematsu v. United States*, which lives on in even greater infamy, extended *Hirabayashi* in two key ways. First, it upheld the actual exclusion order, a holding that, try as it might to avoid the conclusion, also validated the internment. Second, the six-justice majority, though likewise deeming the internment as directly authorized by both the president and Congress, relied more heavily on the judgment of the military authorities.[50]

Bad as they were, these judicial surrenders were not total. The Court did hear the cases, rather than attempt to use various doctrines to hold that they could not. In *Korematsu*, moreover, Justices Owen Roberts and Frank Murphy, neither of whom have gone down as great luminaries of the Court, both dissented on the ground—obvious even to many government lawyers, not to mention the FBI—that the exclusion and internment of an entire population based on race could be deemed neither reasonable or rational.[51] Justice Jackson also dissented, on the separate ground that it would be better for the Court not to have taken the case than to have a bad precedent rattling around its case law to validate future abuses.[52] Though often praised, an approach that suggests the judiciary sit on the sidelines in sensitive national security cases to avoid the possibility of a bad decision itself runs the risk of informally validating any high-stakes foreign policy determination that the political branches may make, no matter the abuses. Nor did Jackson anticipate that a combination of academic commentary, popular activism, and ultimately a 1980 act of Congress compensating the victims of internment would render *Korematsu* a type of "antiprecedent," toxic to any who might cite it.[53]

The Court proved to be truer to its designated role in other major wartime cases. A trilogy involved challenges to trials of enemy combatants accused of war crimes.[54] In *Ex Parte Quirin* a unanimous Court upheld the use of a special military tribunal—with fewer due process protections than a court martial—against eight German spies who came ashore on Long Island, New York, from a submarine. It did so, moreover, under enormous and immediate pressure by the Roosevelt administration. The justices, sitting in emergency session, issued their opinion as the trial proceeded and didn't release a full opinion until three months later, well after all of the spies were convicted and six were executed.[55] As in *Korematsu*, the justices went out of their way to find congressional authorization and so avoided any invitation to rely on executive power exclusively. Conversely, the Court also avoided deferential language regarding the executive's wartime judgment precisely because of its determination that creating military tribunals fell within the president's authority and the violation of fundamental rights had not been asserted.[56] The consideration of General Tomoyuki Yamashita's military commission followed a broadly similar pattern. Citing *Quirin*, the decision once more reasoned that the proceedings fell within the executive's authority. It further rejected claims that the trial violated substantive aspects of U.S. military and international law, but again, it did so without sounding any note of deference to military or executive officials.[57] The third case, *Johnson v. Eisentrager*, raised the different inquiry of whether U.S. statutory and constitutional protections extended to German prisoners captured in China and tried by military commission in Germany. The justices answered no, also rejecting the prisoners' claims of procedural violations of the 1929 Geneva Convention. Although the military—and, therefore, the commander in chief—again prevailed, it did so based upon the Court's independent legal analysis rather any notion that the Court should view its duties differently during wartime.[58]

Rarely, though significantly, the executive during World War II could also lose. Fittingly, perhaps the most significant defeat came in the context of Japanese American internment. Mitsuye Endo was an American citizen of Japanese ancestry imprisoned in the Tule Lake "war relocation center." While there, she applied for a leave to the War Relocation Authority, the executive agency that administered the internment program. The agency granted her a preliminary "leave clearance" as a loyal citizen, but she still needed to make a formal application for indefinite leave, which could be denied on various grounds. Though this application was not made, a unanimous Supreme Court nevertheless held that the War Relocation Authority had no authority to detain her and declared that "we are of the view that Mitsuye Endo should be given her liberty."[59] The justices avoided holding that the federal government directly violated the Constitution. Rather, they unanimously reasoned that neither the executive order nor the related act of Congress authorized the War Relocation Authority to detain a loyal citizen.[60] The otherwise uncelebrated Justice Murphy again went further. In a lone concurrence, he pointed to the "patent facts" that the executive at the highest levels "held the belief in the legality and validity" of the internment program, as did Congress; yet the detention directly "violated the guarantees of the Bill of Rights."[61] Under either approach, a united Court demonstrated it would still stand up to the executive, even as a global war still raged.

The judiciary regained its traditional footing as World War II ended and the Cold War began. Moreover, it showed that it could withstand presidential pressure even when the long battle with communism was at its most heated. Nowhere was this assertion more striking than in the *Youngstown* decision itself. Here the result may be even more important than the reasoning analyzed earlier and is worth pausing to consider. Six judges told a sitting president of the United States that he had no authority to undertake a temporary measure that he believed critical to conduct a major conflict that would lead to the deaths of tens of thousands of American troops. And President Truman, who would assert his own firmness by "firing" the popular but vainglorious General MacArthur, complied. For this alone, *Youngstown* rightly retains its place in marking the historic foreign affairs role for the judiciary. That place is doubly noteworthy in the face of *Curtiss-Wright* coming to mark an opposing vision in which the courts effectively stand aside as the executive asserts the need for increased authority to face seemingly endless foreign threats.

The cooler periods of the Cold War nonetheless involved an unprecedented, sustained projection of American military might throughout the world. Deployed by the president and funded by Congress, the U.S. armed forces stationed tens of thousands of service personnel in bases ranging from the United Kingdom, West Germany, and Turkey to the Philippines, South Korea, and Japan. Even with the fall of the Soviet Union, this "forward strategy" now entails over eight hundred military installations outside the fifty states.[62] Such a massive overseas presence was bound to raise important legal issues, and it did. The most important involved the authority of the executive versus the judicial enforcement of rights overseas.

Clarice Covert had been living on a U.S. airbase in England when she took an axe and murdered her husband, Master Sergeant Edward Covert. Dorothy Smith did much the same to her husband, Army Colonel Aubrey Smith, while living on a base in Japan, only she used a knife. Though civilians, each woman was tried before a court martial, convicted, and sentenced to life imprisonment. Each was sent back to the United States, where they challenged their convictions in federal court on the ground that the courts martial had no jurisdiction over civilians. Two different district courts agreed.

So did the Supreme Court. A plurality led by Justice Black addressed several momentous issues. First, the opinion did not hesitate to "reject the idea that, when the United States acts against citizens abroad, it can do so free of the Bill of Rights."[63] Instead, Black articulated the idea that constitutional rights operated extraterritorially because the Constitution's constraints travelled with its grants of power. As he put it, "the United States is entirely a creature of the Constitution. Its power and authority have no other source. It can only act in accordance with all the limitations imposed by the Constitution."[64] The Constitution did follow the flag, and the judiciary's authority followed the Constitution.

In this way the opinion went well beyond earlier jurisprudence. One set of precedents it exceeded was the *Insular Cases*. That label refers to a series of decisions in which the Court had to deal with the status of island territories that the United States conquered during the Spanish-American War. Of these, two held that the right to trial by jury, and the Bill of Rights more generally, did not automatically apply to the "unincorporated" territories of Puerto Rico and the Philippines, since they were considered not destined to become states, though they might in the future become "incorporated." The Court balked, frankly, because the inhabitants of each acquisition were too alien—read, too Catholic, Hispanic, and/or Asian—to enjoy the full panoply of constitutional rights. The cases did, however, hold that unspecified fundamental rights, at least, did apply.[65] Black's opinion departed even further from *In re Ross*, the closest case on point. This decision permitted an executive U.S. consular court to conduct a nonjury trial of a U.S citizen in nineteenth-century Japan, in part because anything else at the time would have been impractical.[66] Conversely, Black's *Reid v. Covert* plurality did note that the principal limitation at issue was the right to a civilian trial by jury set out in the Fifth and Sixth Amendments, as well as Article III.[67] It also noted that the trials involved American citizens. Black's logic, however, suggested that constitutional rights would follow the flag, which is to say constitutional power, in general.[68]

The *Reid* plurality further made clear that the judiciary would apply the Constitution abroad to a type of international agreement that empowered the president to empower Congress to empower the president. The two homicidal spouses, of course, had been tried by military lawyers in military courts, quintessential components of the executive. Congress, however, had sought to authorize courts martial of "civilian dependents" in the Uniform Code of Military Justice. Congress's power to do that, in turn, derived from provisions in sole-executive agreements that the president had made with the United Kingdom and Japan to maintain U.S. bases. Such accords, now commonly known as Status of Armed Forces Agreements or "SOFAs" were and are the lynchpin of America's overseas "forward strategy."[69] They are also but a subset of the international agreements with other nations that the Court has permitted the president to make with increasing frequency on a range of matters. By extending the Constitution, the *Reid*

Court deployed the judiciary to balance an increasingly important source of executive authority. The justices have not always been as steadfast in following the flag since then, arguably bowing to the consistent pressure exerted by executive actions overseas. *Reid* itself, however, showed how steadfast the Court could be, even at the height of the Cold War.

In a more complex fashion, the Court also pushed back against executive authority from a challenge within its midst in a case involving how to deal with Castro's Cuba. As befits a communist revolution, among Castro's initiatives upon seizing power was nationalizing various industries, including the sugar industry. In this Castro was not alone, nor was the practice confined even to communist regimes. Many newly independent former colonies after World War II appropriated business sectors, especially those with heavy foreign investment. This wave of seizures put substantial pressure on the customary international law rule that required prompt and adequate compensation.[70] Cuba's measures not surprisingly led to conflicts with U.S. investors. In one critical case, *Banco Nacional de Cuba v. Sabbatino*, the state bank laid claim to the purchase price of a cargo of sugar from an American firm on the ground that the cargo was the nationalized property of the Cuban government. The Cuban bank relied on, among other things, the "act of state" doctrine. Derived from customary international law, this principle mandated that the courts of one state would not review the official acts of another state taken within the second state's own borders. The Cuban position was that the nationalization of the sugar industry was an official act within its borders and could not be reviewed by U.S. courts, and so its claim should prevail.[71]

The lower courts held against the Cuban claim. The district court reasoned that the act of state doctrine did not apply to the uncompensated taking of property, which it deemed itself to be a violation of international law. The Court of Appeals for the Second Circuit in essence agreed. Significantly, it based its decision in part on what it believed to be the desires of the executive branch.[72] The State Department had issued two "Bernstein letters," which the court "took as evidence that the Executive Branch had no objection to a judicial testing of the Cuban decree's validity."[73] This type of letter got its name from an early, post–World War II case of the same circuit court, in which that court indicated it would defer to the State Department's recommendations.[74] The Cuban case would test, among other things, whether the Supreme Court would approve the ceding of judiciary authority to determine a question of law rooted in international custom to the executive.

The Supreme Court took back the authority the Second Circuit had ceded, at least in this case. It could do so because the State Department itself made clear it would not seek a "Bernstein" exception in letters to attorneys involved in the case after it had granted review. Writing for the majority, Justice Harlan noted that the justices had never endorsed the Bernstein letter exception and did not need to do so here.[75] Turning to the merits, the Court reversed and held for the Cuban bank, doubtless confirming in the eyes of some critics the orientation of the Court under Chief Justice Earl Warren. First, the Court almost certainly incorrectly decided that government taking of foreign property did not violate customary international law as it then stood. Somewhat less clearly, the Court decided that the judiciary had the power to apply rules rooted in customary international law absent a statute or a treaty, not by bringing it down directly, as the Founders would have understood, but by exercising a version of their own authority to fashion common-law, judge-made rules in matters dealing with foreign affairs.[76]

Even among specialists, *Sabbatino* has a reputation of being as Delphic as it is important.[77] Whatever else, it reflects the postwar judiciary's stance on foreign affairs in an age of perpetual conflict. The decision kept alive the Court's authority to apply rules based on international custom, either indirectly (as a type of judge-made federal common law) or even (where the custom was clear) directly, as it had before. As noted, this type of authority had been used to check both the president and Congress since the early days of the republic. More pointedly, the Court declined to endorse the Bernstein letter approach as a way to defer to the executive branch and refrain from applying a legal rule it otherwise would have brought to bear. That said, and this reflects the so-far "minor" theme of the judiciary's response, neither did the Court reject the device. Since *Sabbatino*, the lower courts have deferred to Bernstein letters with increasing frequency, so that the "exception" threatens to swallow the rule. This is all the more reason for the contemporary judiciary to reconsider and recommit to its Founding position.

Vietnam, for the United States the Cold War's most heated conflict, would also show the Court responding to aggressive presidential assertions in kind. In foreign affairs, few confrontations were more dramatic than the Nixon administration's attempt to prevent the publication of the "Pentagon Papers," a secret Department of Defense study of U.S. involvement in Vietnam after 1945.[78] *New York Times Co. v. United States*[79] began as the *Times* and the *Washington Post* sought to publish the materials, which revealed the inner workings of U.S. policy in Southeast Asia, often in an unflattering light. Relying on the president's inherent "executive authority," Attorney General John Mitchell went to federal court to obtain injunctions against the two newspapers publishing any excerpts from the study on the grounds that doing so might cause irreparable harm to national security.[80] The executive also sought to rely on the 1917 Espionage Act, which made it a criminal offense for anyone having "unauthorized possession" of documents "relating to national defense" to "communicate" such information to others.[81] The trouble here was that even if publication of the Pentagon Papers qualified as a violation—a dubious interpretation—the statute still did not authorize the government to seek a prior restraint on publication, as opposed to punishment after a criminal prosecution, trial, and conviction after printing the documents. The Second Circuit Court of Appeals in New York accepted the administration's position; its sibling tribunal in D.C. did not.[82]

As in *Youngstown*, the Supreme Court handed a wartime president a resounding defeat. Though the justices in the majority broadly agreed, they produced separate opinions emphasizing different concerns. Most obviously, they shared common ground that the First Amendment prohibition of any law abridging freedom of the press all but precluded prior restraints on the publication. Yet they were no less troubled by the aggressive assertion, in the name of national security, by an executive branch that ongoing conflict had made more powerful than any other in the nation's history. As Justice William Brennan noted, "Never before has the United States [executive] sought to enjoin a newspaper from publishing information in its possession."[83] More generally, Justice Potter Stewart noted that awesome power of modern presidents:

> In the governmental structure created by our Constitution, the Executive is endowed with enormous power in the two related areas of national defense and international relations. This power, largely unchecked by the Legislative and Judicial branches, has been pressed to the very hilt since the advent of the nuclear missile age.[84]

Justice Byron White made clear just how far the executive now pressed:

> The Government's position is simply stated: The responsibility of the Executive for the conduct of the foreign affairs and for the security of the Nation is so basic that the President is entitled to an injunction against publication of a newspaper story whenever he can convince a court that the information to be revealed threatens "grave and irreparable" injury to the public interest.[85]

The majority left no doubt that the judiciary would not be commandeered into aiding and abetting the Nixon administration's claims. In some ways the justices did not go as far as *Youngstown*. Central here was the overriding importance of the First Amendment. In other ways, however, the *New York Times* decision went further. The *Youngstown* Court viewed President Truman as operating against the will of Congress. In the *New York Times* case, the justices observed that President Nixon simply operated without congressional approval. Whatever the differences, the Vietnam-era decision, no less than its Korean conflict predecessor, showed that the courts would remain the last, not the first, to leave the illegitimate foreign affairs claims of the executive unchecked.

Vietnam, however, also showed that repeated executive assertions could also take their toll. Not least in this regard was the ongoing assertive behavior of fighting a major conflict without a declaration of war by Congress. Korea is usually cited as the first large-scale war fought without a congressional declaration. There, at least, President Truman had a novel argument, however problematic, that he was implementing a binding UN Security Council resolution, either directly or as prospectively incorporated by Congress through the UN Participation Act.[86] President Johnson had no such innovative basis for Vietnam. Instead, he relied on the infamous 1964 Gulf of Tonkin Resolution, in which Congress authorized the president "to take all necessary steps, including the use of armed force," to support any allied state in Southeast Asia "requesting assistance in defense of its freedom."[87] It would later come to light that Congress in part acted on false reports that North Vietnamese gunships had fired on U.S. Navy vessels. Congress repealed the resolution in 1970.[88]

In another contrast to Korea, unprecedented challenges were brought against this unprecedented type of war. In one such instance, two U.S. servicemen fought transfers to Vietnam on the ground that the president was waging an unconstitutional war in the absence of a formal declaration by Congress.[89] Later, members of Congress made a similar argument. The first challenge, *Orlando v. Laird*, made its way to the Second Circuit Court of Appeals in New York. That court held that numerous congressional measures that supported the war, not least ongoing appropriations, served as sufficient legislative approval.[90] In the second case, *Mitchell v. Laird*, the District of Columbia Circuit disagreed, contending that measures implementing a war did not substitute for a deliberative choice by Congress to authorize a war in the first place. Rather than hold the remaining operations in Cambodia illegal, the D.C. Circuit took a significant step in the direction that has led to the current crossroads in which the judiciary in foreign affairs finds itself. Among other reasons for its sidestep, the judges held that the challenge presented a "political question" beyond the competence of the judiciary—especially because it involved foreign affairs. Specifically, they reasoned that the judiciary was in no position to second-guess President Nixon's efforts to end a war, no matter how protracted, that he had inherited, even if his predecessor began it in violation of the Constitution.[91] In neither case did the Supreme Court itself grant review.[92]

As in many other arenas, Vietnam left a mixed legacy. *New York Times*, like *Youngstown*, showed that the judiciary could still fulfill its envisioned role even in the middle of a hot war, taking place during a period of perpetual conflict, in the context of a permanent national security state. The direct challenges to the conflict, however, indicate that the perspective underlying *Curtiss-Wright* were still strong enough to prompt courts to defer and even sideline themselves.[93] Other judicial responses in other areas during this period suggest that the burdens of a superpower engaged in ceaseless hostilities worked to bolster the *Curtiss-Wright* perspective over time.

The rumblings of possible change manifested in those areas, among others, that determined whether challenges to executive action got to court in the first place. Take the "political question" doctrine, which enabled courts to sidestep consideration of executive adventurism in Southeast Asia. This idea, to be considered in depth later, in essence holds that certain kinds of cases should not be decided by courts because they are more political than legal in nature. One standard example arises when the Constitution expressly commits a matter to be resolved outside the courts, such as impeachment of a president by the House of Representatives and trial in the Senate. Another example, if a vaguer one, is found in instances in which there are insufficient legal standards to permit judicial resolution. Itself a relative newcomer, the "political question" doctrine, further embracing the notion that foreign affairs matters in particular should elude judicial consideration because they are more likely to raise "political" rather than legal issues, predated the Gulf of Tonkin resolution by just a few years. In this there is a certain irony. "Political question" analysis in its current form dates to the Supreme Court's 1962 holding in *Baker v. Carr*, in which the Court effectively coined the term only to reject its application to invalidate the districting of congressional seats as violating the Constitution's implicit mandate of "one person, one vote."[94] Along the way Justice Brennan indicated that one area associated with "political" questions was, as he defined it, "foreign affairs." He did attempt to qualify the point, noting that "it is error to suppose that every case or controversy which touches foreign relations lies beyond judicial cognizance."[95] Unfortunately, Brennan's defensive phrasing planted the seeds for courts to err on the side of avoiding thorny foreign affairs cases.

Other "gatekeeper" doctrines likewise emerged during this period that either insulated or privileged the executive's determinations in matters that typically implicated foreign policy concerns. The modern "state secrets privilege" is one. This arose during the Korean War when the widows of three contractors who were killed in an Air Force B-29 crash sued the federal government. To make their case, the survivors naturally sought the accident reports that had been made as a matter of course. The Supreme Court effectively denied them the critical evidence, holding that when the executive made a claim that certain information was privileged "under circumstances indicating a reasonable possibility that military secrets were involved, there was certainly a sufficient showing of privilege to cut off further demand for the document on the showing of necessity for its compulsion that had then been made."[96] In doing so, the justices more or less created a new shield for governmental activity out of scant English materials, in part because "we cannot escape judicial notice that this is a time of vigorous preparation for national defense."[97] Even then, this initial application of the state secrets privilege was fairly narrow, and the widows managed to get a settlement. As with the "political question," however, the judiciary had articulated a method that could be used to tie its own hands in the face of possible executive wrongdoing.

Nor were these the only self-imposed constraints. In two instances the judiciary developed mechanisms that invited the executive to control judicial review in specific cases. As already seen, the Second Circuit Court of Appeals in New York established the Bernstein letter procedure, which ceded to the State Department the determination of whether to apply the act of state doctrine. Though the Supreme Court's *Sabbatino* decision refused to endorse the device, neither did it reject it, leaving the lower courts free to apply it.[98] The Court more affirmatively approved a similar concession to the executive that came to be known as the "Tate letter." This type of missive deals with an international law principle known as "foreign sovereign immunity," which prevents lawsuits against foreign states or officials in the courts of other countries. In two World War II cases, the Supreme Court declared that it would leave the decision of whether to apply what is a legal standard to the State Department.[99] Several years later, the assistant secretary of state James Tate announced that the United States would join the majority of states and permit suits for private, commercial conduct as opposed to governmental action. The

Tate letter opened the door for endless litigation, since the line between a state's official versus its commercial conduct is often less than clear. This new position nonetheless rightly assumed that the judiciary would still bow to the executive's decisions; only now such a determination would be known as a "Tate letter."[100] As such it would join the Bernstein letter, the state secrets privilege, and modern "political question" doctrine as novel and self-inflicted challenges to the opportunity of hearing the merits of a case in order to say what the applicable law is.

The pressures of checking the national security state also left their mark even when the judiciary did proceed to consider the substance of a case. Probably nothing illustrates this development more clearly than the Supreme Court's apparent growing willingness to defer to the executive's interpretation of treaties under which individuals claimed various rights or protection. Recall that in the first decades of the republic, the Supreme Court neither articulated nor accorded any significance to the executive's interpretations in such instances. As the nation became more engaged in global affairs, and the president became commensurately more powerful, the Court began to articulate deference. Yet, adhering to its original practice, the justices invariably interpreted the relevant international agreement first, and only then would they note their agreement with the president's position, almost as an add-on. The pattern began on the eve of World War I, in a decision holding that an extradition treaty made no exception for U.S. citizens to be delivered up to Italy, the Court famously deployed this statement: "A construction of a treaty by the political department of government, while not conclusive upon a court called upon to construe such a treaty . . . is nevertheless of much weight."[101] That declaration, however, came only after the Court had resolved the matter already, with citation to the treaty's text, principles of international law, comparable U.S. treaties, and treatises.[102] The justices repeated this performance almost exactly—articulating but not actually according deference—just after the Great War.[103]

After the next world war, during the Cold War that followed, the Court raised the bar to saying what the law is, recharacterizing the "much weight" owed to executive interpretations as "great weight."[104] That shift may have reflected the delicacy of the case. Two Oregon residents died without a will, with the only next of kin being relatives in Yugoslavia. State law prevented the property going to the Yugoslavs on the ground that the nonaligned communist state would have denied inheritance to U.S. citizens under the same circumstances. The Court, however, interpreted the treaty in favor of the Yugoslav relatives, the position also taken by the executive.

Once established, where the Court has articulated a standard, it has been "great weight" ever since.[105] Even when the Court applies this standard, however, it nonetheless first undertakes its own interpretation. Yet the concern remains that, sooner or later, articulating deference will in fact result in according it. One recent study suggests that exactly this phenomenon has come about in the lower federal courts.[106]

Judicial deference in this area matters even more in light of related postwar developments. It was after World War II that presidents almost exponentially increased their undertakings of international agreements outside the treaty process requiring two-thirds Senate approval. The nation projected its postwar economic primacy through congressional-executive agreements. Matters dealing with the recognition of new regimes, or the status of the country's military now based throughout the world, took the form of sole-executive agreements. Presidents chose these nontreaty processes precisely because they were far easier to secure. The postwar result was that there were thousands of international agreements, while before there were hundreds.[107] As Paul Stephen has observed, "Legitimizing nontreaty international agreements amplifies executive power."[108] Presidents have an increased number of sources on which to base further executive orders. They also have a vast array of new legal instruments by which they can claim their interpretations are owed "great weight" by the judiciary.

Youngstown *Agonistes*

Of all the postwar landmarks, perhaps none better shows the conflict between the Court's traditional role and the increasing pressures of the executive than a decision that endorsed Justice Jackson's *Youngstown* concurrence even as it diluted it. *Dames & Moore v. Regan* arose out of the Iranian hostage crisis during the Carter administration.[109] Late in 1979, "students" stormed the U.S. embassy in Tehran, outraged by the decision to allow the deposed shah to come to the United States for medical care. The new Iranian government under the Ayatollah Khomeini endorsed the detention of fifty-two American embassy personnel and citizens; this lasted for 444 days.[110]

The U.S. executive's response had little immediate effect. President Carter ordered that Iranian assets in the United States be frozen. He also ordered a rescue attempt that failed. The stalemate showed no real promise of ending until after the election of Ronald Reagan. At that point members of the outgoing and incoming administrations negotiated a deal to resolve the hostage crises through an intermediate sole-executive agreement, with Algeria acting as an intermediary. The Iranians would release the hostages the minute Reagan took the oath of office. In return, the Iranian interests would be able to seek recovery of their assets previously frozen in the United States, in a new Iranian-U.S. claims tribunal to sit in The Hague. To effect this solution, President Carter ordered that the frozen Iranian assets be transferred from the United States to the Federal Reserve Bank in New York, from which the tribunal's judgments could be satisfied.[111]

The trouble was that some U.S. parties had already brought actions against Iranian interests in U.S. courts. In particular, Dames & Moore, an energy company, had contracted with the Iranian government and agencies under the shah to build a nuclear plant. Claiming over $3 million in damages, the company had brought suit in federal court in New York. The trial court duly attached the Iranian assets frozen in the United States pending the trial. Permitting such claims to go forward in U.S. forums, however, directly threated the core idea of the hostage deal. Iran would accept resolutions of claims only before the neutral tribunal in The Hague, not in American courts.[112]

The executive handled this problem by eliminating it. In the waning days of his administration, President Carter ordered that any attachments of Iranian property in the United States be nullified. He further ordered that all frozen Iranian assets be transferred for use by the claims tribunal, pursuant to the sole-executive agreement. To seal the deal, President Reagan shortly after taking office issued an executive order "suspending" all claims against Iranian interests pending in U.S. courts. *Dames & Moore* challenged all three executive actions, and the case eventually made its way to the Supreme Court.[113]

Youngstown provided the relevant analysis. The executive had unilaterally taken steps domestically to deal with a foreign affairs crisis. As a purely formal matter, the justices should have relied primarily, if not exclusively, on the majority opinion of Justice Black, which posited the president's authority could come only from an act of Congress or directly from the Constitution's text. Instead, Justice William Rehnquist began his majority opinion in *Dames & Moore* by endorsing the now-heralded concurrence of Justice Jackson, for whom he had happened to clerk. "We have," he wrote, "in the past found, and do today find, Justice Jackson's classification of executive actions into three general categories analytically useful." But the endorsement came with a substantial caveat: "It is doubtless the case that executive action in any particular instance falls not neatly in one of three pigeonholes, but rather at some point along a spectrum running from explicit congressional authorization to explicit congressional prohibition. This is particularly true as respects cases such as the one before us, involving responses to international crises the nature of which Congress can hardly have been expected to anticipate in any detail."[114]

The Court then applied the "spectral" version of Jackson's categories to the Iranian case. It had no difficulty with President Carter's nullification of the attachment or the transfer of assets. The opinion concludes that Congress had expressly authorized both actions under the International Emergency Economic Powers Act (IEEPA). This statute declares that the president, in order to meet international crises, "may direct and compel, nullify, void, prevent or prohibit, any acquisition, holding, withholding, use, transfer, withdrawal, transportation, importation or exportation of, or dealing in, or exercising any right, power, or privilege with respect to, or transactions involving, any property in which any foreign country or a national thereof has any interest."[115] The plain language was directly on point. The executive would have prevailed even under Justice Black's more limited and mechanical framework.

The more difficult question involved the suspension of a lawsuit pending in a federal court. Even a broad reading of the IEEPA, Justice Rehnquist conceded, did not cover that. Neither did any straightforward reading of the Constitution's textual grants of presidential power. Justice Black therefore almost certainly would have rejected this action. Yet Justice Jackson's framework provided a window of executive opportunity. The suspension of Dames & Moore's suit could have fallen in the "zenith" of power in which the executive enjoyed whatever power it derived implicitly or explicitly from Congress. Or the president might be able to claim authority under the "zone of twilight," in which congressional inaction might count—at least as "a practical matter"—as acquiescence.

How would Jackson have applied his own categories? Any answer, of course, is speculative. Yet most likely the framer of the framework would have concluded that President Reagan, like President Truman, lacked authority. There were no statutes that either expressly or implicitly granted authorization. The IEEPA did not. Nor did the Hostage Act, a statute that granted the president broad powers to recover Americans taken hostage but at no point authorized the suspension of pending claims.[116] Indeed, Jackson might have concluded, as he did in *Youngstown*, that Congress's actions occupied the field without extending the specific power to suspend. Likewise, Jackson would almost certainly not have found any tradition of congressional acquiescence, even if he agreed that Congress's inaction invited the executive to fill the vacuum of authority as a legal, rather than merely "practical," matter. To be sure, presidents had extinguished state court claims under sole-executive agreements made to further their textual authority to recognize the government's powers. That custom, however, did not readily translate to a broader custom of a president relying on such an international agreement to deal with any international matter.

None of this gave pause either to Justice Rehnquist or the majority. Instead, the majority opinion applied the modified Jacksonian "spectrum" in an elliptical manner that has been debated ever since. The president derived authority, more or less, near the "zenith." Even though neither the IEEPA and nor the Hostage Act expressly or implicitly authorized suspension, the opinion nonetheless concluded, "We think both statutes highly relevant in the looser sense of indicating congressional acceptance of a broad scope for executive action in circumstances such as those presented in this case."[117] Precisely because those statutes gave the president an array of powers to deal with international emergencies, their "general tenor" could be taken to "invite" related executive action.[118] While, in short, Jackson found the absence of a specific power in related states to be a decisive omission, his former law clerk found vague approval.

The Court nonetheless accorded more weight to congressional custom nearer to the "zone of twilight." Here Justice Rehnquist noted that Congress had implicitly approved the practice of claim settlement by (sole-) executive agreement. His specific evidence: instances in which Congress extended alternative settlement procedures to facilitate particular presidential initiatives.[119] Once again, the *Dames & Moore* majority inverts the meaning of Congress's actions. Justice Frankfurter, who more than Jackson found authority in constitutional custom, read a tradition of ex post congressional authorizations as demonstrating that a Congress's failure to do so indicated a lack of approval. Justice Rehnquist's analysis all but reverses the presumption. "Where, as here," he writes, 'the settlement of claims has been determined to be a necessary incident to the resolution of a major foreign policy dispute between our country and another, and where, as here, we can conclude that Congress acquiesced in the President's action, we are not prepared to say that the President lacks the power to settle such claims."[120]

What to make of *Dames & Moore*? That, in part, is the point. On one hand, the Court made no attempt to avoid taking the case. More importantly, it endorsed Jackson's now famous framework, which in its original incarnation provided a basic framework that helped check a wartime president. On the other hand, the Court's embrace of Jackson's approach was more apparent than real. Like many commentators, it overlooked the real point of Jackson's jeremiad on congressional inaction, choosing instead to view it as a potential source of presidential authority in the manner of Justice Frankfurter. The opinion also reimagined the distinct categories as fuzzy points on a spectrum. This last move arguably helped enable the majority to shift *Youngstown*'s presumptions about congressional inaction. Back then, Congress's failure to specifically authorize, either through a statute or long, unbroken custom, provided the executive with no authority. In *Dames & Moore*, such failures apparently did grant authority. As the century wore on, the Court ostensibly remained committed to its role in foreign affairs. The pressures of continued presidential assertions, however, were evident.[121]

Leading up to the millennium, then, the judiciary had retreated but by no means surrendered. The rise of the national security state, and the commensurate empowerment of the presidency, necessarily put substantial pressure on the Constitution's commitment to separation of powers in foreign affairs. For the most part, the Court held true to its assigned role. Nothing better reflected nor symbolized this point than the justices' stance in *Youngstown*. Yet in numerous areas during this period the Court applied or introduced principles that suggested a loss of confidence. Rarely, if ever, did it go to the extreme deference articulated in *Curtiss-Wright*. The judiciary was not yet, as the great Yankee jurist not from Olympus Yogi Berra once urged, taking a fork in the road. A path leading away from a robust role for the judiciary in foreign affairs was, however, clearly coming into view. The changing nature of international relations would add to the pressure to follow this route, however misguided it was given the Founders' commitment to separation of powers in matters domestic and foreign.

PART III

Global Imbalance

CHAPTER SEVEN

The New World Order

THE FOUNDING COMMITTED the nation to separation of powers, including and especially in foreign affairs. Subsequent custom has endangered that commitment. Now a new development in international relations threatens to tip the balance away from both separation of powers in general and judicial protection of individual rights in foreign affairs controversies in particular. This novel challenge flows directly from globalization. Classically, international relations—and international law—is premised on the interactions of sovereign nation-states. The past generation of leading international law scholars has contested this view, observing that states today interact less as sovereign units and more through the direct connection of their component parts.

The result is a world of "disaggregated states," in which traditional sovereignty has been eroded by "global networks" comprising the subdivisions of national governments directly connecting with one another. These networks take up an ever-increasing proportion of the interactions that constitute international relations, including sharing information and intelligence, joining forces on particular projects, and creating formal connections, obligations, and institutions. Significantly, these interactions track traditional separation of powers. Executive and administrative regulators of one state connect with their counterparts in other states. Legislators attempt to coordinate with their counterparts. Not least, judges from one jurisdiction will trade opinions with foreign colleagues face to face and rely on one another's opinions in their formal judgments.

The Old Order

The "separate and equal station" that the United States assumed in the Declaration of Independence was as "Free and Independent States." That claim had meaning primarily, if not exclusively, under the law of nations.[1] The ultimate success of that assertion, in turn, meant that the new nation took its place among other "sovereign" states with certain basic characteristics that made them the irreducible and impermeable building blocks of foreign affairs.[2]

The United States was born into an international legal order that was barely a century old. By most accounts, that order emerged with the Treaties of Westphalia of 1648, which ended the Thirty Years War.[3] This conflict displayed a ferocity that matched its duration, in no small part because of the religious rivalries unleashed by the Protestant Reformation. Catholic kings and princes invaded neighbors to promote the one true religion. Their Protestant counterparts did the same, and for the same reasons. The eventual peace helped introduce what was then a progressive concept. Henceforth a sovereign entity would have all but exclusive control over a territory that it ruled, free from interference from outside sovereigns, even and especially those claiming a mandate of God.[4] All sovereign states, moreover, would be presumptively equal. Emer de Vattel, one of the greatest expositors of the law of nations, summarized the idea this way:

> It is an evident consequence of the liberty and independence of nations, that all have a right to be governed as they think proper, and that no state has the smallest right to interfere in the government of another. Of all the rights that can belong to a nation, sovereignty is, doubtless, the most precious, and that which other nations ought the most scrupulously to respect, if they would not do her an injury.[5]

This concept of equal territorial sovereignty meant that states would be both the basic subject and objects of the emerging international framework. Subjects, because they would make the substantive rules through their behavior or agreements, so long as these were congruent with natural law. Objects, because the rules that states made would mainly operate upon them and govern their interaction rather than address anything that went on within their borders.

The American Founders embraced these fundamentals and would come to claim what they offered. Under the law of nations, colonies—not least British North America—counted as no more than subdivisions of Great Britain. Nova Scotia, Massachusetts, New York, Pennsylvania, Virginia, and Barbados enjoyed no separate and distinct status. Still less, under the unwritten British constitution, did they have a formal role in determining Great Britain's foreign affairs, a role in complex ways divided between the monarch, the royal courts, and the Westminster Parliament.[6] Colonial Americans, at least those with a decent legal knowledge, would nonetheless have been familiar with at least the fundamentals of the law of nations. This familiarity would have been a function of English legal doctrine considering the common law, the law of nations, and natural law as interwoven. The common law consisted of judicial decisions, based upon experience, that reflected progressively better understanding of what the law of nature required. The law of nations, likewise, consisted of the decisions of sovereign states, mainly through custom augmented by treaties, which also approximated more faithful adherence to natural law over time. In part for these reasons, English legal doctrine, then and now, considers at least the customary law of nations as a judicially recognized and applicable domestic law.[7] As for then, no legal treatise had more influence throughout the eighteenth-century British Empire than William Blackstone's *Commentaries on the Laws of England*. The great work focused on the infinitely complex aspects of purely domestic doctrine and did not delve deeply into the law of nations itself. Blackstone nonetheless made sure that if his readers took away nothing else, they would grasp the basic idea of state sovereignty. He explained, "As it is impossible for the whole race of mankind to be united in one great society, they must necessarily divide into many . . . entirely independent of each other, and yet liable to a mutual intercourse. Hence arises a . . . law to regulate this mutual intercourse, called 'the law of nations;' which, as none of these states will acknowledge a superiority in the other, cannot be dictated by any."[8]

Yet eighteenth-century Americans did not have to settle for discovering the law of nations through domestic legal sources. They purchased, read, discussed, and quoted the major law of nations writings of the day, including treatises by Samuel Pufendorf, Jean-Louis DeLolme, and Hugo Grotius. None, however, enjoyed more popularity among the Founding generation than the Swiss scholar Vattel.[9] More and more appreciated is the influence of Vattel's *Law of Nations*, which, among other works, rivaled that of better-known thinkers as celebrated as Blackstone, Locke, and Montesquieu.[10] John Adams cited the work in 1773 when debating Governor Thomas Hutchinson of Massachusetts concerning the authority of Parliament.[11] During the Second Continental Congress, Benjamin Franklin thanked a French colleague for sending him an annotated copy of Vattel's work at a time "when the circumstances of a rising state make it necessary frequently to consult the law of nations." He continued, "That copy which I kept (after depositing one in our own public library here, and sending the other to the college of Massachusetts Bay, as you directed) has been continually in the hands of the members of our congress, now sitting."[12] Leading up to the Federal Convention itself, Alexander Hamilton, then literally a Wall Street lawyer, relied extensively on Vattel in arguing *Rutgers v. Waddington*, the case in which he argued that a New York statute violated the law of nations as incorporated by the state's new constitution; the case is therefore seen has helping to establish the idea constitutional judicial review.[13]

As the leading authority of his day, Vattel made clear the bedrock notion of state sovereignty. He began his great treatise by defining states as self-contained, self-organized entities:

> Nations or states are bodies politic, societies of men united for the purpose of promoting their mutual safety and advantage by combined effort of their joint strength.[14]

The law of nations therefore dealt with the rules regulating conduct between states:

> The law of nations is the science which teaches the rights subsisting between nations or states, and the obligations correspondent to those rights.[15]

It followed that neither the law nor other states directly addressed how a particular nation should govern within its own borders:

> Nations being free and independent of each other, in the same manner as men are naturally free and independent, the . . . general law of their society is, that each nation should be left in the peaceable enjoyment of that liberty which she inherits from nature. The natural society of nations cannot subsist, unless the natural rights of each be duly respected. No nation is willing to renounce her liberty: she will rather break off all commerce with those states that should attempt to infringe upon it.[16]

Later, Chief Justice Jay, who conceded nothing to Hamilton in his mastery of the law of nations, echoed the idea, writing that "the United States had, by taking a place among the nations of the earth, become amenable to the laws of nations; and it was their interest as well as their duty to provide, that those laws should be respected and obeyed."[17]

The law of nations that Vattel explicated did not address the type of government a state should constitute for itself. Vattel himself acknowledged that a state could operate in various forms: kingdom, principality, electorate, federation, even a republic or democracy. The law of nations, however, treated a state—regardless of form—as a single sovereign, in no small part because literal sovereigns governed most states.[18] Not surprisingly, eighteenth-century political theory—whether applied to domestic or foreign affairs—defined a core idea of sovereignty as the ultimate decision maker in any government. Where that role fell to a king or prince, as in most of Europe, the law of nations mirrored domestic law exactly. The same held true even in more complex states, such as Great Britain. Parliament, which still theoretically required royal approval of acts, may have enjoyed sovereignty domestically. It nonetheless remained a core tenet of British constitutional doctrine that foreign relations matters remained as prerogative powers of the actual sovereign monarch.[19]

American constitutionalism challenged the prevailing conception. As colonists, Americans rejected the then novel idea that Parliament had the sovereign last word throughout the empire, unconstrained by constitutional limits. Once independent, they struggled with the idea of dividing ultimate sovereign domestic power between the national and state governments. Most of all, they came to see the necessity of separating the basic powers of government—at first state, then federal—among three different institutions. That idea applied as fully to foreign as to domestic affairs. As we have seen, the Federal Constitution carefully, and sometimes not so carefully, allocated foreign affairs powers among Congress, the president, and the Supreme Court. As such, the United States was, radically and self-consciously, different from other contemporary states.[20]

The classic Westphalian system, in other words, may deem the United States as a single sovereign, but the Constitution permits no branch of the national government to claim exclusive sovereign power to make foreign policy, still less to accept and apply international legal obligations. An irony is that these divergent conceptions—unitary state sovereignty under the law of nations; the diffusion of foreign relations authority under the Constitution—were arguably never stronger than in the late eighteenth century. It would therefore be a grave mistake to take the Westphalian idea that each state constitutes a single state sovereign for the purposes of international law and impose it onto the framework established by the Constitution, which was distinctive in dividing the state's powers, including foreign affairs authority. Worse still would be to impose the international law idea of a single sovereign onto the U.S. executive as the closest thing to the type of living and breathing sovereign on which the law of nations was founded.

None of which is to say that the two ideas could not coexist on two different planes, one domestic, the other international. The law of nations did not address a state's internal arrangements precisely because it was premised on state sovereignty. On the national level, the new United States pioneered the idea of divided sovereign authority, including and especially with regard to foreign affairs. On the international plane, however, the nation proceeded as a single state sovereign, subject to the laws regulating its relations with other states, as created in conjunction with other states, either by mutual agreement or common behavior.

So matters proceeded through the nineteenth and twentieth centuries. In particular, both treatises and case law repeated the conventional, almost mundane truism that for the purposes of international affairs the United States operated as a sovereign. Indeed, some commentators, such as St. George Tucker, went so far as to suggest that each of the thirteen states, upon independence, "from that moment became sovereign, and independent, not only of Great-Britain, but of all other powers, whatsoever."[21] Joseph Story, in his 1834 *Commentaries on the Constitution*, which echoed the classic theme of this time, standard national sovereignty, stated that sovereignty "has no admitted superior, and that it gives the supreme law within its own dominions on all subjects appertaining to sovereignty."[22] This classic view remained alive and well through the turn of the century, with Elihu Root nominally asserting that "the Sovereignty of Spain has been withdrawn from Cuba, but the Sovereignty of the United States has not attached thereto, and the sovereignty, declared by the Congress [is rightly] possessed by the people of the island."[23]

The Supreme Court concurred. The *Schooner Exchange v. McFaddon* notably adopted the doctrine of sovereign immunity, observing, among other things, "it cannot be implied where the law of nations is unchanged, nor where the implication is destructive of the independence, the equality, and dignity of the sovereign."[24] Leap forward to the early twentieth century and the song remained the same, as the Court spoke of the "consequence of the absolute independence of every sovereign authority," inducing the "sovereign state to respect the independence and dignity of every other sovereign state."[25]

As it was in law, so it was in international relations. As Anne-Marie Slaughter notes, "In an international legal system premised on unitary states, the paradigmatic form of international cooperation is the multilateral convention. . . . The 'states' participating in [this process] are presumed to speak with one voice—a voice represented by the head of state or foreign minister. Looking at the international system through the lens of the unitary state leads . . . to a focus on traditional organizations and institutions created by and composed of formal state delegations."[26] For decades, if not centuries, this lens yielded a more or less accurate picture. Before air travel, mass communication, and the internet, ambassadors, consuls, and formal delegations did characterize foreign relations in this way. Much of Slaughter's work contrasts this traditional unitary framework with one in which branches, departments, and agencies of states reach out to one another directly. This development, as will be seen, puts profound pressure on any state committed to—and committed to retaining—a separation of powers framework.

Yet even at the time of the Founding, exceptions proved the unitary rule. Ever since the modern law of nations emerged in the seventeenth century, important nonstate actors functioned as subjects, either directly or indirectly influencing the creation of international law. Perhaps most prominent in this regard remains the Roman Catholic Church, which for these purposes operates under the title Holy See. Prominent at the time were large trading companies, such as the British and Dutch East India Companies. Likewise, the law of nations always addressed certain objects other than the relations between sovereign states. At least as far back as Grotius, the law of nations sanctioned humanitarian intervention when a tyrant "should inflict upon his subject such treatment as no one is warranted in inflicting."[27] To this exception, the anti–slave trade movement in the early nineteenth century added an international law prohibition of the slave trade, and eventually of slavery itself.

Exceptions to state sovereignty leapt by a quantum by the mid-twentieth century. New and more subjects capable of directly and indirectly fashioning international rules emerged, especially in the immediate aftermath of World War II. One group comprised transnational organizations, both global and regional, such as the UN, the EU, the Council of Europe, the African Union, and the Organization of American States. Another group, one with less direct but often substantial influence, consists of nongovernmental organizations (NGOs) such as Amnesty International, Human Rights Watch, Human Rights First, Greenpeace, and scores of others.[28] At the same time, international law extensively addresses how states treat persons within their jurisdiction. Human rights law, above all, represents one of the most profound assaults on the idea that state sovereigns are the irreducible, impermeable building blocks of foreign affairs.[29]

The New World Order

Yet the nation-state model has been eroding no less profoundly in less formal ways. Central here is the insight that governments today no longer simply interact state to state, through heads of state, foreign ministers, ambassadors, and consuls. Increasing, if not already dominant, is interaction through global networks in which subunits of governments deal directly with one another.[30] In separation of powers terms, elements of executive branches at all levels—education ministries, intelligence agencies, health bureaus, or other offices—interact less as the representatives of nations than as partner-counterparts. In a similar, though lagging, phenomenon, legislators and committees from different jurisdictions meet to share approaches and discuss common ways forward. Lastly, and least evidently powerful, judges from different nations share approaches in conference, in teaching-abroad programs, and, of course, by formally citing to one another in their opinions. Only recently has pioneering work by Anne-Marie Slaughter, among others, given a comprehensive picture of this facet of globalization.[31] That work, in turn, suggests that one of the results of this process has been a net shift of domestic power in any given state toward the executive and away from the judiciary and the protection of fundamental rights.

Where international human rights lawyers seek directly to pierce the veil of state sovereignty, international relations experts have chronicled the no-less-significant disaggregation of state sovereignty through the emergence of this growing array of subgovernmental networks. Nowhere has this process been more greatly marked than with regard to the interaction of various levels of regulators within the executive branches—in parliamentary systems—of the governments of individual nations.

EXECUTIVE GLOBALIZATION

Starting with groundbreaking work by Robert Koehane and Joseph Nye,[32] and elaborated by Slaughter, current scholarship offers a multifaceted picture of what may be termed "executive globalization." That said, much work remains to be done on how the post-9/11 "global war on terror" has accelerated this process with regard to security agencies. Nor, on a more general level, has significant work been done as to what the net effects of executive networking have been in separation of powers terms.

Slaughter refers to government regulators who associate with their counterparts abroad as "the new diplomats." This characterization immediately raises the question of who they are and in what contexts they operate. Perhaps ironically, disaggregation begins at the top. Presidents, prime ministers, and other heads of state gather in settings such as the G-7 not only as the representatives of their states but as chief executives with common problems, which may include dealing with other branches of their respective governments. Moving down the ladder, there comes an assortment of different specialists who meet across borders with one another both formally and informally: central bankers, finance ministers, environmental regulators, health officials, government educators, prosecutors, and perhaps most importantly today—military, security, and intelligence officials. The frameworks in which these horizontal groups associate are various. One such setting might be seen in transnational organizations under the aegis of the UN, the EU, NATO, or the WTO.[33] Another venue can be networks that meet within the framework of executive agreements, such as the Transatlantic Economic Partnership of 1998. Others meet outside governmental frameworks, at least to begin with, with examples ranging from the Basel Committee to the Financial Crime Enforcement Network.[34]

As important as the matter of which executive officials currently cross borders is the question of what they actually do. The activities that make up "executive transgovernmentalism" may be sliced in various ways. One breakdown divides the phenomenon into (a) information networks; (b) harmonization networks; and (c) enforcement networks. An obvious yet vital activity, many government regulatory networks interact simply to exchange relevant information and expertise. Such exchanges include simple brainstorming on common problems, sharing information on identified challenges, banding together to collect new information, and reviewing how one another's agencies perform.[35] Harmonization networks, which usually arise in settings such as the EU or NAFTA, entail relevant administrators working together to fulfill the mandate of common regulations pursuant to the relevant international instrument.[36]

For present purposes, however, enforcement networks most immediately implicate separation of powers concerns precisely because they generally involve police and security agencies sharing intelligence in specific cases, and, beyond that, in capacity building and training. During the "Troubles" in Northern Ireland, period of ethnic, religious, and ideological violence that plagued the region from the late 1960s to the late 1980s, the Royal Ulster Constabulary maintained "numerous links with other police services, particularly with those in Britain, but also with North American agencies and others elsewhere in the world . . . [including] the Federal Bureau of Investigation."[37] In a relatively benign vain, the independent police commission charged with reforming the RUC recommended further international contact, in part because "the globalisation of crime requires police services around the world to collaborate with each other more effectively and also because the exchange of best practice ideas between police services will help the effectiveness of domestic policing."[38]

It is exactly at this point, moreover, that 9/11-era concerns render this aspect of executive globalization ever more salient—and often more ominous. To take one example, consider the shadowy practice of "extraordinary renditions." Under this model, forces of one country capture a person and send him or her to another nation, where rough interrogation practices are likely to take place; all this occurs outside the usual mechanisms of extradition.[39] To this extent, transnational executive cooperation moves from general mutual bolstering to the expansion of the involved parties' jurisdiction in the most direct and concrete fashion possible.

All this, in turn, suggests a profound shift in power to the executives in any given nation-state. At least in the United States, the conventional wisdom holds that the executive branch has grown in power relative to Congress and the courts, not even counting the rise of administrative and regulatory agencies—with all these developments considered in purely domestic terms.[40] Add to this the specter of enlarged executives worldwide enhancing one another's power, through information and enforcement networks in particular, and the conclusion becomes presumptive. Add further the cooperation of executives in light of 9/11, and the proexecutive implications of government globalization become more troubling still.[41]

LEGISLATIVE GLOBALIZATION

This proexecutive conclusion becomes even harder to resist given the slowness with which national legislators have been interacting with their counterparts. Several factors account for the slower pace of legislative globalization. Membership in a legislature entails, almost by definition, not just representation but representation keyed to national and subnational units. The turnover among legislators typically outpaces that of either executive officials or, for that matter, judges. In further contrast to legislators, regulators need to be specialists. Specialization facilitates cross-border interaction, if only because it is easier to identify counterparts and focus upon common challenges.[42]

Transnational legislative networks exist nonetheless, and they are growing. To take one example, national legislators have begun to work with one another in the context of such international organizations as NATO,

OSCE, and ASEAN. To take another, independent legislative networks have begun to emerge, such as the Inter-Parliamentary Union and Parliamentarians for Global Action. [43]

Yet even were national legislators to "catch up" to their executive counterparts in any meaningful way, the result would not necessarily be more robust or adequate protection of fundamental rights in times of perceived danger or the protection of minority rights at any time. Human rights organizations around the world are all too familiar with the democratic pathology of draconian statutes hastily enacted in response to actual attacks or perceived threats, including the Prevention of Terrorism Act in the United Kingdom, the USA PATRIOT Act in the United States, and the Internal Security Act in Malaysia. It is for this reason that the essential player in the matter of rights protection must remain the courts.

JUDICIAL GLOBALIZATION

Several years ago, then Justice Sandra Day O'Connor visited Queens University Belfast to participate in a summer academic program that also involved schools from the Republic of Ireland and the United States. During the course of her visit, she was able to meet with local leaders of the bench and bar and exchange experiences, compare notes, and talk shop with her UK and Irish counterparts.

This is but one facet of what Slaughter calls the "construction of a global legal system" through both formal and informal transnational judicial networks.[44] Such judicial globalization, broadly conceived, occurs in several ways. The most mundane yet potentially transformative are the increasing number of face-to-face meetings through teaching, conferences, and more formal exchanges. Next, and directly tied to classic economic globalization, courts of different nations have transformed the idea of simple comity to coordination in tackling complex multinational commercial litigation. Of immense regional importance, the ongoing dialogue between the European Court of Justice and national courts constitutes a more formal, horizontal aspect of direct interaction among judiciaries.[45]

For the purposes of present analysis, however, by far the most important aspects of judicial globalization involve national courts' use of comparative materials and international law—above all, international human rights law. Ostensibly new and controversial in the United States, these aspects of globalization are familiar in most other jurisdictions.[46] As noted, national, supreme, and appellate courts have with apparent frequency cited to comparable case law in other jurisdictions as at least persuasive authority to resolve domestic constitutional issues.[47] Likewise, such courts also cite with increasing frequency the human rights jurisprudence of such transnational tribunals as the European Court of Human Rights and its inter-American counterpart.[48] In spectacular fashion, the Supreme Court of the United Kingdom, formally the House of Lords in its judicial capacity, has recently been doing both.[49] Similarly, the still-recent South African Constitution famously requires judges interpreting its Bill of Rights to consult international law while expressly allowing them to consult "foreign," that is, comparative law.[50] So marked is the phenomenon that several comparative constitutional law casebooks that highlight such borrowing have carved out a significant market niche, even in the United States.[51]

It follows that in all these ways the global interaction of judges strengthens their hands within their respective countries. In both theory and in the substance of these interactions, the bolstering of judiciaries generally works toward a greater protection of individual and fundamental rights. But while leading authorities view judicial globalization as outpacing its legislative counterpart, so too do they describe a world in which executive and regulatory interaction outpaces them all.

To this extent, judicial globalization helps identify a problem while also suggesting a solution. The problem, simply, is that transgovernmental globalization, taken as a whole, draws power to national executive branches and away from rights-protecting judiciaries. Against this problem, the solution becomes the fostering of the judicial side of the phenomenon, particularly with regard to the use of comparative and international materials.[52]

CHAPTER EIGHT

Global Imbalance

INTERNATIONAL RELATIONS SCHOLARS have identified an important new phenomenon. But they have yet to pursue its implications. Assume, as is true in almost any constitutional democracy, a given constitution features a commitment to separation of powers. A critical question then follows: Which branch benefits and which loses given globalization, the disaggregated state, and the erosion of sovereignty? The clear winner by any standard is the executive. By far the most "global networking" that modern international relations work documents involves executive and administrative regulators from various states pooling information, taking joint action, and generally augmenting one another's power. This advantage holds true whether the area is economic regulation, environmental protection, or, especially, national security. A somewhat surprising yet still distant second are judiciaries. Judges and courts, as executives and agencies, face fewer collective action problems, and so readily meet and cite foreign colleagues, in part to strengthen their hand at home. Far behind are legislators, who face substantial problems empowering their institutions merely through individuals or delegations coordinating with outside counterparts.

The result is an even greater imbalance among governmental departments in favor of the executive branch.[1] Such an imbalance poses, among other things, a significant and growing threat for the protection of individual rights by domestic courts, whether on the basis of international or national norms. Yet if separation of powers analysis helps identify the problem, it also suggests the solution. If globalization has comparatively empowered executives in particular, it stands to reason that courts should fight to restore balance, all the more so in matters of foreign affairs, the realm that now more than ever threatens the separation of powers foundation of constitutional government. That legislatures appear ever able to keep pace in foreign affairs makes the need for judicial checking all the more urgent.

An Example, Rendered Extraordinarily

Maher Arar was a telecommunications engineer with dual Canadian and Syrian citizenship who had been living and working in Canada for seventeen years. In September 2002, he stopped at New York's JFK Airport for a layover en route home to Canada after a family vacation in Tunisia. Acting on information supplied by the Royal Canadian Mounted Police (RCMP), U.S. authorities detained Arar and interrogated him for two weeks on suspicion that he was a member of al-Qaeda. Arar denied any connection with terrorism and repeatedly asked to see a lawyer and to return to Canada, requests that were denied. Instead, U.S. officials put him on a plane to the Middle East, where he was eventually taken to Syria. There he was beaten, tortured, kept in a shallow grave, and forced to falsely confess that he had attended a training camp in Afghanistan in order to fight against the United States. The detention and mistreatment lasted for ten months, after which Arar was permitted to return to Canada. No charges were ever filed by Canada, Syria, or the United States.[2]

Arar would receive a measure of redress from the Canadian government, but he was met with nothing but stubborn refusal from the United States. Arar's return to Ottawa led to a media frenzy. In a move destined to backfire, the RCMP raided a reporter's home to investigate a suspected leak. A provincial court responded by unsealing the previously secret search warrants, ordering the return of the reporter's materials, and declaring part of the national Security of Information Act as unconstitutionally vague.[3] Ongoing public pressure led the Canadian government to establish a commission of inquiry under the Canadian Inquiries Act, led by an associate chief justice of Ontario. The report concluded, among other things, that Arar had no connection to terrorism, that U.S. authorities had likely acted on erroneous information provided by Canadian officers, and that Arar had been subject to torture during his nearly yearlong detention in Syria. Shortly thereafter, the RCMP issued a formal apology. Eventually, the Canadian government awarded Arar C$10.5 million as a settlement.[4]

Arar did not fare so well in the United States. He brought suit in federal court against former Attorney General John Ashcroft, former FBI Director Robert Mueller, Secretary of Homeland Security Tom Ridge, and a host of federal immigration officials for violations of the Constitution as

well as the Torture Victims Protection Act. The U.S. government moved
to dismiss the action, invoking the state secrets privilege—a doctrine of
problematic origin that enables the government to withhold evidence on
the basis of "national security," even at the cost of dismissing a case. The
district court embraced the government's position and dismissed Arar's
action.[5] The U.S. Court of Appeals for the Second Circuit agreed.[6] The
Supreme Court denied certiorari and let the dismissal stand, effectively
denying Arar his day in court to hold U.S. authorities accountable for violations of federal law, the Constitution, and the nation's international law
obligations. Despite congressional hearings, the U.S. executive has neither
apologized nor offered Arar any compensation.[7]

The Arar fiasco has since become one of the best-known instances of
"extraordinary rendition."[8] Shrouded in secrecy, the practice increased dramatically after 9/11 though, almost by definition, the extent may never be
known.[9] No less important, Arar's case illustrates modern international
relations at their disaggregated worst. Distressing enough were the initial violations. First, executive officials in three countries appear to have
directly colluded to ship an innocent person to what was effectively a torture site: Canadian police (with erroneous information); U.S. immigration
and law enforcement officials (through interrogation, denial of access to
counsel, and deportation); Jordanian officials (effecting a transfer); and,
not least, Syrian security forces (who engaged in months of torture and
mistreatment). Second, this executive "networking" in turn sidestepped
numerous acts of several legislatures. Third, no judiciary—including, most
notably, the U.S. courts—was given a chance to directly intervene. Executive officials, in short, leveraged their transnational counterparts to out-
maneuver any constraints imposed by legislatures or judiciaries, leaving a
clear path to violate the fundamental rights of an innocent man.[10]

Arar's attempts at redress confirm the point yet more strongly. In the
United States, he understandably sought to hold the government accountable through the federal courts. The suit Arar brought aimed at the heart
of the investigative branch, naming Attorney General Ashcroft, Homeland
Security Secretary Ridge, and FBI Director Mueller for violations of his
rights under the Fifth Amendment, the Torture Victims Protection Act,
and customary international law via the Alien Tort Statute. He lost, but
not on the merits. Rather, as noted, the courts accepted the U.S. government's invocation of the dubious state secrets privilege, accepting the argument that public scrutiny of the evidence concerning Arar's rendition
would somehow compromise national security. Even though executives
apparently colluded to violate the edicts of Congress, to say nothing of

the Constitution, the argument was not to be settled judicially. Instead, the courts simply placed themselves on the sidelines. As Arar himself observed:

> After seven years of struggle it was my hope that the court system would listen to my plea and act as an independent body from the executive branch. Unfortunately, this recent decision and decisions taken on other similar cases, prove that the court system in the United States has become more or less a tool that the executive branch can easily manipulate through unfounded allegations and fear mongering. If anything, this decision is a loss to all Americans and to the rule of law.[11]

Nor did the legislative branch do much better. Congress did hold a number of hearings that, to varying degrees, took up Arar's case. Several members of Congress offered apologies.[12] Yet in the end the House and Senate offered no legislation, proposed no structural reform, nor voted Arar any compensation.

In an effective rebuke to the United States, Canada showed separation of powers to greater advantage. The Canadian judiciary played a significant role by safeguarding freedom of the press in response to the RCMP raid on an investigative reporter. The Canadian Parliament's commission of inquiry, in which the United States refused to participate, exposed the RCMP's misinformation. It was in part for these reasons that the Canadian government—which translated into American means "executive"—issued Arar its formal apology, paid the C$10.5 million compensation award, and added an additional C$1 million for legal costs.[13]

The Arar case is outrageous, shameful, and extreme. Yet for all that, it is illustrative. Its very outrageousness serves to cast in higher relief consequences of modern international relations that are underappreciated even by those who first noted the phenomenon of marginalized judiciaries. First, Arar reflects the larger truth that multitrack interactions of disaggregated states afford executive officials around the world striking new and effective means of mutual empowerment. As such, the development adds a powerful entry to Justice Jackson's list of factors that increase the power of the executive. The key difference, one not irrelevant to foreign affairs law, is that this factor is itself international. Second, and more importantly, Arar illustrates that the contemporary mutual empowerment of executives is comparative, outstripping their legislative and judicial counterparts in ways that place ever-increasing pressure on the ideal of balance among the branches of government and, in so doing, threatening fundamental rights, both domestic and international.

For all these reasons, understanding the comparative rise of global-ized executives requires a closer look at who composes them, where they are situated, and, most of all, what they do to generate greater power. This review will confirm not only that executives around the world have gained a comparative edge, but also show by what means—which are numerous, powerful, and often novel—this has been done. The result by definition constitutes a threat to any constitutional system premised on separation of powers. Legislatures alone will seldom be the solution. They cannot serve as a substantial check in parliamentary systems, since there the legislature and executive are fused. As the final part of this volume will indicate, in the United States, at least, the legislature has not served as much of a check, for many of the reasons Justice Jackson identified. Modern international relations, therefore, makes the judicial safeguard all the more important. It also makes self-imposed judicial constraints in cases involving foreign affairs not just counterproductive but downright perverse.

Executive Assertions

How, then, have executives become so comparatively powerful? As noted, modern transgovernmental networks cover nearly the full range of execu-tive officials.[14] This development stands in stark contrast to the traditional model of states cooperating formally through diplomats. Instead of suffer-ing this bottleneck, executive officials increasingly do business with their foreign counterparts. The process starts at the top, as heads of government increasingly meet to pursue various initiatives in groups such as the G-7, G-20, G-34, or subsequent incarnations.[15] Foreign ministers, of course, con-tinue to carry on classical international relations. Yet today the procession does not stop there. Early on came lower meetings and associations of finance ministers and central bankers. So standard has such interaction become that it is now formalized in organizations such as the Basel Com-mittee on Banking Supervision.[16] Likewise, environmental regulators meet directly, in both bilateral and multilateral fora, in part to deal with exter-nalities such as pollution that no one state can address. Counterintuitively or not, such networking has been especially fruitful between the United States and China. [17] That relationship raises the further example of differ-ent militaries also interacting, not simply on joint exercises among allies but also in coordination to prevent misunderstandings and problematic incidents.[18] Networking also occurs among both national and provincial police forces. For better or worse, such interaction had previously occurred when state security forces were addressing domestic terrorism through direct cooperation with their counterparts.[19] For worse, the Arar case shows that since 9/11 the trend continues among multiple security forces, including in the form of extraordinary rendition.

As has also been noted, transnational executive networking occurs in an increasing number of settings. Almost classical by now are ministerial networks within international organizations. As Koehane and Nye put it, when an international agreement establishes an intergovernmental institution, "cabinet ministers or the equivalent, working in the same issue-area, initially from a relatively small number of relatively rich countries, got together to make the rules. Trade ministers dominated GATT [now the WTO]; finance ministers ran the IMF; defense and foreign ministers met at NATO; central bankers at the Bank for International Settlements (BIS)."[20] Other notable international settings for executive interaction include the Organization for Economic Development and Cooperation (OECD) and the EU's Council of Ministers. These and others Koehane and Nye have dubbed examples of the "club model" of international relations.[21]

But there are also less formal clubs. These consist of frameworks instituted among the heads of governments rather than by international agreements. The distinction matters because international agreements typically require approval by branches of government other than the executive. In the United States, for example, treaties need a two-thirds majority of a quorum of the Senate; congressional-executive agreements need a majority of each house. U.S. sole-executive agreements are just that, binding commitments with other states made by the president alone. One set of examples involves sole-executive agreements made with the president of the EU commission to promote economic cooperation. Another example has been the G-22, which the United States helped establish as a way to maintain its influence in international development. In these types of frameworks, the dominant voices range from finance ministers, central bankers, securities regulators, and other economic officials.[22]

Some frameworks occur outside formal clubs—which is to say, international agreements—altogether. Instead, executive officials establish networks with their counterparts on their own. Prominent here are financial groups, such as the Basel Committee, the International Organization of Securities Commissions (IOSCO), and the International Network for Environmental Compliance (INECE).[23] Significantly, even these shade over into law enforcement, notably in the instance of the Financial Crimes Enforcement Network (FINCEN).[24] These spontaneous organizations also feature meetings and consultations among executive officials outside conventional diplomatic channels. Though spontaneous, these networks nonetheless remain executive. That is, their members still answer to the chief executives of their several states. In that sense, these fora expand executive power from the bottom up, even beyond the plans of the presidents and prime ministers who oversee them.

But what really matters is what they do. Perhaps the most basic activity of global executive networks is sharing information. When officials, regulators, and administrators gather, more than anything else they exchange information, swap expertise and approaches, trade studies and techniques, or offer one another best practices. Much of this sharing remains general. Various financial networks, including the Basel Committee and IOSCO, exchange best practices, often by issuing codes. IOSCO has gone a step further by publishing principles for a memoranda of understanding (MOU), "which is essentially a set of best practices for trans-governmental networking."[25] Other forms of information sharing are more targeted. Environmental officials have been especially adept at pooling relevant data, which is not surprising given that externalities such as pollution require multistate cooperation. The surprising cooperation between the U.S. EPA and the Chinese Ministry of Ecology and Environment no less surprisingly features exchange of environmental data.[26] More generally, environmental regulators brought together one another's data to deal (effectively) with the depletion of the ozone layer and, less effectively, with climate change.[27]

Most dramatically, security officials increasingly share intelligence on global crime and terrorism, for better or—as the Arar saga shows—for worse. INTERPOL, which traces its origins to 1914, pioneered the idea of police officials trading information to address cross-border crime, a practice that today entails 190 states and sophisticated databases.[28] EUROPOL implements a similar model regionally under the aegis of the EU.[29] 9/11 has had a double effect in this area. Existing networks, including INTERPOL and EUROPOL, have shifted their emphasis to intelligence for combatting global terrorism. At the same time, new frameworks have formed toward the same end. One example is customs offices. Another is intelligence agencies themselves.[30]

All of this expansion of knowledge, however, comes with a critical caveat, especially with regard to criminal and security matters. In these areas, especially, it is axiomatic that the information executive officials share with their counterparts they endeavor to keep secret from everyone else. A recent study by NYU's Brennan Center for Justice makes a compelling case that "overclassification" by U.S. governmental agencies is "rampant."[31] It further concludes that the problem has existed at least since the Cold

War and has only gotten worse since the advent of global terrorism. Nor is the United States unique. During Northern Ireland's "Troubles," the UK government systematically resisted disclosing information for security reasons.[32] What applies for constitutional democracies goes double, or more, for authoritarian regimes. To pick among the most notorious examples, China not infrequently jails dissidents, lawyers, and even hapless foreign businesspeople for the notoriously vague charge of revealing state secrets—in certain instances even when the government itself has already disseminated the information.[33]

Classified or public, information augments power in part because it facilitates enforcement; this phenomenon is a second major aspect of executive globalization. Law enforcement networks and various police forces have for decades shared potential evidence with regard to specific crimes and suspects. Traditionally, a good deal of this effort went toward financial crime and drug trafficking. Since 1995, for example, the Egmont Group of Financial Intelligence Units has worked to provide a forum for FIUs around the world to strengthen their respective governments in combatting money laundering, terrorist financing, and other financial crimes. Regarding drugs, for example, the U.S. DEA has met with its Chinese counterpart to deal with the growing opioid crisis. [34]

Today, of course, terrorism dominates. The Arar case, however botched, represents just one of the innumerable instances of international police cooperation to track and target specific terrorists, cells, and networks. The incentives for such cooperation are so pervasive that they can bring together unexpected combinations against less obvious threats. To take one striking example, the U.S. Navy coordinated with its Chinese counterpart to monitor and capture an older type of international outlaw—pirates—operating off the Somali coast.[35]

To information and enforcement, add harmonization. Global executive networks more and more work "toward the adoption of an international standard that adjusts the regulatory standards or procedures of two or more countries until they are the same."[36] Often the process arises out of international agreements to produce just this result. Most obvious here are trade agreements such as the WTO or the USMCA (née NAFTA), which are designed to produce single standards. Nor does harmonization stop with trade. Other international agreements currently seek to create more uniform international rules concerning food safety, environmental regulation, consumer protection, and labor conditions. In these and other fields, regulators, officials, and administrators of one state confer with their opposites under formal and informal frameworks with a view to do nothing short of altering their respective domestic laws to converge on a uniform international standard.[37]

Another path to harmonized standards runs through mutual recognition agreements, or MRAs. Under MRAs, "in effect, country A agrees to substitute country B's regulatory apparatus for its own with regard to products and services originating from country B."[38] Regulators in each state necessarily must connect as a result. MRAs have long been standard operating procedure in the EU and have been increasingly employed between the EU and the United States.[39]

Various observers have pointed out that the executive combinations that result from either variant not infrequently produce interest groups in their own right. Aviation officials, for example, have banded together to ensure that standards in their field of expertise do not become the subject of trade negotiations. The same has held true of antitrust and competition officials, who with international scholars and lawyers have formed a community "to improve its power, prestige, and jurisdiction in competition with other bureaucratic and non-governmental interest groups."[40] A similar process has also held true in the areas of food, drug, and environmental regulation, among others. All of which prompts Anne-Marie Slaughter to query whether harmonization—and executive globalization generally—amounts to "beneficial bolstering" of a given state's governmental capacity or, instead, "worrisome collusion" among executives, especially at the expense of other branches of their respective governments that are charged with, among other things, checking concentration of power.[41]

The Impetuous Vortex, Global Division

As a matter of political theory, separation of powers persists as a leading method to address such concentrations. And, at least in the United States, separation of powers likewise remains a central constitutional commitment, which is fitting for the first nation to make such a commitment deliberately. As noted, for Madison the need for the doctrine came from the threat posed by legislatures, which were "everywhere . . . drawing all power into [their] impetuous vortex."[42] And, as we have seen, at the national level the executive long ago assumed that role. Justice Jackson's explanation for this switch has not lost its power. The concentration of executive authority under a single person, unique access to national media, direction of a nationwide political party, the rise of the administrative state, and command of a permanent military establishment all play major roles.[43] In addition to these, consider globalization.

The processes described add an international dimension to the growth of executive power in at least three ways. First, they almost by definition work to expand executive authority within governments around the world, not least that of a globally engaged superpower such as the United States. Second, the ways just recounted that executive globalization proceeds undermine legislative power by either coopting it, bypassing it, or both. Third, and most relevant here, the ways in which transnational regulators, administrators, and officials interact also work to evade the scrutiny of the courts. None of this bodes well for maintaining the type of intragovernmental balance that separation of powers promises. The scope and vigor of modern executives—what Hamilton viewed as their requisite "energy "[44]—suggest that they exploit the possibilities of modern international relations more effectively than their legislative or judicial counterparts. That modern international relations enables executives to poach their legislative and judicial counterparts indicates that this is a zero-sum game in any case. Globalization, in short, aggravates the imbalance of power that, in the United States, has long since tipped in favor of the president.

Consider first mutual executive empowerment. All of the ways administrators, regulators, and other officials interact with their counterparts abroad contribute to this result. Knowledge, as Francis Bacon was not exactly the first to observe, is power.[45] Executive information networks suggest that knowledge shared by multiple actors worldwide is power multiplied. No doubt that pooled data leads to greater efficiency in the legitimate implementation of statutes and judicial decrees. Yet, as the Arar case indicates, increased knowledge can be increasingly corrupting, especially given the corollary that executives around the world tend to keep this source of power to themselves. Collaborative enforcement tips the balance even more directly. Police, military, intelligence officers, administrative investigators and regulators in general increase their capacity by leveraging the resources, personnel, technology, experience, and expertise of their foreign counterparts. Through harmonization, finally, executive officials make accord with one another to go beyond mutually augmenting their power to implement rules and policies made by other governmental actors. In addition, they assume the power of crafting those rules and policies.

Second, executive globalization facilitates displacing legislative authority. Take knowledge. Traditionally, fact-finding for the purpose of making laws has been a province of the legislature through research, studies, and hearings. To be sure, foreign legislatures also traditionally ceded some of this knowledge-gathering role to executive bodies, which, through diplomats, the military, and intelligence officers had a direct claim to information abroad. Today, however, data sharing among regulators not only fosters legislative reliance on executive information; it further extends that reliance to areas traditionally seen as domestic. Whether involving the environment, finance, or security, modern information networks render more powerful the executive's claim for having a fuller picture of a policy challenge in any one state, which in turn pressures legislative fact finders to defer, which then strengthens the executives' hand in shaping any regulations or laws that result.

Mutual enforcement also plays a part. Faced with the challenges of terrorism, or even simple cross-border law breaking, police and security forces face the temptation to evade any applicable domestic limits, be they statutes or court orders, by relying on foreign colleagues to break them in their stead. Extraordinary rendition again furnishes the most dramatic example. Infamous, and only slightly less dramatic, was the collusion between US, Iranian, and Contra forces in Nicaragua to get around congressional prohibitions on certain types of international arms sales.[46] On a more workaday level, the same temptation applies to gathering intelligence despite domestic prohibitions. At the very least, transgovernmental enforcement offers the prospect of muddying responsibility enough to make accountability that much more difficult.

Yet the greater threat to legislative authority arises from harmonization. Since the end of the last century, significant protests against the WTO, NAFTA, the EU, and other multilateral frameworks have objected to, among other things, the ceding of domestic authority to international agreements.[47] This reaction has been strident enough simply when treaties and equivalent instruments displace national laws. Yet, at least in the United States, two of the three processes for making international agreements involve one (in the case of the WTO) or both (in the case of the USMCA) houses of Congress. Fanning the flames, however, is harmonization, the process by which the goal of uniform standards that international regimes set out is ultimately achieved not through the agreements themselves, nor through implementing legislation, but through networked administrators, regulators, and other officials. Concern sometimes issues from corporations and business advocates, as when the U.S. Department of Justice seeks to promote convergence on antitrust standards. More often, opposition comes from groups concerned about the environment, workers, consumers, or all of the above.[48] The point is not which of these interests—businesses or activists—offers the normatively better global position. Rather, it is that each side can and has objected to the achievement of global standards through transnational committees, working groups, and other executive networks instead of more transparent legislative or administrative processes overseen by legislators. As Slaughter succinctly puts it, at worst the result can be nothing short of a "distortion of national political process."[49]

But the most troubling—and so, for present purposes, the most relevant—challenge that modern international relations poses for separation of powers is neither simple mutual executive empowerment or encroachment on legislative authority. It is instead the evasion of judicial accountability. Again, the various forms of contemporary executive interaction contribute. Just as the Arar case introduced the problem, allow another case to illustrate the threat presented to the courts—and to show precisely how the courts should not respond.

Dr. Humberto Alvarez-Machain was a citizen and resident of Mexico. While still living there, he was indicted in the United States for the kidnapping and murder of a U.S. DEA agent, Enrique Camarena-Salazar, who had been working undercover to expose a Mexican drug cartel. According to the indictment, Alvarez-Machain used his medical skills to keep the agent alive for two days so he could be tortured longer before being killed. Several years after the indictment was issued, Alvarez-Machain was himself kidnapped in Mexico, held overnight, and handed over to federal authorities in Texas to stand trial. How this took place is instructive. Initially, U.S. and Mexican federal agents initiated formal yet secret negotiations to exchange Alvarez-Machain for a Mexican national in the United States whom the Mexican authorities sought. The Mexican side, in particular, desired to keep the matter "under the table." Formal negotiations, however, broke down. At that point, the Mexican informant for the DEA who had been attempting to broker the deal offered the services of his "associates" to apprehend and transfer the doctor for the U.S. authorities. This they did. The group performing the abduction was not formally authorized by the Mexican government. It allegedly included, however, former military police and at least two current police officers. For their efforts the DEA paid the abductors a hefty initial reward, helped evacuate a number of them and their families, and paid a weekly stipend.[50]

Alvarez-Machain moved to dismiss the indictment, claiming that the district court lacked jurisdiction to try him because he was abducted in violation of the extradition treaty between the United States and Mexico.[51] The district court and the Ninth Circuit agreed. The Supreme Court did not. Writing for the majority, Chief Justice Rehnquist argued first that the Court's precedents established that a federal court may obtain jurisdiction over a defendant through an abduction when not in violation of an extradition treaty.[52] Second, the majority concluded that nothing in the treaty's text, negotiation history, subsequent practice, or purpose "supports the proposition that [the treaty] prohibits abductions outside of its terms."[53] Finally, the majority rejected the notion that the treaty should be interpreted to conform with the customary international law prohibition on arbitrary detention, not because the norm didn't exist but because, apparently, arbitrary arrest and detention in the context of extradition is a subset of the prohibition generally.[54]

Justice John Paul Stevens, with two others, dissented. First and foremost he argued that it would make little sense to have in place an agreement as comprehensive as the treaty if it could be evaded by state-sanctioned kidnapping. The dissent further pointed out that the Court failed to distinguish between abductions by private individuals, the subject of its previous case law, and instances in which officials from two states collude. With an eye to comparative law, foreign relations, and the rule of law itself, Justice Stevens concluded:

> The significance of this Court's precedents is illustrated by a recent decision of the Court of Appeal of the Republic of South Africa. Based largely on its understanding of the import of this Court's cases— including our decision in *Ker*—that court held that the prosecution of a defendant kidnaped by agents of South Africa in another country must be dismissed. The Court of Appeal of South Africa—indeed, I suspect most courts throughout the civilized world—will be deeply disturbed by the "monstrous" decision the Court announces today. For every nation that has an interest in preserving the Rule of Law is affected, directly or indirectly, by a decision of this character.[55]

Alvarez-Machain, like the Arar case, casts the dire effects of executive globalization in high relief. Of these, especially troubling is the evasion of courts. This facet is doubly worrying when the end run prevents judicial protection of fundamental rights. Worse, by failing to apply a self-executing treaty, the Court allowed collusion by police officials in two states to circumvent international and domestic law in one stroke. Such a result may be all the more striking since it does not reflect harmonization, perhaps the executive's most direct incursion into the authority of another branch. That said, the Alvarez-Machain abduction certainly illustrates the power of transgovernmental information sharing. Given that the doctor was ultimately acquitted, that intelligence was pooled cannot be said to have been sufficient. More powerfully, the case demonstrates how cooperation between respective police and security forces can undermine judicial scrutiny. Those forces, at least on one side, followed the usual executive tendency of seeking to keep certain operations "under the table." As it was, it was the judiciary itself that succumbed to the more recent tendency to allow the executive to escape accountability in any case.

The Last, Not the First

The substantial recent scholarship in international relations describes the emergences of transgovernmental networks on a global scale. This work suggests, though has yet to explore, the comparative institutional results in any given state. The overwhelming evidence nonetheless suggests that the primary comparative beneficiary of the modern disaggregated state has been the executive.

Given this development, transgovernmental globalization violates the core tenets of separation of powers doctrine in any given country. These tenets have long made separation of powers in some form a predicate for properly functioning democratic self-government. Separation of powers theory promises balance among the major branches of government to prevent a tyrannical accretion of power in any one. In the United States, the Founding generation prized this facet of the doctrine above all else. And though they viewed the "most dangerous branch" as the legislature, subsequent history has clearly established the executive as the greatest threat to the type of balance that separation of powers presupposes.[56] Beyond this, the American Founders also believed that separation of powers could facilitate democracy not simply by preserving liberty but by widely dispersing democratic accountability.[57] For this reason they ensured that all three branches of government had a direct or indirect democratic provenance: the House of Representatives through direct elections; the Senate initially through election by the state legislatures; the president through the Electoral College; and, not least, the judiciary through presidential appointment and senatorial approval.[58] Of course, not all liberal democracies, especially in the parliamentary mode, follow the U.S. model in these and other specifics. At a more general and no less relevant level, they do, nonetheless, share with the United States certain foundational principles, especially the idea that an independent judiciary, itself at least indirectly accountable, serves as a check on behalf of individual rights against too-great concentrations of power in the legislature and executive in the service of energetic government. Not only is this idea evident in democratic constitutions, it is also expressed in various international human rights instruments.[59]

Whether reversing the present trend toward foreign affairs deference will suffice to redress the imbalance may be an open question. But to paraphrase Justice Jackson in *Youngstown*, courts concerned with separation of powers should be the last, not the first, to bow to the increasingly powerful executive that globalization promotes.[60]

PART IV

Restoration

CHAPTER NINE

Getting (Foreign Affairs) into Court

COURTS CANNOT PRESERVE balance among the branches unless they hear cases that challenge official actions in the first place. Still less can they protect individual rights from government overreaching. Unfortunately, judges themselves have more and more often shut the courthouse doors in cases that they perceive to have international implications—especially, though not exclusively, since the turn of the millennium. In *Smith v. Obama*, a federal district court used a restrictive view of standing requirements to prevent consideration of President Obama's unilateral decision to undertake military action against ISIS, a determination that echoes Kosovo- and Vietnam-era precedents.[1] The so-called political question doctrine has served as a basis to justify dismissing cases almost solely on the ground that they touch upon foreign policy, mostly notably in *Goldwater v. Carter*, in which the Supreme Court ducked consideration of the Constitution's requirements for treaty termination.[2] Shamefully, in *Kiobel v. Royal Dutch Petroleum*, the Court held that the Alien Tort Statute, a measure designed to protect basic rights under international law, should be presumed not to apply outside the United States.[3] *In re Terrorist Attacks on September 11, 2001* and other decisions have read the Foreign Sovereign Immunity Act to have only the narrowest of exceptions to its general prohibition against suing foreign nations, even for terrorist acts and human rights violations.[4] In the post-9/11 era, the lower federal courts have vastly expanded the state secrets privilege to bar suits against government officials, no matter how outrageous the alleged conduct.

These missteps can and should be reversed. They violate the Founding's commitment to a robust judicial role in the protection of rights, including and especially in foreign affairs. They represent a still-novel departure from that commitment. Finally, in the name of international relations, they exacerbate the very imbalance in favor of the executive that modern international relations fosters. This chapter first considers how courts have become generally conflicted about whether to open their doors to foreign affairs cases, and next demonstrates that the conflict should be resolved in favor of openness.

Closing the Courthouse Doors

The federal courts can fulfill their dual role of checking the rest of the government, and thereby safeguarding liberty, only if they consider the merits of cases brought before them. Some state and foreign judiciaries enjoy additional powers. Several such courts may issue "advisory opinions," passing on the legality of official acts even before anyone affected brings a challenge to court.[5] Remarkably, others have the power to invalidate proposed legislation even before it is enacted. The Constitution, however, extends the judicial power of the United States only to actual "Cases or Controversies."[6] To the extent that foreign affairs cases present the most dramatic instances of both imbalance among the branches and threats to fundamental rights, it follows that exactly here the courthouse doors should be opened widest.

Yet those doors have been closing when access to the courts has been needed most. In several important decisions, the Supreme Court and lower federal courts have employed an array of doctrines to end consideration of cases just as they commence. They have done so, moreover, on the ground that these doctrines most powerfully restrict access to the courts when cases deal with foreign affairs. Conversely, in other, often landmark, cases the Supreme Court in particular has fulfilled its duty. That is, it has rejected arguments against hearing challenges and gone on to consider the merits, often deciding against the government. Perhaps nowhere is it more evident that the Court stands at a crossroads in its foreign affairs jurisprudence than in matters affecting access to the courts. And nowhere is the inconsistency more jarring than in the courts' recent struggles with terrorism.

Here judicial abdication at its most dubious often comes in the face of government at its most egregious. The practice of extraordinary rendition provides a cautionary tale in this regard as well. As the Arar case illustrates, the practice demonstrates how modern international relations empowers state executives to slip whatever checks their constitutional systems provide. The lawless export of persons for torture by other states features the violation of an array of rights, including prolonged arbitrary detention, denial of due process, and torture. What matters at this point, however, is the utter failure of the judicial branch to consider redress. In contrast to Canadian authorities, American courts avoided addressing Arar's claims, and did so on multiple grounds. But it is another instance of extraordinary rendition that more cleanly illustrates how American courts today avoid their responsibilities precisely where their intervention is most needed.

In this case Khalid el-Masri was the victim, and the literal denial of his day in court resulted from a gatekeeping doctrine known as the "state secrets privilege." El-Masri was a German citizen of Lebanese descent. While travelling in Macedonia, authorities there detained him for over three weeks. Macedonian law enforcement then turned him over to CIA operatives, who flew him to Afghanistan, where he was beaten, tortured, and held incommunicado. After five months the CIA apparently concluded that they had captured the wrong individual. They therefore transported him to Albania, where he was left alone in a remote area, from which he made his way back to Germany. El-Masri filed suit in federal court against the director of the CIA, ten other CIA employees, and employees of corporations involved in transporting him in and out of Afghanistan. There he asserted three claims: denial of due process against the CIA director and employees; violation of the customary international law (CIL) prohibition against prolonged arbitrary detention under the Alien Tort Statute; and, also under the ATS, violation of CIL's protections against tortured and cruel, inhuman and degrading treatment—the last two claims against all concerned.[7]

The courts never reached any of these challenges. Instead the U.S. Court of Appeals for the Fourth Circuit affirmed the district court's dismissal of each claim under the ever-dubious state secrets privilege. This was the same basis on which the courts ducked considering the allegations of Maher Arar. Other recent dismissals of significant foreign affairs cases have likewise relied on the need to protect "state secrets."[8] All of which is reason enough to examine the doctrine more closely.

Under this state secrets privilege, the federal government may prevent the disclosure of information in a judicial proceeding if "there is a reasonable danger" that disclosure "will expose military matters which, in the interest of national security, should not be divulged."[9] Debate persists as to the origins of this doctrine. Most courts and commentators date its current version to *United States v. Reynolds*, a case in which the Supreme Court considered a suit by the survivors of three civilians who were killed in the crash of a B-29 bomber.[10] The Court accepted that the executive could refuse to provide certain information on national security grounds, yet it remanded the case in the expectation that in this instance, the suit could go forward. One other state secrets decision cited is *Totten v. United States*,[11] among the earliest cases in which such a principle was invoked. This case dealt with a narrower situation.[12] A Union spy during the Civil War alleged that President Lincoln did not make good on a contract between the two for services rendered. Under what is now known as the "*Totten* bar," the Court held that the judiciary could not entertain a case in which this type of confidential information would be disclosed. The Court recently reaffirmed the *Totten* bar in a suit against a CIA director, though the ruling extended only to disclosure in suits concerning disputes over private agreements.[13]

Considering the general state secrets privilege at issue in *El-Masri* involves three steps. First, several procedural requirements must be met: only the U.S. government may advance the claim; only the head of a relevant department may assert the privilege; and the department head may assert the claim only after actually considering the matter. Though often labeled as an assertion of the "United States," the specific procedural requirements make clear that the privilege rests with the executive. Often courts will not even hold a hearing, on camera or otherwise, but instead defer to the word of a department head without further consideration. Second, a court must decide whether the information constitutes a state secret that presents a reasonable danger of putting national security in danger. Finally, if the court deems the material privileged, it must then decide how or whether a case may proceed. Taken together, these various steps come down to this: the state secrets privilege enables an executive branch official to have a court throw out an individual's claim that the government has violated his or her basic rights by asserting that the case might reveal information that could endanger national security.[14]

The *El-Masri* court noted that the state secrets privilege has a hazy basis. It does not appear in the Constitution; in a statute; in Founding materials; or, for the past century and a half, in consistent case law or tradition. The best the court could say was that it had its origins in English common law and has "constitutional underpinnings." The constitutional basis that the Court apparently had in mind was the executive's need for secrecy as a corollary of the commander in chief clause[15] or under separation of powers more generally, notwithstanding the duty of the judiciary to adjudicate cases under Article III. What the court failed to note was the doctrine's rise from obscurity after World War II. Clearly announced by the Supreme Court only in 1953, the doctrine was invoked almost not at all in the two decades that followed. Since 9/11, however, it has become a regular component of the executive's litigation strategy in national security cases.[16]

El-Masri shows why. Before the case got underway, the "United States" invoked the "state secrets privilege," supported by two statements by the new CIA director, a successor to the principal defendant. El-Masri responded, arguing that numerous officials, from Secretary of State Condoleezza Rice down, had publicly acknowledged that the government had engaged in extraordinary renditions. He further argued that the media, NGOs, and even the European Parliament had thoroughly reported on his story in considerable detail. How, then, could his case jeopardize national security? After a hearing, the district judge nonetheless concluded that the suit could do just that, and dismissed el-Masri's case. The Fourth Circuit affirmed, reasoning that the litigation might add information as to how the specific defendants were involved in his detention, thus exposing how the CIA runs secret operations. Beyond that, the court declared that the state secrets doctrine does not represent "a surrender of judicial control over access to the courts," because it is the court that applies the doctrine.[17] That conclusion was asserted even though, as the court failed to point out, the judiciary has almost invariably applied the doctrine in a way that results in denial of access to the courts for litigants such as Khalid el-Masri.[18]

Yet the courts' use of "gatekeeper" doctrines has not always (or even usually) kept the gates closed, even after 9/11. In stark contrast to *El-Masri*, consider the Supreme Court's first major post-9/11 case, *Rasul v. Bush*.[19] Shafiq Rasul had been among a group of two Australian and twelve Kuwaiti nationals who had been captured in Afghanistan and detained as "unlawful enemy combatants" at the U.S. naval base in Guantánamo, Cuba. Through friends and relatives, the detainees went to the federal district court in Washington, D.C., and filed what the court construed as petitions for writs of habeas corpus. Their fate would turn on the statutory canon against "extraterritoriality"—on whether, in plain English, the habeas statutes applied outside the United States.

Otherwise known as "the Great Writ," habeas corpus has for centuries been the principal device under English common law by which individuals turn to the courts to challenge the lawfulness of their incarceration by the executive. Justice Jackson, not surprisingly, captured its role and pedigree:

> Executive imprisonment has been considered oppressive and lawless since John, at Runnymede, pledged that no free man should be imprisoned, dispossessed, outlawed, or exiled save by the judgment of his

peers or by the law of the land. The judges of England developed the writ of habeas corpus largely to preserve these immunities from executive restraint.[20]

The Founders entrenched the protection in the Constitution's habeas corpus clause, providing that the "Privilege of the Writ of Habeas Corpus shall not be suspended, unless when in cases of Rebellion or Invasion the public Safety may require it."[21] In that spirit, Congress included a provision for habeas in the First Judiciary Act. During Reconstruction, Congress extended the protection of the writ to "all cases where any person may be restrained of his or her liberty in violation of the constitution, or of any treaty or law of the United States."[22]

The question in *Rasul* came down to whether the federal habeas statute applied to the Guantánamo naval base, which lay within the sovereign territory of Cuba, however much it remained subject to U.S. control. Ordinarily, federal statutes are presumed to apply only within U.S. borders. One reason for this longstanding rule is international cooperation and respect, otherwise known as comity. One nation ordinarily should avoid imposing its laws and regulations on another, lest that country do the same. Given that detainees in Guantánamo were seeking habeas writs, *Rasul* presented the specific question "whether the habeas statute confers a right to judicial review of the legality of executive detention of aliens in a territory over which the United States exercises plenary and exclusive jurisdiction, but not [since the naval base is on Cuban territory] 'ultimate sovereignty.' "[23]

The lower courts held that it did not. They did so largely on the basis of a World War II–era Supreme Court decision, *Johnson v. Eisentrager*. There the justices ruled that the constitutional right to habeas review did not extend to German prisoners captured in China and held by U.S. armed forces in Germany, where they had since been moved. The *Eisentrager* court noted, among other things, that these detainees were not U.S. citizens, were neither captured nor detained on U.S territory, and had been tried and convicted for war crimes by a U.S. military tribunal.[24] On this view, the consequences for Guantánamo detainees were stark. Without access to federal court though habeas, they could not challenge the executive's conclusion that they were combatants, nor the torture and inhuman conditions for which Guantánamo has since become known. Without habeas they would languish in what commentators came to call a "law-free zone."[25]

That result was too much for the Supreme Court. In a six to three ruling, the justices held that the habeas statute did provide access to the courts. The

Court first of all distinguished *Eisentrager* on several grounds. Unlike the German prisoners, the Guantánamo detainees were not nationals of countries at war with the United States. They had never been charged, must less convicted, of any wrongdoing. *Eisentrager*, moreover, had dealt with the constitutional right to habeas corpus, not with a considered reading of the statute. No less importantly, the Court rejected a crabbed application of the presumption against extraterritoriality. Technically, Guantánamo did lie within Cuba. Nonetheless, the United States, through the original lease it had more or less imposed upon Cuba, exercised "complete jurisdiction and control" over the Guantánamo base.[26] Conversely, the lower courts have since held that the habeas statute does not extend to more ostensibly temporary installations, such as the detention center at the Bagram air force base in Afghanistan. Even so, *Rasul* stands as a landmark assertion of judicial authority in one of the most fraught areas of foreign affairs. In keeping open the courthouse doors, the decision permitted further challenges which themselves led to landmark Supreme Court rulings on critical military and foreign affairs issues: the basic due process rights that detainees possess; the unlawfulness of military tribunals originally established to try detainees; and even the extraterritorial application of the Constitution's guarantee of habeas review.

The judiciary has many other ways, beyond the state secrets privilege or extraterritoriality, to keep cases in or out. These involve areas that typically fall under the rubric of "justiciability"—threshold limits on when a court may exercise its authority. Such initial constraints include doctrines of subject matter and personal jurisdiction, standing, "political question," and immunity. They extend to issues that may allow litigants into court in order to deal with the substance of claims, but they have the effect of ending cases nearly at the outset. Among these issues are extraterritoriality and act of state considerations. Together these areas might usefully be termed the "gatekeeper" doctrines. The Court's current conflicted stance, as seen in *El-Masri* and *Rasul*, more or less extends across the board. The remainder of this chapter argues that it should not. Instead, the Founders got it right; subsequent custom challenges but does not overturn their commitments; and modern international relations only heightens their concerns. The federal judiciary should throw open its doors to those asserting violation of their rights under the Constitution, laws, and treaties of the United States—especially in foreign affairs.

Opening the Courthouse Doors Once Again

Recall that during the Neutrality Controversy, President Washington desperately needed guidance on international law.[27] In particular, he needed to know whether the nation's earlier 1778 Treaty of Alliance with France would require that the United States assist its erstwhile ally and get dragged into a global conflict between France and Great Britain. In Alexander Hamilton and Thomas Jefferson, his cabinet boasted two of the most brilliant minds to serve in the executive branch, who had offered the president their views as trained lawyers. Washington, Hamilton, and Jefferson nonetheless sought the views of the Supreme Court. Chief Justice Jay properly responded that the Court could render legal opinions only in the context of an actual, litigated case. Jay's refusal, however, only serves to highlight how eager the executive then was to be guided by the views of the Court. More generally, the incident illustrates in striking fashion the centrality of the judiciary's role in foreign affairs as envisioned by the Founding generation.[28]

More general Founding understandings hold this line even if the modern executive, along with several newly minted Supreme Court justices, thinks otherwise. Once more, one of the few ideas upon which there is near consensus in Founding sources is that separation of powers should prevent the dangerous accumulation of power in any one branch of government. In creative tension with that function is the goal of efficiency, to be achieved through each branch's specialization in its relatively distinct function. The executive effectively implements laws, in part because it has the Hamiltonian advantages of energy and dispatch. The judiciary's training and experience positions it to "say what the law is," as *Marbury* later proclaimed. On these general principles, Washington, Hamilton, and Jefferson, on one hand, and Jay, on the other, would agree that it fell to the courts to apply the law in a properly litigated case between two parties, no less when it affected the nation's foreign policy interests. It follows that doctrines employed to avoid adjudicating otherwise justiciable cases at best fail to reflect fidelity to the Founding.

Has subsequent tradition and precedent amended these commitments? The short answer falls between "not yet" and "not even close." Gateway doctrines tend to follow the general pattern of marked yet incomplete judicial retreat in the face of growing assertions by the political branches, the executive especially. As noted, these assertions reflect the nation's emergence as a power, superpower, and hegemon, developments that further benefit the executive. That said, gateway doctrines reflect these trends to varying degrees. Some, such as the so-called political question doctrine, follow the classic pattern. This device, notorious for permitting courts to dodge otherwise justiciable cases, did not appear as such until the mid-twentieth century. Since then it has sometimes been invoked yet has often been rejected. A similar pattern holds for the "state secrets" privilege, which allows a judge to dismiss a case if the government maintains that the litigation will expose information that might damage national security. This too didn't arise as such until after World War II. Compared to the "political question" doctrine, the popularity of the state secrets privilege has spiked, especially after 9/11, though not so consistently that its broad application cannot be turned back. By partial contrast, the presumption that statutes do not apply beyond the nation's borders has taken a longer and more winding road. First articulated by the Supreme Court in the early nineteenth century, over a century later it had appeared to outlive its usefulness precisely because the United States could project strength around the world. The Supreme Court nonetheless revived it as the twentieth century came to a close, though again not so consistently that it could be established as an exception to the Founding vision of the judiciary's role in foreign affairs.

Regardless of the differences, each of these stories has the same conclusion. Even under a theory that gives great weight to evolving constitutional tradition, the commitments of the Founding endure. Separation of powers contemplates as important a role for the judiciary in foreign as in domestic affairs. That role means keeping open access to the courts.

Modern international relations, finally, makes the need to do so only more urgent. Today government officials from each branch meet directly with their counterparts to compare, share, and plan. Scholars who have noted this development further observe the resulting benefits, including increased coordination and efficiency. Regarding the increased power that results, the comparative winner, almost of necessity, has been the executive. At least in the United States, the growing complexity and energy of international relations increases the primacy of an executive that has long been the most powerful branch of government. *El-Masri* and *Rasul* each show how this phenomenon can lead directly to assaults on the most fundamental of liberties. They likewise show the importance of the judiciary allowing (or not allowing) itself to deal with the underlying claims defending these rights.

Founding understandings. The lack of sufficient countervailing custom. The effects of modern international relations on relative executive, legislative, and judicial power. Each of these factors powerfully pushes back against the recent tendency of many judges to close the doors of their courthouse to cases implicating foreign affairs. Just how much they do so is best seen in how they apply to several of the principle doctrines that have more and more been used to dismiss cases just as they are getting started.

WITHDRAWING THE "POLITICAL QUESTION"

Perhaps no gatekeeper principle appears—or should appear—more mystifying than the "political question" doctrine. A standard definition holds that "the Federal courts will refuse to hear a case if they find that it presents a political question."[29] To which remark a person untainted by legal training might respond, "What matters reach the Federal courts that aren't political? Racial discrimination, abortion, sexual orientation, health care, torture?" Legal training may add nuance, but it does not explain away the mystery. In modern form, the political question doctrine arose in the Supreme Court's landmark decision *Baker v. Carr*, ironically, a case in which the justices asserted power in an area—the drawing of state legislative districts—in which they had not previously exerted authority. Justice Brennan famously set out six factors for determining whether an issue presented a political question or not:

> [1] a textually demonstrable constitutional commitment of the issue to a coordinate political department; [2] or a lack of judicially discoverable and manageable standards for resolving it; [3] or the impossibility of deciding without an initial policy determination of a kind clearly for nonjudicial discretion; [4] or the impossibility of a court's undertaking independent resolution without expressing lack of the respect due coordinate branches of government; [5] or an unusual need for unquestioning adherence to a political decision already made; [6] or the potentiality of embarrassment from multifarious pronouncements by various departments on one question.[30]

Even so explicated, the political question doctrine has produced no shortage of critics. Not least among these was Louis Henkin, a founder of modern U.S. foreign relations law.[31] Henkin argued that almost every case lumped under the "political question" heading was not "political" at all. Instead, just about every assertion of the idea involved government action that was "within the powers granted by the Constitution to the political branches . . . and violate[d] no constitutional limitation on that power, either because the Constitution imposes no relevant limitations, or because the action is amply within the limits prescribed."[32] For example, when the judiciary refuses to review the president's determination that a particular regime is the government of a foreign state, the refusal is not made because the decision is "political" but because the president acts within his or (one day) her constitutional authority and violates no constitutional limits. More recent scholarship agrees that "political question" doctrine in its current form is of recent vintage but that, to an extent, it reflects the judiciary asserting power, at least insofar as courts now reserve to themselves the power to decide whether the Constitution commits certain matters to the other branches.[33] Whatever the scholarly take, one thing remains clear beyond the law schools. For too many judges, the temptation to view especially delicate or controversial matters as "political," and therefore beyond their reach, can and has become seductive.

This siren song has been especially powerful in foreign affairs cases. *Baker* itself recognized this problem and sounded a note of caution. Justice Brennan observed that questions touching foreign relations have often been deemed "political," often because of vaguely applicable legal standards, the textual assignment of a particular foreign relations power to the president or Congress, or the ostensible need for the government to speak with one voice. But Brennan went on to caution that "it is error to suppose that every case or controversy which touches foreign relations lies beyond judicial cognizance."[34] Rather, the Court's "cases in this field seem invariably to show a discriminating analysis of the particular question posed, in terms of the history of its management by the political branches, of its susceptibility to judicial handling in the light of its nature and posture in the specific case, and of the possible consequences of judicial action."[35]

In short, as far as "political question" doctrine is concerned—like Oakland, California, there is no there there. As Henkin notes, legal principles, not judicial abdication, account for court decisions unhelpfully grouped under the "political question" label. The trouble is that the label itself can become a handy excuse for judges who would rather avoid considering the relevant law in a complex or controversial case to do just that—duck the matter altogether as nonjusticiable. As Brennan observes, the problem can be especially acute in the context of legal issues that implicate foreign affairs. Not surprisingly, the judicial response in practice has been mixed. Some federal courts have applied the political question doctrine broadly, in effect abdicating their responsibility for matters seen as too hot to handle. The trend, however, has been to employ the doctrine narrowly, which is to say, to use the label when the given decision simply holds that either the executive or the legislature has been acting within its authority, as in any constitutional or statutory case. And yet, in similarly unsurprising fashion, foreign affairs remains one area in which the misuse of "political question" endures, even though the Supreme Court itself has viewed the doctrine with an ever more skeptical eye.

As with other gateway issues, recent high-profile cases suggest a judiciary that is, to borrow from Lincoln, divided against itself. Captain Smith's challenge to the military campaign against ISIS shows how the judiciary can also misuse "political question" doctrine to shut its doors.[36] Not satisfied to block Smith's claims by applying standing narrowly, the court made sure never to reach his underlying argument in employing political question broadly. Recall that those claims asserted that President Obama, in sanctioning military operations against ISIS, violated federal law, namely the War Powers Resolution, and that neither the AUMF nor any other act of Congress authorized the incursion, as federal law required. Deciding these claims would have been straightforward. Did the president seek congressional authorization for the military operations within sixty days of their commencement? Or did the operations fall within the scope of the earlier AUMF, which authorized the president to take "necessary and appropriate action" against the perpetrators of the attacks of 9/11?

Notwithstanding, the trial court decided that these challenges were not legal but "political" questions. It would actually have to decide whether, under the AUMF, an entity that did not exist until over a decade after the attacks on 9/11 was involved in those attacks. The court would also actually have to decide whether the president could plausibly argue that mounting military operations on ISIS, assuming that doing so was covered by the AUMF, was a necessary and appropriate response given that few critics disputed that a full-scale war in Afghanistan was necessary and appropriate to counter al-Qaeda. In addition, the claim was "political" because to decide that a small-scale military campaign was "necessary and appropriate" would require the court to examine information about military matters in a combat zone. Finally, judicial intervention would be inappropriate because Congress has appropriated funds for the campaign against ISIS.[37] This conclusion somehow followed even though, at best, the War Powers Resolution does not equate appropriations for military action with authorizing such action, and, at worst, the matter is a legal question which conventional legal reasoning and materials would appear well equipped to answer. And so, on this basis too, a question of central constitutional importance affecting the lives of hundreds of service personnel and their families went unaddressed by the same judiciary that earlier determined the legality of naval warfare against France, Lincoln's suspension of habeas corpus, and President Truman's efforts to keep the steel mills operating during the Korean War.[38]

Contrast *Smith* with the Supreme Court's own handling of "political question" doctrine in *Zivotofsky v. Clinton*.[39] Menachem Zivotofsky was a U.S. citizen born in Jerusalem to American parents. His mother requested that the birthplace on his passport read, "Jerusalem, Israel." U.S. officials refused, citing the State Department's policy of listing "Jerusalem" only, given the United States' role in seeking to broker a resolution of the city's status in light of competing claims by Israel and the Palestinian Authority. Zivotofsky's parents then went to federal court, relying on a recent U.S. statute that among, other things, mandated that "Israel" be listed at the request of the potential passport holder or a guardian. *Zivotofsky*, in short, presented an important question at the intersection of separation of powers and foreign affairs. Official recognition of a foreign state's sovereignty over a territory could profoundly affect the nation's interests abroad, nowhere was this more pronounced than in the Middle East. Under the Constitution, which branch had the power to do so? The president, Congress, or some combination of both?

Separation of powers cases are a staple of the federal judicial docket. And so held the Supreme Court here—but not before the lower courts evaded the underlying issue by holding that Zivotofsky's case constituted a "political question." They reasoned that resolving the case "would require the Judiciary to define U.S. policy regarding the status of Jerusalem."[40] The justices rightly pointed out that this conclusion misunderstood the issue. Instead, the Court stated, the case merely required a determination on whether Zivotofsky was entitled to have "Jerusalem, Israel" stated as his birthplace under the federal statute.[41] Since neither side disputed what the statute required, the real question became whether the statute was constitutional.

Nothing prevented the Court from deciding this issue. Determining the power to recognize a state's sovereignty over territory was not a determination textually assigned to another branch. Nor was there a lack of judicially discoverable and manageable standards to make this determination, including text, original historical understandings, and subsequent application or tradition. To the contrary, many landmark separation of powers clashes between the president and Congress, such as the question of who has the power to control the removal of federal officials from office, proceed in the absence of constitutional text whatsoever.[42] As Henkin might have pointed out, there existed no legal basis for the Court to avoid considering the constitutional question, regardless of the political or foreign policy implications. Instead, the Court declared that it remained "emphatically the province and duty" of the judiciary to consider Zivotofsky's claim.[43] With this it sent the case back down to the lower courts, effectively telling them to do their job.

After they did so, the challenge returned to the Court, only this time it featured the underlying constitutional question, not to mention a new secretary of state. The resulting decision, in what was now captioned *Zivotofsky v. Kerry*, confirmed the wisdom of the justices' prior rejection of "political question."[44] Now the Court held that the federal statute was unconstitutional based on a fairly standard consideration of text, history, structure, and custom. The Court correctly interpreted the clause empowering the president to "receive Ambassadors" as a grant to recognize a particular regime as the legitimate government of a foreign state.[45] It based this interpretation largely on the contemporary understanding of the Founders, who read the clause in just this way. The Court further reasoned that constitutional structure implied that this power was exclusive to the president, lest confusion arise from different branches recognizing different governments. Finally, the Court pointed to fairly consistent interbranch tradition leaving the matter to previous presidents.[46] Dissents and commentators did challenge certain points. Recognition of a regime is not the same thing as recognizing (or not recognizing) a regime's claim to a certain territory. While the president clearly has the power to recognize a government, less clear is whether this power remains exclusive of any congressional control.[47] These critiques, however, merely confirm the larger point. The second *Zivotofsky* decision presented an almost humdrum example of constitutional interpretation. The law itself may take a matter away from the courts; the "political" nature of a case should never do so, including and especially in foreign affairs.

"Political question" doctrine again reveals a conflicted judiciary. Even more than other "gateway" areas, it should leave no doubt as to which side of the conflict better reflects the Constitution, properly recaptured. First, the Founding leaves little doubt that courts were to "say what the law is" in cases and controversies before them, whether in general or in foreign affairs. *Marbury* itself represents a summing up of the original idea in general. Especially salient, the Neutrality Controversy reflects just how far the Founding generation assumed judicial power would extend in foreign affairs in particular. To be sure, Chief Justice Jay left no doubt when he responded to President Washington's request for an interpretation of the U.S. treaty with France. The Court would interpret the law only in a properly litigated case. Often forgotten is that Jay was articulating a minimum baseline. No lesser figures than Washington, Hamilton, Jefferson, and Randolph assumed that the Court could opine on sensitive foreign relations matters even in the absence of a case. This Founding view represents the opposite end of the spectrum from the idea that the judiciary can dodge rendering a judgment simply because a case touches upon sensitive or difficult foreign affairs matters.

Nor, secondly, has the emergence of "political question" as a separate category amended the basic Founding commitment. The term remains novel, rare, and, most of all, misleading. Unpacked, it refers to legal reasons for a court to decline hearing a case, but wrongly implies that political considerations alone, above all in foreign affairs, may lead to the same result.

Finally, judicial self-abnegation of this sort is inconsistent with the Constitution to the extent that modern international relations empowers an already vastly powerful executive at the expense of the other branches. Taken individually or together, these considerations suggest that the judiciary should consider "political question" doctrine as it has sometimes been used in foreign affairs cases a dubious, if not outright illegitimate, reason to avoid addressing the merits of others justiciable cases or controversies.

PUTTING THE "EXTRA" BACK
IN EXTRATERRITORIALITY

Whether American law applies abroad implicates another gateway consideration that courts often close to avoid foreign affairs cases. The very name of this doctrine—"the presumption against extraterritoriality"—all but ordains that federal courts ordinarily will not apply U.S. law to conduct beyond the nation's borders, including government action that violates protected rights. As most presumptions, it may be rebutted. For that conclusion to obtain, however, courts typically require that the relevant law clearly state an intention or purpose to act extraterritorially.

Strictly speaking, the presumption applies to federal statutes and to the regulations that implement them. Yet it also has a powerful influence in ongoing debates over the extraterritorial force of rights guaranteed under the Constitution. It is just this question that prompted Elihu Root, secretary of state under Theodore Roosevelt, to muse whether the Constitution followed—and kept pace with—the flag.[48] In these debates, the Supreme Court has articulated at least four positions. They are, in no particular order as follows: First, constitutional rights apply abroad, but only to citizens and legal residents, based on an idea that only "members" of the political community should enjoy its fundamental guarantees of liberty. Second, those guarantees should apply wherever the government acts. Constitutional constraints travel with constitutional powers. Third, the Court has frequently employed a multifactor approach, including the practical obstacle to enforcing the right and the nature of the foreign location under consideration. Finally, constitutional rights end at the border, in effect an irrebuttable presumption against extraterritoriality.[49] Different decisions have embraced each of these approaches.[50] But whether based on Constitution or statute, the decision not to extend U.S. law clearly affects the judiciary's role. Especially when the law seeks to constrain government actors, such a decision diminishes the courts in the face of the executive in particular.

For now, a focus on the classic statutory version suffices to illustrate the current choices facing the judiciary and the informed decision it should make. In contrast to the "political question" doctrine, American courts articulated the presumption against extraterritoriality from the earliest days of the republic. Yet in this area as well, both the Supreme Court and the lower federal judiciary today have a mixed, almost conflicted record. This story, however, may be less a matter of courts expanding a restrictive doctrine. Rather, it is more a tale of globalized actors, including government officials, taking actions indifferent to borders while the courts fail to keep pace with the new reality.

Once more, recent prominent cases illustrate the conflict. *Rasul* represents a landmark step toward extraterritoriality. As noted, the question facing the Supreme Court was whether the federal statute authorizing the writ of habeas corpus applied beyond U.S. borders to confer a right "to judicial review of the legality of executive detention of aliens in a territory over which the United States exercises plenary and exclusive jurisdiction, but not 'ultimate sovereignty.'" Deciding that the law did extend to the U.S. base in Cuba required a clear expansion of extraterritoriality that was nonetheless more real than apparent. At least two hurdles stood in the way of applying the habeas statute to Guantánamo. One was the Supreme Court's *Eisentrager* decision concerning Germans captured, tried, and imprisoned abroad. As was also noted, the Court held, among other things, that this case primarily dealt with the Constitution and not the statute. Somewhat more technical was another line of cases that did deal with the statute directly. In a decision involving Germans detained on Ellis Island, the Court held that those seeking the writ had to be within the jurisdiction of the district court to which they were petitioning.[51] The Germans in this instance lost because they wrongly chose to file in the district court in

D.C. In a later case, the Supreme Court rejected this approach. Instead it reasoned that a court could grant habeas review so long as the official allegedly holding someone unlawfully could be served, regardless of whether the detainee was within the court's jurisdiction.[52] The Court moved in this direction, in part, because its intervening case law in many of those cases involved detainees "confined overseas (and thus outside the territory of any district court)," in which the Court "held, if only implicitly, that the petitioners' absence from the district does not present a jurisdictional obstacle to the consideration of the claim."[53] In these ways the Court self-consciously pushed extraterritorial application further.

Paradoxically, when it came time to justify applying the statute to sovereign Cuban territory, the Court muted the significance of its action. Here the Court quickly noted that under the lease, which the United States had more or less imposed, the federal government has complete jurisdiction and control over its military base, sufficing to place it within the territorial jurisdiction of the United States, if not within its sovereign territory. For this reason, the justices argued that the case did not technically implicate the presumption against extraterritoriality. In lay terms, the Court reasoned that the habeas statute reached land over which the United States had effective and exclusive control. But make no mistake. *Rasul* extended the statute to the sovereign territory of another nation. It did so, moreover, even though the law made no clear statement that it should be so applied.

Yet applying statutes abroad has hardly won the day. No sooner had the Court expanded the reach of a statute not obviously extraterritorial to another shore than it ostensibly confined another statute to touching the territory of the United States even though this law was manifestly international. This law is the Alien Tort Statute,[54] or ATS, an enactment that will be considered more fully later. Passed by the First Congress, the ATS provides in full that "the district courts shall have original jurisdiction of any civil action by an alien for a tort only, committed in violation of the law of nations or a treaty of the United States."[55] For nearly forty years, those who have escaped repressive regimes have used this law to sue official torturers, executioners, and kidnappers, mainly for violations of international human rights law, in the federal courts, which are widely perceived worldwide as neutral, fair, and professional. The human rights laws that the ATS incorporates are by definition standards that command almost universal acceptance around the world. This consensus, among other things, means that the chief concern of the presumption against extraterritoriality is absent. When a U.S. court uses the ATS to hold accountable a defendant who has engaged in extrajudicial murder, neither Congress nor the judiciary are imposing distinctive U.S. regulations on other states. Rather, they are enforcing standards that the United States and virtually all other states hold as fundamental.

Neither that fact, nor four decades of modern human rights litigation, stopped the Supreme Court.[56] In *Kiobel v. Royal Dutch Petroleum*,[57] the Court unanimously(!) held that the ATS should apply only to cases "that touch and concern the territory of the United States." The justices came to this conclusion through a straightforward, if not wooden, application of the presumption against extraterritoriality.[58] Chief Justice Roberts did acknowledge that ATS suits could be brought only when the international law violation was "specific, universal, and obligatory." His opinion nonetheless went on to vaguely assert that enforcing such universal norms as prohibitions against slavery, torture, genocide, and extrajudicial killing would implicate important foreign policy concerns, since the courts would have to fashion related rules such as a statute of limitations. For this reason, the Court sought in vain for a "clear statement" that the ATS applied abroad. It found none, in part because it was likely so obvious that Congress expected the statute to be applied beyond the nation's borders that such a statement would have been superfluous. As the Court itself earlier and correctly held, among the violations of "the law of nations" that Congress had in mind in 1789 was piracy. Pirates, then and now, at a minimum operate beyond U.S. borders on the high seas. Lest that fact be taken to show that Congress did not in fact expect the ATS to be applied to the territory of another state, pirates who seized ships technically violated the sovereign territory of the state whose flag the ship was flying.[59]

By applying the presumption, the *Kiobel* court in one stroke cast in doubt the core of modern ATS litigation. Starting in the 1980s, the paradigmatic action consisted of alien refugees in the United States suing officials of foreign authoritarian regimes for gross human rights violations. Such was the first case that established the modern pattern. There the family of a Paraguayan student who had been "disappeared" in Paraguay—that is, kidnapped, tortured, and executed without charge or trial—brought an ATS suit against the Paraguayan colonel, who was in the United States and was served with the complaint, alleged to have been in charge of the death squad.[60] With this case as precedent, dozens of others followed in which the federal courts burnished their global reputation by holding accountable numerous other gross human rights violators on similar facts.[61]

Whether *Kiobel* has sounded the end of such suits remains to be seen. In a useful concurrence, Justice Breyer suggested that the "touch and concern" language be interpreted as permitting ATS actions for violations that

(a) occur on U.S. soil; (b) are committed by a U.S. defendant; or (c) in which "the defendant's conduct substantially and adversely affects an important American national interest, and that includes a distinct interest in preventing the United States from becoming a safe harbor . . . for a torturer or other common enemy of mankind."[62] Justice Breyer's approach would mitigate the damage. *Rasul* notwithstanding, the presumption against extraterritoriality remains another gateway doctrine that can do significant damage, like others, by shutting down attempts to assert fundamental rights in cases that touch and concern foreign affairs.

But this will happen only if the judiciary allows it. Once more, a return to Founding principles, an understanding of custom and precedent, and an appreciation of modern international relations suggest that in modern foreign affairs cases, the courts should marginalize the presumption against extraterritoriality rather than marginalize themselves.

As in some other areas, the Founding sheds little specific light. But as in every area considered, it does provide general guidance. The extraterritorial application of national statutes was not a point of contention during the ratification debates and still less at the Federal Convention. As later cases make clear, to the extent that the presumption against such application existed in American law, it reflected that reciprocal idea that one sovereign state should not project its distinctive legal regulations on the territory of another.[63] This rationale clearly has less force in a globalized world in which activities in one state produce effects in another. More enduring, however, is the general Founding commitment to balanced government, with a judiciary committed to the protection of fundamental rights, whether in domestic or foreign affairs. This is why *Rasul* reflects abiding faith in that commitment, and *Kiobel* does not.

Kiobel notwithstanding, subsequent precedent and custom undermine the presumption in distinctive ways. First, reliance on the doctrine has historically been uneven and has reemerged with force only recently. The rise of other gateway doctrines in foreign affairs have mainly tracked the rise of the United States as a world power. "Political question" and the state secrets privilege are two examples. The same holds true of doctrines employed once parties are in court and arguing the substance of a claim, such as judicial deference to executive branch interpretations of laws bearing on foreign affairs. The presumption against extraterritoriality reflects a slightly different path. It emerged clearly in the Supreme Court as early as 1824.[64] Yet it waned as the twentieth century progressed, to the point that the leading treatise on U.S. foreign relations law omitted the presumption altogether.[65] This eclipse doubtless reflected the presumption's growing irrelevance in an age of increasing globalization, which, among other things, blurs the distinction between purely domestic and foreign regulations. Yet as the century closed, the Supreme Court revived it. Worse, it did so to avoid adjudicating an alleged violation of the Civil Rights Act of 1964 by a U.S. company operating in Saudi Arabia.[66] Since then it has, if anything, fortified the presumption by refusing extraterritorial application of federal law prohibiting securities fraud.[67] The potential wrong turn down at this crossroads, in other words, amounts to barely a step, one that should be easily walked back.

Finally, developments in international relations have eroded the foundation on which the presumption originally rested. As noted, one aspect of this foundation was the relative insularity of nation-states when both the United States and the modern law of nations were still young. It would have been one thing for the United States to extend a law prohibiting a violation of federal right to the Arabian Peninsula in 1800. (Indeed, it would have been an achievement to do so nationally, since Congress did not enact such a law until the Civil Rights Act of 1866.) It is quite another thing for the United States to have extended such an act to Saudi Arabia in 1992, at least to American companies that had long since gone global. Beyond this, modern international relations further undermines the presumption in a manner noted throughout this study. The more frequently executive officials from different states work together directly, the more comparatively empowered the executive becomes, intensifying the threat to a balance among the branches of government that might prevent a concentration of power that threatens liberty. Both *Rasul* and *Kiobel* offer illustrations. Guantánamo detainees of the type seeking habeas in *Rasul* generally got there after Afghan forces cooperating with their U.S. counterparts handed over persons often wrongly suspected of being members of the Taliban or al-Qaeda.

At first glance, *Kiobel* appears less exemplary. There the corporate defendants were accused of collaborating only with Nigerian government officials. There has, however, been no shortage of examples in which foreign governments committing human rights violations have been funded, trained, or otherwise aided by executive counterparts in the United States. Modern international relations would support extraterritorial application even in *Kiobel* itself. Among the core purposes of tort law is deterrence. The ATS, by imposing civil liability on violators of universal human rights norms, is no exception. Deterring human rights violations of executive officials regardless of their state has the effect of, among other things, reducing the pool of potential collaborators with their counterparts elsewhere.

Ensuring the executive is checked in any one state, in other words, can only tend to check its counterparts in all of them, including the United States.

DECLASSIFYING STATE SECRETS

As the *El-Masri* case illustrates, the state secrets privilege offers an especially pernicious example of a gateway doctrine that itself should be shown the door. Recall that this mechanism effectively permits an executive official to keep a case out of court by raising the specter that there would be a reasonable chance that any information made public at trial would harm national security. Recall further that courts have had a difficult time articulating whence this doctrine originates. Ostensibly it derives from the more general idea of absolute executive privilege. Made famous—and rejected—in the Nixon tapes case, this doctrine calls for the judiciary to decline hearing a case if proceedings would reveal presidential communications that compelled secrecy, lest the president be denied frank advice, without which the executive could not function.[68] At least in this instance, the Supreme Court made more or less clear that executive privilege derived from constitutional structure. Each branch has to enjoy certain powers and safeguards necessary to discharge its functions. Moreover, *United States v. Nixon* mandated that a district court itself needed to review the material claimed to be privileged in chambers.[69] The state secrets corollary, by contrast, rests variously on the (English) "common law" or vague constitutional "underpinnings." Worse, courts that employ the policy commonly defer to the say-so not of the president but of a department chief, and without any review. Probably worst of all, the state secrets privilege often juxtaposes claims of truly shocking government actions with broad assertions by the government of potential danger to national interests. The case of Khalid el-Masri, who never had a day in court, demonstrates the consequences.

Such consequences have increased at an alarming rate. For most of the other gateway doctrines, the judiciary appears poised to venture down the wrong path, but it can yet be pulled back. With state secrets, many courts have plowed down the more problematic road as a result of increased executive assertions and misplaced judicial deference. As a recent assessment notes, "The state secrets privilege has strayed far from the narrow evidentiary privilege described in *Reynolds*, and is now being asserted as a basis for dismissal of entire categories of litigation challenging government programs."[70]

Yet even here it is not too late to put matters right. Several decisions have rejected application of the state secrets privilege in important areas. One case, brought against AT&T, alleged that the telecommunications giant collaborated with the National Security Agency in collecting information on millions of citizens. The challenge claimed that AT&T, acting as a government agent, facilitated the massive violation of the First Amendment right of free speech and association and the Fourth Amendment right against unreasonable searches. The United States, which is to say the executive, moved to dismiss on the ground that the information disclosed would damage national security under the *Totten* version of the state secrets doctrine. The district court rejected the government's argument on the ground that the government's surveillance program was already widely reported.[71] The Ninth Circuit Court of Appeals sent the case back, but on other grounds. In a similar case, brought by the ACLU, the district judge similarly rejected the state secrets doctrine, though in this instance the Sixth Circuit reversed.[72] These and similar decisions show that the judiciary's surrender to executive secrecy remains incomplete. In contrast to the *Totten* bar, moreover, the Supreme Court has yet to endorse the expansion of the underlying, broader version of the doctrine that has accelerated since 9/11.

When and if it does, it should reign in the state secrets privilege, if not eliminate it altogether. For this gateway doctrine, the factors at work in this study have salience in reverse order. The background context established by modern foreign relations alone justifies a pushback. El-Masri's case shows why. As any human rights lawyer will testify, the temptations for executive officials to cut corners in the name of national security are substantial. This has been true at various periods in Cuba, in Guatemala, in Northern Ireland, in Turkey, in Kenya, in South Africa, in China, in the Koreas, and in Taiwan. Those temptations grow when multiple sets of executive officials spur each other on, especially when the tradition among other partners is to cut more than corners. This more modern partnership produces, among other things, the abomination of extraordinary rendition of which el-Masri, Arar, and many others were victims. As such, this distinctively international form of mutual executive empowerment accelerates the imbalance that the executive has long enjoyed for a host of other reasons. For courts to shirk their basic duty because the same executive asserts a need for secrecy in the name of national security, an assertion that just happens also to frustrate any attempt to hold officials accountable for the violation of fundamental rights, can only be characterized as the very definition of wrongheaded.

Nor has the judiciary proceeded so far down the path of safeguarding ostensible state secrets that there is no legitimate turning back. The use and approval of the doctrine has grown, but only in the past several decades, and significantly, only since the executive overreach occasioned by 9/11. Even then, as noted, not a few judges continued to resist. Since World War II and the emergence of the national security state, the Supreme Court has endorsed the idea only twice, and then in either the narrow context of private agreements or with a narrow application of the general doctrine.

Founding understandings, finally, powerfully cut against judicial dereliction. Paradoxically, early sources fail to reject the state secrets idea because the idea simply didn't come up. One would search the records of the Federal Convention or the ratification debates in vain for the proposition that an executive official's claim that key information would harm national security would suffice to keep an otherwise justiciable case out of court. Rather, the consistent theme is sounded at a much more general level. And that clear theme emphasizes the need to prevent the concentration of power in any one branch of government, along with the need for the judicial power—bolstered by life tenure and salary protection—to adjudicate cases as one means to do so, without distinction between foreign or domestic affairs. Early practice, moreover, confirms this commitment. Any one of a number of early foreign affairs cases might have been a candidate for dismissal had it been brought today. *Little v. Barreme* might have revealed sensitive information about naval operations. *Murray v. the Schooner Charming Betsy* might have done the same. Likewise, *Brown v. United States*, which dealt with confiscation of the property of aliens of a belligerent power resident in the United States, could have revealed secrets about military intelligence. But in none these instances was the idea of keeping the case out of court on the grounds of secrecy argued, much less applied. To reclaim its proper role, the federal judiciary would do well to follow its earlier lead.

CHAPTER TEN

Saying What Foreign Affairs Law Is

FOR CASES THAT *have* made it into court, a second troubling development consists of doctrines mandating judicial deference to the legal interpretations of the executive, particularly in cases involving foreign affairs. Here, too, the Court appears poised to proceed down a novel and ill-advised path. Recently the Court has faced, and faced down, arguments for deference in cases turning on the Constitution (*Boumediene v. Bush*),[1] statutes (*Rasul v. Bush*),[2] treaties (*Hamdan v. Rumsfeld*),[3] and agency determinations (*Gonzalez v. Reno*).[4] Arguments for courts adopting a subordinate position have, nonetheless, gained ever greater currency, so much so that the Court itself often declares deference to be the norm even as it fails to defer. A similar pattern also appears in related areas. Decades ago the Court rejected deferring to outright executive recommendations with regard to the "act of state" doctrine, yet more recently it preserved space for just such intervention with regard to foreign sovereign immunity.

Once more, custom, history, and international relations considerations should keep the doctrine to its original and proper tack. Current case law, not least in post-9/11 landmarks, shows that whatever the Court says, judicial deference remains an upstart position that has yet to overcome either the commitments of the Founding or the imperatives of modern international relations. That original commitment—to separation of powers in domestic and foreign relations alike—yielded a specific practice of zero deference. Adopting deference today, moreover, would fuel the very pro-executive imbalance that globalization daily accelerates.[5]

The Unbearable Lightness of "Great Weight"

Imagine that you face federal charges for trafficking narcotics. Under one reading of the relevant statute, the "narcotics" in your possession might mean any drug without a current prescription. On a different reading, the term might only mean drugs elsewhere specified as prohibited for use or sale under certain circumstances. The first interpretation means that you have been caught with a large haul of narcotics and so will likely go to jail for a long time. And so the federal prosecutor argues to the Court. Under the second interpretation, you have been caught with fewer narcotics, and you face less time up the river. Your attorney argues this reading. What the judge will—must—do is weigh each argument and then independently decide which reading of the statute is best, based on such tools as the statute's text, its legislative history, its structure and purpose, and previous judicial interpretations. What the judge will not do is automatically give additional weight to the prosecutor's views on the ground that the executive branch knows more about fighting the war on drugs and has, therefore, a unique understanding of the consequences of reading the statute one way rather than the other.

Exactly this argument, however, has commanded a following when the law to be interpreted involves foreign affairs. Judges who would otherwise meet the suggestion as an assault on their most basic duty believe they should defer in some significant way to the executive's interpretation of a treaty, statute, or even the Constitution. The executive, after all, is better placed to assess the actual impact a law may have in foreign affairs, and besides, the stakes are pretty high.

As it is, the modern Supreme Court's adoption of such an approach remains more apparent than real. As with the gatekeeper doctrines, juxtaposing recent, high-profile decisions again reveals a judiciary at odds with itself. *Sanchez-Llamas v. Oregon*, for example, suggests that the doctrine has gained more than a toehold.[6] This case was one of several involving a treaty called the Vienna Consular Convention. This agreement guarantees, among other things, the right of an arrested foreign national to consult with the consular officials of his or her nation. In *Sanchez-Llamas*, the Court affirmed an earlier decision that the convention did not require domestic courts to reconsider a conviction if the defendant had failed to raise his or her treaty claim at trial or on direct appeal. In doing so, it expressly declined to follow a contrary interpretation of the treaty by the International Court of Justice (ICJ). The majority bolstered this particular decision by expressly noting that the executive's interpretation of the convention advanced during the case was owed "great weight."[7] Even Justice Breyer in dissent made clear his agreement with the "great weight" formulation.[8]

The Court dug in further in a follow-up case, *Medellin v. Texas*. There the majority again gave "great weight" to the executive's views that the UN Charter, among other treaties, did not make judgments of the ICJ automatically enforceable in U.S. courts, even when those judgments involved the parties now appearing before federal courts.[9] So much the better to defer to the executive's reading of the treaty, since the majority had already concluded under the contrary interpretation that

> sensitive foreign policy decisions would instead be transferred to state and federal courts charged with applying an ICJ judgment directly as domestic law. And those courts would not be empowered to decide whether to comply with the judgment—again, always regarded as an option by the political branches—any more than courts may consider whether to comply with any other species of domestic law. This result would be particularly anomalous in light of the principle that "[t]he conduct of the foreign relations of our Government is committed by the Constitution to the Executive and Legislative—'the political'—Departments."[10]

In stark contrast, deference was conspicuous by its absence at Guantánamo. *Hamdan v. Rumsfeld* involved the Bush administration's attempt to put an alleged associate of Osama bin Laden on trial before a special military commission rather than a civilian federal court or a court martial. That plan ran up against the Geneva Conventions of 1949. *Hamdan*, in particular, required the Court to interpret the convention's Common Article 3 as incorporated by Congress in the Uniform Code of Military Justice.[11] That provision, among other things, prohibited "the passing of sentences and the carrying out of executions without previous judgment pronounced by a regularly constituted court, affording all the judicial guarantees which are recognized as indispensable by civilized peoples."[12]

On this point the administration vigorously put forward the novel and radical argument that Common Article 3 could not apply to alleged members of al-Qaeda because the "global war on terror" was by definition international, whereas the treaty provision applied only to "armed conflict not of an international character."[13] Justice Stevens's opinion of the Court made short work of this contention. He properly reasoned that the treaties' text, structure, and history all indicated that the protections of Common Article 3 apply as the baseline in any armed conflict.[14] The opinion rejects the president's position, moreover, without any indication that it is doing so notwithstanding a presumption that the executive's interpretation of a treaty is owed substantial weight. The failure to mention this presumption, even if overcome in this case, becomes all the more striking given Justice Thomas's strident reliance on the doctrine in dissent.[15]

Whatever else they suggest, the opinions, and citations, in *Medellin*, *Sanchez-Llamas*, and *Hamdan* make clear that deference may not be established, but it is in play. The doctrine's repeated appearance in recent case law indicates that it has attained at least a rhetorical role, and with that, the prospect for greater gains. For one thing, the doctrine appears ever more frequently as an express judicial trope. In this, *Medellin* and *Sanchez-Llamas* follow *El Al Israel Airlines, Ltd. v. Tseng*,[16] *Sumitomo Shoji America, Inc. v. Avagliano*,[17] *United States v. Stuart*,[18] and *Kolovrat v. Oregon*.[19] The judicial rhetoric, moreover, may well match the reality. From the 1950s through the early 1990s, the executive's interpretation has been the best predictor of at least the Supreme Court's own interpretation, if not that of the lower federal courts.[20] Nonetheless, the modern executive prevails in treaty cases almost in inverse proportion to the frequency with which the executive lost in the early republic.[21] Explicit articulations of deference, moreover, have also accounted for some of the most recent, high-profile lower court opinions. Of note in this regard is *United States v. Lindh*, the "American Taliban" case, in which the district court adopted a deference model based upon *Chevron* and accordingly held that John Walker Lindh was not entitled to POW status under the Third Geneva Convention.[22] Similarly, in *Hamdan* itself the D.C. Circuit cited its obligation to defer in adopting the executive's radical interpretation that Common Article 3 of the Geneva Conventions did not extend to armed conflict that crossed international borders.[23]

The *Sanchez-Llamas/Hamdan* pairing reflects exactly the currently unsettled state of affairs. On one hand, the doctrine has ostensibly shifted the burden onto parties who cling to the historic idea that courts interpreting laws or treaties that touch upon foreign affairs owe an obligation to nothing other than their own sound interpretation. Yet as *Hamdan* shows, this apparent obligation can disappear without a trace, and in among the highest profile cases as well.

From Independence toward Submission

For all the verbal fanfare, the presumption that the judiciary should defer to the executive in foreign affairs cases is a newcomer to the legal landscape. As noted, recent work on early cases confirms that foreign relations deference was neither present at the republic's creation nor evident for a long period thereafter.[24] The Supreme Court applied a "zero deference" approach to the executive in treaty interpretation during the Constitution's first half century. At points, the Court even enunciated a duty *not* to defer.[25] In fact, the first signs of an obligation to defer did not appear until the late nineteenth century. Even then, those signs remained few and far between for almost a century thereafter. Today only a handful of cases discuss a requirement to defer, and most of these do little more than allude to the idea in passing.[26] Despite all the attention deference receives, its actual applications remain as meager as they are late in coming.

The Supreme Court's failure to justify deference may have something to do with its actual status in current jurisprudence. Much like a blimp, the doctrine appears ponderous but in reality has little weight. The leading cases almost always repeat the formula that the executive's treaty interpretations are due "much weight,"[27] "great weight,"[28] "duty to respect,"[29] or, at the very least, "respect . . . ordinarily due."[30] Even a cursory review of the cases, however, demonstrates that the impressive-sounding formula does no actual work.

As if on cue, the story begins as the United States was poised to enter world affairs as a major power. The Court's first decision to articulate a deference standard came only in 1913, with *Charlton v. Kelly*. [31] Holding that an extradition treaty made no exception for U.S. citizens to be delivered up to Italy, the Court stated: "A construction of a treaty by the political department of government, while not conclusive upon a court called upon to construe such a treaty . . . is nevertheless of much weight."[32] That declaration, however, came only after the Court already had resolved the matter. With typical early-twentieth-century economy, Justice Horace Lurton came to the conclusion first based on the plain meaning of the treaty's term "persons"; next based on "accepted principles of public international law," as traced through a brief history of the exemption starting from an eighteenth-century reference by John Bassett Moore to a treatise on extradition; and, finally, based on a survey of U.S. treaties contrasting agreements in which the exception was and was not clearly specified. Only then does the "much weight" statement refer to the executive's interpretation of the treaty at hand, and then only in light of the United States' consistent practice with extradition treaties generally. Even then, the Court returns to Moore, who himself argues plain meaning, the existence of treaties with and without express exceptions, and the apparently joint practice of the United States and United Kingdom following the plain meaning of their own 1842 extradition treaty.[33]

The canon has generally done even less work ever since. Less than a decade after *Charlton*, just after World War I, the Court for the first time recycled the "much weight" standard in *Sullivan v. Kidd*.[34] Yet once again, the Court "deferred" to the executive only after its own careful review of the treaty provisions at hand, general principles of public international law, and the extreme consequences that would result from the opposing interpretation, which would have effectively allowed subjects throughout the British Empire to inherit land in the United States.[35]

The pattern continued in more recent times with *Kolovrat*, where the Court ratcheted up the apparent deference standard to "great weight" for interpretations "by the departments of government particularly charged with [a treaty's negotiation and enforcement]."[36] Notwithstanding this language, the Court turned first to the treaty's text, its general purpose, the canon establishing that a treaty's conveying rights are to be construed liberally, other similar treaties to which the United States was a party, and even the "hope[s]" and "desire[s]" of the nationals of each country for whom the treaty was intended to benefit. Even when Justice Black got to the practice with regard to the treaty under consideration, he referred to the mutual application of the treaty by both the contracting parties.[37] Much the same pattern was repeated in the 1980s in *Sumitomo Shoji America, Inc. v. Avagliano*, another "great weight" case. There Chief Justice Warren Burger considered the executive's interpretation only after pages of textual analysis and, even then, only in conjunction with the parallel interpretation followed by Japan.[38] That decade closed as it opened in *United States v. Stuart*, in which an agency's interpretation of a treaty as a source of deference received exactly one sentence amid paragraphs of more conventional interpretive analysis.[39]

For that matter, the same pattern holds up through *Sanchez-Llamas* and *Medellin*. For all that these decisions affirm deference, the canon still plays an exceptionally modest role. Take *Sanchez-Llamas*. Deference simply does not figure at all in the Court's consideration of the case's first issue: whether the "full effect" language of the Vienna Convention on Consular Relations (VCCR) requires the application of an exclusionary rule. To address this, Chief Justice Roberts relied exclusively on analysis of treaty text in the context of "constitutional common law"[40] remedies for similar domestic rights.[41] Citation to *Kolovrat*'s version of the "great weight" standard does appear with regard to the issue of whether the International Court of Justice's interpretation of the VCCR, or the treaty itself, requires the setting aside of state procedural default rules on habeas,[42] especially in light of the ICJ's contrary rulings.[43] That citation, however, comes only after consideration of the Court's own precedent on this point in *Breard v. Greene*,[44] which itself did not rely on deference; this is followed by reference to the statute of the ICJ, and—ironically for a deference case—to *Marbury's* proposition that the federal courts in the U.S. constitutional system have the duty "to say what the law is."[45] After then devoting a single sentence to the executive's interpretation of the VCCR, the chief justice proceeded to a close and substantive critique of the ICJ's analysis as it applied to the domestic constitutional system of the United States.[46]

Medellin functions as a typical sequel, not quite as inventive and no better crafted than the original. However problematic its interpretations, Chief Justice Roberts's opinion makes clear that it is the Court saying what the relevant treaties—as law—provide. The Protocol to the Vienna Convention does not make ICJ judgments automatically enforceable in domestic courts since it merely extends jurisdiction to the ICJ to hear cases between state parties. Likewise, the UN Charter also fails because it leaves to each state how ICJ judgments will be followed. In both instances, the Court came to its conclusions first through its own review of the relevant treaty texts, an approach it declares to be "hardly novel." The opinion does skimp on other standard methods, not least the purpose, structure, and *travaux*, or drafting history, of the agreements. Conversely, Justice Roberts does augment his analysis with the postratification behavior of the state parties, also standard practice. Only in passing does the opinion refer to the understanding of the executive, and then only to its views when arguing in favor of the UN Charter.[47] Once again, "great weight" proves to be neither great nor weighty.

Ironically, the only case to have produced an opinion in which deference actually drives the analysis is *Hamdan*. The irony diminishes, however, upon noting that the opinion comes from Justice Clarence Thomas in dissent. As on many other points, the Thomas dissent parts company with the majority with regard to whether Common Article 3 of the Geneva Conventions applies to the "conflict with al Qaeda."[48] Before attempting any independent analysis, Justice Thomas found the argument that the provision does apply to be "meritless" based on the Court's "duty to defer" to the conclusion of the Justice (not State) Department, as accepted by the president as commander in chief and chief executive.[49] Only after this did Justice Thomas adopt the argument that the provision's language applying its protections to "conflicts not of any international character" cannot apply since the struggle with al-Qaeda occurs "in various nations around the globe."[50] The dissent does concede that that the majority's position, which follows the treaty's text, history, structure, and near-consensus interpretation, is "plausible"(!)[51] Nevertheless, "where, as here, an ambig-uous treaty provision . . . is susceptible of two plausible and reasonable interpretations, our precedents *require* us to defer to the Executive's inter-pretation."[52] Here, at last, is *real* deference. The only trouble is, it is not actually compelled by the case law to which it alludes.

That case law instead shows that deference in this setting is essentially an add-on, though an add-on that appears with increasing frequency. It mainly appears as a passing reference to conclusions that have already been reached on the basis of significant textual, structural, purposive, com-parative, or general international legal analysis. To the extent the cases diverge from this pattern, they show that deference to executive interpre-tation is not on the table. At times the Court instead has considered early practice as evidence of the treaty-making parties' intent. At other times it has relied on the longstanding practice of treating the assent of all state parties to a treaty as probative of mutual understanding and perhaps reli-ance. Of course, it could be that deference to the executive is really what's driving the case outcomes, notwithstanding what the Court actually says. But were this so, and were this proposition somehow provable, the Court's duty to offer reasoned arguments would require it to say so. And if it is not so, the Court should make *that* stance plain. As it is, the halfway house of announcing a standard that does no real work serves neither the standard's advocates, its detractors, nor the public.

Nor, it should be pointed out, has the Court made out the nominal stan-dard as consistently as is sometimes claimed. Prior to *Sanchez-Llamas*, the Court's previous articulation of the deference standard came in more muted form in *El Al Israel Airlines, Ltd. v. Tseng*.[53] Writing for the majority, Justice Ruth Bader Ginsburg demoted the "great weight" standard considerably with the remark that "respect is ordinarily due the reasonable views of the Executive Branch concerning the meaning of an international treaty."[54] Flipping the usual pattern, she then concluded that "the Govern-ment's construction . . . is most faithful to the [treaty's] text, purpose, and overall structure," devoting the rest of the opinion to demonstrating just that.[55] In this she follows Justice Stone, who himself demoted "great weight" to mere "weight" or "recourse," [56] and then only to negotiating his-tory or diplomatic correspondence by the treaty-making parties rather than executive interpretation more generally.

Of course, blimps do sometimes take flight. But at least for now the clout of deference doctrine remains more potential than actual. That said, appearances sometimes presage reality. *U.S. Reports* is filled with doctrines that began as novelties, became plausible, and are now entrenched. State sovereign immunity is one.[57] The assault on customary international law is underway.[58] Judicial deference to the executive in foreign relations is already far more pronounced than at the Founding. Numerous advocates and commentators strongly press for the doctrine in articles and briefs.[59] Whether they say they are doing it or not, courts today do generally follow the executive's lead.[60] Justice Thomas's dissent may be a first step for the Court both proclaiming and actually following an obligation to defer. Deference, in short, may attain the status its advocates seek, and sooner than may be supposed. All this confirms the importance of the paradoxical obligation to take a feeble doctrine very seriously.

In fact, the reasons for deference to the executive's treaty interpretations are so feeble as not to be taken seriously at all. For its part the Supreme Court has never fully articulated a justification, a failure that suggests either that the doctrine is so well entrenched that a defense would be superfluous or that the doctrine has crept into the case law with little or no thought. Lower courts, commentators, and advocates have therefore had to fill the breach. Two types of defense predominate. One is institutional expertise. The other shows up in the guise of democratic accountability.[61] Of these, far and away the most frequently voiced defenses sound the purported institutional superiority of the "political" branches, in particular the executive, to guide U.S. foreign relations. The executive's comparative advantages are most commonly said to arise from, among other things, the executive's access to information, its comparative decisiveness, and its consequent position as the branch best suited to speak on behalf of the nation with one voice.[62]

Once its expertise is taken as a given, executive practice becomes an all-but-infallible guide to foreign affairs matters, including legal determinations. Starting in the late nineteenth century with *In re Ross*, the Supreme Court has usually, though not always, linked a presumption to defer to those particular treaty interpretations that the executive has "consistently upheld," especially in different settings and circumstances.[63] Of course, emphasis on executive consistency does not necessarily reflect comparative institutional advantage. On the analogy of treaty to contract law, longstanding practice may simply reflect a species of reliance interest, especially when other states that have acceded to an agreement have followed the same interpretation.[64] More narrowly, early and consistent interpretation may be probative of the treaty-making parties' controlling intent,[65] much the same way the Supreme Court privileges the actions of early Congresses as plausible reflections of the original understandings of the Constitution's ratifiers.[66] Yet deference keyed to consistency may also reflect institutional competence nonetheless. A longstanding and unbroken interpretation of a treaty, or provisions in a particular type of treaty, plausibly reflects all the executive's advantages in foreign affairs, on the theory that superior knowledge, decisiveness, and special position as the primary voice of the United States in foreign affairs all pointed to a particular interpretation early on, and have served to confirm that reading since, apart from the vagaries of changes in administration or the need to adopt litigation positions in particular cases.

To the values of expertise may be added an overlapping set of justifications founded on democratic accountability. The strong version of these claims often leads back to an observation of Alexander Hamilton. Treaties may be "the supreme Law of the Land," and so the province of the judicial department. They nonetheless remain contracts between states, and thereby instruments of foreign policy, and are, therefore, the job of the political branches, above all the executive.[67] This division comports with democratic accountability in at least three ways. First, it ostensibly follows the original assignment of tasks by "We the People" as a matter of higher constitutional lawmaking. Second, the assignment places the conduct of foreign policy in the hands of representatives accountable to the people (during normal times) through periodic elections. Third, and with special regard for the president, deference to the executive in part reflects the necessity of designating a primary voice to speak on behalf of the United States in foreign relations combined with the propriety of designating the one policy maker who is elected on a national basis.

A more modest, though influential, democratic argument comes from administrative law.[68] Some deference defenders contend that the judiciary does and should bow to executive interpretation of international agreements in much the same way it follows executive, especially agency, interpretation of statutes under *Chevron U.S.A v. NRDC.*[69] As under *Chevron,* courts interpreting treaties will not resort to deference when the relevant text is unambiguous. Yet as also under *Chevron,* where ambiguity exists, or where the treaty simply fails to address the issue, courts will generally follow the executive's interpretation unless it is unreasonable.[70]

Though *Chevron* deference has much to do with administrative expertise, its ultimate justification rests upon the inference that Congress has delegated authority to resolve ambiguities or fill gaps to the agency assigned with administering a given statute.[71] It follows that for the *Chevron* analogy to work, the theory must be that whoever binds the United States to an international agreement must be presumed to delegate similar authority to either the State Department as a general matter or to specific agencies that a particular treaty designates for implementation.

As critics have pointed out, the *Chevron* analogy is not without problems.[72] The Court has made clear that full *Chevron* deference is most appropriate when an agency has offered an interpretation of a statute based upon the type of deliberation that comes from providing interested parties with notice and a hearing or some form of adjudication. Less formal deliberation ordinarily triggers no more than the lower level of consideration articulated in the Supreme Court's decision in *Skidmore v. Swift*.[73] Mere agency litigation positions do not command even that.[74] It is far from clear how the treaty setting will produce deliberative opportunities to the same extent as domestic statutes, especially in the case of human rights treaties. It is even less clear how a general treaty, at least, is like an organic statute that regulates a particular field and creates an agency to administer the policies that the statute sets out.[75] As will be seen, neither the problems with the *Chevron* analogy, nor with the justifications for deference in general, end here.

Reclaiming the Power to Say What the Law Is

Judicial foreign affairs deference has not been without numerous critics from numerous angles. Most, however, share a common reliance on separation of powers in general and *Marbury* in particular. As the Court reiterated in *Sanchez-Llamas*, it is emphatically the province of the judiciary to declare what the law is. It follows that treaties, both as international law and the "supreme Law of the Land," as well as international agreements more generally, are in the first instance to be interpreted as law. This form of argument is fine as far as it goes. But the formal *Marbury* assertion goes only so far. In particular, it fails to engage the larger, functional separation of powers assumptions that its defenders put forward, above all the argument from executive expertise and efficiency. Confronting these assumptions once more requires looking back, to our Founding commitments, and looking around, to how nations conduct foreign affairs today.

Recall first the Constitution's original and ongoing commitment to separation of powers generally. That general, functional approach to separation of powers that conventional sources confirm better reveals the true potency of the *Marbury* argument against deference. The point is not simply that it is the formal job of the courts, rather than the executive, to interpret the law when parties argue a case. The real point is, rather, twofold. First, and implicit in the judicial function, remains the courts' role in providing a neutral forum for the vindication of individual claims, particularly with regard to fundamental rights, particularly against the government. Second, and no less potent, the courts' insistence on this traditional role serves the core function of preserving balance among the branches to ensure that individual excesses do not become systemic.

The courts' competing functional claim, which is also central to separation of powers, badly needs to be restored to modern separation of powers analysis in foreign affairs, especially in such contested areas as deference. Too often, such values as balance and the Founding conception of accountability get lost in the face of executive reliance, expertise, and efficiency in foreign affairs. Yet even Hamilton himself, the early champion of a strong executive, extolled all of the core purposes that separation of powers offered: effective government, yes, but also a government that was balanced throughout. Shorthand judicial references to *Marbury* simply do not suffice.

Once restored, separation of powers reaffirms the wisdom of "zero deference." Consider simply the core value of balance. Arguably the *primus inter pares* of all separation of powers functions, concern about accretion of power in any one set of hands two hundred years into our history must focus on the executive as "the most dangerous branch" based simply on the growth of the president's domestic authority during that time.[76] This development, the executive's practical increase in foreign affairs authority, at a minimum shifts the burden onto those who would assert that changed circumstances now cut in favor of augmenting presidential power.

In addition, a fully restored approach to separation of powers does more than counter certain sets of functional considerations against others. It also refutes more specific arguments for deference. Take, for example, the ostensible analogy to *Chevron*. As noted, that analogy rests on the fiction of legislative delegation of interpretative and regulatory authority to the executive through statutory ambiguity. The functional purposes of balance bolsters the arguments that this fiction be given credence narrowly, and then only where executive processes mimic deliberation by the legislature, especially in the area of foreign affairs, where the executive is nowhere more potent. Likewise, balance and accountability also put pressure on the *Chevron* analogy to the extent it bases deference on the executive's expertise outright. In this instance, the direct confrontation of functions merely replays itself, with balance in particular, directly countering expertise, a stalemate that at worst would preserve the Founding's "zero deference" approach absent some compelling argument to the contrary.

Yet this conclusion hardly need be left to general inference. True, the conventional materials from the Founding—the debates in the Federal Convention, the ratification debates, general pamphlets and articles—fail to discuss whether or not courts should defer to the president's interpretation of treaties. The issue was simply one of dozens that were too specific and unanticipated to come up. Early practice, however, speaks volumes. As noted, the very first time treaty interpretation sparked controversy, President Washington *first* turned to the Supreme Court for its views.[77] That Chief Justice Jay declined to have the Court offer its views on the Treaty of Alliance with France in no way reflected submission to the greater expertise of the executive branch. Rather, it famously showed the Court's commitment to hearing only "Cases and Controversies" under Article III.[78] In that setting, the Neutrality Controversy suggests, the Courts would say what treaty and international law was without bowing to Congress or the President. This is exactly what happened. Through at least the first half of the nineteenth century, in case after case the Court rendered judgments in cases involving rights claims under treaties, holding against the executive. In none of these cases, moreover, did any justice hint at the idea of deference.

Now consider the changed circumstances wrought by modern international relations. To its proponents, deference follows from the executive branch's ostensibly greater expertise in foreign relations at a time when foreign relations is becoming ever more important. Yet the "new world order" of disaggregated states suggests that this school of thought has it exactly backward. As argued earlier,[79] globalization has not only introduced new modes of conducting international relations. By doing so, it has enhanced the power of the executive relative to the legislature and judiciary throughout the world. Including and especially the United States, the next effect has been to add foreign relations to the long list of factors creating the imbalance that separation of powers seeks to prevent. For just that reason, the Supreme Court should not hasten the process and augment the increasingly powerful executive that globalization promotes.

Over two hundred years ago, Thomas Jefferson anticipated concern about the relevance of a constitution that outlived the generation that created it.[80] His concern would only have grown at the prospect of an eighteenth-century framework in a twenty-first century world. To judge from the many opinions and articles grappling with its implications, globalization highlights Jefferson's concerns about an antique constitution speaking to a far different era as does perhaps no other modern development.

Yet if the strange career of judicial deference is any indication, separation of powers, at least, demonstrates the Constitution's vitality, especially in foreign relations. Contrary to what some formalists aver, the Constitution's founders did not work through the concept so thoroughly or precisely as to effectively freeze its applications to the circumstances of the late 1700s. Yet neither is separation of powers so general that it is merely an invitation to struggle and nothing more. Rather, text, structure, and history yield a structural approach to separation of powers, revealing a principle that spoke to its own day but which remains no less germane to ours. At the Founding, considerations of efficiency led to an executive far more powerful than any of the young country's (domestic) predecessors, yet also one severely constrained by the imperatives of balance and joint accountability. Today, globalization in its transgovernmental form cuts against executive pretensions even further. At least with regard to treaty interpretation, the phenomenon does not particularly add to the executive's traditional claims based on expertise, claims which did not go especially far in the early republic. By contrast, globalization places enormous pressure on the value of balance in particular. It follows that there is even less reason for the courts to defer to the executive now than before—and nowhere is there less cause for deference than in foreign relations.

With this in mind, return to the tension between *Sanchez-Llamas* and *Medellín* on one side versus *Hamdan* on the other. The radically different stances that the two decisions embrace reflect the general stalemate that characterizes the Court's current approach, or rather approaches. What should now be obvious is that *Hamdan*'s refusal to defer to the president better comports with the Founding's commitment to separation of powers in general, and with regard to foreign affairs in particular. Likewise, *Hamdan*'s approach better preserves the balance that separation of powers requires in light of the rising power of globalized executives.[81] Yet *Hamdan* illustrates a step in the right direction in another sense. *Hamdan* just might represent a growing reaction to judicial deference, all the more striking as it has come in the Court's landmark decisions dealing with terrorism after 9/11.[82] Both the president and deference consistently lost, whether the cases involved interpreting treaties, as in *Hamdan* itself, statutes implicating foreign affairs, as in *Rasul*, or even the Constitution, as in *Boumediene*.[83] At the same time, the Court's terrorism cases also show that any victory remains incomplete. The Court may not have deferred to the executive's interpretations, but neither did it reject deference per se. Rather, the majority mainly ignored the doctrine altogether, leaving it to the dissenting justices to rail about its de facto rejection.

This approach may be a step in the right direction, but it is only a step. Fidelity to the Constitution's original vision in a globalized world demands more. Not only should the Court address deference doctrine head on. Doing that first means referring back to the Founders' conception of the Court's foreign relations role. It should also mean looking to current and ongoing developments in international relations that challenge the balance among the branches that separation of powers demands.

TREATIES: *HAMDAN*

It is worth considering what is right about *Hamdan* in greater detail—and why it still did not go far enough. As noted, the case turned in large part on the contest between judicial and executive interpretation of one of the nation's most important treaties—the Third Geneva Convention as incorporated into domestic law by the Uniform Code of Military Justice (UCMJ).[84] This issue arose in light of President Bush's decision to try certain Guantánamo detainees in special military commissions rather than in civilian courts or courts martial. Among the first slated to go on trial was Salim Ahmed Hamdan, who was seized in Afghanistan, turned over to the U.S. military, and ultimately charged with "conspiracy 'to commit offenses . . . triable by military commission,'" namely "attacking civilians; attacking civilian objects; murder by an unprivileged belligerent; and terrorism."[85] Hamdan countered with a habeas petition that claimed, among other things, that the commissions violated basic procedural protections as set forth in Common Article 3 of the Geneva Conventions.

The executive disagreed, and strongly. The president argued that the Third Geneva Convention was "inapplicable to the ongoing conflict with al Qaeda."[86] This result followed thanks to a Catch-22 created by his lawyers' interpretation of the convention. On one hand, "the President has determined that the Geneva Convention does not apply to our conflict with al Qaeda in Afghanistan or elsewhere throughout the world because, among other reasons, al Qaeda is not a High Contracting Party to [the convention]."[87] Since al-Qaeda was a terrorist organization rather than a sovereign state capable of signing and ratifying the treaty, the executive further determined that neither al-Qaeda nor its members could claim the protections the treaty provided. Yet on the other hand, the provision that appeared to address conflicts involving nonstate actors did not do so either. Or so the executive determined. As the solicitor general noted, the president had concluded "that common Article 3 of Geneva does not apply to . . . al Qaeda . . . detainees, because, among other reasons, the relevant conflicts are international in scope and common Article 3 applies only to 'armed conflict not of an international character.'"[88] Lest there be any doubt about the Court's role in interpreting international law, the president contended that its "standard of review would surely be extraordinarily deferential to the President."[89]

These arguments for self-abnegation registered with the Court, or at least among certain justices in dissent. Justice Thomas, writing for Antonin Scalia and Samuel Alito, first invoked the specter that executive interpretations of international agreements are entitled to "great weight." So heavy was that burden that it was the Court's "duty to defer to the President's understanding of the provision at issue," which was "only heightened by the fact that he is acting pursuant to his constitutional authority as Commander in Chief and by the fact that the subject matter of Common Article 3 calls for a judgment about the nature and character of an armed conflict."[90]

Writing for the majority, Justice Stevens rejected these views utterly—but not as such. The majority quickly passed by the president's argument that the convention applied only to forces fighting for "High Contracting Parties" under Article 2 and that al-Qaeda did not qualify. "[We] need not decide the merits of this argument because there is at least one provision of the Geneva Conventions that applies here even if the relevant conflict is not one between signatories"—Common Article 3.[91] The Court made this determination by properly rejecting the executive's key interpretive move. That position read the article's introductory wording, which states that it applies to "armed conflict not of an international character," as not covering conflict with al-Qaeda given that the "global war on terror" clearly crosses national borders.[92]

Justice Stevens rejected this reasoning on several bases. First, he noted that the structure of the conventions was best understood as providing a high level of protection for combatants of classical state-versus-state conflicts, yet in addition as according minimum fundamental rights for participants in conflicts falling short of traditional wars.[93] Second, the majority noted that the use of the term "international" was a term of art literally applying to actions between—"inter"—nation-states. It followed that conflict between the United States and a terrorist organization was not of an "international character" in this sense.[94] Finally, the Court relied on the International Committee of the Red Cross's "commentaries," which confirmed the Court's interpretation.[95]

Having concluded, contrary to the executive, that Common Article 3 applied, the Court found violations at the core of Hamdan's case. Quite simply, the United States violated the Geneva Conventions because the military commissions the president created were illegal under domestic law. Specifically, the military commissions proposed by President Bush ran afoul of the provision's requirement that detainees receive sentences only from "a regularly constituted court."[96] The Court reasoned that the commissions were not regularly constituted on the strength of its conclusion that the UCMJ prohibited them on the record before it, which was also a discrete and independent basis for the Court's judgment.

For all its merits, the *Hamdan* majority could have gone further. It first of all could have relied on the Founding outright. The Founders' commitment to separation of powers in foreign affairs provides the Court with a compelling basis to justify its independent review of treaty provisions in the face of insistent constructions put forth by the president. The same functional commitments apply as fully with international agreements as they do with domestic laws. Certainly, efficiency—or, as Hamilton put it, "secrecy and despatch"—applied to the making of treaties in particular.[97] For this reason the convention transferred the power to negotiate treaties from the Senate to the president, and the too-large House was to get out of the process altogether. Yet balance still remained the core goal. To further this purpose, the Founders included, among other things, the requirement that two-thirds of the senators present approve before a treaty could go into effect.[98] Despite what might be thought today, this supermajority proviso did not have much to do with addressing an ostensible "democratic deficit" left by excluding the House. Rather, it had nearly everything to do with the fear that the president could combine with a regional block of senators to undermine the rights and interests of a particular part of the country— the particular scenario envisioned was the northeastern states' using their majority to protect their fishing rights in the Atlantic at the expense of giving away navigation rights on the Mississippi, which were essential to the prosperity of the growing settlements along the southwestern borders of the nation. In these ways, the Founding desire to prevent an autocratic consolidation of power within the government was both manifest and self-conscious in a core area of foreign affairs.[99]

The same concern applies more specifically to the role of the courts, no less in foreign affairs than in other areas. The *Hamdan* Court could have noted that one of the central problems leading to the Federal Convention was the failure of the U.S. government in maintaining its treaty commitments. Foundational in this regard, of course, was the 1783 Treaty of Paris with Great Britain that ended the Revolution. Of special concern, the Court might have pointed out, were the American undertakings to, first, ensure compensation for loyalists whose property had been confiscated during the war and, second, to prevent the states from impeding British creditors from making good on their valid claims. With no direct power to legislate, the national government had to rely on the states, many of which blithely ignored the obligation to pass any measures protecting such unpopular groups. The solution was the supremacy clause's provision making treaties "the supreme Law of the Land," or, in modern parlance, "self-executing."[100] The no-less-manifest corollary to this decision was that it would fall to the courts, above all the federal courts, to make good on individuals' treaty claims when government officials would not.

Looking forward, the Court's effort in *Hamdan* would have been that much stronger had it further noted the effects of globalization. First, again as a general matter, the ties that executives around the world have been able to forge have outstripped those made by their legislative and judicial counterparts. This broad pattern would be reason enough for courts to maintain their authority *because of* rather than *despite* particular cases having foreign relations implications. For this reason, judicial authority to interpret treaties becomes even more important insofar as this source of law usually deals with foreign relations matters more directly and more often than with statutes and because, in the international context, agreements frequently furnish the primary check on executive action. The stakes become only that much higher when national security and individual rights are implicated. *Arar* and *El-Masri* illustrate the point.

So does *Hamdan* itself. There, executive officials from different states worked together outside the usual checks of domestic law to capture an individual who would be indefinitely detained and made subject to an attempted trial before an irregular court. Hamdan himself landed in Guantánamo after being captured by Afghan militia forces, who then turned him over to the U.S. military. The justification for deeming the resulting detention and trial outside the usual checks was that the capture took place in the course of a war. Yet it is exactly this claim that shows the dangers of globalization in the national security context. First, while the war in Afghanistan may have ended, captures in the new "war on terror" may continue as long as the threat of terrorism persists, which is to say forever. To face this threat, executives around the world will continue to cooperate to detain suspected terrorists and place them in specialized courts wherever and whenever they can find them. In this context, the primary source for the rule of law comes from treaties such as the Geneva Conventions. Given this role, it would come as no surprise that an executive might interpret the resulting strictures either as not applicable or not meaningful. It should, however, be shocking for the courts to cede their authority to interpret treaties just as they would interpret any other body of law. To do so would be to take one of the quickest paths to undermine separation of powers given the realities of modern international relations.

STATUTES: *RASUL*

As it is with treaties, so with statutes. *Rasul,* the first "war on terror" case to reach the Supreme Court, did not only deal with whether a federal law applied beyond sovereign U.S. territory. Along the way, it also pitted judicial authority against judicial deference with regard to statutory interpretation. As noted, *Rasul* involved the claims of fourteen persons captured during the war in Afghanistan and detained at the U.S. naval base at Guantánamo Bay.[101] As all sides made clear, the sole question came to be whether that federal habeas statute extended beyond the sovereign territory of the United States to Guantánamo.[102]

In arguing "no," the president's lawyers did not stop at the merits. They also sought refuge not merely in judicial deference but in judicial self-abnegation. The government first made the ritual prefatory contention that "the conduct of the foreign relations of our Government is committed by the Constitution to the Executive and Legislative—'the political'— Departments."[103] It continued that during armed hostilities, the commander in chief clause made the commitment to the executive in particular that much stronger. It followed, therefore, that what the Constitution gives to the executive it takes away from the courts. "Exercising jurisdiction over habeas actions filed on behalf of Guantánamo detainees would directly interfere with the Executive's conduct of the military campaign against al Qaeda and its supporters."[104] From here the consequences of judicial intervention grew direr. Entertaining claims from Guantánamo would extend jurisdiction of U.S. courts to habeas petitions filed on behalf of aliens captured or detained on the battlefield in Afghanistan or anywhere in the world. Simple review of Guantánamo claims would be enough to "thrust the federal courts into the extraordinary role of . . . superintending the Executive's conduct of an armed conflict. . . ."[105]

Three justices agreed. Writing for Chief Justice Rehnquist and Justice Thomas, Justice Scalia wrote a dissent that made clear that doubts about the courts' fitness to meddle in foreign affairs resonated. The majority's analysis, Scalia declared, "ought to be unthinkable when . . . [it] . . . has a potentially harmful effect upon the Nation's conduct of a war."[106] As if that were not plain enough, he concluded, "For this Court to create such a monstrous scheme in time of war, and in frustration of our military commanders' reliance upon clearly stated prior law, is judicial adventurism of the worst sort."[107]

Establishing a pattern for all the 9/11 cases, the majority rejected deference, yet did so almost passively. Justice Stevens devoted most of his opinion to the specific merits of habeas. Here it was affirmatively asserted that recent habeas decisions held "that the prisoner's presence within the territorial jurisdiction of the district court is not 'an invariable prerequisite' to the exercise of district court jurisdiction under the federal habeas statute."[108] Instead, a district court acts "within [its] respective jurisdiction" within the meaning of section 2241 as long as "the custodian can be reached by service of process" because "the writ of habeas corpus does not act upon the prisoner who seeks relief, but upon the person who holds him in what is alleged to be unlawful custody."[109] What the Court did *not* do was acknowledge, much less address, the arguments against the courts asserting their authority to interpret statutes that bear a significant impact on foreign affairs.

Yet the Court could have done exactly this. Rather than sidestep the issue, the majority first might have reiterated the historical foundations for its intervention. Any such historical case would have to begin with more than just half the story behind separation of powers, let alone the lesser half. At a general, functional level, the Founding generation did agree that a key function of dividing government authority was the type of efficiency borne of specialization. It followed that the president and Congress would be best suited to set policy across the board, including in foreign relations. It even followed further that the executive would enjoy a comparative institutional advantage in responding to national security emergencies. Efficiency, however, was not the only nor the primary function envisioned for the doctrine. If any one purpose had primacy, it was the prevention of tyranny by preventing too great a concentration of power into "the impetuous vortex"[110] of any branch of government. The executive's greater decisiveness and flexibility justifies, among other things, its grant of commander in chief authority, power to recognize governments, and further powers that may be implied for these express authorizations. But in just the same way, the judiciary, in explicating the law where it has jurisdiction and, more generally, in its role as a neutral arbiter of rights, vests within itself an exclusive power to adjudicate the scope of a remedial statute free and clear from any special concern for the executive's views.

Nor did the Founders tailor these fundamentals for cases involving foreign affairs. Instead, they envisaged the courts as key players in the new nation's quest for international respect. *Little v. Barreme* provides a perfect illustration.[111] Recall that in that case the Court considered the capture of a suspected American merchant ship by the frigate USS *Boston* during the so-called quasi war with France. An act of Congress authorized the president to instruct naval commanders to inspect and seize any suspected vessel sailing to a French port.[112] President Adams, however, construed the act to empower him to have American ships seized whether they were going to or coming from French ports. Following these orders, the *Boston* seized the vessel under suspicion even though it was coming from a French island. Writing for the Court, Chief Justice Marshall had no difficulty holding that the capture was not authorized, despite a "construction of the act of congress made by the department to which its execution was assigned"—a construction, moreover, "much better calculated to give it effect."[113] Where Marshall paused at all, it was to consider whether the *Boston*'s captain might have some sort of immunity from damages for following a presidential interpretation, but he declined even to do this.[114] Consistent with the Founding, in short, the chief justice gave zero deference to a federal statute authorizing military action and applied during a period of armed hostilities.

Looking forward, the *Little* Court might also have predicted that the bases for its foreign affairs role would grow stronger, not weaker. Even under George Washington, the eighteenth-century executive paled in relation to the other branches, in stark contrast to its modern counterpart.[115] Even then, this comparative weakness did not mean that the Court would grant the president any special leeway when it determined that a matter fell within the judicial power. As *Little* indicates, the judiciary instead would accord the executive zero deference in statutory interpretation, even when the statute dealt with what was then the nation's only real instrument of national defense, the U.S. Navy, in an armed naval conflict.

Today the executive's comparative power has increased exponentially, making the prima facie case for a strong judicial check correspondingly stronger. Many of the domestic sources for increased presidential power mentioned as long ago as *Youngstown* continue to flourish, including the concentration of authority in a single head, access to media, and the role of the president as head of his or her party.[116] Add to this the further effects of foreign relations. Globalization today works to comparatively enhance executive authority throughout the world, including the United States. This equation gains a multiplier effect once national security becomes the occasion for executives around the world to cooperate.

The facts of *Rasul* itself provide a telling illustration. There, the armed forces of the United States, in the course of a war given only the most general authorization by Congress, teamed up with irregular insurgent forces within Afghanistan to detain hundreds of enemy combatants where the likelihood of misidentification was substantial.[117] Such assertion of joint executive authority provides all the more reason for the judiciary to assert its checking function against the concentration of too much power in any single branch. The conclusion follows with that much greater force when the specific check is the judiciary's core role of interpreting statutes that set forth remedies for the violation of fundamental rights. Otherwise, the central purpose underlying separation of powers would survive merely at the sufferance of the president's claims in foreign affairs.

CONSTITUTION: *HAMDI*

Hamdi v. Rumsfeld,[118] which was decided after *Rasul* and before *Hamdan*, goes beyond, or at least above, the other two decisions by addressing the Constitution. The case arose when Yaser Hamdi, an American citizen, was captured by members of the Northern Alliance in Afghanistan and turned over to the U.S. military.[119] Like Rasul, however, Hamdi was designated an "enemy combatant," and so was subject to indefinite detention. Hamdi's father filed a petition for a writ of habeas corpus claiming, among other things, that he had a right under the Fifth and Fourteenth Amendments to contest the factual basis for his detention through a hearing.[120] In the course of its response, the executive attached a declaration from a Defense Department official.[121]

The Court granted certiorari on two potentially constitutional questions. The first dealt with Hamdi's challenge to the executive's authority to detain citizens as "enemy combatants." With detention authority established, there remained the second question: "What process is constitutionally due to a citizen who disputes his enemy-combatant status?"[122] Here the Court did grapple with the constitutional issue and, with it, the question of judicial deference.

As ever, the president's lawyers argued against the courts having any meaningful role. In *Rasul*, that meant reading a statute consistent with the executive's concerns given its constitutional role in foreign relations. In *Hamdan*, the argument went further to assert that the courts should bow to the president's interpretation of treaties given the president's greater ostensible expertise in dealing with this type of law. With *Hamdi*, the executive rang still another change. Here the White House argued that the Constitution itself acknowledged the president's greater institutional capacity in foreign affairs, especially in the context of national security.[123] In the circumstances, separation of powers principles meant that the courts had to accept the president's determination of who constituted an "enemy combatant."

Taking direct aim at judicial authority, the executive asserted that separation of powers principles compelled it to defer to its factual determinations plain and simple. The solicitor general reminded the Court that it had observed that " 'courts traditionally have been reluctant to intrude upon the authority of the Executive in military and national security affairs,' " and further that 'matters intimately related to foreign policy and national security are rarely proper subjects for judicial intervention.' "[124] The basis for judicial restraint rested in institutional capacity, namely the military's "unmatched vantage point from which to learn about the enemy and make judgments as to whether those seized during a conflict are friend or foe."[125] The president's lawyers did make the apparent concession that while factual determinations muted judicial review, a habeas challenge would give the courts the opportunity to consider challenges concerning the executive's authority to act. As they put it, "Respect for separation of powers and the limited institutional capabilities of courts in matters of military decision-making in connection with an ongoing conflict may well limit courts to the consideration of legal attacks on the detention of captured enemy combatants. . . ."[126] Of course, in *Rasul* and *Hamdan* the executive went on to argue that the president's legal determinations also commanded deference.

Once more, the executive's arguments met with some support from the bench, though again only in dissent and, in this instance, only in the lone effort of Justice Thomas. That opinion nonetheless sets out the case for judicial deference to the executive in almost its purest form. Thomas argued that, once authorized by the Constitution or Congress to take a particular action dealing with national security, the president may make the factual determinations necessary to take that action free and clear of any oversight by the courts—all on grounds of institutional capacity. He made the point as follows: "This detention falls squarely within the Federal Government's war powers, and we lack the expertise and capacity to second-guess that decision."[127] The dissent came to this conclusion by focusing entirely on the capabilities of the "unitary executive" in foreign affairs. Here Justice Thomas proceeded from the well-worn premise that the Constitution's structure aimed to create an energetic executive reflecting the "decision, activity, secrecy, and despatch" that characterizes an individual rather than a group.[128] "These structural advantages are most important in the national-security and foreign-affairs contexts."[129] Congress, Thomas conceded, does have an important role in these realms. "But," he added, "it is crucial to recognize that *judicial* interference in these domains destroys the purpose of vesting primary responsibility in a unitary Executive."[130]

Bolstering this conclusion, according to Thomas, is the judiciary's own and abject lack of expertise in these areas. First, "courts simply lack the relevant information and expertise to second-guess determinations made by the President based on information properly withheld."[131] Second, determining what information may be safely made public is simply too "delicate [and] complex" a matter for courts.[132] Finally, the Court itself has ostensibly recognized the primacy of the political branches in foreign and national security affairs. Unconsidered in this analysis were any special capacities of the courts.[133]

What the dissent did not do was pause to consider the structural counterpoint that an independent judiciary served to check the political branches, especially when individual liberty was at stake. Nor did it discuss the Court's own expertise in making individual factual determinations concerning individual deprivation of liberty. Still less did it talk about the Court's capacity to make such determinations against different levels of proof as set out either by the Constitution or statute.

These tasks would mainly fall to Justice Sandra Day O'Connor's plurality opinion, announcing the judgment that the federal courts did have substantive oversight power over the decision to detain persons as "enemy combatants." Justice O'Connor came to the case with her well-known penchant to struggle with both sides of a question and split the difference with some form of balancing test.[134] It therefore came as no surprise that she did exactly that here. As she said at the outset of her analysis, "It is beyond question that substantial interests lie on both sides of the scale in this case."[135]

On one side, the O'Connor plurality does not ignore either the executive's interests or its institutional advantages. In particular, the opinion noted the "weighty and sensitive governmental interests in ensuring that those who have in fact fought with the enemy during a war do not return to battle against the United States."[136] It also took as a given the Constitution's assignment of military decision-making and policy to the president and Congress. "Without doubt," Justice O'Connor observed, "our Constitution recognizes that core strategic matters of warmaking belong in the hands of those who are best positioned and most politically accountable for making them."[137] Article II concerns, and to some extent Article I considerations as well, had to be taken into account.

Yet in stark contrast to the Thomas dissent, the O'Connor opinion saw another side as well. Justice O'Connor bookended her discussion of the military perspective by looking at the constitutional claims of detainees and the role of the judiciary in safeguarding them. The claims rested squarely on Fifth Amendment due process. The plurality acknowledged that the right at stake "is the most elemental of liberty interests—the interest in being free from physical detention by one's own government."[138] Nor did the wartime setting change the reality that physical detention affected this interest.[139] To the contrary, on that point O'Connor noted a darker side to the institutional capacity of the executive. "History and common sense," she opined, "teach us that an unchecked system of detention carries the potential to become a means for oppression and abuse of others who do not present [a national security] threat."[140]

First and foremost, the check against such potential abuse is "an impartial adjudicator"[141]—and not just any impartial adjudicator, but in this instance the federal courts. As the plurality declared:

> We necessarily reject the Government's assertion that separation of powers principles mandate a heavily circumscribed role for the courts. . . . Indeed, the position that the courts must forgo any examination of the individual case and focus exclusively on the legality of the broader detention scheme cannot be mandated by any reasonable view of separation of powers, as this approach serves only to *condense* power into a single branch of government.[142]

The conclusion reemphasized the judiciary's role as guardian of fundamental rights. As O'Connor put it, "Whatever power the United States Constitution envisions for the Executive in its exchanges with other nations or with enemy organizations in times of conflict, it most assuredly envisions a role for all three branches when individual liberties are at stake."[143] Any other conclusion would "turn our system of checks and balances on its head."[144]

All that said, the plurality's specific unpacking of these principles might have done more to fit the reality to the rhetoric. Under the plurality's analysis, the balance between the Bill of Rights and Article III, on the one hand, and Article II, on the other, would be mediated by *Mathews v. Eldridge*,[145] a case usually associated with the denial of government entitlement benefits.[146] In this setting, a detainee could get notice of the factual basis for the detention; could have a hearing to rebut that factual basis; and at some point could access a lawyer. These specific safeguards may not quite match the plurality's high-flying analysis. That analysis, however, matters insofar as it repudiated judicial deference when constitutional liberties are at stake.

It would fall to Justice Scalia in dissent to point to a better way forward. Joined by Justice Stevens, the dissent argued that the government had only two options to get around Hamdi's habeas petition: it could charge him with treason (or some other similarly grave crime), or it could seek to have Congress suspend the habeas option.[147] No less importantly, the grounds for Scalia's position rested squarely on Founding notions of separation of powers. Of even greater import is that, more than the plurality, this dissent provides a foundation on which to build a better constitutional analysis in the post-9/11 context. That foundation rests first on the dissent's result. For Scalia, the Constitution's concern for basic rights commands "that Hamdi is entitled to a habeas decree requiring his release unless (1) criminal proceedings [most obviously for treason] are promptly brought, or (2) Congress has suspended the writ of habeas corpus."[148] Since neither alternative had occurred, Hamdi should have been held no longer.

More significant is Scalia's reasoning. More fully than the plurality, the dissent rehabilitates the Constitution's concern for individual liberty even in time of national danger. It resurrects this historic commitment, moreover, with a near-complete reliance on history. *Hamdi* gives Scalia a classic opportunity to apply his theory that the Constitution's protection of rights was, for the most part, originally understood to incorporate those protections as manifested in the common law at the time of the Founding. This idea applies with special force when attached to a particular text and with greater force still to habeas corpus since that is "the only common-law writ to be explicitly mentioned [in the Constitution.]"[149] Most of the dissent, therefore, discusses the writ's history. It conducts a 250-year excursion through English history, demonstrating how habeas became the critical check on the English monarch's attempts to incarcerate individuals outside the law.[150]

That said, the dissent does end with a powerful coda suggesting that the Founders' purpose was not simply to replicate common law doctrine but to do so precisely because they understood the threat to fundamental rights that times of national crises entailed:

> The Founders well understood the difficult tradeoff between safety and freedom. 'Safety from external danger,' Hamilton declared, 'is the most powerful director of national conduct.' . . . The Founders warned us about the risk, and equipped us with a Constitution designed to deal

with it. . . . Whatever the general merits of the view that war silences law or modulates its voice, that view has no place in the interpretation and application of a Constitution.[151]

This final flourish should serve as a double reminder. Whatever cavils one might have, it is Justice Scalia, more than any of his colleagues, who here marshals our Founding history in service of a proper framework for considering the roles of the executive and judiciary in light of 9/11. Any consideration of that history indicates that a concern for judicial protection of fundamental liberty is, at a minimum, as important as any solicitude for the executive and national security.

Even then, the dissent has it only half right. Subsequent history has served merely to make these Founding concerns greater. The executive has become infinitely greater than anything the Founders could have envisioned, especially in light of the New Deal and the emergence of the modern national security state. Beyond all of this, however, is the more recent development of globalization, of which countering terrorism is part. To fully play its assigned role, the courts should not just restore the Founding concern for fundamental rights to their analysis, nor simply note that the modern executive has grown so powerful that it puts pressure on any original conception of a balance among the branches. Justices and judges should also make explicit that foreign relations in the twenty-first century does not merely reveal new threats to the nation's external security but furnishes the executive with even greater means to act as an institution that has a "tendency to destroy [a nation's] civil and political rights."[152] To date, the Supreme Court has done a surprisingly good job of resisting calls for deference to the executive. With a deeper understanding of the past and the present, it could do better.

Coda: Boumediene

Much the same assessment applies to the Court's post-9/11 valedictory, *Boumediene v. Bush.* Also a constitutional case, the decision in many ways represented the Court's strongest defense of its foreign affairs authority to date. The justices stood up not only to the president but also to Congress in the face of a united attempt to strip them of the power to hear further challenges from Guantánamo detainees, or anyone else held as "enemy combatant," on the say-so of the executive. More importantly, the Court confirmed the extraterritorial reach of a vital constitutional right. Unfortunately, it did so based on one of the less robust of the available approaches. Even here, a better understanding of past and present might have prompted the Court to go further.

Boumediene arose in response to the other branches' responses to the Court's previous 9/11 rulings. On one hand, the Bush administration did set up something called "combat status review tribunals" (CSRTs) in light of *Hamdi* to determine, or rather confirm, that detainees at Guantánamo were "enemy combatants."[153] Yet, on the other hand, it continued to fight judicial oversight of the detentions. Critically, Congress joined the assault. First, it enacted the Detainee Treatment Act (DTA), which deprived the federal courts of jurisdiction to hear the habeas challenge from any Guantánamo detainee (though it did authorize the D.C. Circuit Court of Appeals to review CSRT determinations.)[154] The Supreme Court counterpunched in *Hamdan*, determining that the DTA did not apply to cases that were already pending when it was enacted. Congress then raised the stakes with the Military Commission Act (MCA), which again stripped the federal courts of habeas jurisdiction over any detainee who had been determined to be an "enemy combatant," to those who were awaiting such a determination, and to any detainees whose cases were still pending.[155]

The president and Congress, in short, presented the Supreme Court with a united front. Together they sought nothing less than to deny the judiciary the power to hear writs of habeas corpus, the centuries-old device to challenge the legality of government detention. Against this assault stood the Constitution's declaration that "the Privilege of the Writ of Habeas Corpus shall not be suspended, unless in Cases of Rebellion or Invasion the public Safety may require it."[156] As the Court stated, *Boumediene* raised the stark question of whether the Guantánamo detainees "have the constitutional privilege of habeas corpus, a privilege not to be withdrawn except in conformance with the Suspension Clause."[157]

Writing for the majority, Justice Anthony Kennedy answered yes. Taking his reasons in reverse order, the Court concluded that Congress had effectively suspended habeas review. Chief Justice Roberts, in dissent, argued that the D.C. Circuit's exclusive review of CSRT determinations only was enough to show that habeas had not been eliminated altogether.[158] But the majority rightly determined this power to be the fig leaf that it was. This conclusion meant that the Court had to determine whether the suspension of the "Great Writ" accorded with the Constitution's requirements. But first, and momentously, it had to determine whether the suspension clause applied outside the territorial limits of the United States.

Here the Court had a choice; indeed, it had too many choices. When it comes to the question "Does the Constitution—especially the freedoms it protects—follow the flag?" for at least one hundred years the justices have been all over the map, or rather, the globe. As noted, previous decisions had set forth no less than four approaches.[159] The narrowest, the "territorial approach," holds simply that constitutional rights stop at the border.[160] The potentially broader "membership" approach would extend the Constitution's protections abroad, but only to citizens and resident aliens as members of the American political community.[161] Most expansive is the "right/powers" school, which argues that just as the Constitution must authorize the government's power wherever it acts in the world, so too must it determine the limits on the power that travels with it.[162] Cutting across all these approaches, sometimes the Court has employed a more or less ad hoc, multifactor test, with the factors often changing from case to case.[163] Different decisions have relied on one or another of these approaches depending upon the right under consideration. The only constant in this inconsistent method has been the persistence of the overall a la carte approach.

For the "Great Writ," Justice Kennedy went with the multipronged approach. This meant "that at least three factors are relevant in determining the reach of the Suspension Clause: (1) the citizenship and status of the detainee and the adequacy of the process through which that status determination was made; (2) the nature of the sites where apprehension and then detention took place; and (3) the practical obstacles inherent in resolving the prisoner's entitlement to the writ." On the first point the majority concluded that the detainees' status as "enemy combatants" was contested and the CSRTs fell far short of habeas review. Justice Kennedy's opinion further noted that the United States possessed effective and indefinite jurisdiction over Guantánamo. Finally, the Court determined that neither the cost nor the effect of habeas review would compromise the military's mission.[164]

Boumediene's analysis is bracing so far as it goes. Yet, like its immediate predecessors, it could have gone further. For starters, turn back to the Founding and early republic. Justice Kennedy noted that the historical sources on application of habeas beyond the nation's borders were at best inconclusive. What remains clear are the more general Founding commitments. First, the Federalists' basic theory held that "We the People of the United States" ordained and established a constitution that both delegated and divided the powers of government. Yet, at the same time, even the original framework also set forth limitations on those powers by recognizing various fundamental rights, soon augmented in the Bill of Rights. It follows that wherever the government asserts its powers, it necessarily must contend with any limitations absent some clear indication to the contrary.[165] Some commentators have argued that such an indication arises from the very idea that the Founders established a sovereign government with fixed borders. This fact somehow means that the Constitution authorizes officials to act abroad but not to be subject to the restrictions that constitutional rights would otherwise impose. Early evidence on this point is meager, in no small part because the government then barely operated abroad in comparison to today. What scattered early evidence does exist is either contradictory or plainly insufficient to rebut that core Founding idea that powers come with constraints.[166] To the contrary, it is at just this point that the Founding materials on foreign affairs and separation of powers come in. As noted, the text, original understandings, and early practice tended to treat separation of powers as fully applicable in foreign as well as domestic affairs. Among other things, that commitment enjoins all the branches to stay within their grants of power and respect the limitations that rights impose, and it compels the judiciary to enforce these injunctions in cases that come before it. Justice Kennedy may have reached the right result. But a deeper understanding of history suggests he got there with the wrong method.

Nor has later custom repealed the idea. Over the last two hundred years, the Court may well have dabbled with additional and often contrary approaches. Yet, almost by definition, the current a la carte approach demonstrates that no one school of thought has prevailed, much less for a sustained period. In that failure, the Court has yet to displace the approach most faithful to the Founding's core ideals. Constitutional custom, in short, has failed to fix an alternative. That includes the ad hoc approach adopted in *Boumediene*.

Modern international relations, finally, reinforces the conclusion. Since the Founding, the national government's ability to assert its powers abroad has grown exponentially. Since World War II, the same can be said of executive officials working directly with their counterparts in other states. The net result is an executive that can assert itself overseas for good or ill as never before. The good need not concern the courts. But the ill can and has ranged from extraordinary rendition, to kidnapping, to prolonged detention, to torture, to targeted killing. In this light, the balance contemplated by separation of powers can be better defended the more the judiciary extends constitutional protections wherever constitutional powers travel. This is one more reason constitutional rights should now, more than ever, keep pace with Old Glory in a new age.

CHAPTER ELEVEN

American Courts, Global Norms

THE FOUNDING DESIGN applied the separation of powers idea without distinction as to domestic or foreign affairs. That commitment assigned a distinctive and robust role to the judiciary even in matters with international implications, particularly when important rights were at stake. This role, among other things, belies the tale of executive hegemony given aid and comfort by *Curtiss-Wright*, instead supporting the judicial duty to say what the law is most strikingly reaffirmed in *Youngstown*.

But the Founders did not stop there. They fully expected that the new federal judiciary would play its part, drawing not only on the nation's law but also the law of nations. Drawing upon this additional source of law would help accomplish two of the central goals that brought the Federal Convention together to begin with. First of all, federal judicial enforcement of international law would bolster separation of powers itself. Where applicable, judges could rely on international law to check the other branches in general, and so maintain an appropriate balance among all three to prevent the tyrannical concentration of power in any one. In particular, international law could furnish an additional source of rights against encroachments by the other branches. Furthermore, judicial reliance on international law would keep the United States in compliance with its obligations to other nations. All things being equal, such compliance would help the country avoid conflict and further promote peace and prosperity by demonstrating that the republic would act as an honorable and reliable member of the international order.

As in other areas, the use of international law, including and especially when rights are at stake, has met with increasing resistance. Part of the pushback, as elsewhere, results from the nation's rise to global power and engagement in near-perpetual conflict. Part of the challenge, in contrast to other issues, ironically stems from the greater protection of rights that international law has been expanding since World War II. The resulting controversies have been notably high profile and high stakes in three areas. Once more, the points of contention deal with (1) treaties; (2) statutes; and (3) the Constitution itself. In this context, the dispute has less to do with the judiciary's distinctive claim to applying these forms of law. Rather, controversy centers on the relationship of these categories and certain aspects of international law. With treaties, the main issue centers on whether and when such international agreements should operate as domestic law without additional legislation. Regarding statutes, contention swirls around the Alien Tort Statute, which, among other things, incorporated customary international law to protect aliens from violations of their rights. Finally, whether foreign legal materials should be used to interpret the Constitution likewise generates controversy.

As before, a restored understanding of the Constitution's text and history, subsequent constitutional custom, and effects of modern international relations suggest that developments have been heading in the wrong direction—and also suggest how they may be put back on proper course.

Supreme Law of the Land: Treaties

You are a Canadian national and Syrian refugee legally residing in the United States. One day you are pulled over by the local police while driving along the highway. Before you know what is happening, you are arrested, severely beaten, and charged with state terrorism offenses. While your trial is pending, you discover that you were swept up as part of a policy instituted by the newly elected local sheriff, who had pledged to be the nation's first line of defense from fundamentalist Islamic, Arab terrorism.

Now several treaties to which the United States has acceded might help you. Article 36 of the Vienna Convention on Consular Relations gives you the right to be notified that you may speak with a member of your country's consulate. Article 5 of the International Covenant on Civil and Political Rights (ICCPR) provides that "no one shall be subjected to torture or to cruel, inhuman or degrading treatment or punishment,"[1] as do articles 1 and 16 of the Convention Against Torture.[2] Any number of treaties—the central feature of international human rights law—prohibit discrimination based upon religion, race, ethnicity, or national origin, not least the ICCPR and the United Nations Charter.[3] The only problem for you is the following:

Can you rely on any of these instruments in a U.S. court? If they applied of their own force, you would be able to rely on them defensively, much as you might find recourse in a provision from the Bill of Rights. Depending on other domestic law provisions, you might even be able to use them against the relevant government agents offensively, in a civil rights suit. If, however, these treaties require implementation by Congress, absent a federal statute probably the best you can hope for is a diplomatic representation from Canada to the United States.

The answer to your dilemma would appear to lie in that part of the supremacy clause that proclaims: "Treaties made, or which shall be made, under the Authority of the United States, shall be the supreme Law of the Land." As noted, this provision reflected one of the principal reasons for creating Constitution in the first place. Madison, in his critical *Vices of the Political Systems of the United States*, had, after all, fretted over the many violations by the several states of the Treaty of Paris as well as treaties with France and the Netherlands.[4] As the new Constitution's text made clear, the solution was to make treaties automatically supreme over state law without any additional action by the Congress. This doctrine of treaty supremacy would remain a bedrock principle of American law for the next century and a half.

Three decades into that period, Chief Justice John Marshall added a notable and today often misunderstood clarification that came to be known as "self-execution."[5] It arose in the widely noted case of *Foster v. Neilson*, which required the Court to resolve a complicated dispute over a tract of land east of the Mississippi River.[6] One set of parties asserted title under a treaty between the United States and Spain. In that agreement Spain ceded the territory in question, which both nations had claimed, and further provided that all grants of land made by Spain "shall be ratified and confirmed" as if they had remained under Spanish dominion.[7] A rival group—and the U.S. government—argued that Spain had already given the land to France, which in turn sold it to the United States in the Louisiana Purchase. Marshall held against those who relied on the treaty with Spain. He reasoned that the treaty "does not declare that all the grants made by [Spain] before the [treaty] shall be valid," noting instead that "its language is that those grants shall be ratified and confirmed to the persons in possession, &c."[8] It followed that "the ratification and confirmation which are promised must be the act of the legislature [that is, Congress, since the land was to be initially under Federal control]. Until such act shall be passed, the Court is not at liberty to disregard the existing laws on the subject."[9] In short, the treaty was not "self-executing," since its language did not indicate automatic application, but rather was "non-self-executing," since the terms indicated that the treaty makers contemplated further action by Congress to perfect the land titles domestically.[10]

As David Sloss has made clear, the idea of "treaty supremacy" and "self-execution" are and were conceptually distinct.[11] Treaty supremacy meant that any treaty made "under the authority of the United States" took precedence over state law whether or not it contemplated further action by Congress. Non-self-execution, by contrast, meant that a treaty whose language did contemplate that Congress incorporate its provisions would not bind the federal government domestically until Congress acted.

Treaty supremacy, as Madison might have expected, played the more important role for much of the nation's history. As early as *Ware v. Hylton*, in 1796, the Supreme Court met the Founding expectation by holding that the Treaty of Paris ending the War of Independence was supreme over a conflicting Virginia statutory scheme.[12] No less importantly, that tradition remained strong through the first half of the twentieth century. So settled was the idea that it applied in instances in which racism might be expected to carry the day. Not long after World War I, Ichi Asakura, a Japanese citizen living in Seattle, challenged a city ordinance that prohibited non–U.S. citizens from obtaining a pawnbroker license. Asakura sued in state court, arguing that the law violated a treaty between the United States and Japan that granted equal treatment to Japanese who practiced a "trade" within the United States. The Supreme Court made short work of the ordinance. It paused mainly to consider whether pawnbroker qualified as a "trade." Perhaps more striking, Justice Pierce Butler's opinion readily accepted that the treaty could reach such local activity, which at the time was almost certainly beyond Congress's power to regulate under the commerce clause or any other grant of federal authority.[13] Most importantly of all, treaty supremacy remained axiomatic. Under the supremacy clause, the treaty operated "of itself without the aid of any legislation, state or national; and it will be applied and given authoritative effect by the courts. . . ."[14]

Today's Syrian-Canadian has far less reason to be confident. In the second half of the twentieth century, two developments heralded a judicial retreat from Madison's vision, the extent of which remains unclear. First, as previously mentioned, was "the death of treaty supremacy" after World War II. The demise occurred with the extension of non-self-execution— more accurately, the possibility that some treaties could be non-self-executing—to the previously automatic operation of treaties on the states. Next came the Senate's consistent practice of declaring nearly all human rights treaties to be non-self-executing. A final blow came more recently, in a case in which the Supreme Court may or may not have raised the bar to finding such treaties self-executing.

In a development almost unnoticed at the time, treaty supremacy expired from at least two major causes. One stemmed from what should by now be the familiar theme of rising U.S. geopolitical power as the twentieth century progressed.[15] As a result, treaty violations were no longer as perilous to the nation as they were during its nascent period. Early in the century, legal scholarship provided the conceptual tools for a change by emphasizing the intent of the treatymakers for domestic application in instances in which it was unclear that Congress had independent authority to enact legislation.[16] This work specifically sought to support the executive's seizure of foreign "rum-running" vessels outside U.S. territorial limits under treaties meant to facilitate Prohibition in precisely an area—the high seas—where it was then contested whether Congress had the power to expand the territorial limits of U.S. criminal law. The executive branch would take advantage of the new emphasis on treaty-maker intent. The premium placed on executive discretion in foreign affairs in the years leading up to World War II prompted State Department lawyers in particular to argue that, because the executive was the branch with special insight into the intent of the treaty makers, treaties that enhanced executive power were self-executing, and those that constrained it were not. In response, the Supreme Court itself began to conflate concepts of supremacy, an idea that suggested automatic superiority to state law, with preemption, a doctrine mainly developed for federal statutes and which, to a significant extent, turned on congressional intent. All these seeds would germinate after 1945, when the intent-based non-self-execution doctrine would be extended to treaty supremacy over state law.

Facilitating, even compelling, this development was the advent of modern international human rights law. Though in significant part a U.S. creation, this development within the United States led to a parochial, nationalist, and racist backlash. As any but the most idiosyncratic account holds, World War II and the Holocaust prompted the international community, led by the United States, to transform international law by addressing how nation-states treated persons within their territory and jurisdiction.[17] The UN Charter established the transformation. The Universal Declaration of Human Rights elaborated it in the form of nonbinding principles. A series of covenants and conventions translated these principles into specific, binding treaty obligations. Of all the freedoms enunciated, the one substantive right that the charter mandated would remain central: enjoyment of the enumerated rights "without distinction as to race, sex, language, or religion."[18] Though it is often overlooked today, domestic civil rights activists pounced on the new international human rights law featuring equality. The NAACP, the ACLU, and other groups filed amicus briefs in numerous cases, challenging racially discriminatory state laws as violating the UN Charter.[19] The Supreme Court generally struck down such laws. When it did, however, it relied on constitutional grounds rather than the Charter.

That did not prevent a nationalist reaction more than incidentally fueled by prejudice. To some observers, U.S. accession to the convention against genocide "threatened" to accord Congress the authority it otherwise would not have had to pass an antilynching law under the logic of *Missouri v. Holland*.[20] Worse was the widely publicized result of an otherwise minor state case that, in certain ways, echoed *Asakura*. In *Fujii v. California*, a California appellate court relied on the UN Charter to invalidate a state law that prohibited (most) East Asians from owning land.[21] Unlike *Asakura*, *Fujii* convinced much of the nation's legal elite to conclude that the idea that treaties that could automatically preempt state segregation laws was simply unacceptable. Accordingly, the American Bar Association began in earnest to propose measures that would either limit the subject matter that treaties could address—meaning human rights would be excluded—or make the treaty supremacy rule subject to the doctrine of non-self-execution based on the intent of the treaty makers. These ideas were taken up in the Senate, most notably by Ohio's John Bricker. Bricker led a movement to amend the Constitution outright, an effort that has borne his name ever since. The so-called Bricker Amendment was actually a multiheaded beast. A key proposal, however, called for the treaty supremacy rule to be abolished, or for its scope to be limited so that most treaties affecting state law would not have any domestic legal effect unless Congress enacted implementing legislation.[22]

Bricker's forces lost, but they exacted a price. The ultimate proposal that went before the Senate stated, "A treaty or other international agreement shall become effective as internal law in the United States only through legislation by the Congress unless in advising and consenting to a treaty, the Senate . . . shall provide that such treaties may become effective as internal law without legislation by Congress."[23] This version went down to defeat by a close vote. A key factor in the result was the Eisenhower administration, which opposed restrictions on the executive's ability to conclude international agreements. Yet Bricker and his supporters won a significant victory along the way. As Sloss notes, "Throughout the Bricker Amendment debates, virtually all the participants . . . framed their arguments in a way that viewed treaty supremacy as a subset of self-execution."[24] In other words, the doctrines that had been distinct for over 150 years were effectively combined. Treaty supremacy's death certificate came in the form of the *Restatement (Second) of the Foreign Relations Law of the United States*,[25] the elite, influential treatise on the subject that otherwise tended to promote international human rights. The *Restatement*'s position reflected, among other things, the conflation of the non-self-execution idea with treaty supremacy doctrine during the Bricker controversy. It enabled the United States during the Cold War to avoid human rights violations if treaty provisions commanding racial equality applied automatically to the states. And it meant that the U.S. legal community would not have to squarely face the reality that international human rights law protected rights more extensively than did the Constitution. In the end, with virtually no public discussion, a "de facto Bricker Amendment"[26] became part of constitutional law. Treaty makers could opt out of the principle of treaty supremacy over state law.

Opt out they did. It would prove ironic that modern international human rights law to a great extent began as an American export. As the first chair of the UN Human Rights Commission and, before that, as a key U.S. member of the General Assembly's Third Committee, Eleanor Roosevelt in particular would channel a strain of progressive U.S. internationalism to promote negative rights such as freedom from torture, positive rights such as education and healthcare, and equal enjoyment of them all without distinction as to race, sex, and national origin.[27] This commitment evaporated with the Eisenhower administration, which generally refrained from developing or even signing human rights agreements produced under UN auspices. This reversal was in part an additional cost of the Bricker controversy. Eisenhower resisted any attempt to curtail the executive's ability to negotiate treaties or other international agreements, but the executive at the same time acknowledged the concerns of Bricker and his supporters by steering the United States clear of any commitments to rights "imposed" from abroad, including and especially racial equality.[28] This new U.S. stance also reflected a hard "realist" approach to foreign policy newly ascendant in the executive, reflected not least by Eisenhower's formidable secretary of state, John Foster Dulles.

Thus began a Janus-faced approach to human rights that has characterized U.S. foreign affairs ever since. At times certain executives, politicians, diplomats, scholars, judges, and lawyers have continued the (Eleanor) Roosevelt tradition, viewing international human rights law as a laudable complement to American constitutional rights as well as American "soft power."[29] Probably more often, foreign policy leaders have sought to have the nation stand aloof from the human rights movement. Louis Henkin, the Columbia law professor who became a leading proponent of U.S. participation in international human rights, summed it up best when he analogized the U.S. stance to a "flying buttress," supporting the idea, but from the outside.[30]

The nation remained on the outside. Either executives did not sign human rights treaties in the first place or, when they did, the Senate failed to approve. When it has assented to treaties, the Senate has nonetheless taken advantage of the death of automatic treaty supremacy over state law and added a declaration of non-self-execution to any approval. The Office of the UN High Commissioner of Human Rights lists eighteen "core human rights" treaties.[31] Of these, the United States has signed only nine. Of these, the Senate has given its constitutional advice and consent to only five. And with these, approval in every instance has come with a declaration of non-self-execution. Since the death of treaty supremacy, that means that they do not preempt even state law absent an act of Congress and so are not subject to judicial enforcement.

One further blow to such enforcement remained. At least in treaties protecting individual rights that the Senate might not have deemed non-self-executing, there remained the possibility, if not the presumption, that the agreement would apply domestically. As traditionally stated, regardless of whether it applies to state law or not, the doctrine holds that treaties will be deemed self-executing absent text or some other indication of the treaty makers' intent to the contrary. This approach may or may not have changed in *Medellin v. Texas*, a recent Supreme Court decision that exemplifies the ambiguous state of modern foreign relations law toward the judicial enforcement of international rights.[32]

On August 8, 2008, the state of Texas executed Jose Medellin, a Mexican national convicted of capital murder. That execution violated the provisions of at least two treaties to which the United States is a party. First was the Vienna Convention on Consular Relations. Article 36 of the convention provides that foreign nationals arrested in one state have a right to be informed that they can meet with members of their state's consulate. [33] This provision was buried in an otherwise obscure agreement dealing with definitions, rights, and duties of consular diplomatic officials. Perhaps for that reason, the Senate did not attach a declaration of non-self-execution, as it does in agreements wholly dedicated to human rights. The Vienna

Convention, in other words, is exactly that mythical beast of a treaty protecting significant individual rights that tests the usual presumptions concerning treaties as the supreme law of the land.

As is typical in most U.S. domestic states, Texas never conveyed this information to Medellin. Unaware of the treaty, Medellin, not surprisingly, failed to raise it at trial or on direct appeal. When, with more informed counsel, he sought to do so on habeas, the Texas courts ruled that he had effectively waived the opportunity by his failure to raise the issue beforehand. In similar circumstances, the Supreme Court had previously ruled that reliance on a domestic U.S. state's "procedural default rule" did not constitute a violation of the convention.[34]

The International Court of Justice begged to differ. In a case known as *Avena*, Mexico brought an action against the United States on behalf of fifty-one Mexicans on death row in the United States who had not been informed of their Vienna Convention rights, including Medellin.[35] The ICJ held that the procedural default rule could not preclude review of cases in which the Vienna Convention had been violated. To the contrary, the ICJ directed the United States to reopen the conviction before a non-executive body. Relying on this decision, Medellin at the Supreme Court argued that the United States had to provide him with such a review. Further, he pointed to article 94 of the UN Charter, which states that "each Member of the United Nations undertakes to comply with the decision of the International Court of Justice in any case to which it is a party."[36]

The Supreme Court rejected Medellin's claim nonetheless. It held, among other things, that the UN Charter provision was not "self-executing," and so an act of Congress was needed for ICJ decisions involving the United States to apply domestically. In particular, Chief Justice Roberts's majority opinion reasoned that the Charter lacked language that clearly expressed that ICJ opinions were to be treated as automatically enforceable— self-executing—in domestic courts.[37] Justice Breyer in dissent aptly replied that a multilateral treaty could never contain such language since many "dualist" nations, such as the United Kingdom and most of its former colonies, required their legislatures to incorporate treaty provisions into domestic law before their courts could consider them.[38] Experts disagree as to whether *Medellin* inverts what had effectively been a presumption of self-execution.[39] Whatever else it accomplished, the decision did nothing to bolster such a presumption.

In any case, the immediate result is clear. As far as the Court was concerned, the UN Charter failed to make the *Avena* decision binding on Texas. Likewise, the Court held, without a federal statute, the executive lacked any power to implement the ICJ decision against Texas. As a leading expert says, with self-conscious understatement, "The Supreme Court based its decision on an understanding of the Constitution that differed sharply from the Framers' understanding."[40]

All of which raises the question: Was the death of treaty supremacy legitimate, or is it an ongoing constitutional violation? Some by no means nationalistic scholars, including David Sloss and Peter Spiro, argue that treaty supremacy's effective repeal has since acquired a measure of validity through subsequent constitutional custom.[41] Yet the death of treaty supremacy is better considered to be exaggerated rather than final. Recent constitutional custom almost certainly affords the best defense for the doctrine's continuing eclipse. In this instance, however, the custom is insufficient, especially as it is made possible by the constitutional anomaly of a minority veto in the Senate, itself a democratic anomaly. More importantly, the bar for a constitutional change through institutional custom would seem higher when the original constitutional position is thoroughly entrenched though specific text, discernable original understanding, and centuries of custom confirming the initial commitment. It follows that the most principled response to the death of treaty supremacy may be simply to revive the doctrine of treaty supremacy.

Of course this conclusion need not follow if the repeal of the rule, however illegitimate initially, really could be said to have gained the status of a new constitutional standard in light of later custom. Justice Frankfurter's *Youngstown* concurrence set out the idea that unbroken, systematic executive action, combined with congressional acquiescence, can help confirm the constitutionality of that practice. Certainly executive branch lawyers during the Bricker Amendment controversy put forward the view that the executive and Senate could sidestep the treaty supremacy rule by stipulating that a treaty was non-self-executing (among other ways), a move that would then enable the United States to sign human rights treaties but avoid the dire consequence of having international legal standards actually upend Jim Crow. These instances, the argument goes, show an ongoing custom that assumes such a declaration suffices as an opt-out of treaty supremacy.[42]

A closer examination suggests not. Even on its own terms, the Senate's practice of attaching non-self-execution declarations is limited and recent. By its count, the Senate has employed such declarations—which, among other effects, deny treaty supremacy—in only about two dozen instances. This custom, moreover, as a consistent matter dates back only to the 1990s.[43] It is further worth noting the idiosyncratic mechanism through which this particular custom occurs. Presumably, one justification for reliance on political branch practice is the democratic basis on which the executive and Congress act. Any custom that consistently establishes a principle in theory reflects more general approval by the American electorate. Now consider the treaty context. Under the treaty clause, the assent of just one-third of the members plus one of a quorum of the Senate, already a seriously flawed body from a democratic perspective, suffices to insist on a non-self-execution declaration for a given treaty.

Such a limited, recent custom, based on such an extreme minority veto, falls short as a basis to amend the Constitution. The point applies more, not less, strongly in foreign affairs matters in light of the relevant text, original understandings, and previous longstanding custom. Justice Frankfurter, and in a roundabout way Justice Jackson as well, discussed constitutional practice at most as a gap-filler in areas in which conventional methods of constitutional interpretation left significant space for the political branches to work out pragmatic understandings. A classic instance in this regard is, or should be, congressional limits on the executive's removal power.[44] That is not the case with treaty supremacy. The most natural reading of the supremacy clause makes the rule mandatory: "*All* Treaties made or which shall be made under the Authority of the United States, *shall be the supreme Law of the Land, and the Judges in every State shall be bound thereby, any Thing in the Constitution or Laws of any State to the contrary notwithstanding.*"[45] The Founding history confirms that the consensus view of this provision was for judges to check violations of U.S. treaty obligations without implementing legislation by Congress.[46] For over a century and a half, moreover, consistent practice took this understanding for granted. A theory of customary constitutional change might allow for so entrenched a doctrine to be amended by later practice. Yet, contrary to what is sometimes assumed, treaty supremacy illustrates that foreign affairs is one area in which the bar to amendment though custom should be set higher, not lower. It follows that legitimate constitutional change in this area at the very least would require a consistent, repeated, longstanding, and open practice that is compelling, far more so than what is on offer currently.

In this light, the better course is not to attempt legitimating a constitutional transformation with no obvious justification. Rather, it is to recognize an unconstitutional transgression and restore the commitment that existed previously—to press for a day when that commitment comes back.

Submitted to a Candid World: Statutes

Until that happens, international human rights law will, for the most part, have to come into our domestic legal system not through treaties but through statutes. Relying on today's polarized Congress for much of anything, much less incorporating international human rights obligations, might seem like an idle hope. Such hope might border on delusional in light of the Senate's historic role in attaching declarations of non-self-execution to any human rights treaty it could lay hold of. Yet the legislature can still, from time to time, surprise. Congress has in fact passed signal statutes that have made some of the most notable modern international human rights American law. The 1968 Refugee Act, for example, carries into execution key provisions of the 1950 Refugee Convention.[47] The Anti-Torture Act served the same function for the Convention Against Torture, a treaty actually signed by Ronald Reagan and incorporated by a Democratic Congress.[48] Beyond treaties, the Torture Victims Protection Act opened the U.S. legal system to civil actions by victims of two of the most heinous violations of customary international law: torture, as the title suggests, and extrajudicial killing, which for some reason did not make it into the statute's title.[49] In these instances, Congress, in its way, submitted to a candid world American administration of international justice.

Yet the human rights statute that has generated the most publicity, scholarship, and case law by far is arguably the earliest—the Alien Tort Statute enacted by the First Congress in 1789. Its long and winding saga, moreover, perfectly illustrates a core argument of this book. On one hand, the federal judiciary, and to a point the Supreme Court, have applied the ATS to uphold international human rights in a manner that maintains fidelity to our Founding commitments. On the other, the Supreme Court in particular has signaled retreat from these initial accomplishments.

The ATS in its totality states that "the district courts shall have original jurisdiction of any civil action by an alien for a tort only, committed in violation of the law of nations or a treaty of the United States."[50] Once upon a time, almost every account of the ATS began with Judge Henry Friendly's observation that it "is kind of a legal Lohengrin; although it has been with us since the first Judiciary Act . . . no one seems to know whence it came."[51] Scholarship has since shed light on the statute's origins, in no small part to meet the demands of modern opponents and proponents. Yet it was true enough that for nearly two hundred years the ATS lay unknown and unused.

Then came *Filartiga*. In 1979, Dr. Joel Filartiga and his daughter, Dolly, both citizens of Paraguay, filed the first modern ATS suit in the U.S. Federal District Court in Brooklyn against Américo Norberto Peña-Irala, also a Paraguayan citizen, for the kidnapping, torture, and murder of Filartiga's seventeen-year-old son, Joelito. They alleged that Peña-Irala, who had been the inspector-general of the local police, had orchestrated the crimes. Dolly asserted that later in the day in question, after the abduction, the police brought her to Peña-Irala's home, "where she was confronted with the body of her brother, which evidenced marks of severe torture. As she fled, horrified, from the house, Peña-Irala followed after her shouting, 'Here you have what you have been looking for for so long and what you deserve. Now shut up.'"[52] The Filartigas claimed that Joelito had been targeted because of his father's opposition to Paraguay's then dictator, Alfredo Stroessner. Dolly had ultimately fled to the United States and settled in Washington, D.C. Not long thereafter, she discovered that Peña-Irala had moved to Brooklyn. After consulting with the Center for Constitutional Rights, the Filartigas decided to attempt a civil action under the ATS.

Their case fell literally within the terms of the statute. They were aliens. They sought to bring an action for a tort only. The violations they asserted, torture and extrajudicial murder, were well established under customary international law as it had developed since World War II. The district court nonetheless dismissed. The Second Circuit, however, reversed and let the suit go forward. The opinion could not have come from a more improbable source. Judge Irving Kaufman had come to national prominence as the district judge who presided over the trial of Ethel and Julius Rosenberg, whom he sentenced to death after their conviction for passing nuclear secrets to the Soviets. Worse, in considering the sentence he had allegedly engaged in impermissible *ex parte* contacts with the federal prosecutors on the case, including the notorious Roy Cohn.[53] Kaufman nonetheless effectively wrote a manifesto for the domestic enforcement of international human rights. The main issue centered on whether customary international law addressed how nations treated persons within their own borders and jurisdiction. Kaufman and the court answered yes, drawing upon numerous sources to satisfy the first main requirement of international custom that a principle command a near consensus of the world's nations. As is typical of American courts, the Second Circuit did not address the other main requirement that international lawyers consider—whether nations have acted out of a sense of legal obligation. That did not prevent the court from rightly concluding that torture in particular was a core violation of international law.

Filartiga ushered in over thirty years of often high-profile international human rights litigation in U.S. courts. The cases came in roughly two waves. The first fifteen years or so witnessed something of a golden age. On the *Filartiga* model, foreign victims of authoritarian regimes used the federal judiciary as a kind of "truth commission" to establish that they or their loved ones had been arbitrarily detained, disappeared, or killed, whether or not they could actually obtain damages. Representative successes, often default judgments, included a suit against an Indonesian general for a summary execution of a New Zealand national in East Timor;[54] an action brought by Kanjobol Indians against a former Guatemalan defense minister for torture, disappearance, and extrajudicial killing;[55] and a suit against Radovan Karadžić, the leader of the Republika Srpska, for, among other things, genocide.[56] Successes in this vein continued in cases such as *Yousuf v. Samantar*, in which the courts stripped a former prime minister of Somalia of immunity from suit for torture, arbitrary detention, and extrajudicial killing.[57]

Every circuit court to consider the new spate of ATS cases approved. Outside the courtroom, Congress lent tacit approval as well in passing the 1992 Torture Victim Protection Act, which opened ATS-type suits to U.S. citizens for torture and extrajudicial killing.[58] Likewise supportive was the executive, Republican and Democratic, in numerous amicus briefs. Among the few prominent dissenting voices was Judge Robert Bork, who argued that that the law of nations violations on which the ATS permitted suit were frozen to those that existed when the act was passed in 1789.[59] That would have meant that even torture, and much of the rest of modern human rights law, would not have been covered. Bork, however, was all but a lone voice.

Then human rights victims started suing corporations. And the pushback began. This second wave of ATS suits reflected a simple reality. Multinational corporations, often more powerful than most states, not infrequently work hand in hand with authoritarian regimes on mutually beneficial projects. And sometimes, pursuing such joint projects involves horrific human rights violations. An early case, *Doe v. UNOCOL*, illustrates the dynamic. In 1996 a group of Burmese villages brought suit against UNOCOL, a multinational oil company, for aiding and abetting the Myanmar military dictatorship in committing human rights violations; the regime, in turn, was to assist UNOCOL in putting an oil pipeline in their region. Among the alleged violations were forced labor, torture, rape, and extrajudicial killing. The parties ultimately settled.[60] Yet cases such as UNOCOL multiplied. As anyone might have predicted, suing major corporations meant more formidable opposition than suing former Paraguayan police officials. For one thing, the position of the executive branch at the highest levels switched from support to opposition. More importantly, corporate defendants could hire the nation's most prestigious law firms. Such firms came complete with, among other assets, former Supreme Court clerks and Justice Department officials more than willing to use their legal talents and creativity to make sure that human rights victims would come nowhere near having their day in court.[61]

The counterattack ultimately reached the Supreme Court. The first ATS case the justices would hear in fact would decide the fate of all litigation under the statute. For proponents of human rights, *Sosa v. Alvarez-Machain* could scarcely have presented either a bolder challenge or worse facts. Dr. Humberto Alvarez-Machain allegedly had kept alive Enrique Camarena-Salazar, a U.S. DEA agent, so he could be tortured longer before being executed by a Mexican drug cartel that discovered he was an undercover agent.[62] Alvarez had already had a case go to the Supreme Court when he challenged his abduction by U.S. officials, who had spirited him out of Mexico to stand trial in the United States rather than obtain custody under a U.S.-Mexican extradition treaty. The doctor did stand trial, and was acquitted. Turning the tables, he then brought suit against his abductors. In the case of the Mexican authorities who aided and abetted their U.S. counterparts, Alvarez brought a claim under the ATS, alleging arbitrary detention in violation of customary international law.[63] His acquittal notwithstanding, his case did not exactly conjure the sympathetic story of a noble dissident crushed and tortured by an authoritarian regime.

Conversely, the challenge to the ATS put forward on behalf of Sosa, the lead Mexican defendant, was far-reaching. Not coincidentally, they reflected the views of the solicitor general as well as an array of corporate associations. The argument was simple, sweeping, and fatal. The only thing that the text of the ATS did was to confer jurisdiction on the federal district courts. It did not, however, further provide for a cause of action—in essence a license to sue—a necessary requirement for any civil action to go forward. The modern legal axiom held that a statute granting jurisdiction without another creating a cause of action meant that the courts could hear a given claim, but no one could bring it.[64] Had the justices accepted this argument, the results would have been momentous. Such a conclusion would have meant that the ATS cases of the previous quarter century had been illegitimate. Looking ahead, it would also have meant that no more ATS suits could have gone forward, whether against corporations *or* the official henchmen of authoritarian regimes.

A majority decided otherwise. In an especially rigorous and nuanced opinion, Justice Souter preserved what had been the first wave of ATS suits and left the door partially open for the second. The *Sosa* Court conceded that had the ATS been enacted today, a jurisdictional grant without an express cause of action would indeed have put an end to the matter. The ATS was, however, passed by the First Congress in the late eighteenth century. Here Souter rightly argued that in that period, a grant of jurisdiction brought with it an expectation that courts would use their common-law-making power to themselves fashion a cause of action. He further followed the dominant view of recent historical scholarship on the ATS to conclude that the First Congress would have specifically expected the federal courts to fashion three causes of action based on the contemporary law of nations: claims by ambassadors who had suffered assault; suits for violation of "safe conduct," basically a guarantee by a national government that specified individuals could travel unmolested through its territory; and actions against pirates. Souter then distilled two features common to these examples that would serve as the prerequisites for new causes of action as customary international law evolved. Any new judge-made causes of this kind would have to command a "consensus" of the international community. They would also have had to develop with a degree of specificity.

Whatever else it indicated, this formula meant that the "classic" *Filartiga*-type ATS suits were safe. Torture, extrajudicial killing, slavery, genocide, and prolonged arbitrary detention all easily meet both prerequisites. Also clear was that Alvarez might have won the war for the statute, but he would lose the battle for himself. The Court correctly observed that prolonged arbitrary detention was an established violation of international custom, but it no less correctly held that the doctor's twenty-four-hour detention could in no way be construed as "prolonged." Less clear would be the idea that private corporations could "aid and abet" such state-sanctioned human rights violations.[65]

For just this reason, the opponents of the ATS were far from done. For them the promise of salvation came, out of the blue, from the same court of appeals that had handed down *Filartiga* decades before. In fact as recently as 2007, the Second Circuit had endorsed the idea that a victim of human rights abuses could allege that a corporation had aided and abetted state human rights violations.[66] Then, just three years later, came *Kiobel*. This case involved a group of Nigerian nationals suing Dutch, British, and Nigerian oil companies for, among other things, torture and extrajudicial killing in connection with the running of a pipeline. In a stunning exercise of judicial activism, the majority baldly declared that corporations could not be sued under the statute. It reached this conclusion notwithstanding the absence of supporting statutory text and the usual presumption that tort liability runs to both natural and corporate persons under domestic law.[67] As Judge Leval's masterful separate opinion makes clear, the majority mainly relied on the irrelevant determination that customary international law does not impose criminal, as opposed to civil, liability on corporations for human rights violations.[68]

The Supreme Court took on the case but not, ultimately, the issue it originally presented. It did grant cert, accept briefs, and hear oral argument on corporate liability. But in a rare move, it ordered the case be held over and reargued on a different issue—whether and to what extent the ATS applied extraterritorially. In a greater blow to human rights accountability, the Court answered with a qualified no.

Writing for the majority, Chief Justice Roberts began his analysis with the presumption against applying federal statutes abroad. Curiously, he noted that this rule "'serves to protect against unintended clashes between our laws and those of other nations which could result in international discord.'"[69] He further suggested that this concern weighed even more heavily when, as *Sosa* concluded, Congress left it to the courts to craft the cause of action. Why any of this mattered when the only causes of action the courts could create were, by definition, universal, the opinion did not address. The chief justice stumbled even more badly over the statute's history. Among other challenges, he ran into obvious difficulties arguing that piracy, one of the three law of nations violations that the First Congress had in mind when enacting the ATS, was not extraterritorial. Likewise, he could not fully reconcile the 1795 statement of Attorney General Edmund Bradford that suggested that causes of action under the ATS applied to conduct in Africa. Despite all these difficulties, the presumption carried the day. According to the Court, future claims would have to "touch and concern the territory of the United States."[70] On this view, *Filartiga* itself arguably should have been dismissed.

Justice Breyer, joined by three others, concurred, but with an alternative approach. He rejected outright applying the presumption against extraterritoriality, for the obvious reasons. It does not square either with the Bradford opinion or the contemporary concern about piracy. More obviously, judicial authorization of a suit for the violation of a universal norm by definition cannot create clashes between U.S. law and the laws of other nations. Instead, Breyer argued that any limits to applying the ATS abroad should come from international law. On this basis, he suggested that he would find jurisdiction under the statutes where "(1) the alleged tort occurs on American soil, (2) the defendant is an American national, or (3) the defendant's conduct substantially and adversely affects an important American national interest," including the interest of ensuring that the United States does not become a safe harbor for torturers and other violators of fundamental international human rights.[71] In this instance, Kiobel's claim did not fit into any of the three categories. Nonetheless, on *this* view, *Filartiga* and many of the cases in its wake could have gone forward.

Justice Breyer's approach is at once more faithful to the ATS and, no less importantly, to the separation of powers. First consider the relevant history. As Breyer points out, the presumption cannot be easily reconciled with the role of piracy or the views of Attorney General Bradford. Nor can it be easily reconciled with scholars who stress the Founding generation's desire for the United States to be seen as fully committed to the law of nations. Beyond this, Justice Breyer might also have pointed out that the First Congress's expectation that the judiciary fashion cause of action based on international law in no way cuts against judges limiting these cases to U.S. territory. The Founding generation, to the contrary, expressed confidence in the ability of the judiciary to say what the law is, including international law, as a further power allowing it to maintain balance among all three branches. Second, nothing in intervening constitutional custom undercuts this role. If anything, two generations of current ATS jurisprudence point the other way. Finally, modern international relations has only made the need for judicial accountability that much greater. The mutual empowerment of executives worldwide, especially in ways that put pressure on fundamental rights and evade domestic checks, makes those domestic checks even more essential. For that reason, a more expansive reading of Breyer's third category would ideally include Kiobel's claim as well.

Much the same critique applies to the Court's even more recent blow to the ATS, which adds insult to *Kiobel II*'s injury. For the opponents of human rights litigation, even *Kiobel II* left untied one substantial loose end. Left unresolved was whether corporations could be sued when a claim touched and concerned the territory of the United States. The Court finally decided this issue in 2018's *Jesner v. Arab Bank*.[72] The case involved mainly foreign nationals alleging that a New York branch of a Jordanian bank aided and abetted multiple acts of terrorism in the Middle East. Not surprisingly, a majority held that no matter how heinous the human rights violation, a corporation could not be sued.

Apart from this conclusion, the justices for the most part went their separate ways. Justice Kennedy wrote the main opinion, only slivers of which commanded a majority. His principal rationale, endorsed by only

Chief Justice Roberts and Justice Thomas, asserted that international law controlled the issue of corporate liability, and that there was no universal, specific, or obligatory norm that held corporations directly accountable for human rights violations.[73] For his part, Justice Gorsuch, in a lone, partial concurrence, sought to have set the clock back entirely. Gorsuch would have (1) ideally overruled *Sosa* on the ground that federal courts should not create causes of action; (2) held that foreigners suing foreigners under the ATS went beyond Article III of the Constitution; and (3) at most allowed suits by aliens against U.S. defendants.[74] On this view, the ATS originally would not even have contemplated piracy or assaults on ambassadors, but only violations of safe conduct.

Whatever the problems with these assertions, more problematic from a separation of powers perspective are the few passages that did command a majority. From the Kennedy opinion, these mainly recycle the trope that arose with the nation's rise as a global power and the corresponding ascent of the executive. The courts should hesitate to create new ATS causes of action because "the political branches, not the Judiciary, have the responsibility and institutional weight to weigh foreign-policy concerns."[75] The courts should not allow suits against corporations because they "are not well suited to make the required policy judgments that are implicated by corporate liability in cases like this one."[76] To this extent, what majority in *Jesner* that did exist has kept the possibility of the Court's retreat from its historic foreign affairs role alive and well.

Justice Sonia Sotomayor, in a four-justice dissent, offered a corrective based upon international law, statutory text, history, purpose, and, finally, foreign policy concerns. First, the dissent at great length plausibly argues that international law focuses on conduct, such as extrajudicial killing, not on the mechanisms for penalizing such conduct, such as tort liability against corporate persons who facilitate such conduct. Next, the dissent pointedly notes that the text of the ATS places no limits on possible defendants, that tort suits against corporate persons have a long history under federal common law, and that allowing suit against corporations who assist in wanton violations of international law surely furthers the statute's manifest purpose. Laudably, the dissent also directly ventures into foreign affairs. Among other points, Justice Sotomayor asserts that there is no "reason to believe that the corporate form in itself raises serious foreign policy concerns" any more than does suits against natural persons.[77] In all, the only significant specific argument that the dissent overlooks goes back to the statute's immediate history. At the time the First Congress convened, English common law already had numerous precedents of early corporations, such as the British East India Company, being sued for violations of the law of nations.[78] Otherwise, Justice Sotomayor's opinion is as rigorous as it is forceful in concluding:

> We permit a civil suit to proceed against a paint company that long knew its product contained lead yet continued to sell it to families, or against an oil company that failed to take requisite safety checks of a pipeline that subsequently burst. There is no reason why a different approach should obtain in the human rights context.[79]

Jesner reflects, among other things, the Supreme Court's drift toward at once empowering and shielding corporations. The Sotomayor dissent concludes by hitting just this mark. "Immunizing corporations that violate human rights from liability under the ATS," she writes," undermines the system of accountability for law-of-nations violations that the First Congress endeavored to oppose." But more than that, doing so "allows these entities to take advantage of the significant benefits of the corporate form and enjoy fundamental rights [for example, free speech and free exercise of religion(!) under the First Amendment] without having to shoulder attendant fundamental responsibilities."[80] Among the "other things" *Jesner* reflects is the complementary drift toward judicial self-abnegation in foreign affairs. Together these trends proved to be toxic to much of what was left of the ATS.

For present purposes, what matters more is the drift toward judicial retreat. The saga of the Alien Tort Statute once more shows a conflicted Court threatening to more and more cede its proper role. Whatever else it does, the statute demonstrates that the Founding generation had some concern about judicial enforcement of individual rights guaranteed under international law. Since its rediscovery in *Filartiga*, much has been written about its specific legislative history. While not the only plausible reading, Justice David Souter's take in *Sosa* reflects what can be fairly said to represent the majority view among scholars. Likewise, there is every reason to believe that the First Congress would have expected suits against corporations. Yet more generally, and no less importantly, nothing in the Founding's history justifies the current judicial timidity on display in the fragments that commanded a majority in *Jesner*.

After a hiatus of a century and a half, what custom had emerged in the lower courts now consistently upheld a broad reading of the ATS. Exactly this record both *Kiobel II* and *Jesner* utterly ignored. So too did they ignore the judiciary's commitment to customary international law outside the ATS during this hiatus. Especially suggestive in this regard was

Justice Story's opinion in *La Jeune Eugenie*. There, recall that the justices reasoned that an American court could rightfully uphold the seizure of a French ship engaged in that form of commercial activity known as the slave trade. Story, moreover, based his conclusion on the ground that such trade violated a universal law of nations prohibition, a ban that, not incidentally, stands as one of the early examples of what is now deemed international human rights law.[81]

Finally, modern international relations further serves to confirm the need for precisely the type of international human rights litigation that the ATS represents. Executive officials worldwide increasingly interact to empower one another. This development has, among other things, increased their power compared to other domestic institutions and has, accordingly, made it easier for them to evade the constraints of those institutions, even when they violate fundamental rights. This is all the more reason to maintain the ability of domestic checks in any given nation, including the United States, to hold violators and their accomplices accountable for flouting universal norms.

A Decent Respect for Mankind: The Constitution

For at least the past several decades, judges around the world have been looking beyond their own nations' jurisprudence to international law and the decisions of foreign courts in order to apply domestic law. The practice has been especially pronounced when it comes to judicial protection of fundamental rights. This widespread practice is part of a phenomenon that Anne-Marie Slaughter calls "judicial globalization."[82] The American judiciary, however, has exhibited a distinct diffidence toward the use of comparative and international law to decide domestic cases, a diffidence that extends to many elected officials as well.

To a non-American audience, opposition to judicial borrowing of international and comparative legal materials might appear mystifying. Outside the United States, judicial globalization of this sort is all but taken for granted. Leading national courts in this regard cut across all imaginable lines: India, Canada, Zimbabwe, Hong Kong, South Korea, and Botswana all borrow from legal sources outside their borders. Some states, most notably South Africa, constitutionally require reference to international and comparative law for domestic interpretation.[83] Last, and here not least, other courts of other states frequently cite the case law of the U.S. Supreme Court, including, among others, the Irish Supreme Court and the UK House of Lords.[84]

As in so many other areas, the U.S. Supreme Court approaches the matter with ambivalence. This had not always been true. For over a century the Court relied extensively on international and foreign sources (at least for common law in the latter case) before entering an isolationist phase, which it only lately appears to be leaving.[85] With the exception of *Fujii*, the American judiciary pointedly declined to rely on international human rights instruments in the post–World War II civil rights struggle even though NAACP lawyers at least initially provided courts with the opportunity. Recently, the Supreme Court in particular has again embraced non-U.S. legal materials in certain high-profile cases. That embrace, however, remains, tentative and contested. Widely noted have been recent allusions to outside sources in important decisions on privacy,[86] affirmative action,[87] and the death penalty.[88]

Wide, too, has been the opposition. Some objections have come from within the judiciary itself. Other objections have come from more expected quarters, such as the academy, the executive, and the legislature—in the last case, even to the point of a congressional bill to prohibit judicial reliance on foreign law.[89] There are various rationales behind this opposition, ranging from the ease with which unfamiliar sources can be manipulated to the concern that looking abroad may diminish certain fundamental rights at home. But by far the greatest source of hostility flows from a potent mix of American exceptionalism and democratic theory. The Constitution of the United States, and the laws made pursuant thereto, derive their force from the positive consent of the American people. Interpreting U.S. law with reference to international and comparative standards empowers an unelected judiciary to privilege the views of outsiders at the expense of the American people, and so is inconsistent with our fundamental conceptions of self-government. At no time does this inconsistency become more insufferable than when unelected judges apply a Constitution ordained by "We the People of the United States" to invalidate laws enacted by our elected representatives based upon legal materials in whole or in part foreign to American democracy. Put in European terms, the practice suffers from a near-total "democratic deficit."[90]

The United States Supreme Court has cited "foreign law" with gusto since the early days of the republic. As used here, "foreign" means "international" law, whether treaties or customs, as well as comparative sources, such as the jurisprudence of other national courts, and common-law jurisdictions especially. Often the Court's invocation of foreign law has been tightly cabined, as in cases that turned on "the law of nations" or demanded the application of other nations' jurisprudence on conflict-of-laws grounds.

Yet, to a surprising degree, the federal courts also relied on foreign law when applying purely domestic standards. What all this meant, to what extent it has continued, and its relevance to current practices are questions to which scholars are only now turning.[91]

Nonetheless, for the past several generations the conventional wisdom has been that the Supreme Court has been parochial, or at least a net exporter of legal ideas rather than an importer—that is, until recently.[92] In the past several years, U.S. justices and judges have begun to "borrow" foreign law in a series of high-profile cases that have required interpretation of the Constitution on many of the most controversial issues of the day. Not surprisingly, the combination of what appears to be a new practice, arriving with the adjudication of hot-button controversies, has drawn strident opposition.

Among the most telling examples occurred when Justice Stevens made the barest reference to global practice (or nonpractice) in *Atkins v. Virginia*, where he observed: "Within the world community, the imposition of the death penalty for crimes committed by mentally retarded offenders is overwhelmingly disapproved."[93] That passing comment drew the extended wrath of Chief Justice Rehnquist and Justice Scalia, jurists who acknowledged reference to evolving domestic traditions, however grudgingly. Justice Scalia in particular put his contempt on full display: "But the Prize for the Court's Most Feeble Effort to fabricate 'national consensus' must go to its appeal (deservedly relegated to a footnote) to the views of . . . members of the so-called 'world community.' . . . Irrelevant are the practices of the 'world community,' whose notions of justice are (thankfully) not always those of our people."[94]

The type of judicial globalization that Justice Scalia attacked has continued to infiltrate the United States nonetheless.[95] To great fanfare the Court, or at least individual justices, has cited international and comparative law sources in a number of recent and high profile cases.[96] In *Lawrence v. Texas*, the Court relied in part on European Human Rights Court jurisprudence when declaring unconstitutional a state law criminalizing sodomy.[97] For Justice Ginsburg, international human rights treaties mattered in deciding to uphold law school affirmative action programs.[98] As noted, the Court, however fleetingly, referred to comparative law in voiding the death penalty for the mentally challenged.[99] Though this is less widely noted, Justice Breyer looked to European Union practice in seeking, unsuccessfully, to justify federal "commandeering" of local officials.[100]

As with globalization in general, the phenomenon—and the reactions to it—promises only to continue. In *Roper v. Simmons*, the Court not only declared that the execution of prisoners convicted of capital crimes committed as minors violated the Eighth Amendment's prohibition on "cruel and unusual punishment,"[101] but Justice Kennedy's majority opinion also did so with a discrete section devoted to both international human rights instruments and comparative practice, including discussion of the International Covenant on Civil and Political Rights and the Convention on the Rights of the Child, as well as a global survey of state practice.[102] On cue, sharp disagreement and defense followed both within and outside the Court. Justice Scalia's dissent reserved special disdain for the majority's reliance on international and comparative materials, declaring: "Though the views of our own citizens are essentially irrelevant to the Court's decision today, the views of other countries and the so-called international community take center stage,"[103] and continuing: "That American law should conform to the laws of the rest of the world—ought to be rejected out of hand."[104] While the Court's most recent term did not produce any fresh examples of judicial borrowing on this scale, it did show the Court engaged in an exceptionally careful interpretation of rights protections in treaties that the United States has ratified. The most noted example is *Hamdan v. Rumsfeld*, in which the Court held, among other things, that Common Article 3 of the Geneva Conventions, at the very least incorporated into domestic law by Congress in the Uniform Code of Military Justice, affords protections to alleged members of al-Qaeda.[105]

Outside the Court the debate continued as Justices Scalia and Breyer famously joined issue in a debate at the U.S. Association of Constitutional Law.[106] American scholars, as will be discussed, have done the same. Congress did so as well, and not for the first time—that body more than once ominously considered a bill that would have prohibited the federal judiciary from committing similar sins in the future.[107]

Perhaps most important of all, the question of the legitimacy of judicial globalization arose during the hearings for two recent justices. Chief Justice Roberts appeared to betray a degree of Scalia-like skepticism without committing himself. To take the most suggestive example, he firmly rejected the possibility of relying on a hypothetical interpretation of the U.S. Constitution by a German judge. Roberts mentioned two concerns with regard to reliance on foreign precedents to interpret the U.S. Constitution: first, "democratic theory," suggesting that only the views of those who participate in American democratic processes should count; second, the concern that "relying on foreign precedent doesn't confine judges" to the extent that domestic precedent does.[108] Of course, even the most wild-eyed internationalist has yet to make an argument that goes that far, which is almost certainly one reason the nominee felt he could oppose it without causing anyone offense. The signal was nonetheless clear enough. Justice Alito left less to the imagination. He summed up his views on constitutional interpretation by stating simply, "We have our own law. We have our own traditions. We have our own precedents. And we should look to that in interpreting our Constitution."[109]

The path ahead may be even less promising than even these statements suggest. The replacement of Justice Kennedy with Brett Kavanaugh, whatever else it augurs, heralds a near-complete reversal with regard to the use of foreign legal materials. As foreign relations scholar Stephen Vladeck points out, Justice Kennedy "routinely looked to international law in interpreting, among other texts, the Eighth Amendment." But, he adds, "Kavanaugh, in contrast, has consistently questioned the relevance of international law in shaping the executive's war powers and construing legislative authorizations."[110] Kavanaugh's questioning came in controversial opinions that specifically dealt with whether the Constitution incorporated international law limits rather than using international law and comparative law as an interpretive guide to the Constitution itself. The appointee's record on the one issue, however, does not exactly bode well with regard to the other.[111]

The ongoing rise of such judicial isolationism makes defenses of the Supreme Court's reliance on international and comparative sources all the more imperative. Such defenses have been made, not least by some of the Supreme Court justices themselves.[112] Few, however, have met the democratic objections head-on, though there are important exceptions. Most notable in this regard is Jamie Meyerfeld, who argues that reference to and application of international human rights enhances domestic constitutional government.[113] Still, justifications have mainly defended the general utility of referencing additional sources rather than the specific legitimacy of referencing sources from outside the U.S. legal system.[114] The defenses to date fall short. They fail to grapple with legitimate concerns about the practice. In consequence, they offer no reasons for those opposed to this practice to reconsider their resistance.

Those reasons at this point should come as no surprise. Judicial globalization first draws support from Founding commitments. Subsequent constitutional custom, far from undermining reference to foreign legal materials, powerfully confirms it. The effects of modern international relations, finally, confirm that courts should draw upon their global counterparts to keep pace with executive officials and legislators around the world doing much the same thing to mutually empower themselves.

Start at the beginning, with Founding commitments. There is ample evidence to suggest that the Founding generation, especially its Federalist leadership, held the law of nations in sufficient regard as to create a presumption that the Constitution should be interpreted consistently with international law where possible.[115] A parallel idea with regard to statutes under the *Charming Betsy* canon has, in fact, been settled doctrine almost since the Founding. Were the appropriateness of resort to foreign legal materials to have been approved by the Founding generation, then this practice would be as democratic as the Constitution itself.

As set forth earlier, the rule enunciated in *Charming Betsy* requires U.S. judges interpreting ambiguous federal statutes to adopt a plausible meaning that avoids conflict with international law over an interpretation that would result in an international law violation. [116] In a somewhat softer version, the canon has remained part of U.S. foreign relations law ever since.[117] Marshall's opinion did not elaborate the basis for the canon that bears its name. Yet Marshall's very authorship suggests an originalist foundation. A young but significant member of the Virginia Ratifying Convention, Marshall commonly articulated mainstream Federalist defenses of the new Constitution.[118] Marshall, in short, articulated views widely held by the Constitution's supporters in the state conventions who ordained and established the document as the nation's supreme law.

Let there be no mistake that arguing for the application of a *Charming Betsy* rule to the *Constitution* is a bold if not audacious claim. For starters, current debate centers on the mere use of foreign legal materials when interpreting the Constitution. A constitutional *Charming Betsy* canon could actually accord such sources dispositive weight, at least if two requirements were met. First, the constitutional provision or doctrine at issue, as with statutes, would have to be ambiguous. In addition, a constitutional *Charming Betsy* rule further would require consistency with comparative law only when global practice reflected the type of international consensus that raises a norm to international custom. Put another way, when comparative legal materials reflect near-universal practice, they reflect not just enlightening factoids about what other nations do but actual customary international law. *Roper*, in noting the world's overwhelming rejection of the juvenile death penalty, was on the road to putting this type of rule in place.[119]

A constitutional *Charming Betsy* rule is audacious in another sense. Curtis Bradley has explained why through focusing, appropriately enough, upon separation of powers. An internationalist presumption applied to statutes is subject to formal democratic check by the president and Congress, who can make clear their intent to depart from international law by passing a statute that clearly does so. If the Supreme Court interprets an ambiguous statute to comport with international law, Congress is always free to pass a new one with a clear meaning that would result in an international law violation if it so desires. In this way, the so-called political branches remain free to determine that, in certain instances, violation of international law may better promote justice or, more likely, further U.S. interests in a stable world. As with any statutory presumption, the canon's accommodation of other concerns ultimately bows to the demands of self-government in a fairly straightforward and transparent fashion.[120]

The balance shifts in the constitutional context. Should the Supreme Court interpret an ambiguous constitutional provision in a way that comports with international law, it would be infinitely more difficult to overturn that interpretation even if a clear majority of the nation so desired. This comparative lack of democratic checks in this setting weakens the case of an internationalist presumption from a self-government perspective. It does not mean, however, that the possibility of a democratic response is wholly absent. Dissatisfaction at the polls could always lead to the election of a president and Senate who approved a less internationally inclined judiciary.[121] Then there is the difficult option of constitutional amendment. The possibility of these weaker democratic checks would, at least, provide some justification of a *Charming Betsy* canon in the constitutional context, but not to the same extent as with more readily enacted statutes.

Finally, applying the *Charming Betsy* standard to the Constitution would have to be necessarily bold in another way. Interpreting a statute to be inconsistent with "the law of nations" means, all but by definition, that it violates the international norm. By contrast, interpreting a constitutional right in a manner that diverges from international law may not itself be a violation. Saying that the Eighth Amendment does not bar the juvenile death penalty does not itself bar an international prohibition on the practice. That would occur only if the states or the federal government mandated capital punishment for juvenile offenders. That said, interpreting the Eighth Amendment not to bar the practice would effectively act as an invitation to the states or Congress to violate the international rule. Exactly this occurred with the juvenile death penalty, where a significant minority of states persisted with the practice. It follows that in the constitutional setting, the *Charming Betsy* canon should be strengthened as a prophylactic measure to head off such violations.

Bold claims ideally should have firm foundations. As noted, the *Charming Betsy* canon itself, which applies only to statutes, has at least formally been settled for centuries and likely goes back further to reflect a Founding understanding. Even more important, then, becomes the question "Were 'We the People' understood to have anticipated a version of the same idea for the Constitution?" There is reason to suppose that "We the People" did just that—or were understood to have done so. Toward this end, it is worth reviewing the relevant Founding commitments with which this study began, as well as more specific evidence.

The law of nations exerted an enormous influence over the Founding generation in part because the "science" of government proceeded together with the "science" of international law. Historians and legal scholars commonly reference Vattel, Burlamaqui, Puffendorf, and Grotius as comparable to Locke, Montesquieu, and Blackstone in their influence on American thinkers.[122] Among others, Franklin, Hamilton, Jefferson, Jay, and John Adams cited the work of the era's great international jurists, and not only for international propositions. As Bernard Bailyn notes, "In pamphlet after pamphlet the American writers cited . . . Grotius, Puffendorf, Burlamaqui, and Vattel on the laws of nature and of nations, and on the principles of government."[123]

The law of nations and domestic constitutional thought complemented one another in purpose, method, and result. Each project sought, among other things, to reconcile and develop general propositions about law and government with consideration of actual human and institutional behavior—with constitutional thought focusing on the place of the individual, and international law on the place of the relatively new nation-state. This parallel orientation led not only to substantial cross-fertilization but also to mutually reinforcing conclusions. This is not to ignore the primacy of national sovereignty, perhaps the chief legacy of international law during this period. Yet sovereignty—especially the idea that how states treated those subject to its jurisdiction within its borders was generally not a concern of international law—did not then mean the same type of impermeable barriers that the concept would come to mean later for at least two reasons. First, the principles of justice that informed the law of nations also informed domestic thought precisely because of the two projects' parallels. Second, Vattel's work in particular emphasized a fairly robust conception of both legal and moral obligations nations assumed with regard to established international law rules.[124]

Independence augmented this theoretical commitment to international law for several practical reasons. The revolutionary act of the American people assuming "among the Powers of the Earth, the separate and Equal Station to which the Laws of Nature and Nature's God entitle them"[125] of necessity reoriented thinking about the direct applications of international law from questions of how constituent units fit within an empire to the place of the new republic itself within the law of nations. In addition, Vattel, especially, sought to adapt the classical law of nations in ways that promoted the interests of comparatively weak republics in the face of aggrandizing empires.[126] Relatedly, the United States' violations of its treaty obligations as a result of the Confederation Congress's inability to secure the compliance of the several states posed a tangible threat to national security by giving the Great Britain and other powers the pretext to commit their own violations, often with military force.

It would fall to the Federal Constitution to determine how far to translate the general affinity for the law of nations seen so far into lasting imperatives. As is a basic feature of U.S. foreign relations law, the document itself deals with international law—and foreign affairs generally—in a scattered fashion. Nor does the text deal specifically with the matter at hand—that is, the interpretive weight for international law; this is the type of textual gap that is a common feature of constitutional law in general. Added up, however, the various specific provisions demonstrate an internationalist bent. Most striking, of course, is the treaty clause.[127] Significant as well was the further decision to facilitate treaty-making by involving the executive and omitting the House of Representatives while impeding involvement in conflict by vesting the war power in Congress. Worth remembering, in addition, is Article III's express grant of jurisdiction for maritime and admiralty cases as well as for an array of possible cases involving foreign envoys and nations. On a strict reading, of course, these provisions may be seen as exhaustive, and so leave no place for judicial appeal to international law in other instances. The larger context, however, suggests that these clauses instead reflect a more general commitment.

Such a commitment specifically emerges in the Federal Convention debates. Although the delegates did not discuss international law frequently, the statements they made reveal a pronounced affinity. Madison set the tone in focusing upon the volatile mix of the states' violations of international law and national security. Critiquing the rival Pinckney Plan, Madison asked, "Will it prevent those violations of the law of nations & of Treaties which if not prevented must involve us in the calamities of foreign wars? . . . The existing confederacy does not sufficiently provide against this evil."[128] Whatever their differences, moreover, Madison and Pinckney both supported Madison's pet dream of a congressional veto on state legislation, in part as a way to police local laws violating treaty commitments in particular.[129] To Congress, moreover, was given the power to "define and punish Piracies and Felonies committed on the high Seas, and Offences against the Law of Nations."[130]

The ratification debates—for many originalists the most authoritative source—address the need for the nation to play the part of good international citizen both more clearly and more extensively. Two venerable sources must suffice to convey the general picture. One is the ratification debates in Virginia, which dealt with international law and foreign relations more thoroughly than any other state. Despite sharp disagreements over questions such as whether the treaty-making process safeguarded regional interests, Federalists and anti-Federalists alike agreed on the necessity of the United States honoring its specific obligations and comporting with the law of nations generally.[131] In one colloquy, one of the Constitution's defenders went so far as to assure opponents that the executive and Senate could not make a treaty ceding territory without approval of Congress because such an action would violate the law of nations.[132]

The Federalist, that popular chestnut source, likewise stresses the urgency for good international citizenship.[133] As in the Virginia debates, certain passages proceed fairly far down the road. While he stopped short of a *Charming Betsy* presumption for the Constitution, John Jay, for example, clearly anticipated the rule that the federal courts shall expound customary international law, even though the Constitution itself makes no express incorporation. Arguing for the primacy of the national government in foreign affairs, Jay declared that "treaties, as well as the law of nations, will always be expounded in one sense, and executed in the same manner" by the federal judiciary, as opposed to the thirteen judiciaries of the several states.[134]

Then again, perhaps constitutional custom slowly but inexorably moved away from this initial orientation. As it is, the Founding merits further study, whether on the question of a constitutional *Charming Betsy* rule or with regard to the use of foreign legal materials more generally. Conversely, "further study" concerning the Supreme Court's practice for the last two centuries has already in large measure proceeded. In a landmark study, Sarah Cleveland has addressed—if not exactly the issue of a constitutional *Charming Betsy* canon—then the more general question of whether and to what extent the justices have drawn upon international law and foreign legal materials in constitutional analysis. Her "thorough, though not exhaustive" comprehensive survey conclusively demonstrates that the practice is multifaceted and longstanding.[135]

The Court's longstanding use of international law and related sources in constitutional analysis falls into three general categories. The first comprises cases in which the Constitution's text refers to international law or legal concepts. Direct references include the treaty power; Congress's authority to "define and punish Offenses against the Law of Nations"; and the states' ability to enter into international "Compacts" subject to congressional approval. Among references to international legal terms or concepts are war, military commissions, admiralty, citizenship, and foreign commerce.[136] Not surprisingly, examples date to the early republic. *Ware v. Hylton*,[137] applying the 1783 Treaty of Paris in 1796, is among the earliest. Such recent cases as *Zivotofsky*, dealing with a contested Jerusalem, passports, and the power to recognize a nation-state,[138] show that the Court's resort to international law is alive and well.

Much the same pattern holds for the Court's use of international law as a background principle for constitutional analysis. Among other reasons, it has done so to determine borders and territoriality; aspects of "sovereignty" such as regulating immigration; and analogizing the relationship between the several states with the law regulating nation-states. Once again, exemplary cases date back to the nation's earliest days and continue into this century.[139]

Most relevant to the modern pushback, the Court has long and consistently drawn upon international law to interpret constitutional rights. Here the range is truly wide. Justices have turned to international law when applying "Fifth and Sixth Amendment criminal protections, habeas corpus, Fourteenth Amendment citizenship, freedom of contract, due process in the personal jurisdiction and foreign taxation contexts, the application of individual rights in the territories, and extraterritorial limits on the scope of individual rights protections."[140] Add to this analysis of the takings clause, Thirteenth Amendment involuntary servitude, the Eighth Amendment prohibition against "cruel and unusual Punishment," and procedural and substantive due process.[141] The custom, moreover, has been as time-honored as it has been far-reaching. Notable opinions go at least as far back as the early nineteenth-century decision *Ogden v. Saunders*, in which Justice Bushrod Washington observed that the law of contractual rights and obligations derives from the law of nations.[142] As noted, examples continue up to such cases as *Lawrence* and *Roper*—the very decisions that have prompted calls for the Court to turn a blind eye to international legal materials on the ground that they are somehow deeply at odds with American constitutionalism.

Like other areas involving judicial foreign affairs authority, modern international relations offers a further reason for judicial empowerment. Assume, as argued earlier, that executive officials directly interacting with their counterparts worldwide have left judges running a distant second, while legislators around the globe are barely in the race.[143] It follows that any judicial practice that helps make up the distance should not only be permitted but outright encouraged. Or at least this is so in any system that remains committed to separation of powers and the corollary of relative balance among the branches of government. It follows with that much more force in systems in which the executive for other reasons has already become dangerously dominant. If anything, the case is more obvious when viewed in negative terms. Executive branches around the world have used the tools of globalization in a world of disaggregated states to outstrip their domestic competitors. In that light, it appears all but perverse to deny the judiciary, as it invades foreign affairs, parallel tools of globalization that might help maintain the very balance that separation of powers seeks to establish.

CHAPTER TWELVE

Conclusion

RESTORING THE JUDICIARY to its proper place in foreign affairs comports with Founding understandings. It accords with subsequent constitutional tradition that has stalled but not yet changed course. It is, finally, ever more urgent in light of the modern workings of international relations. For all these reasons, the position the Supreme Court staked out in the *Youngstown* case should endure as a source of judicial resolve. To the extent it does, it may be offered with pride in places such as China, where the rule of law, constitutionalism, and separation of powers remain grassroots aspirations yet deemed officially to be threats.

Then again, the proper course may well no longer be practical. Whether legitimate or not, matters may have proceeded too far to be reversed. Exactly this concern animated *Youngstown*, or at least Justice Jackson's signal concurrence, in the first place. This foreboding, then and now, bears two interrelated aspects. First, the executive could have become so powerful already that matters have passed the point of no return. Individuals and institutions do not readily give away authority once secured. It may be that the modern presidency has already drawn sufficient power into its "impetuous vortex"[1] that neither Congress nor—the focus of this study—the courts, could either check it or, much less, wrest it back, even if they did prove willing and able to do so. Second, even if it is not too late, all the forces that have rendered an over-powerful executive a threat remain in place. Madison set out certain factors, including the advantage of individual presidential command or collective legislative action. Justice Jackson added others that by now are familiar, including national party politics, an executive's ability to dominate the press, and, most of all, concerns about national security and foreign affairs. To add to these preoccupations, this examination has sought to point out the nature of modern international relations. It may be a contribution of sorts to point out an emerging challenge. But should the process be inexorable, and should the challenge in short order become insurmountable, then any prescription is beside the point. To put it bluntly, what a recent attorney general said about the Geneva Conventions arguably applies to the judiciary as a check to the abuse of power in foreign affairs: the developments that created the problem render the solution "quaint" and "obsolete."[2]

And yet. The nation's rise as a world power, the corollary shift toward national power, and the growing primacy of the executive, far from heralding the eclipse of judicial foreign affairs power may instead serve as the trigger for its restoration. This more hopeful possibility is precisely the reason Justice Jackson undertook sounding the alarm about the dangers of the modern presidency. As noted, Jackson's *Youngstown* concurrence is often taken to secure the possibility that ongoing constitutional custom may provide the executive a source of legitimate authority, much as Justice Frankfurter's own concurrence is seen to have done. The Supreme Court gave Jackson just this reading by ostensibly adopting his framework thirty years later in *Dames & Moore v. Regan*.[3] But in truth, Jackson's real aim was to alert first Congress, and then the courts, to the practical consequences of inaction in the face of executive assertions that appeared concerning as long as half a century ago. His effort rested on the truism that democracies are notoriously slow to awaken to threats but, once roused, can also be especially effective in meeting grave challenges. For that reason, a quiescent Congress was his principal audience. He nonetheless called upon his fellow judges to undertake their responsibilities as well, presidential claims of national security and foreign affairs expertise notwithstanding. He sought to do so precisely by highlighting the growth of the American executive, and he did this after casting his net more widely to consider the recent constitutional histories of Europe, the dangers of executive authority outside law made by parliamentary deliberations and adjudicated by independent courts.[4]

For all its singularity, the Trump administration in this regard merely doubles down on a problem already long in the making. How his tenure will end defies rational prediction. How it began, however, has offered a litany of potential, alleged, and actual instances of presidential overreach beyond the imagination of the executive's staunchest critics—or, for that matter, defenders—especially in foreign affairs: the "Muslim ban"; a border wall to be paid through declaration of a national emergency when not financed by Congress or by another sovereign state; the restoration of torture; a ban on transgendered military personnel; withdrawal from the global climate regime; continuing military intervention in the Middle East without clear congressional authorization; cover-up of collusion with a foreign state in a presidential election; and initiation of hostilities with a newly-minted nuclear power. Whatever else they portend, these actions illustrate the dangers of an out-of-control executive as never before. Ideally, they should trigger checks both from within the executive branch and from Congress. Whether they will, or will do so sufficiently, is another matter.

Regardless of the answer to that question, the main argument of this study remains. Assuming that anything resembling a constitutional commitment to separation of powers still holds, clearly a key part of the solution to the imbalance of authority among the three branches of government is the judiciary in general, and the Supreme Court, literally, above all. This assumption rests on, among other things, an initial understanding that applies as fully to foreign as to domestic matters, has on balance been confirmed rather than repealed by subsequent constitutional tradition, and has further been rendered more urgent in light of the workings of modern international relations. To play its necessary and proper role will require a recommitment by the judiciary in several regards. Such a recommitment first of all will mean hearing cases even though, or perhaps better, precisely because, they implicate foreign affairs. It will further require, once a case is taken up, "saying what the law is" without deferring to other parts of the government simply because the matter deals with foreign affairs. The recommitment advocated here will also mean, at the very least, a more accommodating stance to the applications of international law protecting fundamental rights.

But even if these solutions should yet be timely, they themselves are open to a variant of the initial objection. The presidency may still be sufficiently powerful to counter the judiciary as a check in foreign affairs, not so much because its growth has reached a point of no return but because no one has a greater capacity to shape the courts than the executive. This capacity, moreover, falls within the executive's enumerated power to appoint federal judges with the advice and consent of the Senate. Presidents of either party have every incentive to nominate judges whom they believe will err on the side of executive power in constitutional controversies. The incentive is that much greater in foreign affairs, where executives have pressed the vision that came to be embodied in *Curtiss-Wright* decades before that decision was handed down. As in so many other areas, the Trump administration commenced by raising the stakes. Of course, that executive's first encounters with the courts resulted in unprecedented personal attacks on federal judges who dared to apply the law against White House policies in foreign affairs—in particular, the attempted ban on immigration from majority-Muslim nations. Entirely consistent with these assaults is filling the judicial vacancies left open by the Senate's refusal to confirm the appointments made by President Obama. More consistent still is the ideology that unites the nominees that the Trump administration has put forward. Not surprisingly, one key criterion is a predilection to defer to the executive, especially in matters of foreign affairs and national security.[5] The point applies in particular to Justice Gorsuch and, more obviously still, to Brett Kavanaugh.[6]

What point, then, in calling upon the courts to reclaim their historic roll when the appeal is destined to fall upon deaf ears? Direr still, would it not be worse for such judges to follow this volume's advice, reach out, and hear foreign-affairs-related cases only to produce decisions that confirm executive assertions?

Against such jurists' objections are corresponding responses. First, presidential nominations, particularly to the Supreme Court, are always subject to what might be termed the "Brownell effect." The name refers to Herbert Brownell, attorney general under President Eisenhower. It was under Brownell's stewardship that Ike famously nominated Earl Warren and William Brennan to the high court.[7] Ever since, the two have been talismanic examples of justices who did not behave as expected. Eisenhower never went so far as to say that his two biggest mistakes in office were sitting on the Supreme Court, a story that endures despite having been refuted.[8] Warren and Brennan nonetheless proved to be far more progressive than the executive who appointed them. Enough other examples exist before and after. Justices Harry Blackmun, Stevens, and Souter also turned out to be more liberal than Presidents Nixon, Ford, or George H. W. Bush anticipated. And just to cite one earlier example, striking is the concern about executive power shown by Robert Jackson, who was, after all, attorney general for Franklin Roosevelt. Of course, the extent to which judicial appointments diverge from presidential expectations can be exaggerated. The point remains, however, that the insulation of life tenure has the potential of mitigating a proexecutive bias even in a judiciary nominated by Donald Trump.

Second, likewise exaggerated is the fear that the courts will still remain deferential enough to the executive to produce bad precedents, and would do less damage by not taking foreign-affairs-related cases in the first place. Justice Jackson, with typical eloquence, made this point not in *Youngstown* but in *Korematsu*, the Japanese internment case. Better, he wrote, not to take the case at all than render an abusive government measure into a judicial precedent.[9] Within the Supreme Court, the justices often act on this assumption through the practice of "defensive denial." Typically, the Court hears cases when four of the nine vote to grant "cert"—formally, a writ of certiorari. According to the Court's internal rules, a case merits cert when there is a lower court split on the interpretation of federal law or simply when a case involves obvious national importance. Not infrequently, however, a justice will vote against hearing a "certworthy" case if he or she believes that any decision that would likely result would undermine a precedent that should stand or would otherwise send the law in the wrong direction. Better to render no decision than a bad one.

Though far from trivial, this concern is overblown for several reasons. To begin with, the Constitution is rightly premised on the idea that having a potential institutional check is better than not having none at all. Taken to its conclusion, worry that the courts may produce bad precedents becomes an argument for not having courts in the first place. Yet at least with the judiciary, and a judiciary willing to take cases properly before it, there remains the potential for a check on government abuse. Without it, that potential vanishes.

All things being equal, institutional loyalty also mitigates the potential for decisions that do more harm than good. Separation of powers proceeds on the notion that the members of the different branches of government will usually seek to expand, or at the very least defend, their power. "Ambition," as Madison's oft-quoted observation posits, "must be made to counteract ambition."[10] The judiciary may not always be counted on to avoid bad precedents when it comes to considering the relative powers of Congress and the executive, the federal government, and the states, or even the scope of individual rights. Judges tend to be more reliable when defending their own authority. Early conceptions of judicial review applied more forcefully when courts sought to defend their jurisdiction. Scholars such as Larry Kramer[11] and Mark Tushnet[12] have forcefully argued that defense over time has become offense, as the Supreme Court in many areas has expanded its power well beyond early practice. This tendency may well explain why the courts have resisted the political branches' aggrandizement in foreign affairs as long and as well as they have. Equipped with a restored understanding of their role, that resistance should persist and, ideally, prevail.

At least the Supreme Court, moreover, can more readily overrule itself than the rest of the federal judiciary for the simple reason that it does not consider itself bound by the edicts of any other tribunal when construing federal law. In *National League of Cities v. Usery*,[13] for example, the Court upheld the fiction of state sovereignty against federal regulation. Just nine years later, in *Garcia v. San Antonio MTA*,[14] it reversed itself. Likewise, in *Bowers v. Hardwick*[15] the Court rejected the idea that the Constitution protected the right to same-sex consensual relations. A decade later, in *Lawrence v. Texas*,[16] it effectively upheld exactly that right.

Finally, the Court itself is susceptible to correction should the populace become sufficiently mobilized. The election of a new executive can result in different judicial nominations, however much some of those nominated may not perform as expected. On a grander scale, the American people may unite even further against the Court's constitutional vision to produce a formal amendment under Article V, as has formally happened four times in our history,[17] or what Bruce Ackerman termed a "constitutional moment," either of which fundamentally alter the Constitution as previously understood.[18]

Objections aside, a restoration of the judiciary to its proper role in foreign affairs carries an additional benefit that literally goes beyond our borders. Of course, reestablishing the balance among the branches of the U.S. government in the area in which that balance is most tipped would be no small feat. But return to consider the effects in places like China. In this regard, a case such as *Youngstown* illustrates the potential that constitutional separation of powers offers to the many human rights advocates and democratic reformers in such authoritarian regimes who sacrifice for a system that can limit the excesses of rulers, especially when undertaken in the name of national security and projecting strength abroad. For exactly this reason, *Youngstown* and what it represents made for a better introductory case in Beijing than *Marbury*, and for exactly this reason the increasingly authoritarian regime of Xi Jinping condemned "western constitutionalism."[19] China, moreover, is hardly alone. Increasingly, the United States confronts of world of strong men, regimes in which executive power overawes legislatures, courts, and fundamental rights, from Russia to Hungary to Egypt to Turkey to Venezuela. Justice Jackson's protean *Youngtown* concurrence noted the emergence of a similarly dangerous world disorder. He did so there to draw lessons for applying the U.S. Constitution. Yet he could just as easily have projected his insights abroad. Today not a few commentators argue that the nation has lost its influence as an exemplar of democratic, constitutional values for a host of reasons, most recently the prospect of an unqualified, ill-informed, and unstable chief executive. It follows, however, that in the converse possibility lies hope. To the extent that the United States reclaims its commitment to balanced government, of which judicial engagement in foreign affairs is a piece, it will also reclaim its influence and appeal as a model for like-minded nations in a stable world order.

Whether we are considering the domestic or the foreign benefits of this approach, Justice Jackson deserves the last word, just as he merited the first: "It is the duty of the Court to be the last, not first, to give ... up"[20] its responsibility to confront political powers that undermine the Constitution and, with it, the idea of free government under the law.

NOTES

Chapter One: Introduction

1. XIANFA (1982) (China). On courageous Chinese legal activists who have tried raising the xianfa in court, *see* Martin S. Flaherty, Introduction, *Facing the Unraveling of Reform: Domestic and International Perspectives on the Changing Role of China's Rights Lawyers*, 41 FORDHAM INTERNATIONAL LAW JOURNAL 1091 (2018); Eva Pils, HUMAN RIGHTS IN CHINA: A SOCIAL PRACTICE IN THE SHADOWS OF AUTHORITARIANISM (2018); Sida Liu and Terrance C. Halliday, CRIMINAL DEFENSE IN CHINA: THE POLITICS OF LAWYERS AT WORK (2016); Mark Jia, *China's Constitutional Entrepreneurs*, 64 AMERICAN JOURNAL OF COMPARATIVE LAW 619 (2016); Teng Biao, *The Sun Zhigang Incident and the Future of Constitutionalism: Does the Chinese Constitution Have a Future?* (occasional paper, Centre for Rights and Justice, Faculty of Law, the Chinese University of Hong Kong, Dec. 30, 2013). *See also* Yan Lin and Tom Ginsburg, *Constitutional Interpretation in Lawmaking: China's Invisible Constitutional Enforcement Mechanism*, 63 AMERICAN JOURNAL OF COMPARATIVE LAW 467 (2015) (arguing that the Chinese Constitution plays a coordinating role within the party-state despite its unenforceability); Eric C. Ip, *The Supreme People's Court and the Political Economy of Judicial Empowerment in Contemporary China*, 24 COLUMBIA JOURNAL OF ASIAN LAW 367 (2011) (discussing the evolution of the Supreme People's Court's expansion of power); Larry Cata Backer, *A Constitutional Court for China Within the Chinese Communist Party: Scientific Development and a Reconsideration of the Institutional Role of the CCP*, 43 SUFFOLK UNIVERSITY LAW REVIEW 593 (2010) (discussing the debate over the Chinese power of constitutional review).

2. 5 U.S. 137 (1803).

3. 343 U.S. 579 (1952).

4. Adam Liptak, *The Reach of War: Penal Law; Legal Scholars Criticize Memos on Torture*, NEW YORK TIMES, June 25, 2004, http://www.nytimes.com/2004/06/25/world/the-reach-of-war-penal-law-legal-scholars-criticize-memos-on-torture.html?_r=0.

5. THE FEDERALIST No. 75 at 452 (Alexander Hamilton) (Clinton Rossiter ed., 1961).

6. THE FEDERALIST No. 78 at 465 (Alexander Hamilton) (Clinton Rossiter ed., 1961).

7. *See, e.g.*, Anthony J. Bellia, Jr. and Bradford R. Clark, THE LAW OF NATIONS AND THE UNITED STATES CONSTITUTION (2017); Jack Goldsmith, POWER AND CONSTRAINT: THE ACCOUNTABLE PRESIDENCY AFTER 9/11 (2012); Andrew Kent, *Congress's Under-Appreciated Power to Define and Punish Offenses Against the Law of Nations*, 85 TEXAS LAW REVIEW 843 (2007); Julian Ku, *The Prospects for the Peaceful Co-existence of Constitutional and International Law*, 119 YALE LAW JOURNAL ONLINE 15 (2009); Saikrishna Bangalore Prakash, IMPERIAL FROM THE

BEGINNING: THE CONSTITUTION OF THE ORIGINAL EXECUTIVE (2015); Eric A. Posner and Adrian Vermeule, THE EXECUTIVE UNBOUND: AFTER THE MADISONIAN REPUBLIC (2011); Michael D. Ramsey, THE CONSTITUTION'S TEXT IN FOREIGN AFFAIRS (2007); John C. Yoo, CRISIS AND COMMAND: A HISTORY OF EXECUTIVE POWER FROM GEORGE WASHINGTON TO GEORGE W. BUSH (2010).

8. *See, e.g.*, Bruce Ackerman, THE DECLINE AND FALL OF THE AMERICAN REPUBLIC (2010); Curtis A. Bradley and Martin S. Flaherty, *Executive Power Essentialism and Foreign Affairs*, 102 MICHIGAN LAW REVIEW 545 (2004); David M. Golove and Daniel J. Hulsebosch, *A Civilized Nation, the Early American Constitution, the Law of Nations, and the Pursuit of International Recognition*, 85 NEW YORK UNIVERSITY LAW REVIEW 932 (2010); Heidi Kitrosser, RECLAIMING ACCOUNTABILITY: TRANSPARENCY, EXECUTIVE POWER, AND THE U.S. CONSTITUTION (2015); Thomas Lee, *The Safe-Conduct Theory of the Alien Tort Statute*, 106 COLUMBIA LAW REVIEW 830 (2006); Julian Mortenson, *Executive Power and the Discipline of History*, 78 UNIVERSITY OF CHICAGO LAW REVIEW 377 (2011); Deborah Pearlstein, *After Deference: Formalizing the Judicial Power in Foreign Relations Law*, 159 UNIVERSITY OF PENNSYLVANIA LAW REVIEW 784 (2010); David Rudenstine, THE AGE OF DEFERENCE: THE SUPREME COURT, NATIONAL SECURITY, AND THE CONSTITUTIONAL ORDER (2016); Gordon Silverstein, IMBALANCE OF POWER: CONSTITUTIONAL INTERPRETATION IN THE MAKING OF FOREIGN POLICY (1996); David L. Sloss, THE DEATH OF TREATY SUPREMACY: AN INVISIBLE CONSTITUTIONAL CHANGE (2016); Beth Stevens and Paul Hoffman, *International Human Rights Cases Under State Law and in State Courts*, 3 UC IRVINE LAW REVIEW 9 (2013).

9. Stephen Breyer, THE COURT AND THE WORLD: AMERICAN LAW AND THE NEW GLOBAL REALITIES (2015).

10. *See* Harold Hongju Koh, THE TRUMP ADMINISTRATION AND INTERNATIONAL LAW (2018); Koh, *The Legal Adviser's Duty to Explain, in* THE ROLE OF LEGAL ADVISERS IN INTERNATIONAL LAW (Andraž Zidar and Jean-Pierre Gauci eds., 2016); Koh, THE NATIONAL SECURITY CONSTITUTION: SHARING POWER AFTER THE IRAN-CONTRA AFFAIR (1990).

11. *See* chapter 2.

12. *See* chapter 3.

13. *See* chapter 4.

14. *See* Louis Fisher, SUPREME COURT EXPANSION OF PRESIDENTIAL POWER: UNCONSTITUTIONAL LEANINGS 5 (2017) ("It was not until World War II that we first see American scholars trumpeting the need for bold and unchecked presidential leadership").

15. Legal casebooks in U.S. foreign relations law typically feature lower court decisions in significantly greater numbers than do their constitutional law counterparts, which tend to focus on more obviously domestic matters. *See, e.g.*, FOREIGN RELATIONS LAW (Curtis A. Bradley and Jack L. Goldsmith eds., 6th ed. 2017).

16. Speech given by Attorney General Edwin Meese III before the American Bar Association on July 9, 1985.

17. *See, e.g.*, Martin S. Flaherty, *History Right? Historical Scholarship, Original Understanding, and Treaties as "Supreme Law of the Land,"* 99 COLUMBIA LAW REVIEW 2095 (1999) (arguing for the need for greater historical exploration than that

used by the legal community); John C. Yoo, *Globalism and the Constitution: Treaties, Non-Self-Execution, and the Original Understanding*, 99 COLUMBIA LAW REVIEW 1955 (1999) (retracing the seventeenth- and eighteenth-century British political history); Martin S. Flaherty, *History "Lite" in Modern American Constitutionalism*, 95 COLUMBIA LAW REVIEW 523 (1995) (exploring the narrow historical context most legal scholars have used to analyze the Founding); Edmund S. Morgan, INVENTING THE PEOPLE: THE RISE OF POPULAR SOVEREIGNTY IN ENGLAND AND AMERICA (1988); H. Jefferson Powell, *Rules for Originalists*, 73 VIRGINIA LAW REVIEW 659 (1987); Martin S. Flaherty, Note, *The Empire Strikes Back: Annesley v. Sherlock and the Triumph of Imperial Parliamentary Supremacy*, 87 COLUMBIA LAW REVIEW 593 (1987); Liam S. O'Melinn, Note, *The American Revolution and Constitutionalism in the Seventeenth-Century West Indies*, 95 COLUMBIA LAW REVIEW 104 (1995). *See also* Julian Davis Mortenson, *Article II Vests the Executive Power, Not the Royal Prerogative*, 119 COLUMBIA LAW REVIEW __ (2019).

18. Bruce Ackerman, THE FAILURE OF THE FOUNDING FATHERS: JEFFERSON, MARSHALL, AND THE RISE OF PRESIDENTIAL DEMOCRACY (2005).

19. George Santayana, THE LIFE OF REASON: REASON IN COMMON SENSE 284 (1905); NATIONAL LAMPOON'S ANIMAL HOUSE (1978).

20. *See* Annette Gordon-Reed, THE HEMINGSES OF MONTICELLO: AN AMERICAN FAMILY (2009).

21. For a sampling of work on the Founding generation, *see* Michael J. Klarman, THE FRAMERS' COUP: THE MAKING OF THE UNITED STATES CONSTITUTION (2016); Martin S. Flaherty, *History "Lite" in Modern American Constitutionalism*, 95 COLUMBIA LAW REVIEW 523 (1995); John Phillip Reid, CONSTITUTIONAL HISTORY OF THE AMERICAN REVOLUTION (1986–93) (the project consists of four volumes: 1 THE AUTHORITY OF RIGHTS [1986]; 2 THE AUTHORITY TO TAX [1987]; 3 THE AUTHORITY TO LEGISLATE [1991]; 4 THE AUTHORITY OF LAW [1993]); Forrest McDonald, NOVUS ORDO SECLORUM: THE INTELLECTUAL ORIGINS OF THE CONSTITUTION (1985); Gordon S. Wood, THE CREATION OF THE AMERICAN REPUBLIC, 1776–1787 153–54 (1969); Bernard Bailyn, THE IDEOLOGICAL ORIGINS OF THE AMERICAN REVOLUTION (1967); Edmund S. Morgan and Helen M. Morgan, THE STAMP ACT CRISIS: PROLOGUE TO REVOLUTION (1953).

22. David McCulloch, JOHN ADAMS (2001); R. B. Bernstein, THE EDUCATION OF JOHN ADAMS (forthcoming 2019).

23. THE FEDERALIST No. 78 at 466–69 (Alexander Hamilton) (Clinton Rossiter ed., 1961); *see also* Bruce Ackerman, 1 WE THE PEOPLE: FOUNDATIONS (1991).

24. For a sampling of perspectives, *see* Martin S. Flaherty, *Historians and the New Originalism: Contextualism, Historicism, and Constitutional Meaning*, 94 FORDHAM LAW REVIEW 905 (2015); Randy Barnett, RESTORING THE LOST CONSTITUTION: THE PRESUMPTION OF LIBERTY 94–96 (2014); Keith E. Whittington, *Originalism: A Critical Introduction*, 82 FORDHAM LAW REVIEW 378 (2013); Flaherty, *History "Lite"*; McDonald, NOVUS ORDO; Willi P. Adams, THE FIRST AMERICAN CONSTITUTIONS: REPUBLICAN IDEOLOGY AND THE MAKING OF THE STATE CONSTITUTIONS IN THE REVOLUTIONARY ERA (1980); Wood, CREATION 153–54; Jack N. Rakove, ORIGINAL MEANINGS: POLITICS AND IDEAS IN THE MAKING OF THE CONSTITUTION (1996).

25. *Youngstown*, 343 U.S. at 634–35 (Jackson, J., concurring).

26. Jack M. Balkin, LIVING ORIGINALISM 6–7 (2011).

27. Martin S. Flaherty, *"But Maybe Everything That Dies Someday Comes Back,"* 33 CONSTITUTIONAL COMMENTARY 9 (2018).

28. *See* Ronald Dworkin, LAW'S EMPIRE (1986); *see also* Ronald Dworkin, *The Arduous Virtue of Fidelity: Originalism, Scalia, Tribe, and Nerve*, 65 FORDHAM LAW REVIEW 1249 (1997).

29. Eighteenth-century commentators used both the terms "English constitution" and "British constitution." Technically, the term for the framework in place after the 1707 Act of Union uniting England, Wales, and Scotland into the Kingdom of Great Britain should be "British constitution." While it should be emphasized that, substantively, the principles to which writers referred were those developed under the English constitution, I shall defer to the Act of Union and refer to the constitution after 1707 as the "British constitution."

30. On English, British, and imperial constitutionalism in the late seventeenth and early eighteenth centuries, *see* Martin S. Flaherty, *The Empire Strikes Back:* Annesley v. Sherlock *and the Triumph of Imperial Parliamentary Supremacy*, 87 COLUMBIA LAW REVIEW 593 (1987).

31. *Youngstown*, 343 U.S. at 610 (Frankfurter, J., concurring).

32. William Michael Treanor, *Fame, the Founding, and the Power to Declare War*, 82 CORNELL LAW REVIEW 695 (1997); *see also* John C. Yoo, *The Continuation of Politics by Other Means: The Original Understanding of War Powers*, 84 CALIFORNIA LAW REVIEW 167 (1996); Louis Fisher, PRESIDENTIAL WAR POWER (1995); John Hart Ely, WAR AND RESPONSIBILITY: CONSTITUTIONAL LESSONS OF VIETNAM AND ITS AFTERMATH 3–10, 139–52 (1993); Harold Hongju Koh, THE NATIONAL SECURITY CONSTITUTION: SHARING POWER AFTER THE IRAN-CONTRA AFFAIR 74–77 (1990); Leonard W. Levy, ORIGINAL INTENT AND THE FRAMERS' CONSTITUTION 30–53 (1988); Charles A. Lofgren, *On War-Making, Original Intent, and Ultra-Whiggery*, 21 VALPARAISO LAW REVIEW 53 (1986); Francis D. Wormuth and Edwin B. Firmage, TO CHAIN THE DOG OF WAR: THE WAR POWER OF CONGRESS IN HISTORY AND LAW 17–28 (1986); Edward Keynes, UNDECLARED WAR: TWILIGHT ZONE OF CONSTITUTIONAL POWER 31–40 (1982); W. Taylor Reveley III, WAR POWERS OF THE PRESIDENT AND CONGRESS: WHO HOLDS THE ARROWS AND THE OLIVE BRANCH? 50–115 (1981); Abraham D. Sofaer, WAR, FOREIGN AFFAIRS AND CONSTITUTIONAL POWER: THE ORIGINS 25–38 (1977); Arthur M. Schlesinger, Jr., THE IMPERIAL PRESIDENCY 1–26 (1973); Charles A. Lofgren, *War-Making Under the Constitution: The Original Understanding*, 81 YALE LAW JOURNAL 672 (1972); Raoul Berger, *War-Making by the President*, 121 UNIVERSITY OF PENNSYLVANIA LAW REVIEW 29 (1972); William Van Alstyne, *Congress, the President, and the Power to Declare War: A Requiem for Vietnam*, 121 UNIVERSITY OF PENNSYLVANIA LAW REVIEW 1 (1972); Alexander M. Bickel, *Congress, the President and the Power to Wage War*, 48 CHICAGO KENT LAW REVIEW 131 (1971).

33. Curtis A. Bradley and Trevor W. Morrison, *Historical Gloss and the Separation of Powers*, 126 HARVARD LAW REVIEW 411 (2012).

34. *Cf.* Larry Kramer, THE PEOPLE THEMSELVES: POPULAR CONSTITUTIONALISM AND JUDICIAL REVIEW (2004).

35. Edmund Burke, REFLECTIONS ON THE REVOLUTION IN FRANCE (1790).

36. *Youngstown*, 343 U.S. at 610 (Frankfurter, J., concurring).

37. *Youngstown*, 343 U.S. at 593, 610 (Frankfurter, J., concurring).

38. 299 U.S. 304 (1936).

39. Fisher, SUPREME COURT EXPANSION 69–78; Louis Fisher, THE LAW OF THE EXECUTIVE BRANCH: PRESIDENTIAL POWER 3 (2014).

40. 343 U.S. 579 (1952).

41. *See generally* A. V. Dicey, INTRODUCTION TO THE STUDY OF THE LAW OF THE CONSTITUTION (1889); Bruce Ackerman, *The New Separation of Powers*, 113 HARVARD LAW REVIEW 633 (2000).

42. *See* Daniel Abebe and Eric A. Posner, *The Flaws of Foreign Affairs Legalism*, 51 VIRGINIA JOURNAL OF INTERNATIONAL LAW 507 (2011); Eric A. Posner and Cass R. Sunstein, *Chevronizing Foreign Relations Law*, 116 YALE LAW JOURNAL 1170 (2007).

43. Anne-Marie Slaughter, A NEW WORLD ORDER (2004).

44. *Id. see also* Robert O. Koehane and Joseph S. Nye, Jr., *The Club Model of Multilateral Cooperation and Problems of Democratic Legitimacy, in* EFFICIENCY, EQUITY, AND LEGITIMACY: THE MULTILATERAL TRADING SYSTEM AND THE MILLENNIUM 3 (Roger B. Porter, Pierre Sauve, Arvind Subramanian, and Americo Beviglia Zampetti eds., 2001).

45. Erwin Chemerinsky, CLOSING THE COURTHOUSE DOOR: HOW YOUR CONSTITUTIONAL RIGHTS BECAME UNENFORCEABLE 114–36 (2017); Rudenstine, THE AGE OF DEFERENCE at 4–8; Kent Greenawalt, INTERPRETING THE CONSTITUTION 146–50 (2015).

46. Koh, THE TRUMP ADMINISTRATION AND INTERNATIONAL LAW 2, 12, 148–52.

Chapter Two: Inventing Separation of Powers

1. John Phillip Reid, CONSTITUTIONAL HISTORY OF THE AMERICAN REVOLUTION, 4 vols. (1986–93); Robert L. Schuyler, PARLIAMENT AND THE BRITISH EMPIRE: SOME CONSTITUTIONAL CONTROVERSIES CONCERNING IMPERIAL JURISDICTION (1929); Charles H. McIlwain, THE AMERICAN REVOLUTION: A CONSTITUTIONAL INTERPRETATION (1923). *See also* Barbara A. Black, *The Constitution of Empire: The Case for the Colonists*, 124 UNIVERSITY OF PENNSYLVANIA LAW REVIEW 1157 (1976); Liam S. O'Melinn *The American Revolution and Constitutionalism in the Seventeenth-Century West Indies*, 95 COLUMBIA LAW REVIEW 104 (1995).

2. Bernard Bailyn, THE IDEOLOGICAL ORIGINS OF THE AMERICAN REVOLUTION 22–54 (1967); Forrest McDonald, NOVUS ORDO SECLORUM: THE INTELLECTUAL ORIGINS OF THE CONSTITUTION 57–97 (1985); Gordon S. Wood, THE CREATION OF THE AMERICAN REPUBLIC, 1776–1787 3–45 (1968).

3. John Adams, *The Earl of Clarendon to William Pym, in* 3 THE WORKS OF JOHN ADAMS 477 (Charles F. Adams ed., 1851).

4. Bailyn, IDEOLOGICAL ORIGINS 70.

5. *Id.* at 76.

6. *Id.* at 71.

7. John Adams, *Novanglus and Massachusettensis, in* THE POLITICAL WRITINGS OF JOHN ADAMS 26, 59–70, 74–79 (George Peek Jr. ed., 1954).

8. McDonald, NOVUS ORDO 83.

9. Bailyn, IDEOLOGICAL ORIGINS 274–82.

10. Gordon S. Wood, THE RADICALISM OF THE AMERICAN REVOLUTION 229–43 (1992).

11. Wood, CREATION 65–70.

12. Benjamin Franklin, *Information to Those Who Would Remove to America, in* NOT YOUR USUAL FOUNDING FATHER: SELECTED READINGS FROM BENJAMIN FRANKLIN 278 (Edmund S. Morgan ed., 2006)

13. *Id.*

14. Samuel Adams, 4 THE WRITINGS OF SAMUEL ADAMS 238 (Harry Cushing ed., 1908).

15. Wood, CREATION 150–58.

16. *Id.* at 65–70, 118–24.

17. Bailyn, IDEOLOGICAL ORIGINS 55–93; Edmund S. Morgan, INVENTING THE PEOPLE: THE RISE OF POPULAR SOVEREIGNTY IN ENGLAND AND AMERICA 239–62 (1988).

18. Lance Banning, THE SACRED FIRE OF LIBERTY: JAMES MADISON AND THE FOUNDING OF THE FEDERAL REPUBLIC 84 (1995).

19. "Curtius," untitled essay, THE POLITICAL INTELLIGENCER AND NEW JERSEY ADVERTISER, January 4, 1786.

20. Frederick Chase, *The People the Best Governors, in* 1 A HISTORY OF DARTMOUTH COLLEGE AND THE TOWN OF HANOVER, NEW HAMPSHIRE 654 (John Lord ed., 1891).

21. Reid, 3 CONSTITUTIONAL HISTORY 276–81.

22. *Id.* at 26–27.

23. John Phillip Reid, IN DEFIANCE OF THE LAW: THE STANDING-ARMY CONTROVERSY, THE TWO CONSTITUTIONS, AND THE COMING OF THE AMERICAN REVOLUTION 228–39 (1981).

24. One important exception, to be discussed, was the New York Constitution of 1777.

25. Wood, CREATION 163.

26. Willi Paul Adams, THE FIRST AMERICAN CONSTITUTIONS 178–80 (1980).

27. *2d Charter of Virginia of 1606, sec. XV, reprinted in* CHARTERS OF THE OLD ENGLISH COLONIES IN AMERICA 14 (Samuel Lucas ed., 1850); Bernard Bailyn, ORIGINS OF AMERICAN POLITICS 66–70 (1968).

28. Del. Const. of 1776, art. X; Pa. Const. of 1776, § 20; Vt. Const. of 1777, ch. II, § XVIII; Va. Const. of 1776, para. 9.

29. Del. Const. of 1776, art. VII; Pa. Const. of 1776, § 20; Vt. Const. of 1777, ch. II, § XVIII; Va. Const. of 1776, para. 9.

30. H. Lowell Brown, THE AMERICAN CONSTITUTIONAL TRADITION: COLONIAL CHARTERS, COVENANTS, AND REVOLUTIONARY STATE CONSTITUTIONS, 1578–1780 146–48 (2017); M.J.C. Vile, CONSTITUTIONALISM AND THE SEPARATION OF POWERS 155–59 (2d ed. 1967).

31. N.Y. Const. of 1777, art. XXXIII; N.C. Const. of 1776, art. XXIII; Vt. Const. of 1777, art. XXVII.

32. Ga. Const. of 1777; N.H. Const. of 1776; N.J. Const. of 1776.

33. Morgan, INVENTING THE PEOPLE 245–54; Wood, CREATION 162–73, 209–14.

34. Del. Const. of 1776, art. III; Ga. Const. of 1777, arts. II, III, XVI, XXIII; Md. Const. of 1776, arts. XXV, XXVI, XXVII; Pa. Const. of 1776, §§, 9, 31; Vt. Const. of 1776, ch. II, § X; Va. Const. of 1776, para 5.

35. Del. Const. of 1776, art. XV; Ga. Const. of 1777, art. XXIII; Md. Const. of 1776, art. XXVII; N.Y. Const. of 1777, arts. XXIII, XXVI; Pa. Const. of 1776, §§ 8, 11; Vt. Const. of 1777, ch. II, § X; Va. Const. of 1776, para. 5.

36. Adams, FIRST AMERICAN CONSTITUTIONS 293–307.

37. *Id.* at 248; N.C. Const. of 1776; Declaration of Rights art. XVIII.

38. Pa. Const. of 1776, §§ 13, 14, 15.

39. *See* Saikrishna Bangalore Prakash, IMPERIAL FROM THE BEGINNING: THE CONSTITUTION OF THE ORIGINAL EXECUTIVE 31–34 (2015).

40. Va. Const. of 1776, paras. 14, 10, 8.

41. Va. Const. of 1776, paras. 8, 16.

42. Pa. Const. of 1776, § 19.

43. Robert A. East, JOHN QUINCY ADAMS, THE CRITICAL YEARS, 1785–1794 85 (1962). For a discussion of the Critical Period and the lead-up to the Constitutional Convention, *see* Aaron N. Coleman, THE AMERICAN REVOLUTION, STATE SOVER-EIGNTY, AND THE AMERICAN CONSTITUTIONAL SETTLEMENT, 1765–1800 67–91 (2016).

44. Wood, CREATION 393.

45. *Id.* at 405–9.

46. Moses Hemmenway, A SERMON, PREACHED BEFORE HIS EXCELLENCY JOHN HANCOCK 40 (1784).

47. McDonald, NOVUS ORDO 154; Wood, CREATION 409–29.

48. Wood, CREATION, 449.

49. Vile, CONSTITUTIONALISM 120–22.

50. John Locke, *An Essay Concerning the True Original, Extent, and End of Civil Government, in* TWO TREATISES OF GOVERNMENT 283, 382–83 (Peter Laslett ed., 1967). By "federative" power, Locke meant the conduct of foreign relations (*id.* at 365).

51. W. B. Gwyn, THE MEANING OF THE SEPARATION OF POWERS: AN ANALYSIS OF THE DOCTRINE FROM ITS ORIGIN TO THE ADOPTION OF THE UNITED STATES CONSTITUTION 53–55, 101–11 (1965).

52. Morgan, INVENTING THE PEOPLE 248–55.

53. Baron de Montesquieu, THE SPIRIT OF THE LAWS 151 (Thomas Nugent trans., 1949). *See* Act of Settlement, 1701, 12 & 13 Will. 3; C. H. McIlwain, *The Tenure of English Judges*, 7 AMERICAN POLITICAL SCIENCE REVIEW 217 (1913).

54. Martin S. Flaherty, *The Most Dangerous Branch*, 105 YALE LAW JOURNAL 1725 (1996).

55. Prakash, IMPERIAL FROM THE BEGINNING.

56. Eric Nelson, THE ROYALIST REVOLUTION: MONARCHY AND THE AMERICAN FOUNDING (2017).

57. Montesquieu, THE SPIRIT OF THE LAWS 151.

58. Wood, CREATION 150–61.

59. Ga. Const. of 1777, art. I.

60. N.J. Const. of 1776, art. XX.

61. Wood, CREATION 153–54; *see also* Bruce P. Frohnen and George W. Carey, CONSTITUTIONAL MORALITY AND THE RISE OF QUASI LAW 96–97 (2016).

62. *Quoted in id.* at 441.

63. Thomas Jefferson, *Notes on the State of Virginia, in* THOMAS JEFFERSON: WRITINGS 123, 245 (Merrill D. Peterson ed., 1984).

64. Adams, FIRST AMERICAN CONSTITUTIONS 275.

65. *Id.*

66. *E.g.,* THE FEDERALIST No. 47 at 302–4 (James Madison) (Clinton Rossiter ed., 1961).

67. Aedanus Burke, AN ADDRESS TO THE FREEMAN OF THE STATE OF SOUTH-CAROLINA 23 (1783).

68. James Madison, *Vices of the Political Systems of the United States* (Apr. 1787), *in* 9 PAPERS OF JAMES MADISON 347, 353 (Robert A. Rutland and William M. E. Rachal eds., 1975).

69. Mass. Const. of 1780, pt. I, art. V.

70. Vt. Const. of 1777, ch. II, § XIV.

71. Wood, CREATION 412.

72. Charles C. Thach, THE CREATION OF THE PRESIDENCY, 1775–1789: A STUDY IN CONSTITUTIONAL HISTORY 51–53 (1969).

73. *Id.* at 34–41; Prakash, IMPERIAL FROM THE BEGINNING 33.

74. *E.g.,* the New Hampshire Constitution of 1784.

75. Mass. Const. of 1780, pt. I, art. XXX.

76. *Id.* at pt. II, ch. II, § 1, art. I.

77. *Id.* at pt. II, ch. II, § 1, art. XIII & pt. II, ch. 1, § 1, art. II.

78. N.Y. Const. of 1777, arts. XVII, III.

79. Mass. Const. of 1780, pt. II, ch. II, § 1, art. IX & ch. III, art. I.

80. N.Y. Const. of 1777, arts. XXIII, XXIV.

81. William E. Nelson, 4 THE COMMON LAW IN AMERICA: LAW AND THE CONSTITUTION ON THE EVE OF INDEPENDENCE, 1735–1776 117–28 (forthcoming 2018).

82. Austin Scott, *Holmes v. Walton: The New Jersey Precedent,* 4 AMERICAN HISTORICAL REVIEW 456 (1899); Commonwealth v. Caton 8 Va. (4 Call) 5 (1782); Symsbury Case, 1 Kirby 444 (Conn. Superior Ct. 1785); Trevett v. Weeden (R.I. 1786); Bayard v. Singleton 1 N.C. (Mart.) 5 (1787). It should be noted that the court in *Trevett* held unconstitutional an act of the legislature based upon a Rhode Island Constitution which, like its British counterpart, remained as yet unwritten.

83. (N.Y. Mayor's Ct. 1784). *See* Peter Charles Hoffer, RUTGERS V. WADDINGTON: ALEXANDER HAMILTON, THE END OF THE WAR FOR INDEPENDENCE, AND THE ORIGINS OF JUDICIAL REVIEW (2016).

84. Julius Goebel, Jr., 1 THE LAW PRACTICE OF ALEXANDER HAMILTON: DOCUMENTS AND COMMENTARY (1964).

85. N.H. Const. of 1776, para. 3; S.C. Const. of 1776, art. II; Mass. Const. of 1780, pt. II, ch. II, § 1, art. III.

86. Ga. Const. of 1777, art. II; Pa. Const. of 1776, § 2; Vt. Const. of 1777, ch. II, § 1.

87. N.Y. Const. of 1777, arts. X, XI; Mass. Const. of 1780, pt. II, ch. I, § 2, art. I.

88. N.Y. Const. of 1777, art. XVII; Mass. Const. of 1780, pt. II, ch. II, §1, art. I.

89. Wood, CREATION at 435–36, 451–53; Adams, FIRST AMERICAN CONSTITU-TIONS at 271–72.

90. N.Y. Const. of 1777, art. XVIII.

91. Mass. Const. of 1780, pt. II, ch. II, § 1, art. VII.

92. N.Y. Const. of 1777, art. XIX.

93. U.S. Const. art. III, § 1.

94. U.S. Const. art. I, §1, cl.1.

95. Wood, CREATION 521.

96. U.S. Const. art. II, § 2, cls. 1–3; art. II, § 3. *See* Flaherty, *The Most Dangerous Branch*; Curtis A. Bradley and Martin S. Flaherty, *Executive Power Essentialism and Foreign Affairs*, 102 MICHIGAN LAW REVIEW 545 (2004).

97. U.S. Const. art I, § 7, cl. 2.

98. 1 RECORDS OF THE FEDERAL CONVENTION 98 (June 4) (Max Farrand ed., 1966).

99. U.S. Const. art. III, § 1.

100. Abner S. Greene, *Checks and Balances in the Era of Presidential Lawmaking*, 61 UNIVERSITY OF CHICAGO LAW REVIEW 123, 177 (1994).

101. U.S. Const. art. II, § 1, cls. 2–3, *amended by* U.S. Const. amend. XII.

102. 2 RECORDS OF THE FEDERAL CONVENTION 501 (Sept. 4) (Max Farrand ed., 1966).

103. *Id.* at 498–99.

104. 1 RECORDS OF THE FEDERAL CONVENTION at 65 (James Wilson) (June 1) (Max Farrand ed., 1966).

105. U.S. Const. art. II, § 3.

106. U.S. Const. art. I, § 8, cls. 11–18.

107. U.S. Const. art. III, §§ 1–2.

108. *See* William E. Nelson, *MARBURY V. MADISON*: THE ORIGINS AND LEGACY OF JUDICIAL REVIEW (2d ed., 2018); William Michael Treanor, *The* Case of the Prisoners *and the Origins of Judicial Review*, 143 UNIVERSITY OF PENNSYLVANIA LAW REVIEW 491 (1994).

109. U.S. Const. art. III, § 1.

110. U.S. Const. art. II, § 4.

111. Christopher L. Eisgruber, CONSTITUTIONAL SELF-GOVERNMENT 64–78 (1995).

112. U.S. Const. art. III, § 10, cl. 20.

113. U.S. Const. art. VI, cl. 2.

114. Judiciary Act of 1789, ch. 20, 1 Stat. 73.

115. Wood, CREATION 291–92.

116. Treanor, *The* Case of the Prisoners 491–93; *see also* Robert L. Clinton, MARBURY V. MADISON AND JUDICIAL REVIEW 48–55, 166–75 (1989); William W. Crosskey, POLITICS AND THE CONSTITUTION IN THE HISTORY OF THE UNITED STATES 944 (1953) (listing nine Revolutionary-era cases as possible precedents for judicial review); Charles B. Elliot, *The Legislatures and the Courts: The Power to Declare Statutes Unconstitutional*, 5 POLITICAL SCIENCE QUARTERLY 224, 233–39 (1890); Julius Goebel, Jr., 1 HISTORY OF THE SUPREME COURT OF THE UNITED STATES:

ANTECEDENTS AND BEGINNINGS TO 1801 125–42 (1971); Charles G. Haines, THE AMERICAN DOCTRINE OF JUDICIAL SUPREMACY 88–121 (2d ed. 1959).

117. Treanor, *The* Case of the Prisoners at 557 ("Federal judicial review of state legislatures was deemed necessary to ensure consistency with the United States Constitution"); Sylvia Snowiss, JUDICIAL REVIEW AND THE LAW OF THE CONSTITUTION 34, 45–52 (1990).

118. Dred Scott v. Sanford, 60 U.S. 393 (1857).

119. Marbury v. Madison, 5 U.S. (1 Cranch) 137, 177 (1803).

120. 5 U.S. (1 Cranch) 299 (1803).

121. Ackerman, THE FAILURE OF THE FOUNDING FATHERS 188–89.

Chapter Three: Separation of Powers in Foreign Affairs

1. Letter from Thomas Jefferson to George Rogers Clark (Dec. 25, 1780), *in* 4 PAPERS OF THOMAS JEFFERSON 237–38 (Julian P. Boyd ed., 1951).

2. The Declaration of Independence para. 32 (1776).

3. David M. Golove and Daniel J. Hulsebosch, *A Civilized Nation: The Early American Constitution, the Law of Nations, and the Pursuit of International Recognition*, 85 NEW YORK UNIVERSITY LAW REVIEW 932, 946–52 (2010).

4. *See* David Armitage, *The Declaration of Independence and International Law*, 59 THE WILLIAM AND MARY QUARTERLY 39 (2002).

5. Richard B. Morris, THE FORGING OF THE UNION, 1781–1789 32–44 (1987); Edmund S. Morgan, INVENTING THE PEOPLE: THE RISE OF POPULAR SOVEREIGNTY IN ENGLAND AND AMERICA 54–67 (1988).

6. Morgan, INVENTING THE PEOPLE 54–67.

7. *See* David C. Hendrickson, PEACE PACT: THE LOST WORLD OF THE AMERICAN FOUNDING (2003).

8. George C. Herring, FROM COLONY TO SUPERPOWER: U.S. FOREIGN RELATIONS SINCE 1776 35 (2008).

9. *See* Robert Middlekauff, THE GLORIOUS CAUSE: THE AMERICAN REVOLUTION, 1763–1789 (1976).

10. Herring, FROM COLONY TO SUPERPOWER 102–7.

11. Jack N. Rakove, THE BEGINNINGS OF NATIONAL POLITICS: AN INTERPRETIVE HISTORY OF THE CONTINENTAL CONGRESS 185–90 (1979).

12. Articles of Confederation art. VI.

13. Articles of Confederation art. IX.

14. *Id.*

15. *Id.*

16. *Id.*

17. *See* Thomas H. Lee, *Making Sense of the Eleventh Amendment: International Law and State Sovereignty*, 96 NORTHWESTERN UNIVERSITY LAW REVIEW 1027, 1028 (2002).

18. Articles of Confederation art. II.

19. Golove and Hulsebosch, *A Civilized Nation* 954.

20. James Madison, *Vices of the Political Systems of the United States* (Apr. 1787), *in* 9 PAPERS OF JAMES MADISON 347, 348.

21. Frederick W. Marks III, Independence on Trial: Foreign Affairs and the Making of the Constitution 13 (1973).

22. *See* Lee, *Making Sense of the Eleventh Amendment* 1033–45.

23. Treaty of Paris (1783) arts. 1, 2, 3, 7, 8.

24. *Id.* at art. 4.

25. *Id.* at art. 6.

26. Jack N. Rakove, *The Confederation: A Union Without Power, in* Major Problems in the Era of the American Revolution, 1760–1791 415, 422 (Robert D. Brown ed., 1992).

27. *See* Michael J. Klarman, The Framers' Coup: The Making of the United States Constitution 11–12 (2016).

28. Gazette of the State of Georgia, September 6, 1787.

29. Letter from John Adams to John Jay (May 25, 1786), *in* 8 The Works of John Adams 394–95 (Charles F. Adams ed., 1850–56).

30. "The Grand Committee, consisting of Mr. Livermore, Mr. Dante, Mr. Manning, Mr. Johnson, Mr. Smith, Mr. Symmes, Mr. Pettit, Mr. Henry, Mr. Lee, Mr. Bloodworth, Mr. Pinckney and Mr. Houstoun, appointed to report such Amendments to the Confederation, and such Resolutions as it may be necessary to recommend to the several States, for the Purpose of obtaining from them such Powers as will render the Federal Government adequate to the Ends for which it was instituted" (Articles of Confederation art. XIX [Aug. 7, 1786], http://cdn.loc.gov/service/rbc/bdsdcc/19701/19701.pdf).

31. *See* Daniel J. Hulsebosch, *A Discrete and Cosmopolitan Minority: The Loyalists, the Atlantic World, and the Origins of Judicial Review*, 81 Chicago-Kent Law Review 825 (2006).

32. Alexander Hamilton, *The Rutgers Briefs*, Brief No. 6, *in* 1 The Law Practice of Hamilton: Documents and Commentary 331, 368–73 (Julius Goebel, Jr. ed., 1964).

33. *Id.* at 378–79.

34. Golove and Hulsebosch, *A Civilized Nation* 962–67.

35. *Id.* at 963 (*quoting Opinion of the Mayor's Court, in* 1 The Law Practice of Alexander Hamilton at 413).

36. Marks, Independence on Trial 14.

37. *Id.* at 19–24; *see also* Joseph J. Ellis, The Quartet: Orchestrating the Second American Revolution, 1783–1789 84–93 (2015).

38. Brown v. Maryland, 25 U.S. (12 Wheat.) 419, 446 (1827).

39. Marks, Independence on Trial 13.

40. *Id.* at 55–60.

41. *Id.* at 60–66.

42. Golove and Hulsebosch, *A Civilized Nation* 952–62.

43. Letter from William Smith to John Jay (Apr. 1, 1787), *in* 3 Diplomatic Correspondence of the United States of America, 1783–89 67 (1837).

44. John Lord Sheffield, Observations on the Commerce of the American States 199–200 ([1784] 1970).

45. Marks, Independence on Trial 69–72.

46. Ellis, The Quartet 98–99.

47. *Id.* at 86–90.

48. Klarman, THE FRAMERS' COUP 29.

49. THE FEDERALIST No. 48, at 308 (James Madison) (Clinton Rossiter ed., 1961).

50. THE FEDERALIST No. 66, at 390–96 (John Jay) (Clinton Rossiter ed., 1961).

51. THE FEDERALIST No. 48, at 309 (James Madison) (Clinton Rossiter ed., 1961).

52. U.S. Const. art. I, § 8.

53. *See* introduction, n. 32.

54. 2 RECORDS OF THE FEDERAL CONVENTION OF 1787 (Aug. 17) at 318–19 (Max Farrand ed., 1966); *see* John Hart Ely, WAR AND RESPONSIBILITY: CONSTITUTIONAL LESSONS FROM VIETNAM AND ITS AFTERMATH (1993).

55. *See* Stephen M. Griffin, LONG WARS AND THE CONSTITUTION 35 (2013).

56. William Michael Treanor, *Fame, the Founding, and the Power to Declare War* 82 CORNELL LAW REVIEW 695 (1997).

57. U.S. Const. art. II.

58. Andrew Kent and Julian Davis Mortenson, *The Search for Authorization: Three Eras of the President's National Security Power, in* THE CAMBRIDGE COMPANION TO THE U.S. CONSTITUTION 265–66 (Karen Orren and John W. Compton eds., 2018).

59. Curtis A. Bradley and Martin S. Flaherty, *Executive Power Essentialism and Foreign Affairs,* 102 MICHIGAN LAW REVIEW 545, 679–82 (2004).

60. U.S. Const. art. III, §§ 1, 2.

61. Rakove, BEGINNINGS OF NATIONAL POLITICS at 344, *quoting* Charles Thomson, Memorandum (n.d. probably 1784 or 1785); *see* Letter from Alexander Hamilton to George Clinton (June 1, 1783), *in* 3 THE PAPERS OF ALEXANDER HAMILTON 367–72 (Harold C. Syrett and Jacob E. Cooke eds., 1962).

62. U.S. Const. art VI, cl. 2.

63. 2 RECORDS OF THE FEDERAL CONVENTION OF 1787 164–68 (Max Farrand ed., 1966); Letter from James Madison to Thomas Jefferson (Oct. 24, 1787), *in* 12 THE PAPERS OF THOMAS JEFFERSON 270–86 (Julian P. Boyd ed., 1955).

64. Thomas H. Lee, *The Law of Nations and the Judicial Branch,* 106 GEORGE-TOWN LAW JOURNAL 1707 (2017).

65. THE FEDERALIST No. 81 at 487(Alexander Hamilton) (Clinton Rossiter ed., 1961).

66. *Id. See* Thomas Lee, *The Supreme Court as a Quasi-International Tribunal,* 104 COLUMBIA LAW REVIEW 1765 (2004).

67. U.S. Const. art. III, § 2, cl. 1.

68. THE FEDERALIST No. 81 (Alexander Hamilton).

69. Golove and Hulsebosch, *A Civilized Nation* 1004, 1001–10.

70. THE FEDERALIST No. 3 (John Jay).

71. *Id.*

72. *Id.*

Chapter Four: Holding Steady

1. Martin S. Flaherty, *The Neutrality Controversy: Struggling Over Presidential Power Outside the Courts, in* PRESIDENTIAL POWER STORIES (Christopher H. Schroeder and Curtis A. Bradley eds., 2009).

2. *Id.*

3. George Washington, *The Proclamation of Neutrality* (Apr. 22, 1793), available at http://avalon.law.yale.edu/18th_century/neutra93.asp.

4. Louis Fisher, PRESIDENTIAL WAR POWER 27–28 (3d ed. 2013); Chris Edelson, EMERGENCY PRESIDENTIAL POWER: FROM THE DRAFTING OF THE CONSTITUTION TO THE WAR ON TERROR 20–23 (2013).

5. For a criticism of Helvidius's arguments, *see* Saikrishna Bangalore Prakash, IMPERIAL FROM THE BEGINNING: THE CONSTITUTION OF THE ORIGINAL EXECUTIVE 125–26 (2015).

6. Curtis A. Bradley and Martin S. Flaherty, *Executive Power Essentialism and Foreign Affairs*, 102 MICHIGAN LAW REVIEW 545, 682–84 (2004).

7. Flaherty, *Neutrality Controversy*.

8. Washington, *A Proclamation*.

9. *Id.*

10. James Wilson, *Charge to the Jury, quoted in* Francis Wharton, STATE TRIALS OF THE UNITED STATES DURING THE ADMINISTRATIONS OF WASHINGTON AND ADAMS 84 (1849).

11. Flaherty, *Neutrality Controversy*.

12. Edgar J. McManus and Tara Helfman, 1 LIBERTY AND UNION: A CONSTITUTIONAL HISTORY OF THE UNITED STATES 105 (2014).

13. Letter from Thomas Jefferson to John Jay (July 18, 1793) *in* 6 THE DOCUMENTARY HISTORY OF THE SUPREME COURT OF THE UNITED STATES 747–51 (Maeva Marcus ed., 1998).

14. Letter from Supreme Court justices to George Washington (Aug. 8, 1793) *in* 6 THE DOCUMENTARY HISTORY OF THE SUPREME COURT OF THE UNITED STATES 755–57 (Maeva Marcus ed., 1998); Robert G. McCloskey, THE AMERICAN SUPREME COURT 20 (6th ed. 2016); *but see* Prakash, IMPERIAL FROM THE BEGINNING 281–82 (arguing that there is nothing seemingly unconstitutional about extrajudicial advice giving).

15. Letter from Thomas Jefferson to the justices of the Supreme Court (July 18, 1793), *in* 26 PAPERS OF THOMAS JEFFERSON 520 (John C. Catanzariti ed., 1995); *Questions for the Supreme Court, in id.* at 534–35.

16. For general accounts, *see* Thomas P. Slaughter, THE WHISKEY REBELLION: FRONTIER EPILOGUE TO THE AMERICAN REVOLUTION (1986); Saul Cornell, THE OTHER FOUNDERS: ANTI-FEDERALISM AND THE DISSENTING TRADITION IN AMERICA, 1788–1822 195–220 (1999); Andrew Kent and Julian Davis Mortenson, *The Search for Authorization: Three Eras of the President's National Security Power, in* THE CAMBRIDGE COMPANION TO THE U.S. CONSTITUTION 265–66 (Karen Orren and John W. Compton eds., 2018).

17. Act of May 2, 1792, ch. 23, 1 Stat. 264, codified as amended at 10 U.S.C. § 334.

18. George Washington, *A Proclamation* (Aug. 11, 1784), available at http://avalon.law.yale.edu/18th_century/gwproc03.asp.

19. David L. Sloss, Michael D. Ramsey, and William S. Dodge, *International Law in the Supreme Court to 1860, in* INTERNATIONAL LAW IN THE U.S. SUPREME COURT: CONTINUITY AND CHANGE 38 (David L. Sloss, Michael D. Ramsey, and William S. Dodge eds., 2011).

20. Richard J. Regan, A CONSTITUTIONAL HISTORY OF THE SUPREME COURT 10 (2015); Julie Novkov, THE SUPREME COURT AND THE PRESIDENCY: STRUGGLES FOR SUPREMACY 274–75 (2013).

21. Ware v. Hylton, 3 U.S. 199, 277 (1796).

22. Paul Finkleman, *Race and Domestic International Law in the United States*, 17 NATIONAL BLACK LAW JOURNAL 25, 38–43 (2003).

23. Elkison v. Deliesseline, 8 F. Cas. 493 (C.C.D.S.C. 1823) (No. 4,366).

24. *Elkison*, 8 F. Cas. at 495.

25. *Id.*

26. 28 U.S.C. § 1350 (2012).

27. An Act Concerning Letters of Marque, Prizes, and Prize Goods, 2 Stat. 759 (June 26, 1812).

28. *See, e.g.*, *The Adeline*, 13 U.S. (9 Cranch.) 244 (1815).

29. An Act to Protect the Commerce of the United States and Punish the Crime of Piracy, Pub. L. No. 15–77, 3 Stat. 510 (Mar. 3, 1819).

30. Ian W. Toll, SIX FRIGATES: THE EPIC HISTORY OF THE FOUNDING OF THE U.S. NAVY (2006).

31. An Act Further to Suspend the Commercial Intercourse Between the United States and France, and Dependencies Thereof, 2 Stat. 7 (Feb. 27, 1800).

32. Murray v. The Schooner Charming Betsy, 6 U.S. (2 Cranch.) 64, 67 (1804).

33. *Id.* at 64.

34. The Appollon, 22 U.S. (9 Wheat.) 362, 370 (1824).

35. *Id.*

36. Sloss, Ramsey, and Dodge, *International Law* 38.

37. Curtis A. Bradley, INTERNATIONAL LAW IN THE U.S. LEGAL SYSTEM (2d ed. 2015).

38. 11 U.S. 116 (1812).

39. 5 U.S. (1 Cranch) 103 (1801).

40. 6 U.S. 170 (1804).

41. *Id.* at 177.

42. *Id.*

43. *Id.* at 178.

44. Louis Fisher, SUPREME COURT EXPANSION OF PRESIDENTIAL POWER: UNCONSTITUTIONAL LEANINGS 28 (2017).

45. 1 NAVAL DOCUMENTS RELATING TO THE UNITED STATES WARS WITHIN THE BARBARY POWERS 467 (1939).

46. *See generally* Toll, SIX FRIGATES.

47. 12 U.S. 110 (1814).

48. *Id.* at 128.

49. *Id.* at 129

50. Finley Peter Dunne's fictional bartender, Mr. Dooley, stated the point most famously in commenting on the *Insular Cases*, which determined the extent to which constitutional rights applied to territories wrested from Spain during the Spanish-American War: "No matter whether the constitution follows the flag or not, the Supreme Court follows the election returns" (*quoted in* Elmer Ellis, MR. DOOLEY'S AMERICA: A LIFE OF FINLEY PETER DUNNE [1969 ed.]). For a scholarly

articulation, *see* Michael J. Klarman, BROWN V. BOARD OF EDUCATION AND THE CIVIL RIGHTS MOVEMENT (2007).

51. Joel Richard Paul, WITHOUT PRECEDENT: CHIEF JUSTICE MARSHALL AND HIS TIMES 319–25 (2018).

52. United States v. *La Jeune Eugenie*, 26 F. Cas. 832 (Circuit Ct., D. Mass. 1821).

53. *Id.*

54. *Id.*

55. David Sloss, *Judicial Deference to Executive Branch Treaty Interpretations: A Historical Perspective*, 62 NYU ANNUAL SURVEY OF AMERICAN LAW 497 (2007).

56. Letter from Edmund Randolph to Joseph Fauchet (June 13, 1795), *in* AMERICAN STATE PAPERS: FOREIGN RELATIONS 617–18 (Walter Lowrie and Matthew St. Clair Clarke eds., 1833).

57. *See, e.g.*, Fleming v. Page, 50 U.S. (9 How.) 603, 615 (1850) (holding that the president may invade a country that Congress has declared war against, but any conquests made do not enlarge the territory of the United States). For a discussion of the Court's role during the Mexican War, *see* Fisher, SUPREME COURT EXPANSION 37–38.

58. 133 U.S. 258 (1889).

59. *Id.* at 267.

60. 100 U.S. 483 (1880).

61. Duncan Hollis, *Treaties in the Supreme Court, 1861–1900*, *in* INTERNATIONAL LAW IN THE U.S. SUPREME COURT: CONTINUITY AND CHANGE 86 (David L. Sloss, Michael D. Ramsey, and William S. Dodge eds., 2011).

62. Whitney v. Robertson, 124 U.S. 190 (1888).

63. Head Money Cases, 112 U.S. 580, 598–99 (1884) (emphasis added).

64. Reichart v. Felps, 73 U.S. 160, 165–66 (1867).

65. 124 U.S. at 194.

66. Chew Heong v. United States, 112 U.S. 536 (1884).

67. Thomas H. Lee and David L. Sloss, *International Law as an Interpretive Tool in the Supreme Court, 1861–1900*, *in* INTERNATIONAL LAW IN THE U.S. SUPREME COURT: CONTINUITY AND CHANGE 129 (David L. Sloss, Michael D. Ramsey, and William S. Dodge eds., 2011).

68. *Id.* at 163.

69. *Id.* at 129.

70. *In re* Baiz, 135 U.S. 403 (1890).

71. *See, e.g.*, U.S. v. Klein, 80 U.S. 128 (1871); U.S. v. Padelford, 76 U.S. 531 (1869).

72. Prize Cases, 67 U.S. 635, 684 (1863).

73. *Id.* at 670; Regan, A CONSTITUTIONAL HISTORY 43–44.

74. Prize Cases, 67 U.S. 635, at 674, 680.

75. David J. Bederman, *Customary International Law in the Supreme Court, 1861–1900*, *in* INTERNATIONAL LAW IN THE U.S. SUPREME COURT: CONTINUITY AND CHANGE 121 (David L. Sloss, Michael D. Ramsey, and William S. Dodge eds., 2011).

76. *See* Gary Lawson and Guy Seidman, THE CONSTITUTION OF EMPIRE: TERRITORIAL EXPANSION AND AMERICAN LEGAL HISTORY 33–77 (2004).

77. Louis Fisher, *The Mexican War and Lincoln's "Spot Resolutions,"* August 18, 2009, https://www.loc.gov/law/help/usconlaw/pdf/Mexican.war.pdf.

78. Earl M. Maltz, *The Constitution and the Annexation of Texas*, 23 CONSTITU-TIONAL COMMENTARY 391 (2006).

79. *See* Kal Raustiala, DOES THE CONSTITUTION FOLLOW THE FLAG?: THE EVOLUTION OF TERRITORIALITY IN AMERICAN LAW (2010); Carmen F. Randolph, *Constitutional Aspects of the Annexation of Hawaii*, 12 HARVARD LAW REVIEW 291 (1898).

80. 175 U.S. 677, 700 (1900).

81. Novkov, THE SUPREME COURT, 276.

82. *Id.*

83. Bederman, *Customary International Law* 120–21.

84. *Id.* at 122.

85. 71 U.S. 404, 408 (1866).

86. 140 U.S. 453 (1891).

Chapter Five: Curtiss-Wright *versus* Youngstown

1. 299 U.S. 304 (1936).

2. 343 U.S. 579 (1952).

3. The point holds even if it is conceded that Truman was at the time especially unpopular. *See* Stephen M. Griffin, LONG WARS AND THE CONSTITUTION 92 (2013) ("[*Youngstown*] functioned more as a rebuke to an unpopular president who had over-reached than a decisive check that forced the executive branch to reassess what the Cold War was doing to the Constitution").

4. 299 U.S. at 312.

5. *Id.* at 312.

6. *Id.* at 315.

7. *Id.*

8. *Id.* at 316.

9. *Id.* at 318.

10. *Id.*

11. Chae Chan Ping v. United States, 130 U.S. 581 (1889).

12. *Curtiss-Wright*, 299 U.S. at 319.

13. *Id.*

14. *Id.*

15. *Id.* at 320.

16. *Id.*

17. *Id.* at 320.

18. *Id.*

19. Harold Hongju Koh, THE NATIONAL SECURITY CONSTITUTION: SHAR-ING POWER AFTER THE IRAN-CONTRA AFFAIR 94 (1990); *see also* Kimberley L. Fletcher, *Unilateral Executive Power Enshrined in Law: The* Zivotofsky *Court Stays the Course* 37 NORTHERN ILLINOIS UNIVERSITY LAW REVIEW 307, 314 (2017).

20. For a discussion of the historical errors in *Curtiss-Wright*, *see* Louis Fisher, *The Staying Power of Erroneous Dicta: From* Curtiss-Wright *to* Zivotofsky 31 CONSTITU-TIONAL COMMENTARY 149, 159–63, 170–73 (2016).

21. Ruth Wedgewood, *The Revolutionary Martyrdom of Jonathan Robbins* 100

YALE LAW JOURNAL 229 (1990); *see also* Louis Fisher, SUPREME COURT EXPANSION OF PRESIDENTIAL POWER: UNCONSTITUTIONAL LEANINGS 67–69 (2017).

22. *See* Fletcher, *Unilateral Executive Power* at 318.

23. Edward A. Purcell, Jr., *Understanding Curtiss-Wright*, 31 LAW AND HISTORY REVIEW 653, 656 (2013). For a brief biography of Justice Sutherland, *see* David G. Savage, 2 GUIDE TO THE U.S. SUPREME COURT 984–85 (4th ed. 2004).

24. Purcell, *Understanding Curtiss-Wright* at 656.

25. *Id.*

26. *Id.* at 668.

27. *Id.* at 713.

28. 343 U.S. at 583.

29. Patricia L. Bellia, *The Story of the Steel Seizure Case, in* PRESIDENTIAL POWER STORIES 9 (Christopher H. Schroeder and Curtis A. Bradley eds., 2009); *see also* Maeva Marcus, TRUMAN AND THE STEEL SEIZURE CASE: THE LIMITS OF PRESIDENTIAL POWER (1977); *Youngstown at Fifty: A Symposium* 19 CONSTITUTIONAL COMMENTARY 1 (2002).

30. President Truman also personally believed that it was appropriate for the courts to review his executive order. Chris Edelson, EMERGENCY PRESIDENTIAL POWER: FROM THE DRAFTING OF THE CONSTITUTION TO THE WAR ON TERROR 104 (2013).

31. In doing so, the Court rejected the president's argument that democracy needed to be able to effectively respond to modern crises that become manifest at a much greater speed. *See* David Rudenstine, THE AGE OF DEFERENCE: THE SUPREME COURT, NATIONAL SECURITY, AND THE CONSTITUTIONAL ORDER 286–87 (2016).

32. 343 U.S. at 585.

33. *Id.* at 587.

34. *Id.* at 585–86.

35. *Id.* at 589.

36. *Id.* at 593.

37. *Id.* at 610–11.

38. Bellia, *Steel Seizure Case* 2; Fletcher, *Unilateral Executive Power* at 324; Daniel Bodansky and Peter Spiro, *Executive Agreements+*, 49 VANDERBILT JOURNAL OF TRANSNATIONAL LAW 885, 890 (2016) ("The *Youngstown* framework has represented a dominant heuristic for assessing the constitutionality of presidential action in recent decades"). For a discussion of the other, less influential concurrences, *see* Fisher, SUPREME COURT EXPANSION 121–22.

39. 343 U.S. at 634.

40. *Id.*

41. *Id.* at 635.

42. *Id.* at 637.

43. *Id.*

44. The closest he comes is in a footnote that attempts, to some extent, to reconcile *Youngstown* with *Curtiss-Wright*. There Jackson correctly points out that the earlier case involved congressional delegation, not freestanding executive power, and goes on to argue that delegations to the president should be broadly construed when they involve external affairs. *Id.* at 635–36, n. 2.

45. Dames & Moore v. Regan, 453 U.S. 654 (1981). Significantly, the Court at the

same time arguably flipped Jackson's presumptions about congressional silence in a proexecutive direction. *See* chapter 6.

46. 343 U.S. 579 (1952).

47. *Id.* at 651–52.

48. *Id.* at 636–38.

49. *Id.* at 635–36, n. 2.

50. *Id.* at 639.

51. *Id.* at 642.

52. *Id.* at 642–43, n. 10. *See* chapter 4.

53. *Id.* at 654.

54. *Id.* at 655.

55. *Id.* (emphasis added).

Chapter Six: Article III versus the National Security State

1. George C. Herring, FROM COLONY TO SUPERPOWER: U.S. FOREIGN RELATIONS SINCE 1776 484 (2008).

2. Mary L. Dudziak, WAR TIME: AN IDEA, ITS HISTORY, ITS CONSEQUENCES (2012).

3. *See* Herring, FROM COLONY TO SUPERPOWER 436, 482. *See also* Warren I. Cohen, EMPIRE WITHOUT TEARS: AMERICA'S FOREIGN RELATIONS, 1921–1933 (1987); Brian J. C. McKercher, *Reaching for the Ring: The Recent Historiography of Interwar American Foreign Relations*, 15 DIPLOMATIC HISTORY 565–98 (1991); Arthur M. Schlesinger, *Back to the Womb? Isolationism's Renewed Threat*, 74 FOREIGN AFFAIRS (1995).

4. Herring, FROM COLONY TO SUPERPOWER 484.

5. Garry Wills has referred to this phenomenon as a "permanent war in peace": Wills, BOMB POWER: THE MODERN PRESIDENCY AND THE NATIONAL SECURITY STATE 57 (2010); *see also* David Rudenstine, THE AGE OF DEFERENCE: THE SUPREME COURT, NATIONAL SECURITY, AND THE CONSTITUTIONAL ORDER 64–65 (2016).

6. *See* Herring, FROM COLONY TO SUPERPOWER 908–13, 958–63. *See also* Philip Bobbitt, TERROR AND CONSENT: THE WARS FOR THE TWENTIETH CENTURY (2008); Robert Kagan, THE RETURN OF HISTORY AND THE END OF DREAMS (2008); James Mann, RISE OF THE VULCANS: THE HISTORY OF BUSH'S WAR CABINET (2004); Robert A. Divine, *The Persian Gulf War Revisited: Tactical Victory, Strategic Failure*, 24 DIPLOMATIC HISTORY 129 (2004); Michael R. Gordon and Bernard E. Trainor, THE GENERAL'S WAR: THE INSIDE STORY OF THE CONFLICT IN THE GULF (1995); Raymond L. Garthoff, THE GREAT TRANSITION: AMERICAN-SOVIET RELATIONS AND THE END OF THE COLD WAR (1994); Lawrence Freedman and Efraim Karsh, THE GULF CONFLICT, 1990–1991: DIPLOMACY AND WAR IN THE NEW WORLD ORDER (1993).

7. *See, e.g.*, De Lima v. Bidwell, 182 U.S. 1 (1901); Goetze v. United States, 182 U.S. 221 (1901); Dooley v. United States, 182 U.S. 222 (1901); *see also* Gerald L. Neuman, *Whose Constitution?*, 100 YALE LAW JOURNAL 909 (1991).

8. Harold Hongju Koh, THE NATIONAL SECURITY CONSTITUTION: SHARING POWER AFTER THE IRAN-CONTRA AFFAIR 101–5 (1990); *see also* Authorization for Use of Military Force Against Terrorists, S.J. Res. 23, 107th Congress (2001); Authorization for Use of Military Force Against Iraq Resolution of 1991, H.R.J. 77, 102d Congress; Multinational Force in Lebanon Resolution, H.R.J. Res. 364, 98th Congress (1983); Gulf of Tonkin Resolution, H.R.J. Res. 1145, 88th Congress (1964); Joint Resolution to Promote Peace and Stability in the Middle East, H.R.J. Res. 117, 85th Congress (1957); Joint Resolution Authorizing the President to Employ the Armed Forces of the United States for Protecting the Security of Formosa, the Pescadores and Related Positions and Territories of that Area, H.R.J. Res. 159, 84th Congress (1955).

9. The executive branch argued that the deal was valid based in part on the commander in chief clause as well as the president's broad power to act independently regarding foreign policy. The attorney general who wrote this opinion was Robert Jackson, who would later write his famous concurrence in *Youngstown*. Chris Edelson, EMERGENCY PRESIDENTIAL POWER: FROM THE DRAFTING OF THE CONSTITUTION TO THE WAR ON TERROR 64 (2013).

10. *Compare* Harold Hongju Koh, THE NATIONAL SECURITY CONSTITUTION, *with* Rebecca Thorpe, THE AMERICAN WARFARE STATE: THE DOMESTIC POLITICS OF MILITARY SPENDING (2014).

11. It is important to note that such isolationism was not absolute. For example, even after the Spanish-American War, Presidents Roosevelt and Wilson ordered interventions in the Dominican Republic, Mexico, and Haiti. Louis Fisher, SUPREME COURT EXPANSION OF PRESIDENTIAL POWER: UNCONSTITUTIONAL LEANINGS 56–57 (2017). For a discussion of the Supreme Court's role in civil liberties during World War I and the first Red Scare, *see* Arthur H. Garrison, SUPREME COURT JURISPRUDENCE IN TIMES OF NATIONAL CRISIS, TERRORISM, AND WAR: A HISTORICAL PERSPECTIVE 91–120 (2011).

12. Herring, FROM COLONY TO SUPERPOWER at 597–98; *see also* Koh, THE NATIONAL SECURITY CONSTITUTION at 38–40; Arnold A. Offner, ANOTHER SUCH VICTORY: PRESIDENT TRUMAN AND THE COLD WAR, 1945–1953 (2000) James T. Patterson, GRAND EXPECTATIONS: THE UNITED STATES, 1945–1974 (1996); Melvyn P. Leffler, A PREPONDERANCE OF POWER: NATIONAL SECURITY, THE TRUMAN ADMINISTRATION, AND THE COLD WAR (1992); Michael S. Sherry, PREPARING FOR THE NEXT WAR: AMERICA'S PLANS FOR POSTWAR DEFENSE, 1941–1945 (1977); Thomas G. Paterson, SOVIET-AMERICAN CONFRONTATION: POSTWAR RECONSTRUCTION AND THE ORIGINS OF THE COLD WAR (1973).

13. The National Security Act of 1947, 50 U.S.C. §3002 (2013) (formerly cited as 50 U.S.C. §401); *see also* Koh, THE NATIONAL SECURITY CONSTITUTION 102; Saul Landau, THE DANGEROUS DOCTRINE: NATIONAL SECURITY AND U.S. FOREIGN POLICY (1988). The National Security Act also created and defined the duties of the Central Intelligence Agency. NATIONAL SECURITY LAW IN THE NEWS: A GUIDE FOR JOURNALISTS, SCHOLARS, AND POLICYMAKERS 127 (Paul Rosenzweig et al. eds., 2012).

14. Rachel Ward Saltzman, *Executive Power and the Office of Legal Counsel*, 28 YALE LAW & POLICY REVIEW 439, 449–51 (2009).

15. *See, e.g.,* Mary Ann Glendon, A WORLD MADE NEW: ELEANOR ROOSEVELT

AND THE UNIVERSAL DECLARATION OF HUMAN RIGHTS (2001); Townsend Hoopes and Douglas Brinkley, FDR AND THE CREATION OF THE U.N. (1997); Koh, THE NATIONAL SECURITY CONSTITUTION; Edward R. Stettinius, diary entry of September 27, 1944, *in* 1 FOREIGN RELATIONS OF THE UNITED STATES: DIPLOMATIC PAPERS, 1944 842 (Ralph Perkins and Edward Gleason eds., 1966); Edward R. Stettinius, ROOSEVELT AND THE RUSSIANS (1949).

16. George F. Kennan, AMERICAN DIPLOMACY, 1900–1950 95–99 (1951); *see* John Lewis Gaddis, GEORGE F. KENNAN: AN AMERICAN LIFE 494 (2011) (stating that international law, while useful, played a small part in the conduct of foreign diplomacy). According to Louis Henkin, the popular perception that Kennan dismissed international law is overstated. Louis Henkin, HOW NATIONS BEHAVE: LAW AND FOREIGN POLICY 325–29 (1979).

17. U.N. Charter arts. 55–56. *See also* Universal Declaration of Human Rights art. 7, G.A. Res. 217A (III), U.N. Doc. A/810 at 71 (1948); American Declaration of the Rights and Duties of Man, OEA/Ser.L./V.II.23, doc. 21, rev. 6 (1948), *reprinted in* Basic Documents Pertaining to Human Rights in the Inter-American System, OEA/Ser.L.V./II.82, doc. 6, rev. 1 at 17.

18. *See generally* Mary L. Dudziak, COLD WAR CIVIL RIGHTS: RACE AND THE IMAGE OF AMERICAN DEMOCRACY (2000).

19. David L. Sloss, THE DEATH OF TREATY SUPREMACY: AN INVISIBLE CONSTITUTIONAL CHANGE 237–48 (2016); *see also* David L. Sloss, *Taming Madison's Monster: How to Fix Self-Execution Doctrine*, 2015 BYU LAW REVIEW 1691, 1721–33 (2016); Egon Schwelb, *The Influence of the Universal Declaration of Human Rights on International and National Law*, 53 AMERICAN SOCIETY OF INTERNATIONAL LAW PROCEEDINGS 217 (1959); 77 ABA Ann. Rep., 425, 447–48 (1952).

20. William S. Dodge, *Customary International Law in the Supreme Court, 1946–2000, in* INTERNATIONAL LAW AND THE SUPREME COURT: CONTINUITY AND CHANGE 355–57 (David L. Sloss, Michael D. Ramsey, and William S. Dodge eds., 2011); *see also* Theodor Meron and Jean Galbraith, *Nuremberg and Its Legacy, in* INTERNATIONAL LAW STORIES 13 (John E. Noyes, Laura A. Dickinson, and Mark W. Janis eds., 2007); Louis B. Sohn, *The New International Law: Protection of the Rights of Individuals Rather than States*, 32 AMERICAN UNIVERSITY LAW REVIEW 1 (1982); Quincy Wright, *Legal Positivism and the Nuremberg Judgment*, 42 AMERICAN JOURNAL OF INTERNATIONAL LAW 405 (1948).

21. *See* Erie Railroad Co. v. Tompkins, 304 U.S. 64, 78 (1938) (holding that there is no general federal common law and that, in any case, the laws to be applied when rendering a decision should be the laws of the state).

22. Koh, THE NATIONAL SECURITY CONSTITUTION at 135.

23. *See, e.g.*, Bruce Ackerman, *Bush Can't Operate as a One-Man Act*, LOS ANGELES TIMES, December 16, 2001, http://articles.latimes.com/2001/dec/16/opinion/oe-ackerman16.

24. G. Edward White, *The Transformation of the Constitutional Regime of Foreign Relations*, 85 VIRGINIA LAW REVIEW 1 (1999).

25. Paul B. Stephen, *Treaties in the Supreme Court, 1946–2000, in* INTERNATIONAL LAW AND THE SUPREME COURT: CONTINUITY AND CHANGE 321 (David L. Sloss, Michael D. Ramsey, and William S. Dodge eds., 2011).

26. *Id.* at 322.

27. Dodge, *Customary International Law* 353.

28. 3 U.S. 199 (1796) (invalidating a Virginia land statute pursuant to a provision in the 1783 Treaty of Paris under the supremacy clause of the Constitution).

29. American Law Institute, RESTATEMENT (THIRD) OF FOREIGN RELATIONS LAW § 303 (1987). *See also* Michael J. Glennon and Robert D. Sloane, FOREIGN AFFAIRS FEDERALISM: THE MYTH OF NATIONAL EXCLUSIVITY 311 (2016); Michael D. Ramsey, *Executive Agreements and the (Non)Treaty Power*, 77 NORTH CAROLINA LAW REVIEW 133 (1998).

30. Glennon and Sloane, FOREIGN AFFAIRS FEDERALISM at 312.

31. United States v. Belmont, 301 U.S. 324, 331 (1937).

32. United States v. Pink, 315 U.S. 203, 230 (1942).

33. *See, e.g.*, Kolovrat v. Oregon, 366 U.S. 187 (1961) (imputing the right of inheritance under an 1881 treaty with Serbia to the citizens of Yugoslavia); Clark v. Allen, 331 U.S. 503 (1947) (holding that the right to inherit property under a 1923 treaty with Germany had not been abrogated by the war).

34. Zschernig v. Miller, 389 U.S. 429, 441 (1968) (preventing states from "establishing [their] own foreign policy"). *Cf.* Ioannou v. New York, 371 U.S. 30, 32 (1962) (Douglas, J., dissenting) ("Admittedly the several States have traditionally regulated the descent and distribution of estates within their boundaries. This does not mean, however, that their regulations must be sustained if they impair the effective exercise of the Nation's foreign policy.")

35. Crosby v. National Foreign Trade Council, 530 U.S. 363 (2000) (holding that a Massachusetts law designed to undermine military dictatorship in Burma was preempted by a federal statute giving the president wide discretion as to how best to deal with the regime).

36. *See* Foster v. Neilson, 27 U.S. 253 (1829).

37. Fujii v. State of California, 38 Cal.2d 718 (1952).

38. *See* Sloss, THE DEATH OF TREATY SUPREMACY.

39. Brown v. Board of Education, 347 U.S. 483, 495 (1954) (stating that racial segregation in the school systems clearly violated the equal protection clause of the Fourteenth Amendment). *See* Dudziak, COLD WAR CIVIL RIGHTS 95–114.

40. EEOC v. Arabian American Oil Co., 499 U.S. 244, 258 (1991).

41. *See* Perez v. Brownell, 356 U.S. 44 (1958) (recognizing Congress's power to revoke citizenship).

42. *See, e.g.*, Afroyim v. Rusk, 387 U.S. 253 (1967) (holding that a process of denaturalization for citizens who voted in foreign elections violated the Fourteenth Amendment); Schneider v. Rusk, 377 U.S. 163 (1964) (relying upon the Fifth Amendment of the Constitution to strike down a provision of the INA which denaturalized citizens not residing in the country for three years); Kennedy v. Mendoza-Martinez, 372 U.S. 144 (1963) (relying upon procedural guarantees of the Fifth and Sixth Amendments despite noting the presence of international standards).

43. *See* Douglas T. Stuart, CREATING THE NATIONAL SECURITY STATE: A HISTORY OF THE LAW THAT TRANSFORMED AMERICA (2008).

44. For a general discussion of U.S. military detentions during World War II, including the *Quirin* and *Eisentrager* cases, *see* Amanda DiPaolo, ZONES OF TWILIGHT: WARTIME PRESIDENTIAL POWERS AND FEDERAL COURT DECISION MAKING 56–68 (2010).

45. Exec. Ord. No. 9066, February 19, 1942, General Records of the Unites States Government, Record Group 11, National Archives, available at https://www.archives .gov/historical-docs/todays-doc/?dod-date=219.

46. *See* Garrison, SUPREME COURT JURISPRUDENCE 201–29.

47. Pub. L. No. 77–503, 56 Stat. 173 (1942).

48. *Japanese Relocation During World War II*, NATIONAL ARCHIVES, https:// www.archives.gov/education/lessons/japanese-relocation.

49. Hirabayashi v. United States, 320 U.S. 81, 96–99 (1943); *see also* Edelson, EMERGENCY PRESIDENTIAL POWER 86–90.

50. "But hardships are part of war, and war is an aggregation of hardships. All citizens alike, both in and out of uniform, feel the impact of war in greater or lesser measure. Citizenship has its responsibilities as well as its privileges, and in time of war the burden is always heavier. Compulsory exclusion of large groups of citizens from their homes, except under circumstances of direst emergency and peril, is inconsistent with our basic governmental institutions. But when under conditions of modern warfare our shores are threatened by hostile forces, the power to protect must be commensurate with the threatened danger." Korematsu v. United States, 323 U.S. 214, 219–20 (1944).

51. *Id.* at 225 (Roberts, J., dissenting) (stating that this was a case of discrimination based solely on ancestry); *see also id.* at 233 (Murphy, J., dissenting) (stating that this case goes "over the very brink of constitutional power and falls into the ugly abyss of racism").

52. *Id.* at 248

53. For further discussion of the aftermath of *Hirabayashi* and *Korematsu*, *see* Fisher, SUPREME COURT EXPANSION 99–101.

54. *See* Robert J. Pushaw, Jr., *The "Enemy Combatant" Cases in Historical Context: The Inevitability of Pragmatic Judicial Review*, 82 NOTRE DAME LAW REVIEW 1005 (2007).

55. William W. Wiecek, 12 HISTORY OF THE SUPREME COURT OF THE UNITED STATES; THE BIRTH OF THE MODERN CONSTITUTION: THE UNITED STATES SUPREME COURT, 1941–53 306–27 (Oliver Wendell Holmes Devise, 1993).

56. *Ex Parte* Quirin, 317 U.S. 1, 47 (1942). For criticisms of the *Quirin* decision, *see* Edelson, EMERGENCY PRESIDENTIAL POWER 80–81.

57. *In re* Yamashita, 327 U.S. 1 (1946); *Quirin*, 317 U.S. at 45–48.

58. Johnson v. Eisentrager, 339 U.S. 763 (1953).

59. *Ex Parte* Endo, 323 U.S. 283, 297 (1944).

60. *See* Cass R. Sunstein, *Minimalism at War*, 2004 SUPREME COURT REVIEW 47, 83–84.

61. 323 U.S. at 309 (Roberts, J., concurring).

62. David Vine, *The United States Probably Has More Foreign Military Bases Than Any Other People, Nation, or Empire in History*, THE NATION, September 14, 2015, https://www.thenation.com/article/the-united-states-probably-has-more-foreign -military-bases-than-any-other-people-nation-or-empire-in-history/.

63. Reid v. Covert, 354 U.S. 1, 5 (1957).

64. *Id.* at 5, 6.

65. Balzac v. Porto Rico, 258 U.S. 298 (1922); Dorr v. United States, 195 U.S. 138 (1904).

66. *Compare Reid*, 354 U.S. 1, *with In re* Ross, 140 U.S. 143 (1891) (noting that there was a historical precedent which had allowed consular officials to determine how cases were to be held in their territories.)

67. *See* Vincent J. Samar, *The Treaty Power and the Supremacy Clause: Rethinking* Reid v. Covert *in a Global Context*, 36 OHIO NORTHERN UNIVERSITY LAW REVIEW 287, 300–301 (2010).

68. *Reid*, 354 U.S. at 14; *see also* Kal Raustiala, *The Geography of Justice*, 73 FORD-HAM LAW REVIEW 2501 (2005).

69. *See* International Security Advisory Board, Report on Status of Forces Agreements (2015).

70. Francis J. Nicholson, *The Protection of Foreign Property Under Customary International Law*, 6 BOSTON COLLEGE LAW REVIEW 391, 400–404 (1965).

71. Banco Nacional de Cuba v. Sabbatino, 376 U.S. 398 (1964).

72. Banco Nacional de Cuba v. Sabbatino, 307 F.2d 845 (2d Cir. 1962).

73. *Id.* at 407.

74. Bernstein v. N.V. Nederlandsche-Amerikaansche Stoomvaart-Maatschappij, 210 F.2d 375 (2d Cir. 1954).

75. *Sabbatino*, 376 U.S. at 420.

76. *Id.* at 428; *see also* Glennon and Sloane, FOREIGN AFFAIRS FEDERALISM at 251–56.

77. For criticism of the *Sabbatino* decision and the Act of State doctrine, *see* Harold Hongju Koh, *Transnational Public Law Litigation*, 100 YALE LAW JOURNAL 2347 (1991); Michael J. Bazyler, *Abolishing the Act of State Doctrine*, 134 UNIVERSITY OF PENNSYLVANIA LAW REVIEW 325 (1986); Louis Henkin, *The Foreign Affairs Powers of the Federal Courts*, 64 COLUMBIA LAW REVIEW 805 (1964).

78. *See* Kevin J. McMahon, NIXON'S COURT: HIS CHALLENGE TO JUDICIAL LIBERALISM AND ITS POLITICAL CONSEQUENCES 202–4 (2011).

79. New York Times Co. v. United States, 403 U.S. 713 (1971).

80. *See* Nancy Kassop, *Reverse Effect: Congressional and Judicial Restraints of Presidential Power, in* PRESIDENT OR KING? EVALUATING THE EXPANSION OF EXECUTIVE POWER FROM ABRAHAM LINCOLN TO GEORGE W. BUSH 71–72 (Meena Bose ed., 2011).

81. *See id.* at 733–34; *see also* Espionage Act of 1917, 40 Stat. 217.

82. *See* United States v. New York Times Co., 444 F.2d 544 (2d Cir. 1971); *see also* United States v. Washington Post Co., 446 F.2d 1327 (D.C. Cir. 1971).

83. *New York Times*, 403 U.S. at 725.

84. *Id.* at 727–28 (Stewart, J., concurring).

85. *Id.* at 732 (White, J., concurring).

86. S/Res/84, S/1588 (1950); Pub. L. No. 79–264, 59 Stat. 619 (1945).

87. Pub. L. No. 88–408, 78 Stat. 384 (1964).

88. S. Con Res. 64 (1970).

89. For a discussion of instances in which the United States has used military force without declaring war, *see* Ellen C. Collier, Instances of Use of United States Forces Abroad, 1798–1993, Congressional Research Service Report (1993).

90. Orlando v. Laird, 443 F.2d 1039 (2d. Cir. 1971), *cert. denied* 404 U.S. 869 (1971).

91. Mitchell v. Laird, 488 F.2d 611 (D.C. Cir. 1973), *rehearing en banc denied* (1973).

92. *See supra* n. 487 and n. 489.

93. *See, e.g.,* United States v. United States District Court, 407 U.S. 297 (1972) (holding that electronic surveillance for domestic intelligence was not a reasonable exercise of presidential authority, but expressing no opinion regarding the president's surveillance power over foreign activities inside or outside the United States.)

94. Baker v. Carr, 369 U.S. 186; *see* Tara Leigh Grove, *The Lost History of the Political Question Doctrine,* 90 NEW YORK UNIVERSITY LAW REVIEW 1908 (2015).

95. 369 U.S. at 211.

96. United States v. Reynolds, 345 U.S. 1, 10 (1953).

97. *Id.*

98. *See supra.*

99. Republic of Mexico v. Hoffman, 324 U.S. 30 (1945); *Ex Parte* Republic of Peru, 318 U.S. 578 (1943).

100. Luke Ryan, *The New Tate Letter: Foreign Official Immunity and the Case for a Statutory Fix,* 84 FORDHAM LAW REVIEW 1773, 1777–79; *see also* Chimene I. Keitner, *The Forgotten History of Foreign Official Immunity,* 87 NEW YORK UNIVERSITY LAW REVIEW 704 (2012); Ingrid Weurth, *Foreign Official Immunity Determinations in U.S. Courts: The Case Against the State Department,* 51 VIRGINIA JOURNAL OF INTERNATIONAL LAW 915 (2011).

101. Charlton v. Kelly, 229 U.S. 447, 467 (1913).

102. *Id.* at 466–49.

103. Sullivan v. Kidd, 254 U.S. 433, 435–43.

104. Kolovrat v. Oregon, 366 U.S. 187, 194 (1961).

105. *See also* Sumitomo Shoji America, Inc. v. Avagliano, 457 U.S. 176, 180–84 (1982); United States v. Stuart, 489 U.S. 353, 389 (1982).

106. David J. Bederman, *Revivalist Canons and Treaty Interpretation,* 41 UCLA LAW REVIEW 953 (1994). *But see* Robert M. Chesney, *Disaggregating Deference: The Judicial Power of Executive Treaty Interpretation,* 92 IOWA LAW REVIEW 1723 (2006–07).

107. INTERNATIONAL LAW: NORMS, ACTORS, PROCESS: A PROBLEM-ORIENTED APPROACH 225 (Jeffrey L. Dunoff, Steven R. Ratner, and David Wippman eds., 4th ed. 2015).

108. Stephen, *Treaties in the Supreme Court* at 332.

109. 453 U.S. 654 (1981).

110. *See* David Patrick Houghton, U.S. FOREIGN POLICY AND THE IRAN HOSTAGE CRISIS (2015).

111. *Dames & Moore,* 453 U.S. at 662–66.

112. *Id.*

113. *Id.* at 666–68.

114. *Id.* at 669.

115. 50 U.S.C. § 1702(a)(1)(B).

116. 22 U.S.C. § 1732.

117. 453 U.S. at 677.

118. *Id.* at 678.

119. *Id.* at 681.

120. *Id.* at 688.

121. *See* Koh, THE NATIONAL SECURITY CONSTITUTION at 140.

Chapter Seven: The New World Order

1. David Armitage, *The Declaration of Independence and International Law*, 59 WILLIAM AND MARY QUARTERLY 39 (2002).

2. *Cf.* Harold Hongju Koh, *Complementarity Between International Organisations on Human Rights / The Rise of Transnational Networks as the "Third Globalization,"* 21 HUMAN RIGHTS LAW JOURNAL 307 (2000).

3. For a discussion of the history of sovereignty beginning with the ancient world, *see* Jorge E. Núñez, SOVEREIGNTY CONFLICTS AND INTERNATIONAL LAW AND POLITICS: A DISTRIBUTIVE JUSTICE ISSUE 24–33 (2017).

4. Antonio Cassese, INTERNATIONAL LAW 22–24 (2d ed. 2005); *see also* Dieter Grimm, SOVEREIGNTY: THE ORIGIN AND FUTURE OF A POLITICAL AND LEGAL CONCEPT (Belinda Cooper trans., 2015).

5. Emer de Vattel, 2 THE LAW OF NATIONS ch. IV, § 54, 289–90 (Bela Kapossy and Richard Whatmore eds., 2008).

6. Martin S. Flaherty, *History "Lite" in Modern American Constitutionalism*, 95 COLUMBIA LAW REVIEW 523, 535–49 (1996)

7. *See* Ian Brownlie, PRINCIPLES OF PUBLIC INTERNATIONAL LAW 41 (6th ed. 2003).

8. William Blackstone, 1 COMMENTARIES OF THE LAWS OF ENGLAND: A FACSIMILE OF THE FIRST EDITION OF 1765–1769 § 2, 43 (1979).

9. Grimm, SOVEREIGNTY.

10. Thomas Lee, *Theorizing the Foreign Affairs Constitution*; *see also* Robert Trout, *Life, Liberty, and the Pursuit of Happiness: How the* Natural Law *Concept of G. W. Leibniz Inspired America's Founding Fathers*, 6 FIDELIO MAGAZINE 6 (1997).

11. *Reply of the House to Hutchinson's First Message (Mar 1, 1773), in* 1 PAPERS OF JOHN ADAMS 315, 327 (Robert Taylor et al. eds., 1977).

12. Letter from Benjamin Franklin to Charles-Guillaume-Frédéric Dumas (Dec. 9, 1775), *in* 22 THE PAPERS OF BENJAMIN FRANKLIN: MARCH 23, 1775, THROUGH OCTOBER 27, 1776 287–91 (William B. Willcox ed., 1982).

13. 1 THE LAW PRACTICE OF ALEXANDER HAMILTON 282–392 (Julius Goebel ed., 1964); *see also* Forrest MacDonald, ALEXANDER HAMILTON: A BIOGRAPHY 52–57 (1979).

14. Vattel, 1 THE LAW OF NATIONS preliminaries, § 1, 67.

15. *Id. at* § 3, 67.

16. *Id. at* § 4, 68.

17. Chisholm v. Georgia, 2 U.S. 419, 474 (1793) (opinion of Jay, C.J.); *see also* Ware v. Hylton, 3 U.S. 199, 281 (1796) (Wilson, J.) ("When the United States declared their independence, they were bound to receive the law of nations, in its modern state of purity and refinement").

18. *See* 1 Vattel, THE LAW OF NATIONS preliminaries, § 20; Martin Loughlin, *Why Sovereignty?, in* SOVEREIGNTY AND THE LAW: DOMESTIC, EUROPEAN, AND INTERNATIONAL PERSPECTIVES 42–43 (Richard Rawlings et al. eds., 2013).

19. *See* R. R. Palmer, THE AGE OF DEMOCRATIC REVOLUTION: A POLITICAL HISTORY OF EUROPE AND AMERICA, 1760–1800 (2014); Martin Flaherty, *History Right? Historical Scholarship, Original Understanding, and Treaties as "Supreme Law of the Land,"* 99 COLUMBIA LAW REVIEW 2095, 2109–12 (1999).

20. *See* chapter 1.

21. St. George Tucker, VIEW OF THE CONSTITUTION OF THE UNITED STATES: WITH SELECTED WRITINGS 340 (1803).

22. Joseph Story, COMMENTARIES ON THE CONFLICT OF LAWS 12 (1834).

23. Charles E. Magoon on behalf of Elihu Root, REPORTS ON THE LAW OF CIVIL GOVERNMENT IN TERRITORY SUBJECT TO THE MILITARY OCCUPATION BY THE MILITARY FORCES OF THE UNITED STATES 31 (1902).

24. 11 U.S. (7 Cranch) 116, 123 (1812).

25. Berizzi Bros. Co. v. The Pesaro, 271 U.S. 562 (1926).

26. Anne-Marie Slaughter, A NEW WORLD ORDER 12–13 (2004).

27. Hugo Grotius, II DE JURE BELLI AC PACIS ch. 25, § 8, 584 (1625).

28. *See* Tana Johnson, ORGANIZATIONAL PROGENY: WHY GOVERNMENTS ARE LOSING CONTROL OVER THE PROLIFERATING STRUCTURES OF GLOBAL GOVERNANCE 3–10 (2014).

29. *Cf.* Koh, *Complementarity*; Grimm, SOVEREIGNTY; James Turner Johnson, SOVEREIGNTY: MORAL AND HISTORICAL PERSPECTIVES 138–42 (2014); Jean L. Cohen, GLOBALIZATION AND SOVEREIGNTY: RETHINKING LEGALITY, LEGITIMACY, AND CONSTITUTIONALISM 159–222 (2012).

30. *See* Neil Walker, *Sovereignty Frames and Sovereignty Claims, in* SOVEREIGNTY AND THE LAW: DOMESTIC, EUROPEAN, AND INTERNATIONAL PERSPECTIVES 24–28 (Richard Rawlings et al. eds., 2013).

31. Slaughter has developed her previous writings on the subject in A NEW WORLD ORDER (2004).

32. *See, e.g.,* Robert O. Koehane and Joseph Nye, Jr., *Transgovernmental Relations and International Organizations*, 39 WORLD POLITICS 27 (1974).

33. For an argument that sovereignty will survive the challenge of globalization, *see* Stephen D. Krasner, *Think Again: Sovereignty*, FOREIGN POLICY, November 20, 2009, http://foreignpolicy.com/2009/11/20/think-again-sovereignty/.

34. Slaughter, A NEW WORLD ORDER 36–64.

35. *See* Kal Raustiala, *The Architecture of International Cooperation: Transgovernmental Frameworks and the Future of International Law*, 43 VIRGINIA JOURNAL OF INTERNATIONAL LAW 1 (2002).

36. *See* Sydney A. Shapiro, *International Trade Agreements, Regulatory Protection, and Public Accountability*, 54 ADMINISTRATIVE LAW REVIEW 435 (2002).

37. The Independent Commission for Policing in Northern Ireland, A NEW BEGINNING: POLICING IN NORTHERN IRELAND 101 (1999).

38. *Id.*

39. For a discussion of the practice with regard to international human rights law, *see* Association of the Bar of the City of New York and Center for Human Rights and Global Justice, New York University Law School, TORTURE BY PROXY: INTERNATIONAL AND DOMESTIC LAW APPLICABLE TO "EXTRAORDINARY RENDITIONS" (2004).

40. *See* Martin S. Flaherty, *The Most Dangerous Branch*, 105 YALE LAW JOURNAL 1725 (1996).

41. *See* Aida Torres Pérez, *The Internationalization of Lawmaking Processes: Constraining or Empowering the Executive?*, 14 TULSA JOURNAL OF COMPARATIVE AND INTERNATIONAL LAW 1 (2004); *but see* Alasdair Roberts, *Globalization and the*

Growth of Executive Power: An Old Story, 24 INDIANA JOURNAL OF GLOBAL LEGAL STUDIES 497 (2017) (arguing that the issue of executives strengthened by globalization is overstated).

42. Slaughter, A NEW WORLD ORDER 104–6.

43. *See id.* at 104–30.

44. *Id.* at 65. Slaughter earlier has written about this phenomenon extensively. *See* Anne-Marie Slaughter, *Judicial Globalization*, 40 VIRGINIA JOURNAL OF INTERNATIONAL LAW 1103 (2000); Anne-Marie Slaughter, *Court to Court*, 92 AMERICAN JOURNAL OF INTERNATIONAL LAW 708 (1998).

45. Slaughter, A NEW WORLD ORDER 82–99.

46. For a discussion of the use of comparative analysis in the United States, *see* Julia Salvatore et al., *Sotomayor and the Future of International Law*, 45 TEXAS INTERNATIONAL LAW JOURNAL 487 (2009); Lisa Sofio, *Recent Developments in the Debate Concerning the Use of Foreign Law in Constitutional Interpretation*, 30 HASTINGS INTERNATIONAL AND COMPARATIVE LAW REVIEW 131 (2006).

47. *See, e.g.*, Catholic Commission for Justice and Peace in Zimbabwe v. Attorney-General, Judgment No. S.C. 73/93, 14 HUMAN RIGHTS LAW JOURNAL 323 (1993) (surveying comparative and international law in interpreting the Zimbabwean Constitution regarding delay in application of the death penalty).

48. *See, e.g.*, HKSAR v. Ng Kung Siu, [1999] 2 HKC 10 (opinion of the Court of Appeal of Hong Kong).

49. *See, e.g.*, A (FC) and others (FC) v. Secretary of State for the Home Department, [2005] UKHL 71. For a study of the use of foreign law by other courts, *see* David S. Law, *Judicial Comparativism and Judicial Diplomacy*, 163 UNIVERSITY OF PENNSYLVANIA LAW REVIEW 927 (2015).

50. Constitution of the Republic of South Africa art. 39(1) b & c (1996).

51. *See, e.g.*, Vicki C. Jackson and Mark Tushnet, COMPARATIVE CONSTITUTIONAL LAW (3d ed. 2014); Norman Dorsen et al., COMPARATIVE CONSTITUTIONALISM CASES AND MATERIALS (2003).

52. *See* Eyal Benvenisti and George W. Downs, *Democratizing Courts: How National and International Courts Promote Democracy in an Era of Global Governance*, 46 NEW YORK UNIVERSITY JOURNAL OF INTERNATIONAL LAW AND POLITICS 741 (2014).

Chapter Eight: Global Imbalance

1. For a discussion of how disaggregation is also increasing the influence of NGOs, *see* Christopher P. Banks and John C. Blakeman, THE U.S. SUPREME COURT AND NEW FEDERALISM: FROM THE REHNQUIST TO THE ROBERTS COURT 203–7 (2012).

2. Association of the Bar of the City of New York and Center for Human Rights and Global Justice, NYU Law School, TORTURE BY PROXY: INTERNATIONAL AND DOMESTIC LAW APPLICABLE TO "EXTRAORDINARY RENDITIONS" 11–12 (2004).

3. *See* Ian Austen, *Court Overturns Parts of Secrecy Law in Canada*, NEW YORK TIMES, October 20, 2006, http://query.nytimes.com/gst/fullpage.html?res=950DEE DF163FF933A15753C1A9609C8B63.

4. TORTURE BY PROXY at 11–12.

5. Arar v. Ashcroft, 414 F. Supp. 2d 250 (E.D. N.Y. 2006).

6. Arar v. Ashcroft, 532 F.3d 157 (2d Cir. 2008).

7. TORTURE BY PROXY at 11–12.

8. *Id.* For a list of other individuals who have been subject to extraordinary rendition, *see* Amrit Singh, GLOBALIZING TORTURE: CIA SECRET DETENTION AND EXTRAORDINARY RENDITION 30–60 (2013). Singh also lists the foreign governments that have participated in extraordinary rendition programs (62–118). Alan Clarke gives another list of cases of extraordinary renditions that triggered significant legal or policy debates. Alan W. Clarke, RENDITION TO TORTURE 91–116 (2012).

9. For a description of extraordinary rendition and its evolution before and after 9/11, *see* Peter Jan Honigsberg, OUR NATION UNHINGED: THE HUMAN CONSEQUENCES OF THE WAR ON TERROR 179–84 (2009).

10. *Id.*

11. *No Justice for Canadian Rendition Victim Maher Arar*, CENTER FOR CONSTITUTIONAL RIGHTS, November 2, 2009, http://ccrjustice.org/home/press-center/press-releases/no-justice-canadian-rendition-victim-maher-arar-0.

12. TORTURE BY PROXY at 11–12.

13. *Id.* at 11–12.

14. For a discussion of executive transgovernmental networks in North America, *see* Neil Craik and Debora van Nijnatten, *"Bundled" Transgovernmental Networks, Agency Autonomy, and Regulatory Cooperation in North America*, 41 NORTH CAROLINA JOURNAL OF INTERNATIONAL LAW 491 (2016).

15. Anne-Marie Slaughter, A NEW WORLD ORDER 37 (2004).

16. *Id.* at 38. *See* the committee's website at https://www.bis.org/bcbs/.

17. Woodrow Wilson School Policy Task Force, CHINA'S LEADERSHIP TRANSITION AND THE RULE OF LAW IN CHINA 8–9, 137–61 (2015).

18. Karen Ku, *The Role of U.S. Military Engagement in Shaping China's Legal Development on the International Level* (2016) (unpublished B.A. thesis, Princeton University).

19. *See* Graham Ellison and Nathan W. Pino, GLOBALIZATION, POLICE REFORM, AND DEVELOPMENT: DOING IT THE WESTERN WAY? 131–46 (2012).

20. Robert O. Koehane and Joseph S. Nye, Jr., *The Club Model of Multilateral Cooperation and Problems of Democratic Legitimacy, in* EFFICIENCY, EQUITY, AND LEGITIMACY: THE MULTILATERAL TRADING SYSTEM AND THE MILLENNIUM 3 (Roger B. Porter et al. eds., 2001).

21. *Id.* at 4.

22. Slaughter, A NEW WORLD ORDER 47.

23. *See* Anne-Marie Slaughter, *Governing the Global Economy through Government Networks, in* THE ROLE OF LAW IN INTERNATIONAL POLITICS (Michael Byers ed., 2000); *see also* Jacint Jordana, *Transgovernmental Networks as Regulatory Intermediaries: Horizontal Collaboration and the Realities of Soft Power* 670 ANNALS OF THE AMERICAN ACADEMY OF POLITICAL AND SOCIAL SCIENCE 245 (2017).

24. *See* FINCEN's website at https://www.fincen.gov.

25. Slaughter, A NEW WORLD ORDER 54.

26. Woodrow Wilson School Policy Task Force, BUILDING THE RULE OF LAW IN CHINA: IS THERE A ROLE FOR THE UNITED STATES? 9–10 (2014).

27. *See* Helmut Philipp Aust, *Shining Cities on the Hill? The Global City, Climate*

Change, and International Law, 26 EUROPEAN JOURNAL OF INTERNATIONAL LAW 255 (2015) (describing international agreements between cities to combat climate change).

28. http://www.interpol.int/en.

29. https://www.europol.europa.eu.

30. *See* Adam D. M. Swendsen, UNDERSTANDING THE GLOBALIZATION OF INTELLIGENCE (2012).

31. Elizabeth Goitein and David M. Shapiro, REDUCING OVERCLASSIFICATION THROUGH ACCOUNTABILITY (2011).

32. *See* Geoffrey Bennett and Russell L. Weaver, *The Northern Ireland Broadcasting Ban: Some Reflections on Judicial Review*, 22 VANDERBILT JOURNAL OF TRANSNATIONAL LAW 1119 (1989).

33. Committee to Support Chinese Lawyers, LEGAL ADVOCACY AND THE 2011 CRACKDOWN IN CHINA: ADVOCACY, REPRESSION, RESILIENCE (2011).

34. United States Drug Enforcement Agency, *U.S. and Chinese Drug Enforcement Agencies Meet on Synthetic Opioid Efforts* (Sept. 29, 2016), available at https://www.dea.gov/press-releases/2016/09/29/us-and-chinese-drug-enforcement-agencies-meet-synthetic-opioid-efforts.

35. The Associated Press, *U.S. and China Cooperation Strong in Fighting Somali Pirates*, NEW YORK DAILY NEWS, April 19, 2009, http://www.nydailynews.com/news/world/u-s-china-cooperation-strong-fighting-somali-pirates-article-1.361791.

36. Slaughter, A NEW WORLD ORDER 54.

37. *Id.* at 59.

38. *Id.* at 60.

39. *Id.*

40. *Id.*

41. *Id.*

42. THE FEDERALIST No. 48 at 309 (James Madison) (Clinton Rossiter ed., 1961).

43. Youngstown Sheet & Tube Co. v. Sawyer, 343 U.S. 579, 653–54 (1952) (Jackson, J., concurring).

44. THE FEDERALIST No. 70 at 424 (Alexander Hamilton) (Clinton Rossiter ed., 1961).

45. Francis Bacon, MEDITATIONES SACRAE (1597).

46. Harold Hongju Koh, THE NATIONAL SECURITY CONSTITUTION: SHARING POWER AFTER THE IRAN-CONTRA AFFAIR 48–53 (1990).

47. *See, e.g., G20 in Hamburg: Who are the Protesters?*, BBC, July 7, 2017, http://www.bbc.com/news/world-europe-40534768; Margot Hornblower, *The Battle in Seattle*, CNN, November 22, 1999, http://www.cnn.com/ALLPOLITICS/time/1999/11/22/seattle.battle.html.

48. *See* Ian Bremmer, *Why Trump and Sanders Supporters are So Angry About Globalization*, TIME, April 26, 2016, http://time.com/4299604/globalization-free-trade-trans-pacific-partnership/.

49. Slaughter, A NEW WORLD ORDER 221.

50. United States v. Caro-Quintero, 745 F. Supp. 599, 600–605 (C.D. Cal. 1990).

51. Extradition Treaty, May 4, 1978 [1979], United States-United Mexican States, 31 U. S.T. 5059, T.I.A. S. No. 9656.

52. United States v. Alvarez-Machain, 504 U.S. 655, 659–62 (1992).

53. *Id.* at 663–66.

54. *Id.* at 666–70.

55. *Id.* at 687–88 (Stevens, J., dissenting). For a discussion of the application of the Alien Tort Statute to the decision, *see* Julian Ku and John Yoo, TAMING GLOBALIZATION: INTERNATIONAL LAW, THE U.S. CONSTITUTION, AND THE NEW WORLD ORDER 179–88 (2012).

56. THE FEDERALIST No. 48 at 309 (James Madison) (Clinton Rossiter ed., 1961); Martin S. Flaherty, *The Most Dangerous Branch*, 105 YALE LAW JOURNAL 1725 1810–39 (1996).

57. Flaherty, *The Most Dangerous Branch* at 1767–68, 1821–26; *see* Peter M. Shane, *Political Accountability in a System of Checks and Balances: The Case of Presidential Review of Rulemaking*, 48 ARKANSAS LAW REVIEW 161, 212 (1995).

58. U.S. Const. art. I, §§ 2, 3; art. II, §§ 1, 2.

59. *See, e.g.*, Universal Declaration of Human Rights art. 21.

60. *Youngstown*, 343 U.S. at 655 (Jackson, J., concurring).

Chapter Nine: Getting (Foreign Affairs) into Court

1. No. 16–843 (CKK) (D.D.C. Nov. 21, 2016). The Court of Appeals for the D.C. Circuit later affirmed the dismissal on the ground that the case had become moot. Smith v. Trump, 731 F. App'x 8, 9 (D.C. Cir. 2018) (per curiam).

2. 444 U.S. 996 (1979).

3. 569 U.S. 108 (2013).

4. 03-MDL-1570 (GBD) (S.D.N.Y. Sept. 29, 2015).

5. *See* Sarah Wright Sheive, Note, *Central and Eastern European Constitutional Courts and the Antimajoritarian Objection to Judicial Review*, 26 LAW AND POLICY IN INTERNATIONAL BUSINESS 1201, 1203–4, 1209–10 (1995).

6. U.S. Const. art. III, § 2, cl. 1.

7. El-Masri v. United States, 479 F.3d 296, 300–301 (4th Cir. 2007).

8. *See, e.g.*, Mohamed v. Jeppesen Dataplan, Inc., 614 F.3d 1070 (9th Cir. 2010) (holding that actions would be dismissed pursuant to the state secrets privilege in cases involving foreign nationals who were victims of extraordinary rendition); Tenenbaum v. Simonini, 372 F.3d 776 (6th Cir. 2004) (holding that the state secrets doctrine mandated dismissal of claims that federal agency employees conducted a criminal espionage investigation of the plaintiff solely because he was Jewish); Terkel v. AT&T Corp., 441 F. Supp. 2d 899 (N.D. Ill. 2006) (in which the state secrets privilege was invoked to bar a request to compel a telephone company to confirm or deny whether it had disclosed records to the National Security Agency).

9. United States v. Reynolds, 345 U.S. 1, 10 (1953).

10. Barry Siegel argues that while the state secrets privilege had been used for decades, *Reynolds* marked the first time that the Supreme Court formally recognized and established the framework for the privilege. Barry Siegel, CLAIM OF PRIVILEGE: A MYSTERIOUS PLANE CRASH, A LANDMARK SUPREME COURT CASE, AND THE RISE OF STATE SECRETS ix (2008). David Rudenstine argues that the Court in *Reynolds* created doctrinal rules for state secrets that had no antecedent in U.S. law. Such rules were therefore not a restatement of previously announced state secrets rules.

David Rudenstine, THE AGE OF DEFERENCE: THE SUPREME COURT, NATIONAL SECURITY, AND THE CONSTITUTIONAL ORDER 85 (2016).

11. 92 U.S. 105 (1875).

12. For a further discussion of the distinction between *Totten* and the modern state secrets privilege, *see* Louis Fisher, THE CONSTITUTION AND 9/11: RECURRING THREATS TO AMERICA'S FREEDOMS 255–56 (2008).

13. Tenet v. Doe, 544 U.S. 1 (2005); *see also* Rudenstine, THE AGE OF DEFERENCE 102 (arguing that the Court's decision in *Tenet* blurred the distinction between *Reynolds* and *Totten*).

14. *El-Masri*, 479 F.3d at 304–8.

15. U.S. Const. art. II, § 2.

16. *See, e.g.*, Mohamed v. Jeppesen Dataplan, Inc., 614 F.3d 1070 (9th Cir. 2010).

17. *El-Masri*, 479 F.3d at 312.

18. Fazaga v. FBI, 884 F. Supp. 2d 1022 (S.D. Cal. 2012); *Jeppesen Dataplan*.

19. 542 U.S. 466 (2004).

20. Shaughnessy v. United States *ex rel.* Mezei, 345 U.S. 206, 218–19 (1953) (Jackson, J., dissenting).

21. U.S. Const. art. I, § 9, cl. 1.

22. Habeas Corpus Act of 1867, sess. 2, ch. 28, 14 Stat. 385 (Feb. 5, 1867).

23. 542 U.S. at 475.

24. 339 U.S. 763, 778–81 (1950).

25. Perhaps the earliest use of this now-common descriptor of the Bush Guantánamo policy is in Chris Hedges, *Public Lives: Ex-Judge vs. the Government's Law-Free Zone*, NEW YORK TIMES, February 6, 2004, http://www.nytimes.com/2004/02/06/nyregion/public-lives-ex-judge-vs-the-government-s-law- free-zone.html (profiling John J. Gibbons, former chief judge of the Third Circuit, who argued *Rasul v. Bush* in the Supreme Court; Gibbons describes a cartoon depicting Guantánamo as a "No Law Zone" and remarks, "I am uncomfortable with no-law zones"). *See* Janet Cooper Alexander, *The Law-Free Zone and Back Again*, 2013 UNIVERSITY OF ILLINOIS LAW REVIEW 551, 553 (2013); Fisher, THE CONSTITUTION AND 9/11 at 219–20.

26. *Rasul*, 542 U.S. at 476–77, 487–88.

27. *See* chapter 4. {~?~PE: note new cross-reference.}

28. Letter from Supreme Court justices to George Washington (Aug. 8, 1793), *in* 13 THE PAPERS OF GEORGE WASHINGTON 392 (Theodore J. Crackel et al. eds., 2007).

29. *Political Question Doctrine*, WEX LEGAL DICTIONARY, https://www.law.cornell.edu/wex/political_question_doctrine.

30. 369 U.S. 186, 217 (1962).

31. *See* Erwin Chemerinsky, CLOSING THE COURTHOUSE DOOR: HOW YOUR CONSTITUTIONAL RIGHTS BECAME UNENFORCEABLE 122–24, 127–36 (2017).

32. Louis Henkin, *Is There a Political Question Doctrine?*, 85 YALE LAW JOURNAL 597, 601 (1976).

33. Tara Leigh Grove, *The Lost History of the Political Question Doctrine*, 90 NEW YORK UNIVERSITY LAW REVIEW 1908 *passim* (2015).

34. *Baker*, 369 U.S. at 211.

35. *Id.* at 211–12.

36. Smith v. Obama, No. 16–843 (CKK) (D.D.C. Nov. 21, 2016). As noted, the D.C. Circuit later affirmed the dismissal on the ground that the case had become moot. Smith

v. v. Trump, 731 F. App'x 8, 9 (D.C. Cir. 2018) (per curiam). For another case involving the war on terror and the "political question" doctrine, *see* Al-Aulaqi v. Obama, 727 F. Supp. 2d 1 (D.D.C. 2010) (holding that a case involving the targeted killing of an American member of al-Qaeda was nonjusticiable as a political question); *but see* Al-Aulaqi v. Panetta, 35 F. Supp. 3d 56 (D.D.C. 2014) (holding that the political question doctrine did not bar the citizens' suit against government officials for the deaths of their relatives in drone strikes). *See also* El-Shifa Pharmaceutical Industries Co. v. United States, 607 F.3d 836 (D.C. Cir. 2010) (holding that a case involving the destruction of a Sudanese pharmaceuticals plant by an American cruise missile was nonjusticiable as a political question).

37. 607 F.3d at 24–25, 28–30.

38. *See also* Luftig v. McNamara, 373 F.2d 664 (D.C. Cir. 1967), *cert. denied*, 387 U.S. 945 (1967).

39. No. 10-699, slip op. (Mar. 26, 2012).

40. *Id.* at 2.

41. *Id.* at 6.

42. *See, e.g.*, Humphrey's Executor v. United States, 295 U.S. 602 (1935); Myers v. United States, 272 U.S. 52 (1926).

43. *Zivotofsky v. Clinton*, 566 U.S. 189, 196 (2012).

44. 575 U.S. __ (2015).

45. *Id.*, at slip op. 7–14.

46. *Id.*

47. *See* Steven V. Mazie, AMERICAN JUSTICE 2015: THE DRAMATIC TENTH TERM OF THE ROBERTS COURT 119 (2015) ("*Zivotofsky* does not hand exclusive foreign policy powers to the executive").

48. *See* Kal Raustiala, DOES THE CONSTITUTION FOLLOW THE FLAG? THE EVOLUTION OF TERRITORIALITY IN AMERICAN LAW (2009).

49. Curtis A. Bradley and Jack L. Goldsmith, FOREIGN RELATIONS LAW: CASES AND MATERIALS 685–86 (3d ed. 2009).

50. *See* Boumediene v. Bush, 553 U.S. 723 (2008) (employing the multifactor test in determining whether the right to habeas corpus review extends to Guantánamo Bay); United States v. Verdugo-Urquidez, 494 U.S. 259 (1990) (holding that the Fourth Amendment does not apply to searches of foreign citizens occurring outside the United States); Reid v. Covert, 354 U.S. 1 (1957) (holding that the Fifth and Sixth Amendments apply to U.S. citizens abroad); *Verdugo-Urquidez*, 494 U.S. at 279–80 (Brennan, J., dissenting) (arguing that the Fourth Amendment should apply abroad to searches of foreign citizens suspected of violating U.S. laws).

51. Ahrens v. Clark, 335 U.S. 188 (1948).

52. Braden v. 30th Judicial Circuit of Kentucky, 410 U.S. 484 (1973).

53. *Id.* at 498.

54. 28 U.S.C. § 1350 (2012).

55. *Id.*

56. For further discussion of extraterritoriality and human rights, *see* Tonya L. Putnam, COURTS WITHOUT BORDERS: LAW, POLITICS AND U.S. EXTRATERRITORIALITY 202–54 (2016).

57. 569 U.S. 108, 114–25 (2013).

58. For a discussion of the "touch and concern" test and its resulting circuit split,

see Clarifying Kiobel's *"Touch and Concern" Test*, 130 HARVARD LAW REVIEW 1902 (2017); *see also* Edward T. Swaine, *Kiobel and Extraterritoriality: Here, (Not) There, (Not Even) Everywhere*, 69 OKLAHOMA LAW REVIEW 23 (2016); Ursula Tracy Doyle, *The Evidence of Things Not Seen: Divining Balancing Factors from* Kiobel's *"Touch and Concern" Test*, 66 HASTINGS LAW JOURNAL 443 (2015).

59. *See* 133 S. Ct. at 1667.

60. Filártiga v. Peña-Irala, 630 F.2d 876 (2d Cir. 1980).

61. *See, e.g.*, Doe v. Saravia, 348 F. Supp. 2d 1112 (E.D. Cal. 2004); Kadic v. Karadžić, 70 F.3d 232 (2d Cir. 1995).

62. *Kiobel*, 569 U.S. at 127, 132–33 (Breyer, J., concurring).

63. *Cf.* The Apollon, 22 U.S. (9 Wheat.) 362, 370 (1824).

64. *See id.*

65. American Law Institute, RESTATEMENT (THIRD) OF FOREIGN RELATIONS LAW (1987); William S. Dodge, *Understanding the Presumption Against Extraterritoriality*, 16 BERKELEY JOURNAL OF INTERNATIONAL LAW 85 (1998).

66. EEOC v. Arabian American Oil Co., 499 U.S. 244 (1991).

67. Morrison v. National Australia Bank Ltd., 561 U.S. 247 (2010).

68. *See* Lackland H. Bloom, Jr., Do GREAT CASES MAKE BAD LAW? 332–36 (2014).

69. 418 U.S. 683 (1974).

70. Amanda Frost and Justin Florence, *Reforming the State Secrets Privilege*, ADVANCE: THE JOURNAL OF ACS ISSUE BRIEFS 111, 120 (2007).

71. Henting v. AT&T Corp., 439 F. Supp. 2d 974 (N.D. Cal. 2006).

72. American Civil Liberties Union v. National Security Agency, 438 F. Supp. 2d 754 (E.D. Mich. 2006), *rev'd*, 493 F.3d 644 (6th Cir. 2007).

Chapter Ten: Saying What Foreign Affairs Law Is

1. 553 U.S. 723 (2008).

2. 542 U.S. 466 (2004).

3. 548 U.S. 557, 629–30 (2006).

4. 212 F.3d 1338 (2000), *cert. denied*, 530 U.S. 1270 (2000).

5. *See* Julian Arato, *Deference to the Executive: The US Debate in Global Perspective*, *in* THE INTERPRETATION OF INTERNATIONAL LAW BY DOMESTIC COURTS: UNIFORMITY, DIVERSITY, CONVERGENCE 198–217 (Helmut Philipp Aust and George Nolte eds., 2016).

6. 548 U.S. 331 (2006).

7. 548 U.S. 331, 355–56 (2006) (*quoting* Kolovrat v. Oregon, 366 U.S. 167 [1961]).

8. 548 U.S. at 378 (Breyer, J., dissenting).

9. Medellin v. Texas, 552 U.S. 491, 513 (2008).

10. *Id.* at 512 (*citing* Oetjen v. Central Leather Co., 246 U.S. 276, 302 [1918]).

11. Hamdan v. Rumsfeld, 548 U.S. 557 (2006). *See* Martin S. Flaherty, *More Real than Apparent: Separation of Powers, the Rule of Law, and Executive "Creativity" in Hamdan v. Rumsfeld*, 2005–06 CATO SUPREME COURT REVIEW 51 (2006).

12. Geneva Convention Relative to the Treatment of Prisoners of War (Third Geneva Convention), art. 3(1)(d), 75 UNTS 135 (1949).

13. *See* Brief for Respondents at 48, Hamdan v. Rumsfeld (No. 05–184), 2006

U.S. S. Ct. Briefs LEXIS 292 at **88 (emphasis omitted) (*citing* Geneva Convention Relative to the Treatment of Prisoners of War, Aug. 12, 1949, 6 U.S.T. 3316, 75 U.N.T.S. 135).

14. *See Hamdan*, 548 U.S. at 630–32.

15. *Compare id.* at 635 (stating assumptions made by the majority; deference to the executive is not one of these), *with id.* at 678–80 (Thomas, J., dissenting) (affirming a "well-established duty" to defer to executive interpretations in reference to the military and foreign affairs).

16. 525 U.S. 155 (1999). In contrast to its predecessors, however, *El Al* expressly softens the degree of deference to be accorded from "great weight" owed executive interpretations to "respect . . . ordinarily due the reasonable views of the Executive Branch concerning the meaning of an international treaty." *Id.* at 168.

17. 457 U.S. 176 (1982).

18. 489 U.S. 353 (1989).

19. 366 U.S. 187 (1961).

20. David J. Bederman, *Revivalist Canons and Treaty Interpretation*, 41 UCLA LAW REVIEW 953 (1994). Subsequent work by Robert Chesney for the federal courts generally demonstrates that the executive's success may not be as pronounced as Bederman's initial work suggests. *See generally* Robert M. Chesney, *Disaggregating Deference: The Judicial Power and Executive Treaty Interpretations*, 92 IOWA LAW REVIEW 1723 (2007).

21. *See* Deborah N. Pearlstein, *After Deference: Formalizing the Judicial Power for Foreign Relations Law*, 159 UNIVERSITY OF PENNSYLVANIA LAW REVIEW 783, 793–96 (2011).

22. United States v. Lindh, 212 F.Supp.2d 541, 556 (E.D. Va. 2002).

23. Hamdan v. Rumsfeld, 415 F.3d 33 (D.C. Cir. 2005).

24. David Sloss, *Judicial Deference to Executive Branch Treaty Interpretations: A Historical Perspective*, 62 NYU ANNUAL SURVEY OF AMERICAN LAW 497, 506–7 (2007); *see also* Joshua Weiss, *Defining Executive Deference in Treaty Interpretation Cases*, 79 GEORGE WASHINGTON LAW REVIEW 1592, 1593–94 (2011).

25. *See* The Amiable Isabella, 19 U.S. (6 Wheat.) 1, 92 (1821) (Johnson, J., dissenting) ("The views of the administration, are wholly out of the question in this Court. What is the just construction of the treaty is the only question here. And whether it chime in with the views of the Government or not, this individual is entitled to the benefit of that construction").

26. *See generally* Chesney, *Disaggregating Deference*.

27. Charlton v. Kelly, 229 U.S. 447, 468 (1913).

28. Kolovrat v. Oregon, 366 U.S. 187, 194 (1961).

29. *Hamdan*, 548 U.S. at 678 (Thomas, J., dissenting).

30. El Al Israel Airlines, Ltd. v. Tseng, 525 U.S. 155, 168 (1999).

31. *In re* Ross, 140 U.S. 453 (1891). Sometimes said to be the first deference case, it did not actually articulate a standard. Moreover, the Court's analysis relied not simply on the executive's interpretation of the relevant treaty but on the consistent practice of both treaty-making parties, and only after close consideration of the treaty's text. *Id.* at 466–69.

32. *Charlton*, 229 U.S. at 467.

33. *Id.* at 466–49.

34. Sullivan v. Kidd, 254 U.S. 433 (1921).

35. *Id.* at 435–43.

36. *Kolovrat*, 366 U.S. at 194.

37. *Id.* at 191–95.

38. Sumitomo Shoji America, Inc. v. Avagliano, 457 U.S. 176, 180–84 (1982).

39. "Although not conclusive, the meaning attributed to treaty provisions by the Government agencies charged with their negotiation and enforcement is entitled to great weight." United States v. Stuart, 489 U.S. 353, 369 (1989) (*citing Sumitomo*, 457 U.S. at 184–85; *Kolovrat*, 366 U.S. at 194).

40. *See* Henry P. Monaghan, *Constitutional Common Law*, 89 HARVARD LAW REVIEW 1 (1974).

41. *Sanchez-Llamas*, 548 U.S. at 355.

42. *See id.* at 337–39 (2006); Vienna Convention on Consular Relations art. 36, ¶ 2, April 24, 1963, 21 U.S.T. 77, 100–101.

43. Mexico v. United States (Case Concerning Avena and other Mexican Nationals), 2004 I.C.J. No. 128 (Judgment of Mar. 31); Federal Republic of Germany v. United States (The LaGrand Case), 2001 I.C.J. 466 (Judgment of June 27).

44. 523 U.S. 371 (1998).

45. Marbury v. Madison, 5 U.S. (1 Cranch) 137, 177 (1803).

46. *See Sanchez-Llamas*, 548 U.S. at 350–60.

47. *Medellin*, 552 U.S. at 506–19.

48. *Hamdan*, 548 U.S. at 718–19 (Thomas, J., dissenting).

49. *Id.*

50. *Id.*

51. *Id.*

52. *Id.* (emphasis added).

53. 525 U.S. at 155 (1999).

54. *Id.* at 168.

55. *Id.* at 168–77.

56. Factor v. Laubenheimer, 290 U.S. 276, 295 (1933); Neilson v. Johnson, 279 U.S. 47, 51 (1929).

57. *See* Martin S. Flaherty, *Are We to Be a Nation? Federal Power vs. "States' Rights" in Foreign Affairs*, 70 UNIVERSITY OF COLORADO LAW REVIEW 1277, 1283–86 (1999). One classic example related to "state sovereignty" is the so-called anticommandeering principle, which holds that the Congress cannot enact statutes that compel nonjudicial state officials to implement federal laws. The doctrine is made of whole cloth, with no basis in text, history, structure, or custom. *Id.* Yet the Court again recently relied on it to strike down a congressional attempt to limit state-authorized betting on sports. Murphy v. NCAA, slip. op., at 14–24 (2018).

58. *See* Sosa v. Alvarez-Machain, 542 U.S. 692, 735–38 (2004).

59. *See, e.g.,* Brief for Appellants at 30, Center for National Security Studies v. United States Department of Justice (No. 02–5254), 2002 WL 34576620 ("When a court examines the government's assessment of the ways in which terrorist organizations will use information gleaned about the government's ongoing investigations, substantial deference . . . is plainly proper"); Eric A. Posner and Cass R. Sunstein, *Chevronizing Foreign Relations Law*, 116 YALE LAW JOURNAL 1170 (2007); Julian Ku and

John Yoo, Hamdan v. Rumsfeld: *The Functional Case for Foreign Affairs Deference to the Executive Branch*, 23 CONSTITUTIONAL COMMENTARY 179 (2006); Oren Eisner, Note, *Extending* Chevron *Deference to Presidential Interpretations of Ambiguities in Foreign Affairs and National Security Statutes Delegating Lawmaking Power to the President*, 86 CORNELL LAW REVIEW 411 (2001).

60. For a discussion of why some judges tend to favor deference to the executive, *see* David Rudenstine, THE AGE OF DEFERENCE: THE SUPREME COURT, NATIONAL SECURITY, AND THE CONSTITUTIONAL ORDER 293–307 (2016).

61. For a survey, *see* Robert Knowles, *American Hegemony and the Foreign Affairs Constitution*, 41 ARIZONA STATE LAW JOURNAL 87, 127–38 (2009).

62. *See* John Yoo, *Politics as Law? The Anti–Ballistic Missile Treaty, the Separation of Powers, and Treaty Interpretation*, 89 CALIFORNIA LAW REVIEW 851 (2001); John Yoo, *Federal Courts as Weapons of Foreign Policy: The Case of the Helms-Burton Act*, 20 HASTINGS INTERNATIONAL AND COMPARATIVE LAW REVIEW 747, 748 (1997) ("Foreign policy is best executed by institutions that are united, swift and rational"); *but see* L. A. Powe, Jr., *The Role of the Court, in* SECURITY V. LIBERTY: CONFLICTS BETWEEN CIVIL LIBERTIES AND NATIONAL SECURITY IN AMERICAN HISTORY 182 (Daniel Farber ed., 2008) (arguing that the Bush administration's incompetence defeats Yoo's argument for deference based on institutional competence).

63. Charlton v. Kelly, 229 U.S. 447, 468 (1913). *Cf. In re* Ross, 140 U.S. 453, 468 (1891) (*quoting* a communication made in 1881 by the U.S. minister for Japan to the secretary of state: "The President and the department have always construed the treaty of 1858" in a certain manner).

64. *See Charlton*, 229 U.S. at 472–74.

65. *See, e.g., Ross*, 140 U.S. at 475–76; *Charlton*, 229 U.S. at 467–68. *See also* Chesney, *Disaggregating Deference* at 1741–43 (distinguishing executive interpretive authority and executive practice as evidence of intent).

66. *See, e.g.*, Eldred v. Ashcroft, 537 U.S. 186, 222 (2003) (rejecting a challenge to the extension of copyright terms, with heavy reliance on the actions of the First Congress); Utah v. Evans, 536 U.S. 452, 455, 457 (2002) (rejecting Utah's challenge to a census method undertaken by North Carolina based in part on the meaning of the phrase "actual enumeration" in the First Congress); Marsh v. Chambers, 463 U.S. 783 at 783, 790–91 (1983) (finding the legislative chaplaincy does not violate the establishment clause in part because the First Congress made use of such a chaplaincy ["Standing alone, historical patterns cannot justify contemporary violations of constitutional guarantees, but there is far more here than simply historical patterns. In this context, historical evidence sheds light not only on what the draftsmen intended the *Establishment Clause* to mean, but also on how they thought that Clause applied to the practice authorized by the First Congress—their actions reveal their intent"] [emphasis added]); McCulloch v. Maryland, 17 U.S. (4 Wheat.) 316 at 316, 401–2 (1819) (relying on the actions of the First Congress in part to uphold the establishment of the national bank); *see also* Michael Bhargava, *The First Congress Canon and the Supreme Court's Use of History*, 94 CALIFORNIA LAW REVIEW 1745, 1746–47 (2006).

67. *See* THE FEDERALIST No. 75 at 449–54 (Alexander Hamilton) (Clinton Rossiter ed., 1961).

68. Curtis A. Bradley, Chevron *Deference and Foreign Affairs*, 86 VIRGINIA LAW REVIEW 649 (2000); *see also* Weiss, *Defining Executive Deference* at 1603–7; Joseph

Landau, Chevron *Meets* Youngstown: *National Security and the Administrative State*, 92 BOSTON UNIVERSITY LAW REVIEW 1917, 1928–33 (2012).

69. 467 U.S. 847 (1984).

70. Bradley, Chevron *and Foreign Affairs* at 669.

71. *Id.* at 670–71. That said, Bradley rightly notes that in reality, considerations of executive expertise and, at least on the surface, democratic accountability also obtain a theory of delegation. *Id.* at 669–70.

72. *See, e.g.*, Derek Jinks and Neal Kumar Katyal, *Disregarding Foreign Relations Law*, 116 YALE LAW JOURNAL 1230, 1249–82 (2007).

73. Skidmore v. Swift & Co., 323 U.S. 134 (1944).

74. Bowen v. Georgetown Univ. Hosp. 488 U.S. 204 (1998). *See* Evan Criddle, Note, *Chevron Deference and Treaty Interpretation*, 112 YALE LAW JOURNAL 1927 (2003).

75. Here the leading analysis is Michael P. Van Alstine, *The Death of Good Faith in Treaty Jurisprudence and a Call for Resurrection*, 93 GEORGETOWN LAW JOURNAL 1885 (2005).

76. *See* Martin S. Flaherty, *The Most Dangerous Branch*, 105 YALE LAW JOURNAL 1725, 1810–39 (1996).

77. *See* William R. Casto, FOREIGN AFFAIRS AND THE CONSTITUTION IN THE AGE OF FIGHTING SAIL 103–21 (2006).

78. The Constitution grants power to the judiciary to hear all cases in "Law or Equity, arising under the Constitution, Laws of the United States, Treaties made, or which shall be made, under their Authority." U.S. Const. art. III, § 2.

79. *See* chapter 8 {~?~PE: note new cross-reference}.

80. *See* Letter from Thomas Jefferson to James Madison (Mar. 27, 1789), *in* 15 THE PAPERS OF THOMAS JEFFERSON 392–98 (Julian B. Boyd ed., 1958).

81. One interesting example of the increased power of globalized and coordinated executives comes from the war in Afghanistan. Before the war, Huzaifa Parhat, a Uighur from China's Xinjiang region, fled Chinese oppression and settled in Afghanistan. After his camp was destroyed in a U.S. air attack, Parhat and other Uighurs fled to Pakistan, where they were apprehended by Pakistani authorities. The Pakistanis then transferred the Uighurs to the U.S. military, who then detained the Uighurs at Guantánamo. Rudenstine, THE AGE OF DEFERENCE at 259–60.

82. *See also* Powe, *The Role of the Court* at 186 (arguing that *Hamdan* may suggest a more aggressive protection of individual rights); Samuel Walker, PRESIDENTS AND CIVIL LIBERTIES FROM WILSON TO OBAMA: A STORY OF POOR CUSTODIANS 482–83 (2012) (arguing that the Court's terrorism decisions have made it the most consistent defender of fundamental civil liberties among the three branches). For an overview of how other nations' courts have handled terrorism, *see* COURTS AND TERRORISM: NINE NATIONS BALANCE RIGHTS AND SECURITY (Mary L. Volcansek and John F. Stack, Jr. eds., 2011).

83. *See* Julius Lobel, *The Rhetoric and Reality of Judicial Review of Counter-Terrorism Actions: The United States Experience, in* CRITICAL DEBATES ON COUNTER-TERRORISM JUDICIAL REVIEW 98–104 (Fergal F. Davis and Fiona De Londras eds., 2014); Scott M. Matheson, Jr., PRESIDENTIAL CONSTITUTIONALISM IN PERILOUS TIMES 141–45 (2009).

84. *See generally* 10 U.S.C. § 801 *et seq.*; *see also* Hamdan v. Rumsfeld, 548 U.S. 557 (2006).

85. *Hamdan*, 548 U.S. at 566, 605 (*quoting* Appendix to Brief for Petitioner at 65a, Hamdan v. Rumsfeld, 548 U.S. 557 [2006] [No. 05–184]).

86. Brief for Respondents at 37–38, Hamdan v. Rumsfeld, 548 U.S. 557 (2006) (No. 05–184).

87. *Id.* at 38.

88. *Hamdan*, 548 U.S. at 718.

89. Brief for Respondents at 38, *Hamdan*.

90. *Hamdan*, 548 U.S. at 718–19 (Thomas, J., dissenting) (emphasis added); *see also* United States v. Curtiss-Wright Export Corp., 299 U.S. 304, 320 (1936).

91. *Hamdan*, 548 U.S. at 562.

92. *Id.* at 718 (*quoting* the Geneva Convention Relative to the Treatment of Prisoners of War, Aug. 12, 1949, 6 U.S.T. 3316).

93. *Hamdan*, 548 U.S. at 562.

94. *Id.*

95. *Id.* at 619–20.

96. *Id.* at 630, 631–33. As the Court points out, Article 3(1)(d) prohibits "the passing of sentences and the carrying out of executions without previous judgment pronounced by a regularly constituted court affording all the judicial guarantees which are recognized as indispensable by civilized peoples." *Hamdan*, 548 U.S. at 630 (*quoting* the Geneva Convention Relative to the Treatment of Prisoners of War art. 3, ¶ 1(d), Aug. 12, 1949, 6 U.S.T. 3316).

97. The Federalist No. 70 at 424 (Alexander Hamilton) (Clinton Rossiter ed., 1961).

98. U.S. Const. art. II, § 2.

99. *See* Martin S. Flaherty, *Judicial Foreign Relations Authority After 9/11*, 56 New York Law School Law Review 119, 155 (2011/2012).

100. *See id.* at 155–56.

101. *See* Rasul v. Bush, 542 U.S. 466, 470–71 (2004); *see also* 28 U.S.C. §§ 2241–43 (2006).

102. *See* Transcript of Oral Argument at 5, Rasul v. Bush, 542 U.S. 466 (2004) (Nos. 03–334, 03–343), 2004 WL 943637 at *4, http://www.supremecourt.gov/oral_argu ments/argument_transcripts/03–334.pdf ("Question: . . . We are here debating the jurisdiction under the Habeas Statute, is that right? [Answer]: That's correct . . ."). *Cf. Rasul*, 542 U.S. at 489 (Scalia, J., dissenting).

103. *Id.* at *41 (*quoting* Oetjen v. Central Leather Co., 246 U.S. 297, 302 [1918]).

104. *Id.* at *42.

105. *Id.* at *43.

106. *Rasul*, 542 U.S. at 506 (Scalia, J., dissenting).

107. *Id.* (Scalia, J., dissenting).

108. *Id.* at 478 (*quoting* Braden v. 30th Judicial Circuit Court of Kentucky, 410 U. S. 484, 495 [1973]).

109. *Rasul*, 542 U.S. at 478–79 (*quoting Braden*, 410 U. S. at 494–95).

110. The Federalist No. 48 at 309 (James Madison) (Clinton Rossiter ed., 1961).

111. 6 U.S. (2 Cranch) 170 (1804).

112. An Act Further to Suspend the Commercial Intercourse Between the United States and France, and the Dependencies Thereof, 1 Story's L.U.S. 558 (expired) 1 Stat.

578 (expired), available at http://memory.loc.gov/cgi-bin/ampage?collId=llsl &fileName=001/llsl001.db&recNum=701.

113. *Little*, 6 U.S. (2 Cranch) at 178.

114. *Id.* at 179.

115. *See* Flaherty, *Judicial Foreign Relations* at 149.

116. Youngstown Sheet & Tube Co. v. Sawyer, 343 U.S. 579, 653–54 (1952).

117. Seton Hall Law School's Center for Policy and Research has done extensive research and analysis concerning the detainees held in Guantánamo based upon evidence presented at proceedings before the combat status review tribunals, which are the bodies set up to establish that those individuals held in detention qualify as "unlawful enemy combatants." The reports the center has issued have indicated that the evidence for this designation is meager or nonexistent in the vast majority of instances. *See* Mark Denbeaux et al., Seaton Hall Law Center for Policy and Research, THE MEANING OF "BATTLEFIELD": AN ANALYSIS OF THE GOVERNMENT'S REPRESENTATIONS OF "BATTLEFIELD" CAPTURE AND "RECIDIVISM" OF THE GUANTÁNAMO DETAINEES 2 (Dec. 10, 2007), http://law.shu.edu/publications/GuantánamoReports/meaning_of_battle field_final_121007.pdf. For further discussion of the combat status review tribunals, *see* A. Naomi Paik, RIGHTLESSNESS: TESTIMONY AND REDRESS IN U.S. PRISON CAMPS SINCE WORLD WAR II 156–74 (2016). For a discussion of the use of military commissions in general, *see* THE MILITARY COMMISSIONS ACT AND DETAINEE TRIALS (Joshua Segel and Soto Kimura eds., Defense, Security, and Strategies series, 2011).

118. 542 U.S. 507 (2004).

119. *Hamdi*, 542 U.S. at 510 (O'Connor, J., plurality opinion).

120. *Id.* at 510–11.

121. *Id.* at 512–13.

122. *Id.* at 524.

123. The government maintains that no explicit congressional authorization is required because the executive possesses plenary authority to detain pursuant to Article II of the Constitution. *Id.* at 516.

124. Brief for Respondents at 25, Hamdi v. Rumsfeld (No. 03–6696), 2004 WL 724020.

125. *Id.*

126. *Id.* at 26.

127. *See Hamdi*, 542 U.S. 507, 579 (Thomas, J., dissenting).

128. *Id.* at 581 (*quoting* THE FEDERALIST No. 70 at 471 [Alexander Hamilton] [Jacob E. Cooke ed. 1961]).

129. *Hamdi*, 542 U.S. at 581.

130. *Id.* at 582.

131. *Id.* at 583.

132. *Id.*

133. *Id.*

134. Justice O'Connor, for example, long advocated an "undue burden" test that fell between strict scrutiny and rational relationship analysis for abortion cases. *See* Planned Parenthood v. Casey, 505 U.S. 833, 871–74 (1992). Likewise, in the affirmative action context, while she asserted a strict scrutiny standard, she was at pains to indicate that the test would not be as "fatal" to government measures as generally understood. Adarand Constructors, Inc. v. Pena, 515 U.S. 200, 237 (1995).

135. *See Hamdi*, 542 U.S. at 529 (O'Connor, J., plurality opinion).

136. *Id.* at 531.

137. *Id.*

138. *Id.* at 529.

139. *Id.* at 530.

140. *Id.*

141. *Id.* at 535.

142. *Id.* at 535–36

143. *Id.* at 536.

144. *Id.* at 536–37. For further discussion of the plurality opinion in *Hamdi, see* Chris Edelson, EMERGENCY CONSTITUTIONAL POWER: FROM THE DRAFTING OF THE CONSTITUTION TO THE WAR ON TERROR 179–83 (2013).

145. *Hamdi*, 542 U.S. at 529.

146. *See* Mathews v. Eldridge, 424 U.S. 319 (1976).

147. *See Hamdi*, 542 U.S. at 554 (Scalia, J., dissenting).

148. *See id.* at 573.

149. *Id.* at 558.

150. *Id.* at 554–58.

151. *Id.* at 578–79.

152. *Hamdi*, 542 U.S. at 578 (*quoting* THE FEDERALIST No. 8 at 33 [Alexander Hamilton] [George W. Carey and James McClellan eds. 2001]).

153. *Boumediene*, 553 U.S. at 733.

154. *Id.* at 735.

155. *Id.*

156. U.S. Constitution, art. I, § 9, cl. 2.

157. *Boumediene*, 553 U.S. at 732.

158. *Id.*

159. These are concisely set out in Curtis A. Bradley and Jack L. Goldsmith, FOREIGN RELATIONS LAW: CASES AND MATERIALS 558 n.3 (3d ed. 2009).

160. *See, e.g.*, United States v. Verdugo-Urquidez 494 U.S. 259 (1990) (holding that the Fourth Amendment did not apply to aliens when they were subject to an alleged violation extraterritorially).

161. *Id.* Additionally, the *Reid v. Covert* plurality, which did apply the right to a jury trial in a criminal prosecution extraterritorially, also made note that the two accused were U.S. citizens, though it did not expressly make their status the basis of the decision.

162. If anything, the *Reid* plurality emphasizes a presumption that where federal power is asserted, federal rights should follow. *Reid*, 354 U.S. at 15 (opinion of Black, J.) ("The concept that the Bill of Rights and other constitutional protections against arbitrary government are inoperative when they become inconvenient or when expediency dictates otherwise is a very dangerous doctrine and, if allowed to flourish, would destroy the benefit of a written Constitution and undermine the basis of our Government. If our foreign commitments become of such nature that the Government can no longer satisfactorily operate within the bounds laid down by the Constitution, that instrument can be amended by the method which it prescribes"). *See also Verdugo-Urquidez*, 494 U.S. 279, 282 (Brennan, J., dissenting) ("The Court today creates an

antilogy: the Constitution authorizes our Government to enforce our criminal laws abroad, but when Government agents exercise this authority, the Fourth Amendment does not travel with them. This cannot be").

163. *Eisentrager* itself emphasized territorial factors, but also considered whether the habeas petitioners were U.S. citizens. 399 U.S. at 773.

164. *Boumediene*, 553 U.S. at 766–71.

165. *See* chapter 2.

166. *But see* Andrew Kent, *Against a Global Constitution*, 95 GEORGETOWN LAW JOURNAL 463 (2007).

Chapter Eleven: American Courts, Global Norms

1. International Covenant on Civil and Political Rights art. 5, Dec. 16, 1966, 999 U.N.T.S. 171.

2. Convention Against Torture and Other Cruel, Inhuman or Degrading Treatment or Punishment arts. 1, 16, Dec. 10, 1984, 1465 U.N.T.S. 85.

3. *See* UN Charter art. 1, ¶ 3.

4. James Madison, *Vices of the Political Systems of the United States* (Apr. 1787), *in* 9 PAPERS OF JAMES MADISON 347 (Robert A. Rutland and William M. E. Rachal eds., 1975).

5. For a discussion of the misunderstandings, *see* David L. Sloss, *Executing* Foster v. Neilson: *The Two-Step Approach to Analyzing Self-Executing Treaties*, 53 HARVARD INTERNATIONAL LAW JOURNAL 135 (2012).

6. 27 U.S. 253, 274 (1829).

7. *Id.* at 254.

8. *Id.*

9. *Id.*

10. For a further discussion of the U.S. history of treaty implementation and execution, *see* John T. Parry, *Congress, the Supremacy Clause, and the Implementation of Treaties*, 32 FORDHAM INTERNATIONAL LAW JOURNAL 1209 (2009).

11. *See* David L. Sloss, THE DEATH OF TREATY SUPREMACY: AN INVISIBLE CONSTITUTIONAL CHANGE 149 (2016).

12. 3 U.S. 199 (1796).

13. Asakura v. City of Seattle, 265 U.S. 332, 343 (1924).

14. *Id.* at 341.

15. Sloss, THE DEATH OF TREATY SUPREMACY at 153.

16. Edwin D. Dickinson, *Are the Liquor Treaties Self-Executing?*, 20 AMERICAN JOURNAL OF INTERNATIONAL LAW 444, 452 (1926); Edwin D. Dickinson, *Jurisdiction at the Maritime Frontier*, 40 HARVARD LAW REVIEW 1–29 (1926).

17. *See* Mark Philip Bradley, THE WORLD REIMAGINED: AMERICANS AND HUMAN RIGHTS IN THE TWENTIETH CENTURY 70–86 (2016); Christopher N. J. Roberts, *Human Rights Lost: The (Re)Making of an American Story*, 26 MINNESOTA JOURNAL OF INTERNATIONAL LAW 1 (2017).

18. UN Charter art. 55.

19. *See, e.g.*, Bob-Lo Excursion Co. v. Michigan, 333 U.S. 28 (1948) (with briefs filed by the NAACP, the ACLU, and the National Lawyers Guild); Hurd v. Hodge, 334

U.S. 24 (1948) (with briefs filed by the NAACP and the Japanese American Citizens League); Oyama v. California, 332 U.S. 633 (1948) (with briefs filed by the ACLU and the National Lawyers Guild).

20. For a discussion of *Missouri* and the related case *U.S. v. Bond, see* Michael J. Glennon a Robert D. Sloane, FOREIGN AFFAIRS FEDERALISM: THE MYTH OF NATIONAL EXCLUSIVITY 193–235 (2016); Joshua Muha, *Treaty Power and the Constitution: A Question of Sovereignty,* 17 THOMAS M. COOLEY JOURNAL OF PRACTICAL AND CLINICAL LAW 1 (2015).

21. 38 Cal.2d 718 (1952).

22. Sloss, THE DEATH OF TREATY SUPREMACY at 249.

23. *See* 1 FOREIGN RELATIONS OF THE UNITED STATES, 1952–1954, GENERAL: ECONOMIC AND POLITICAL MATTERS part 2, document 360 (David M. Baehler et al. eds., 1983), *see also* Duane Tanenbaum, THE BRICKER AMENDMENT CONTROVERSY: A TEST OF EISENHOWER'S POLITICAL LEADERSHIP 152–53 (1988).

24. Sloss, THE DEATH OF TREATY SUPREMACY at 253.

25. American Law Institute, RESTATEMENT (SECOND) OF THE FOREIGN RELATIONS LAW OF THE UNITED STATES (1965).

26. Sloss, THE DEATH OF TREATY SUPREMACY at 319.

27. *See* Mary Ann Glendon, A WORLD MADE NEW: ELEANOR ROOSEVELT AND THE UNIVERSAL DECLARATION OF HUMAN RIGHTS (2002).

28. *See* Bradley, THE WORLD REIMAGINED at 86–91.

29. Joseph Nye coined the term to mean the ability of a state to attract and persuade, rather than coerce, in foreign affairs. Joseph S. Nye, Jr., SOFT POWER: THE MEANS TO SUCCESS IN WORLD POLITICS 5–11 (2004).

30. Anne-Marie Slaughter and Catherine Powell, *Louis Henkin (1917–2010): The Power of His Ideas Live On,* OPINIO JURIS, October 27, 2010, http://opiniojuris .org/2010/10/22/louis-henkin-1917–2010-the-power-of-his-ideas-live-on/.

31. *The Core International Human Rights Instruments and Their Monitoring Bodies,* UNITED NATIONS HUMAN RIGHTS OFFICE OF THE HIGH COMMISSIONER, http://www.ohchr.org/EN/ProfessionalInterest/Pages/CoreInstruments.aspx.

32. 552 U.S. 491 (2008).

33. Vienna Convention on Consular Relations art. 36, April 24, 1963. *See also* Sloss, THE DEATH OF TREATY SUPREMACY 311.

34. *Medellin,* 552 U.S. 491 (2008).

35. Avena and Other Mexican Nationals, Mexico v. United States, Judgment on Jurisdiction, Admissibility and Merits [2004] ICJ Rep 12.

36. UN Charter art. 94.

37. *Medellin,* 552 U.S. at 504–6.

38. *Id.* at 547–48 (Breyer, J., dissenting).

39. *See, e.g.,* John Quigley, *A Tragi-Comedy of Errors Erodes Self-Execution of Treaties:* Medellin v. Texas *and Beyond,* 45 CASE WESTERN RESERVE JOURNAL OF INTERNATIONAL LAW 403 (2012); Curtis A. Bradley, *Intent, Presumptions, and Non-Self-Executing Treaties,* 102 AMERICAN JOURNAL OF INTERNATIONAL LAW 540 (2008); Carlos M. Vasquez, *Less Than Zero?,* 102 AMERICAN JOURNAL OF INTERNATIONAL LAW 563 (2008).

40. Sloss, THE DEATH OF TREATY SUPREMACY at 1.

41. *See* Peter J. Spiro, *Treaties, International Law, and Constitutional Rights*, 55 STANFORD LAW REVIEW 1999 (2003)

42. Sloss further notes that there is no similarly clear custom that assumes an NSE declaration can mean something else: that is, that a treaty is federal law but cannot be enforced by the courts (what he calls non-judicially enforceable or NJE doctrine). Sloss, THE DEATH OF TREATY SUPREMACY at 296–99.

43. The Carter administration also proposed adding NSE declarations to human rights treaties as early as 1978. David Sloss, *The Domestication of International Human Rights: Non-Self-Executing Declarations and Human Rights Treaties*, 24 YALE JOURNAL OF INTERNATIONAL LAW 129, 132 (1999).

44. Martin S. Flaherty, *The Most Dangerous Branch*, 105 YALE LAW JOURNAL 1725 (1996).

45. U.S. Const. art. VI, § 2 (emphasis added).

46. *See* Jordan J. Paust, Medellin, Avena, *the Supremacy of Treaties, and Relevant Executive Authority*, 31 SUFFOLK TRANSNATIONAL LAW REVIEW 301, 315–16 (2008).

47. 8 U.S.C. §§ 1101, 1108.

48. 18 U.S.C. § 2340A.

49. 28 U.S.C. § 1350.

50. 28 U.S.C. §1350.

51. ITT v. Vencap, 519 F.2d 1001, 1015 (2d Cir. 1975).

52. *Filartiga*, 630 F.2d at 878.

53. *An Open Letter to Judge Irving Kaufman*, NEW YORK TIMES, June 19, 1977, available at https://www.nytimes.com/1977/06/19/archives/an-open-letter-to-judge -irving-r-kaufman.html.

54. Todd v. Panjaitan, CIV.A. 92–12255-PBS, 1994 WL 827111 (D. Mass. 1994).

55. Xuncax v. Gramajo and Ortiz v. Gramajo, 886 F. Supp. 162 (D. Ct. Mass. 1995).

56. Kadic v. Karadžić, 70 F.3d 232 (1995).

57. 699 F.3d 763 (2012).

58. 28 U.S.C. § 1350.

59. Tel-Oren v. Libyan Arab Republic, 726 F.2d 774 (D.C. Cir. 1984) (Bork, J., concurring in the judgment).

60. Doe v. UNOCOL Corp., 395 F.3d 932 (9th Cir. 2002). *See* Business and Human Rights Resource Centre, *Unocal Lawsuit (re Myanmar)*, available at https://www.busi ness-humanrights.org/en/unocal-lawsuit-re-myanmar.

61. *See, e.g.*, https://www.weil.com/global-search?searchstring=ATS.

62. Sosa v. Alvarez-Machain, 542 U.S. 692, 697–99 (2004).

63. United States v. Alvarez-Machain, 594 U.S. 655 (1993).

64. *Sosa*, 542 U.S. at 712–24.

65. *Sosa*, 542 U.S. at 725–38.

66. Khulumani v. Barclay National Bank, Ltd., 504 F.3d 254 (2d Cir. 2007).

67. Kiobel v. Royal Dutch Shell, 621 F.3d 111 (2d Cir. 2010).

68. *Kiobel*, 621 F.3d at 140 (Leval, J., concurring).

69. Kiobel v. Royal Dutch Petroleum (*Kiobel II*), 569 U.S. 108, 115, *quoting* EEOC v. Arabian American Oil Co., 499 U.S. 244, 248 (1991).

70. *Kiobel II*, 569 U.S. at 119–24.

71. *Kiobel II*, 569 U.S. at 127 (Breyer, J., concurring).

72. 584 U.S. __ (2018).

73. *Jesner*, 584 U.S. at __, slip op. at 11–17 (opinion of Kennedy, J.)

74. *Jesner*, 584 U.S. at __, slip op. at 1–14 (Gorsuch, J., concurring in part and concurring in the judgment).

75. *Jesner*, 584 U.S. at __, slip op. at 19.

76. *Jesner*, 584 U.S. at __, slip op. at 26–27.

77. *Jesner*, 584 U.S. at __, slip op. at 1–34 (Sotomayor, J., dissenting).

78. *See* Brief of Amici Professors of Legal History Barbara Aronstein Black, William R. Casto, Nasser Hussain, Stanley N. Katz, and Anne-Marie Slaughter, *Jesner v. Arab Bank* (2d Cir. Apr. 14, 2014)

79. *Jesner*, 584 U.S. at __, slip op. at 34 (Sotomayor, J., dissenting).

80. *Jesner*, 584 U.S. at __, slip op. at 34 (Sotomayor, J., dissenting). The dissent alluded to the Court's grant of First Amendment rights to corporations in *Citizens United v. Federal Election Commission*, 558 U.S. 310 (2010) (free speech) and Burwell v. Hobby Lobby Stores, Inc., 573 U.S. __ (2014).

81. *See* chapter 4.

82. Anne-Marie Slaughter, A NEW WORLD ORDER 66 (2004). Other aspects of judicial globalization include judges meeting with their foreign counterparts or taking advantage of international sojourns, and courts of different national jurisdictions coordinating with one another in complex international litigation. *Id.* at 65–103.

83. Constitution of the Republic of South Africa arts. 39, 233.

84. *See* Martin S. Flaherty, *Aim Globally*, 17 CONSTITUTIONAL COMMENTARY 285 (2000). *See also Report of Judicial Colloquium on the Domestic Application of International Human Rights Norms, Bangalore, India, reproduced as an appendix to* Michael Kirby, *The Role of the Judge in Advancing Human Rights by Reference to International Human Rights Norms*, 514 AUSTRALIAN LAW JOURNAL 531–32 (1988) (the "Bangalore Principles" Kirby reproduces commend the "growing tendency for national courts to have regard to" international norms in cases where "domestic law— whether constitutional, statute or common law—is uncertain or incomplete").

85. *See* Sarah H. Cleveland, *Our International Constitution*, 31 YALE JOURNAL OF INTERNATIONAL LAW 1 (2006).

86. Lawrence v. Texas, 539 U.S. 558 (2003).

87. Grutter v. Bollinger, 539 U.S. 306, 344 (2003) (Ginsburg, J., concurring).

88. Roper v. Simmons, 543 U.S. 551 (2005); *Atkins v. Virginia*, 536 U.S. 304, 316–17 (2002).

89. *See* H.R. 973, 112th Cong. (2011).

90. *See* Andrew Moravcsik, *In Defense of the "Democratic Deficit": Reassessing Legitimacy in the European Union*, 40 JOURNAL OF COMMON MARKET STUDIES 603 (2002).

91. *See* Cleveland, *Our International Constitution*.

92. *See* Flaherty, *Aim Globally*.

93. 536 U.S. at 304 (2002); *see also* Roth v. United States, 354 U.S. 476 (1957) (relying in part on international treaties and consensus when upholding a federal obscenity statute); Wilkerson v. Utah, 99 U.S. 130 (1879) (rejecting a challenge to a death sentence by firing squad in part because other countries permit execution by shooting).

94. 536 U.S. at 337, 347–48 (Scalia, J., dissenting). In less flamboyant fashion, the

chief justice agreed, stating: "For if it is evidence of a *national* consensus for which we are looking, then the viewpoints of other countries are simply not relevant." *Id.* at 312, 325 (Rehnquist, C.J., dissenting).

95. *See* Anne-Marie Slaughter, *Judicial Globalization*, 40 VIRGINIA JOURNAL OF INTERNATIONAL LAW 1103 (2000); Harold Hongju Koh, *Bringing International Law Home*, 35 HOUSTON LAW REVIEW 623 (1998) (noting and advocating the phenomenon).

96. For a discussion of the Supreme Court's use of foreign law since 1793, *see* Steven G. Calabresi and Stephanie Dotson Zimdahl, *The Supreme Court and Foreign Sources of Law: Two Hundred Years of Practice and the Juvenile Death Penalty Decision*, 47 WILLIAM & MARY LAW REVIEW 743 (2005).

97. *Lawrence*, 539 U.S. at 576–77 (2002).

98. *Grutter*, 539 U.S. at 344 (Ginsburg, J., concurring).

99. *Atkins*, 536 U.S. at 316.

100. Printz v. United States, 521 U.S. 898, 976–78 (1997) (Breyer, J., dissenting).

101. *Roper*, 543 U.S. at 576.

102. *Id.* at 567–68.

103. *Id.* at 622 (Scalia, J., dissenting).

104. *Id.* at 624.

105. 548 U.S. 557 (2006). For an approving commentary, *see* Martin S. Flaherty, *More Real than Apparent: Separation of Powers, the Rule of Law, and Comparative Executive "Creativity" in* Hamdan v. Rumsfeld, 2006 CATO SUPREME COURT REVIEW 51 (2006). Conversely, the Court rejected claims that the Vienna Convention on Consular Relations mandated either the exclusionary rule for a state party's failure to advise a foreigner placed under arrest of the right to see a consular official of his or her own country or that the treaty precluded a state's reliance on procedural default rules to preclude assertion of such a claim. *Sanchez-Llamas v. Oregon*, 548 U.S. 331 (2006).

106. *See* Norman Dorsen, *The Relevance of Foreign Legal Materials in U.S. Constitutional Cases: A Conversation Between Justice Antonin Scalia and Justice Stephen Breyer*, 3 INTERNATIONAL JOURNAL OF CONSTITUTIONAL LAW 519 (2005).

107. In response to *Roper*, resolutions were introduced in the House and Senate indicating that U.S. judges should not rely on foreign legal materials in interpreting the U.S. Constitution unless these reflect the Constitution's "original understanding." H. Res. 97, 109th Cong., 1st Sess. (Feb. 15, 2005); S. Res. 92, 109th Cong., 1st Sess. (Mar. 20, 2005). A year before, a similar resolution had been introduced in the House: H. Res. 568, 108th Cong., 2d Sess. (Mar. 17, 2004). None of these resolutions, however, passed.

108. Testimony of John Roberts before the Senate Judiciary Committee, September 13, 2005 (responding to a question from Senator Jon Kyl); *see also* Richard Posner, *No Thanks, We Already Have Our Own Laws*, LEGAL AFFAIRS, July 2004 ("Even decisions rendered by judges in democratic countries, or by judges from those countries who sit on international courts, are outside the U.S. democratic orbit"), https://www.legalaffairs.org/issues/July-August-2004/feature_posner_julaug04.msp.

109. Peggy McGuinness, *Alito Responds to Senator Kyl on the Use of Foreign Law: Siding with the Anti-Internationalists?*, OPINIO JURIS, January 10, 2006, lawofnations.blogspot.com/2006/01/alito-responds-to-senator-kyl-on-use.html.

110. Stephen I. Vladeck, *One Huge Difference Between Kavanaugh and Kennedy: Their Guantanamo Records*, WASHINGTON POST, July 11, 2018.

111. *See, e.g.*, Al-Bahlul v. United States, 767 F.3d 1 (2016) (Kavanaugh, concurring); Al-Bihani v. Obama, 590 F.3d 866 (2010).

112. Justices Scalia and Breyer debated the practice at American University. *A Conversation on the Relevance of Foreign Law for American Constitutional Adjudication*, (Jan 13, 2005), video available at https://www.c-span.org/video/?185122-1/constitutional-relevance-foreign-court-decisions. Justice Ginsburg has also weighed in, stating: "In the area of human rights, experience in one nation or region may inspire or inform other nations or regions. . . . In my view, comparative analysis emphatically is relevant to the task of interpreting constitutions and enforcing human rights. We are the losers if we neglect what others can tell us about endeavors to eradicate bias against women, minorities, and other disadvantaged groups." Ruth Bader Ginsburg, *Affirmative Action as an International Human Rights Dialogue*, 18 BROOKINGS REVIEW 1 (2000).

113. Jamie Meyerfeld, THE PROMISE OF HUMAN RIGHTS: CONSTITUTIONAL GOVERNMENT, DEMOCRATIC LEGITIMACY, AND INTERNATIONAL LAW (2016).

114. *See* Eric A. Posner and Cass R. Sunstein, *The Law of Other States*, 59 STANFORD LAW REVIEW 131 (2006).

115. *See* Daniel A. Farber, *The Supreme Court, the Law of Nations, and Citations of Foreign Law: The Lessons of History*, 95 CALIFORNIA LAW REVIEW 1335, 1344–54 (2007) (discussing the influence of foreign law on the Founding generation); Jules Lobel, *Fundamental Norms, International Law, and the Extraterritorial Constitution*, 36 YALE INTERNATIONAL LAW JOURNAL 307, 343–49 (2011).

116. 6 U.S. (2 Cranch) 64, 118 (1804) (emphasis added); *see also* Brown v. United States, 12 U.S. (8 Cranch) 110 (1814) (holding that the scope of the president's war powers should be construed consistently with the law of nations).

117. *See* American Law Institute, RESTATEMENT (THIRD) OF THE FOREIGN RELATIONS LAW OF THE UNITED STATES § 114 (1986) ("Where fairly possible, a United States statute should be construed so as not to conflict with international law or with an international agreement of the United States"). This modern version replaces Marshall's "if any other possible construction obtains" with the less demanding "where fairly possible." *See also* Rebecca Crootof, Note, *Judicious Influence: Non-Self-Executing Treaties and the* Charming Betsy *Canon*, 120 YALE LAW JOURNAL 1784 (2011). For a general discussion of how *Charming Betsy* has been applied, *see* Ralph G. Steinhart, *The Role of International Law as a Canon of Domestic Statutory Interpretation*, 43 VANDERBILT LAW REVIEW 1103, 1139–45 (1990).

118. *Compare* Martin S. Flaherty, *John Marshall*, McCulloch v. Maryland, *and We the People: Revisions in Need of Revising*, 43 WILLIAM & MARY LAW REVIEW 1339 (2002).

119. The *Roper* Court noted that since 1990, only Iran, Pakistan, Saudi Arabia, Yemen, Nigeria, the Democratic Republic of Congo, and China had executed juvenile offenders, and that each of these nations had since either abolished the penalty or made a public disavowal of the practice. *Roper*, 543 U.S. at 577.

120. Curtis A. Bradley, *The* Charming Betsy *Canon and Separation of Powers: Rethinking the Interpretive Role of International Law*, 86 GEORGETOWN LAW JOURNAL 479 (1998).

121. Christopher L. Eisgruber, CONSTITUTIONAL SELF-GOVERNMENT 64–66 (2001).

122. Bernard Bailyn, THE IDEOLOGICAL ORIGINS OF THE AMERICAN REVOLUTION 27 (1967).

123. *See* Curtis A. Bradley and Martin S. Flaherty, *Executive Power Essentialism and Foreign Affairs*, 102 MICHIGAN LAW REVIEW 545 (2004). The early American legal scholars James Kent and Henry Wheaton also relied on Grotius in the years following the formation of the republic. *See* Mark Weston Janis, AMERICA AND THE LAW OF NATIONS, 1776–1939 49–71 (2010).

124. *See* Daniel George Lang, FOREIGN POLICY IN THE EARLY REPUBLIC: THE LAW OF NATIONS AND THE BALANCE OF POWER (1985); Thomas H. Lee, *Making Sense of the Eleventh Amendment: International Law and State Sovereignty*, 96 NORTHWESTERN UNIVERSITY LAW REVIEW 1027 (2002).

125. Declaration of Independence para. 1 (1776).

126. *See* Thomas H. Lee, *International Law, International Relations Theory, and Preemptive War: The Vitality of Sovereign Equality Theory Today*, 67 LAW & CONTEMPORARY PROBLEMS 147 (2004).

127. U.S. Const. art. VI, cl. 2. *See* Marin S. Flaherty, *History Right? Historical Scholarship, Original Understanding, and Treaties as "Supreme Law of the Land,"* 99 COLUMBIA LAW REVIEW 2095 (1999).

128. 1 RECORDS OF THE FEDERAL CONVENTION OF 1787 316 (Max Farrand ed., 1966).

129. *Id.* at 164.

130. U.S. Const. art. I, § 8, cl. 10.

131. *See* Flaherty, *History Right?* at 2140–49.

132. *Id.*

133. *See* THE FEDERALIST Nos. 78–83 at 464–527 (Alexander Hamilton) (Clinton Rossiter ed., 1961).

134. THE FEDERALIST No. 3, at 41–45 (John Jay) (Clinton Rossiter ed., 1961).

135. Cleveland, *Our International Constitution* 7.

136. *Id.* at 12–33.

137. 3 U.S. (3 Dall.) 199 (1796).

138. 576 U.S. ___ (2015).

139. *See, e.g.*, Pennoyer v. Neff, 95 U.S. 714 (1878) (using law of nations principles to establish limits on states asserting jurisdiction over defendants outside their territory). Cleveland, *Our International Constitution*, 33–49.

140. Cleveland, *Our International Constitution*, 63 (citations omitted).

141. *Id.* at 63–88.

142. 25 U.S. (12 Wheat.) 213, 258–59 (1827).

143. *See* chapter 8.

Chapter Twelve: Conclusion

1. THE FEDERALIST No. 48 at 309 (James Madison) (Clinton Rossiter ed., 1961).

2. Memorandum from Alberto R. Gonzales to the President (Jan. 25, 2002).

3. 453 U.S. 654 (1981).

4. Youngstown Sheet & Tube Co. v. Sawyer, 343 U.S. 579, 654–55 (Jackson, J., concurring).

5. Lydia Wheeler and Jordan Fabian, *Trump Reveals First Slate of Judicial Nominees*, THE HILL, May 8, 2017, http://thehill.com/regulation/court-battles/332388-trump-reveals-first-slate-of-judicial-nominees.

6. Charlie Savage, *Neil Gorsuch Helped Defend Disputed Bush-Era Terror Policies*, NEW YORK TIMES, March 15, 2017, https://www.nytimes.com/2017/03/15/us/poli tics/neil-gorsuch-torture-Guantánamo-bay.html.

7. *See* Albert Lawrence, *Herbert Brownell, Jr.: The "Hidden Hand" in the Selection of Earl Warren and the Government's Role in* Brown v. Board of Education, 37.1 JOURNAL OF SUPREME COURT HISTORY 75 (2012).

8. Theo Lippman Jr., *Anecdotes Are Dangerous to Biographers and Truth Mistakes: When Essential Little Stories Are Distorted, Vast Damage is Done*, BALTIMORE SUN, September 7, 1997, http://articles.baltimoresun.com/1997-09-07/news/1997250003_1_brennan-eisenhower-eisler.

9. Korematsu v. United States, 323 U.S. 214, 242–48 (Jackson, J., dissenting).

10. THE FEDERALIST No. 51, at 322 (James Madison) (Clinton Rossiter ed., 1961).

11. Larry Kramer, *Foreword: We the Court*, 115 HARVARD LAW REVIEW 5 (2001).

12. *See* Mark Tushnet, WEAK COURTS, STRONG RIGHTS: JUDICIAL REVIEW AND SOCIAL WELFARE RIGHTS IN COMPARATIVE CONSTITUTIONAL LAW (2008); Mark Tushnet, TAKING THE CONSTITUTION AWAY FROM THE COURTS (1999).

13. 426 U.S. 833 (1976).

14. 469 U.S. 528 (1985).

15. 478 U.S. 186 (1986).

16. 539 U.S. 558 (2003).

17. *See* Eleventh Amendment, overruling Chisholm v. Geogia, 2 U.S. 419 (1793); Thirteenth and Fourteenth Amendments, overruling Dred Scott v. Sanford, 60 U.S. 393 (1857); Nineteenth Amendment, overruling Minor v. Happersett, 88 U.S. 162 (1875); Twenty-Fourth Amendment, overruling Breedlove v. Suttles, 302 U.S. 277 (1937); Twenty-Sixth Amendment, overruling Oregon v. Mitchell, 400 U.S. 112 (1970). For a list of other amendments and the cases they overruled, *see* Elliot Mincberg, *America's History of Amending the Constitution to Expand Democracy (and Overturn the Supreme Court)*, PEOPLE FOR THE AMERICAN WAY, June 18, 2014, http://www.pfaw.org/blog-posts/americas-history-of-amending-the-constitution-to-expand-democracy-and-overturn-the-supreme-court. For a discussion of the amendment process in general, *see* Richard B. Bernstein, AMENDING AMERICA: IF WE LOVE THE CONSTITUTION SO MUCH, WHY DO WE KEEP TRYING TO CHANGE IT? (1993).

18. Bruce Ackerman, 1 WE THE PEOPLE: FOUNDATIONS (1991).

19. *See* Chris Buckley, *China Takes Aim at Western Ideas*, NEW YORK TIMES, August 19, 2013, http://www.nytimes.com/2013/08/20/world/asia/chinas-new -leadership-takes-hard-line-in-secret-memo.html.

20. *Youngstown*, 343 U.S. at 655 (Jackson, J., concurring).